Criminal Justice Communications

Custom Edition

Material selected from:

Essentials of Human Communication, Fourth Edition
by Joseph A. DeVito

Written and Interpersonal Communication: Methods for Law Enforcement, Second Edition
by Harvey Wallace, Cliff Roberson, and Craig Steckler

Communication: Principles for a Lifetime
by Steven A. Beebe, Susan J. Beebe, and Diana K. Ivy

Police Talk: A Scenario-Based Communications Workbook for Police Recruits and Officers
by Jean Reynolds and Major Mary Mariani

Communication: Making Connections, Study Edition, Fifth Edition
by William J. Seiler and Melissa L. Beall

Writing for Law Enforcement
by Christopher Thaiss and John E. Hess

Report It In Writing, Second Edition
by Debbie J. Goodman

Painless Police Report Writing: An English Guide for Criminal Justice Professionals
by Barbara Frazee and Joseph N. Davis

With additional contributions from, and as compiled by, Dr. Jean Goodall

PEARSON
Custom Publishing

Cover credit to come

Taken from:

Essentials of Human Communication, Fourth Edition
by Joseph A. DeVito
Copyright © 2002 by Allyn & Bacon
A Pearson Education Company
Boston, Massachusetts 02116

Written and Interpersonal Communication Methods for Law Enforcement,
Second Edition
by Harvey Wallace, Cliff Roberson, and Craig Steckler
Copyright © 2001, 1997 by Prentice-Hall, Inc.
A Pearson Education Company
Upper Saddle River, New Jersey 07458

Communication: Principles for a Lifetime
by Steven A. Beebe, Susan, J. Beebe, and Diana K. Ivy
Copyright © 2001 by Allyn & Bacon

Police Talk: A Scenario-Based Communications Workbook for Police Recruits and Officers
by Jean Reynolds and Major Mary Mariani
Copyright © 2002 by Prentice-Hall, Inc.

Communication: Making Connections, Study Edition, Fifth Edition
by William J. Seiler and Melissa L. Beall
Copyright © 2003 by Pearson Education, Inc.
Published by Allyn & Bacon

Writing for Law Enforcement
by Christopher Thaiss and John E. Hess
Copyright © 1999 by Allyn & Bacon

Report It In Writing, Second Edition
by Debbie J. Goodman
Copyright © 1999, 1995 by Prentice-Hall, Inc.

Painless Police Report Writing: An English Guide for Criminal Justice Professionals
by Barbara Frazee and Joseph N. Davis
Copyright © 1993 by Prentice-Hall, Inc.

Copyright © 2004 by Pearson Custom Publishing
All rights reserved.

Printed in the United States of America

10   9   8   7   6   5   4

ISBN 0-536-75865-4

BA 998589

SS

Please visit our web site at *www.pearsoncustom.com*

PEARSON CUSTOM PUBLISHING
75 Arlington Street, Suite 300, Boston, MA 02116
A Pearson Education Company

CONTENTS

CHAPTER 1

Introduction to Human Communication

O f all the knowledge and skills you have, those concerning communication are among your most important and useful. Whether in your personal, social, or work life, your communication ability is and will continue to be your most vital asset. Through **intrapersonal communication,** you talk with, learn about, and judge yourself. You persuade yourself of this or that, reason about possible decisions to make, and rehearse messages that you plan to send to others. Through **interpersonal communication,** you interact with others, learn about them and yourself, and reveal yourself to others. Whether with new acquaintances, old friends, lovers, family members, or colleagues at work, it is through interpersonal communication that you establish, maintain, sometimes destroy, and sometimes repair personal relationships. Interpersonal communication also occurs during interviews—in, for example, applying for a job, gathering information, and counseling.

Through **small group communication,** you interact with others in groups. You solve problems, develop new ideas, and share knowledge and experiences. You live your work and social life largely in groups, from the employment interview to the executive board meeting, from the informal social group having coffee to the formal meeting discussing issues of international concern. Through **public communication,** others inform and persuade you. And you, in turn, inform and persuade others—to act, to buy, or to think in a particular way or to change an attitude, opinion, or value.

This book focuses on these forms of communication and on you as both message sender and receiver (see Table 1.1). It has three major purposes. First, it explains the concepts and principles, the theory and research in human communication so that you'll have a firm foundation in what communication is and how it works. Second, it explains the skills of human communication helpful in increasing your own communication competence and effectiveness in the real world. Lots of social interaction and workplace examples are integrated throughout the book to further emphasize that the skills and principles discussed here are useful as well as practical techniques that you will take with you when you leave the classroom and the college. Unlike the children in the cartoon, you will have no question about the usefulness of what you'll learn here. Third, it provides guidance to increase your ability to think critically in general and about communication in particular.

"Finger painting is fun, but will we ever use it in real life?"
© Bob Zahn

You can see the differences between effective and ineffective communication all around you. They're the differences between

- the self-confident and the self-conscious speaker
- the person who gets hired and the one who gets passed over because of a poor showing in a job interview
- the couple who argue constructively and the couple who argue by hurting each other and eventually destroying their relationship

TABLE 1.1   Areas of Human Communication

This table identifies and arranges the forms of communication in terms of the number of persons involved, from one (in intrapersonal communication) to hundreds, thousands, and even millions (public speaking on television, for example). It also echoes (in general) the development of topics in this book.

	AREAS OF HUMAN COMMUNICATION	SOME COMMON PURPOSES	SOME THEORY-RELATED CONCERNS	SOME SKILLS-RELATED CONCERNS
	Intrapersonal: communication with oneself	To think, reason, analyze, reflect	How does self-concept develop? How does it influence communication? How can problem-solving and analyzing abilities be improved and taught? What's the relationship between personality and communication?	Increasing self-awareness, improving problem-solving and analyzing abilities, increasing self-control, reducing stress, managing interpersonal conflict
	Interpersonal: communication between two people	To discover, relate, influence, play, help	What's interpersonal effectiveness? What holds friends, lovers, and families together? What tears them apart? How can relationships be repaired? How do online relationships compare to those established face-to-face?	Increasing effectiveness in one-to-one communication, developing and maintaining effective relationships, improving conflict resolution abilities, interviewing for information or employment
	Small group: communication within a small group of people	To share information, generate ideas, solve problems, help	What makes a leader? What type of leadership works best? What roles do members serve in groups? How can groups be made more effective? How can virtual groups be used most effectively in the organization?	Increasing effectiveness as a group member, improving leadership abilities, using groups to achieve specific purposes (for example, solving problems, generating ideas)
	Public: communication of speaker to audience	To inform, persuade, entertain	How can audiences be analyzed and adapted to most effectively? How can ideas best be developed for communication to an audience? How can public postings be made more effective?	Informing and persuading more effectively; developing, organizing, styling, and delivering messages with greater effectiveness; communicating on the Internet

- the group member who is too self-focused to listen openly and contribute to the group and the member who serves both the task and the interpersonal needs of the group
- the public speaker who lacks credibility and persuasive appeal and the speaker audiences believe and follow

A good way to begin your study of human communication is to examine your own beliefs about communication by taking the self-test, "What do you believe about communication?"

What Do You Believe About Communication?

Instructions: Respond to each of the following statements with T (true) if you think the statement is always or usually true and F (false) if you think the statement is always or usually false.

_____ 1. Good communicators are born, not made.

_____ 2. The more you communicate, the better your communication will be.

_____ 3. Unlike effective speaking, effective listening really cannot be taught.

_____ 4. Opening lines such as "Hello, how are you?" or "Fine weather today" serve no useful communication purpose.

_____ 5. The best way to communicate with someone from a different culture is exactly as you would with someone from your own culture.

_____ 6. When verbal and nonverbal messages contradict each other, people believe the verbal message.

_____ 7. Complete openness should be the goal of any meaningful interpersonal relationship.

_____ 8. Interpersonal conflict is a reliable sign that your relationship is in trouble.

_____ 9. Like good communicators, small group leaders are born, not made.

_____ 10. Fear of speaking is detrimental and the effective speaker must learn to eliminate it.

■ **HOW DID YOU DO?**   If you're like most people, you have probably been told lots of things about communication that—like the statements above—are simply not true. In fact, none of the above statements are true, so hopefully you answered "False" to all or most of them. As you read this book, you'll discover not only why these statements are false, but also some of the problems that can arise when you act on the basis of such misconceptions.

■ **WHAT WILL YOU DO?**   This is, then, a good place to start practicing the critical thinking skill of questioning commonly held assumptions—about communication and about yourself as a communicator. What other beliefs do you hold about communication and about yourself as a communicator? How do these influence your communication behavior?

COMMUNICATION MODELS AND CONCEPTS

In early models or theories, the communication process was seen as linear. In this _linear_ view of communication, the speaker spoke and the listener listened. Communication was seen as proceeding in a relatively straight line. Speaking and listening were seen as taking place at different times; when you spoke, you didn't listen, and when you listened, you didn't speak (Figure 1.1).

The linear view was soon replaced with an **interactional** view in which the speaker and listener were seen as exchanging turns at speaking and listening. For example, A spoke while B listened, and then B spoke in response to what A said and A listened (Figure 1.2). Speaking and listening were still viewed as separate acts that did not overlap and that were not performed at the same time by the same person.

A more satisfying view, the one held currently, sees communication as a **transactional** process in which each person serves simultaneously as speaker and listener. At the same time that you send messages, you're also receiving messages from your own communications and from the reactions of the other person (see Figure 1.3).

The transactional viewpoint sees each person as both speaker and listener, as simultaneously communicating and receiving messages (Watzlawick, Beavin, & Jackson, 1967; Watzlawick, 1977, 1978; Barnlund, 1970; Wilmot, 1995). Also, the transactional view sees the elements of communication as interdependent (never independent). Each exists in relation to the others. A change in any one element of the process produces changes in the other elements. For example, you're having a meeting with a group of your coworkers and your boss enters the room. This change in "audience" will lead to other changes. Perhaps you'll change what you're saying or how you're saying it. Regardless of what change is introduced, other changes will be produced as a result.

Through communication, people act and react on the basis of the present situation as well as on the basis of their histories, past experiences, attitudes, cultural beliefs, and a host of related factors. One implication of this is that actions and reactions in communication are determined not only by what is said, but also by the way the person interprets what is said. Your responses to a movie, for example, don't depend solely on the words and pictures in the movies; they also depend on your previous experiences, present emotions, knowledge, physical well-being, and lots more. Another implication is that two people listening to the same message will often derive two very different meanings. Although the words and symbols are the same, each person interprets them differently.

Communication occurs when you send or receive messages and when you assign meaning to another person's signals. All human communica-tion is distorted by noise, occurs within a context, has some effect, and involves some opportunity for feedback. We can expand the basic transactional model of communication by adding these essential elements, as shown in Figure 1.4.

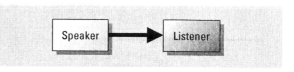

FIGURE 1.1
The Linear View of Human Communication
Communication researchers Paul Nelson and Judy Pearson (1996) suggest that you think of the speaker as passing a ball to the listener, who either catches it or fumbles it. Can you think of another analogy or metaphor for this view of communication?

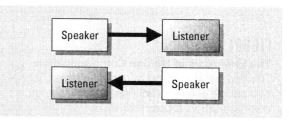

FIGURE 1.2
The Interactional View of Human Communication
In this view, continuing with the ball-passing analogy, the speaker passes the ball to the listener, who then either passes the ball back or fumbles it (Nelson and Pearson, 1996). What other analogy would work here?

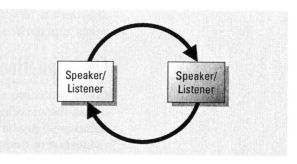

FIGURE 1.3
The Transactional View of Human Communication
In this view, a complex ball game is under way. Each player can send and receive any number of balls at any time. Players are able to throw and catch balls at the same time (Nelson & Pearson, 1996). Can you think of other analogies for this view?

COMMUNICATING WITH POWER

Increasing and Decreasing Power

The power you wield is not static; rather, it varies from one time to another and from one situation to another. You can increase or decrease your power on the basis of what you do or don't do. For example, you can increase your physical power by lifting weights, your power in group situations by learning negotiation techniques, and your persuasive power by mastering the principles of communication.

You can also decrease or lose power. Probably the most common way is by unsuccessfully trying to control another's behavior. For example, if you threaten someone with punishment and then fail to carry out your threat, you'll most likely lose power. Other ways to lose power include allowing others to control you or to take unfair advantage of you and not effectively confronting the unfair power tactics of others.

How would you explain it?

Can you identify specific instances in which you lost power through unsuccessful attempts to control another's behavior or allowed someone to take unfair advantage of you?

---

the evening. Nonverbal messages may also metacommunicate about other nonverbal messages. The individual who, upon meeting a stranger, both smiles and extends a totally lifeless hand shows how one nonverbal behavior may contradict another.

Feedback Messages   When you send a message—say, in speaking to another person—you also hear yourself. That is, you get **feedback** from your own messages; you hear what you say, you feel the way you move, you see what you write. In addition to this self-feedback, you also get feedback from others. This feedback can take many forms. A frown or a smile, a yea or a nay, a pat on the back or a punch in the mouth are all types of feedback.

Feedback tells the speaker what effect he or she is having on listeners. On the basis of this feedback—for example, boos or wild applause in public speaking—the speaker may adjust, modify, strengthen, de-emphasize, or change the content or form of the messages. Similarly, the message you get back from a robot-administered mailing list informing you that it doesn't understand your "plain English" is feedback. When the robot answers your "Please enter my subscription to the communication and gender mailing list" with "Command 'please' not recognized," it is giving you negative feedback—information that tells you something is wrong. Sometimes negative feedback comes with advice on how to correct the problem. A good example of this is the robot's "Commands must be in message BODY, not in HEADER."

Listening to Communicate

Communication is frequently viewed as synonymous with speaking. Listening is either neglected or regarded as something apart from "real communication." But, as emphasized in the model of communication presented earlier and as stressed throughout this book, listening is integral to all communication; it is a process that is coordinate with speaking.

If you measured importance by the time you spend on an activity, listening would be your most important communication activity. In a study conducted by Rankin (1929), listening occupied 45 percent of a person's communication time, speaking 30 percent, reading 10 percent, and writing 9 percent. In another study of college students (Barker, Edwards, Gaines, Gladney, & Holley, 1980), listening also occupied the most time, 53 percent, when compared to reading (17 percent), speaking (16 percent), and writing (14 percent).

Suggestions?

Your supervisor, who has read these statistics, wants you to conduct a two-day seminar in communicating for on-the-job effectiveness. What percentage of these 16 hours would you devote to listening? What types of listening experiences would you seek to incorporate?

Feedforward Messages   **Feedforward** is information you provide before sending your primary messages (Richards, 1951). Feedforward reveals something about the messages to come and includes, for example, the preface or table of contents to a book, the opening paragraph of a chapter, movie previews, magazine covers, and introductions in public speeches.

Feedforward may be verbal ("Wait until you hear this one") or nonverbal (a prolonged pause or hands motioning for silence to signal that an important message is about to be spoken). Or, as is most often the case, it is some combination of verbal and nonverbal. Feedforward may refer to the content of the message to follow ("I'll tell you exactly what they said to each other") or to the form ("I won't spare you the gory details"). In e-mail, feedforward is given in the header, where the name of the sender, the date, and the subject of the message are identified. Caller-ID is another good example of feedforward.

Channel

The communication channel is the medium through which messages pass. Communication rarely takes place over only one channel. Rather, two, three, or four channels may be used simultaneously. In face-to-face conversations, for example, you speak and listen (vocal channel), but you also gesture and receive these signals visually (visual channel). You also emit and smell odors (olfactory channel) and often touch one another, and this, too, is communication (tactile channel).

Another way to classify channels is by the means of communication. Thus, face-to-face contact, telephones, e-mail, movies, television, smoke signals, and telegraph would be types of channels.

Noise

Noise interferes with your receiving a message someone is sending or with their receiving your message. Noise may be physical (others talking loudly, cars honking, illegible handwriting, "garbage" on your computer screen), physiological (hearing or visual impairment, articulation disorders), psychological (preconceived ideas, wandering thoughts), or semantic (misunderstood meanings). Technically, noise is anything that distorts the message, anything that prevents the receiver from receiving the message.

A useful concept in understanding noise and its importance in communication is "signal-to-noise ratio." *Signal* refers to information that you'd find useful and *noise* refers to information that is useless (to you). So, for example, a mailing list or newsgroup that contains lots of useful information would be high on signal and low on noise; one that contains lots of useless information would be high on noise and low on signal.

Because messages may be visual as well as spo-ken, noise, too, may be visual. For example, thesunglasses that prevent someone from seeing the nonverbal messages sent by your eyes would be considered noise, as would blurred type on a printed page. Table 1.2 identifies the four types of noise in more detail.

All communications contain noise. Noise can't be totally eliminated, but its effects can be reduced. Making your language more precise, sharpening your skills for sending and receiving nonverbal messages, and improving your listening and feedback skills are some ways to combat the influence of noise.

TABLE 1.2 Four Types of Noise

One of the most important skills in communication is recognizing the types of noise and developing ways to combat them. Consider, for example, what kinds of noise occur in the classroom. What kinds of noise occur in your family communications? What kinds occur at work? What can you do to combat these kinds of noise?

TYPE OF NOISE	DEFINITION	EXAMPLES
Physical	Interference that is external to both speaker and listener; it interferes with the physical transmission of the signal or message.	Screeching of passing cars, hum of computer, sunglasses
Physiological	Physical barriers within the speaker or listener.	Visual impairments, hearing loss, articulation problems, memory loss
Psychological	Cognitive or mental interference, biases and stereotypes.	Biases and prejudices in senders and receivers, closed-mindedness, inaccurate expectations, extreme emotionalism (anger, hate, love, grief)
Semantic	Speaker and listener assigning different meanings.	People speaking different languages, use of jargon or overly complex terms not understood by listener, dialectical differences in meaning

Effects

Communication always has some effect on those involved in the communication act. For every communication act, there is some consequence. For example, you may gain knowledge or learn how to analyze, synthesize, or evaluate something. These are intellectual or cognitive effects. You may acquire new attitudes or beliefs or change existing ones (affective effects). You may learn new bodily movements, such as how to throw a curve ball, paint a picture, give a compliment, or express surprise (psychomotor effects).

PRINCIPLES OF COMMUNICATION

Several communication principles are essential to understanding interpersonal, small group, and public communication. These principles, although significant in terms of explaining theory, also have practical applications. They provide insight into practical issues such as

- why some people communicate quickly and effectively while others have difficulty even after a long acquaintance
- why some messages are easily believed and others disbelieved
- why disagreements seem to center on trivial issues and yet prove so difficult to resolve
- why people can experience the same event and yet disagree on what happened
- why people can sometimes understand and at other times so easily misunderstand each other's intentions
- why things said in anger or haste have such lasting effects

You may want to try your hand at analyzing an interaction before reading about these principles and then again after reading this section.

Communication Is a Process of Adjustment

Communication may take place only to the extent that the communicators use the same system of signals (Pittenger, Hockett, & Danehy, 1960). You will be unable to communicate with another person to the extent that your language systems differ. In reality, however, no two people use identical signal systems, so this principle is relevant to all forms of communication. Parents and children, for example, have not only largely different vocabularies, but also different meanings for the terms they do share. Different cultures, even when they use a common language, often have greatly different nonverbal communication systems. To the extent that these systems differ, meaningful and effective communication will not take place.

Part of the art of communication is identifying the other person's signals, learning how they're used, and understanding what they mean. Those in close relationships will realize that learning the other person's signals takes a great deal of time and often a great deal of patience. If you want to understand what another person means (by a smile, by saying "I love you," by arguing about trivia, by self-deprecating comments) rather than just

OK sign

France: you're a zero; **Japan:** please give me coins; **Brazil:** an obscene gesture; **Mediterranean countries:** an obscene gesture

Thumbs up

Australia: up yours; **Germany:** the number one; **Japan:** the number five; **Saudi Arabia:** I'm winning; **Ghana:** an insult; **Malaysia:** the thumb is used to point rather than the index finger

Thumbs down

Most countries: something is wrong or bad

Thumb and forefinger

Most countries: money; **France:** something is perfect; **Mediterranean:** a vulgar gesture

Open palm

Greece: an insult dating to ancient times; **West Africa:** "You have five fathers," an insult akin to calling someone a bastard

FIGURE 1.5

Cultural Meanings of Gestures

Cultural differences in the meanings of nonverbal gestures are often significant. The over-the-head clasped hands that signify victory to an American may signify friendship to a Russian. To an American, holding up two fingers to make a V signifies victory or peace. To certain South Americans, however, it is an obscene gesture that corresponds to the American's extended middle finger. This figure highlights some additional nonverbal differences. Can you identify others?

acknowledge what the other person says or does, you have to learn that person's system of signals.

This principle is especially important in intercultural communication, largely because people from different cultures use different signals and sometimes similar signals to mean quite different things. Focused eye contact means honesty and openness in much of the United States. But that same behavior may signify arrogance or disrespect in Japan and in many Hispanic cultures, particularly if engaged in by a youngster with someone significantly older. Figure 1.5 illustrates how the same signals can mean quite different things in other cultures.

Communication Accommodation An interesting theory revolving largely around adjustment is communication accommodation theory. This theory holds that speakers adjust to, or accommodate to, the speaking style of their listeners to gain, for example, social approval and greater communication efficiency (Giles, Mulac, Bradac, & Johnson, 1987). For example, when two people have a similar speech rate, they seem to be more attracted to each other than to those with dissimilar rates (Buller, LePoire, Aune, & Eloy, 1992). Speech rate similarity has also been associated with greater sociability and intimacy between communicators (Buller & Aune, 1992).

Similarly, the speaker who uses language intensity similar to that of his or her listeners is judged to have greater credibility than the speaker who uses different intensity (Aune & Kikuchi, 1993). Still another study found that roommates who had similar communication attitudes (both roommates were high in communication competence and willingness to communicate and low in verbal aggressiveness) were highest in roommate liking and satisfaction (Martin & Anderson, 1995). Although this theory has not been tested on computer communication, it would predict that styles of written communication in e-mail or chat groups would also evidence accommodation.

As you'll see throughout this text, communication characteristics are influenced greatly by culture (Albert & Nelson, 1993). Thus, the communication similarities that lead to attraction and more positive perceptions are more likely to be present in *intra*cultural communication than in *inter*cultural encounters. This may present an important (but not insurmountable) obstacle to intercultural communication.

Communication Is a Package of Messages

Communication normally occurs in "packages" of verbal and nonverbal behaviors or messages (Pittenger, Hockett, & Danehy, 1960). Usually, verbal and nonverbal behaviors reinforce or support each other. You don't usually express fear with words while the rest of your body relaxes. You don't normally express anger with your bodily posture while your face smiles. Your entire being works as a whole—verbally and nonverbally—to express your thoughts and feelings.

Usually, little attention is paid to the packaged nature of communication. But when the messages contradict each other—when the weak handshake belies the confident verbal greeting, when the nervous posture belies the focused stare—you notice. Invariably, you begin to question the communicator's sincerity and honesty. Consider, for example, how you would react to mixed-message situations such as these:

- "Well, we've finally decided to break up after seven years. I think it's all for the best."
- "Even if I do fail the course, so what? I don't need it for graduation."
- "I haven't had a date in the last three years. Men/women are jerks."

Communication Involves Content and Relationship Dimensions

Communication exists on at least two levels. Communication can refer to something external to both speaker and listener (for example, the weather) as well as to the relationships between speaker and listener (for example, who is in charge). These two aspects are referred to as **content and relationship dimensions** of communication (Watzlawick, Beavin, & Jackson, 1967).

For example, let's say that a marketing manager at a Web design firm asks a worker to see him or her after the meeting. The content aspect refers to what the manager wants the worker to do, namely see him or her after the meeting. The relationship aspect, however, is different and refers to the

**"If you want to talk, get a paper, and we'll
talk about what's in the paper."**

©The New Yorker Collection 1981 Boris Drucker from
cartoonbank.com. All Rights Reserved.

relationship between the manager and the worker; it states how the communication is to be dealt with. For example, the use of the command indicates a status difference between the two parties: the manager can command the worker. If the worker commanded the manager, it would appear awkward and out of place simply because it would violate the normal relationship between manager and worker.

Some research shows that women engage in more relationship talk than men; they talk more about relationships in general and about the present relationship in particular. Men engage in more content talk; they talk more about things external to the relationship (Wood, 1994; Pearson, West, & Turner, 1995). Based on your own experience, do you find this cartoon a generally accurate depiction of the male's preference for talking about matters external to the relationship? Would the cartoon be humorous if the woman were the speaker?

Problems often result from failure to distinguish between the content and the relationship levels of communication. Consider a couple, Pat and Chris. Pat made plans to attend a rally with friends during the weekend without first asking Chris, and an argument ensued. Both would probably have agreed that attending the rally was the right choice to make. Thus, the argument is not centered on the content level. The argument, instead, centers on the relationship level. Chris expected to be consulted about plans for the weekend. Pat, in not doing this, rejected this definition of the relationship.

Examine the following interchange and note how relationship considerations are ignored.

> **Pat:** I'm going to the rally tomorrow. The people at the health center are all going to voice their protest and I'm going with them. [Pat focuses on the content and ignores any relational implications of the message.]
>
> **Chris:** Why can't we ever do anything together? [Chris responds primarily on a relational level and ignores the content implications of the message, expressing displeasure at being ignored in this decision.]
>
> **Pat:** We can do something together anytime; tomorrow's the day of the rally. [Again, Pat focuses almost exclusively on the content.]

Here is essentially the same situation, but with something added: sensitivity to relationship messages.

> **Pat:** The people at the center are going to the rally tomorrow and I'd like to go with them. Would that be all right with you? [Although Pat focuses on content, there is always an awareness of the relational dimensions by asking if this would be a problem. Pat also shows this in expressing a desire rather than a decision to attend this rally.]
>
> **Chris:** That sounds great, but I'd really like to do something together tomorrow. [Chris focuses on the relational dimension but also acknowledges Pat's content orientation. Note, too, that Chris does not respond defensively.]

Pat: How about meeting me at Luigi's for dinner after the rally? [Pat responds to the relational aspect—without abandoning the desire to attend the rally. Pat tries to negotiate a solution that will meet the needs of both parties.]

Chris: That sounds great. I'm dying for spaghetti and meatballs. [Chris responds to both messages, approving of both Pat's attending the rally and of their dinner date.]

Communication Sequences Are Punctuated

Communication events are continuous transactions that have no clear-cut beginning or ending. As a participant in or an observer of communication, you divide this continuous, circular process into causes and effects, or stimuli and responses. That is, you segment or **punctuate** this continuous stream of communication into smaller pieces (Watzlawick, Beavin, & Jackson, 1967). Some of these you label causes (or stimuli) and others effects (or responses).

Consider this example: The manager of a local supermarket lacks interest in the employees, seldom offering any suggestions for improvement or any praise for jobs well done. The employees are apathetic and morale is low. Each action (the manager's lack of involvement and the employees' low morale) stimulates the other. Each serves as the stimulus for the other but there is no identifiable initial stimulus. Each event may be seen as a stimulus or as a response.

If you're to understand what the other person means from his or her point of view, you have to see the sequence of events as punctuated by the other person. Further, recognize that your punctuation does not reflect what exists in reality. Rather, it reflects your own unique, subjective, and fallible perception.

Communication Is Purposeful

You communicate for a purpose; there is some motivation that leads you to communicate. When you speak or write, you're trying to send some message and trying to accomplish some goal. Although different cultures emphasize different purposes and motives (Rubin, Fernandez-Collado, & Hernandez-Sampieri, 1992), five general purposes seem relatively common to most if not all forms of communication:

- to learn: to acquire knowledge of others, the world, and yourself
- to relate: to form relationships with others, to interact with others as individuals
- to help: to assist others by listening, offering solutions
- to influence: to strengthen or change the attitudes or behaviors of others
- to play: to enjoy the experience of the moment

You can gain a different perspective on communication purposes by looking at Figure 1.6, which integrates these five purposes with the motives that energize your communication and the results you hope to achieve when you communicate.

FIGURE 1.6

The Multipurpose Nature of Human Communication

The innermost circle contains the general purposes of communication. The middle circle contains the motivations. The outer circle contains the results that you might hope to achieve by engaging in communication. A similar typology of purposes comes from research on motives for communicating. In a series of studies, Rubin and her colleagues (Graham, 1994; Graham, Barbato, & Perse, 1993; Rubin, Fernandez-Collado, & Hernandez-Sampieri, 1992; Rubin & Martin, 1994, 1998; Rubin, Perse, & Barbato, 1988; and Rubin & Rubin, 1992) have identified six primary motives for communication: pleasure, affection, inclusion, escape, relaxation, and control. How do these compare to the five purposes discussed here?

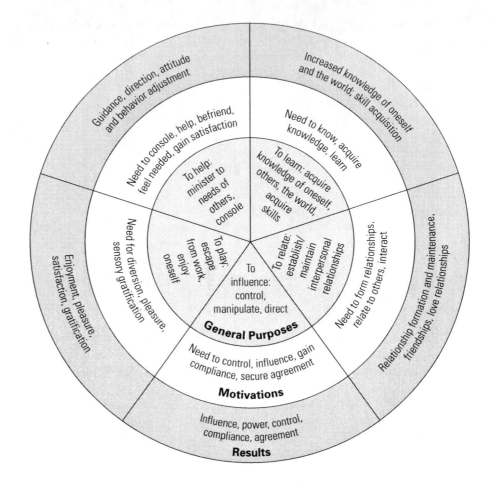

Communication Is Inevitable, Irreversible, and Unrepeatable

Communication is **inevitable** and often takes place even though a person does not intend or want to communicate. Take, for example, a student sitting in the back of the room with an expressionless face, perhaps staring out the window. Although the student might claim not to be communicating with the instructor, the instructor may derive a variety of messages from this behavior. Perhaps the instructor assumes that the student lacks interest, is bored, or is worried about something. In any event, the teacher is receiving messages even though the student might not intentionally be sending any (Watzlawick, Beavin, & Jackson, 1967; Motley, 1990a, 1990b; Bavelas, 1990). This does not mean that all behavior is communication. For instance, if the student looked out the window and the teacher didn't notice, no communication would have taken place. The two people must be in an interactional situation and the behavior must be perceived for the principle of inevitability to operate.

Notice, too, that when you're in an interactional situation, you cannot *not* respond to the messages of others. For example, if you notice someone winking at you, you must respond in some way. Even if you don't respond actively or openly, your lack of response is itself a response, and it communicates.

Communication is an **irreversible** process. Once you say something or press that send key on your e-mail, you cannot uncommunicate it. You can, of course, try to reduce the effects of your message. You can say, for example, "I really didn't mean what I said." Regardless of how hard you try to negate or reduce the effects of your message, the message itself, once it has been received, cannot be taken back. In a public speaking situation in which the speech is recorded or broadcast, inappropriate messages may have national or even international effects. Here, attempts to reverse what one has said (in, say, trying to offer clarification) often have the effect of further publicizing the original statement.

In face-to-face communication, the actual signals (the movements in the air) are evanescent; they fade almost as they are uttered. Some written messages, especially computer-mediated messages such as those sent through e-mail, are unerasable. E-mails that are sent among employees in a large corporation or even at colleges are often stored on disk or tape and may not be considered private by managers and administrators (Sethna, Barnes, Brust, & Kaye, 1999). Much litigation is currently proceeding using the evidence of racist or sexist e-mails that senders thought had been erased but hadn't.

Because of irreversibility (and unerasability), be careful not to say things you may be sorry for later. Especially in conflict situations, when tempers run high, avoid saying things you may later wish to withdraw. Commitment messages—"I love you" messages and their variants— also need to be monitored. Messages that can be interpreted as sexist, racist, or homophobic that you thought private might later be retrieved by others and create all sorts of problems for you and your organization. In group and public communication situations, when the messages are received by many people, it's especially crucial to recognize the irreversibility of communication.

Communication is also *unrepeatable*. A communication act can never be duplicated. The reason is simple: everyone and everything is constantly changing. As a result, you can never recapture the exact same situation, frame of mind, or relationship dynamics that defined a previous communication act. For example, you can never repeat meeting someone for the first time, comforting a grieving friend, leading a small group for the first time, or giving a public speech. You can never replace this initial impression; you can only try to counteract this initial (and perhaps negative) impression by going through the motions again.

CULTURE AND HUMAN COMMUNICATION

Culture refers to the beliefs, ways of behaving, and artifacts of a group that are transmitted through communication and learning rather than through genes. Gender is considered a cultural variable largely because cultures teach boys and girls different attitudes, beliefs, values, and ways of communicating and relating to one another. This means that you act like a man or a woman in part because of what your culture has taught you about how men and women should act. This does not, of course, deny that biological differences also play a role in the differences between male and female behavior. In fact, recent research continues to uncover biological roots of behavior we once thought was entirely learned—acting happy or shy, for example (McCroskey, 1997).

Because your communication is heavily influenced by the culture in which you were raised, culture is emphasized throughout this text. This section explains the relevance of culture to communication and the aims and benefits of a cultural perspective.

A walk through any large city, many small towns, or just about any college campus will convince you that the United States is largely a collection of lots of different cultures (Figure 1.7). These cultures coexist somewhat separately but all influence each other. This coexistence has led some researchers to refer to these cultures as cocultures (Shuter, 1990; Samovar & Porter, 1991; Jandt, 2001). Here are a few random facts that further support the importance of culture generally and of intercultural communication in particular (*Time*, December 2, 1993, p. 14):

- Over 30 million people in the United States speak languages other than English in their homes.
- In some school systems, such as New York City; Fairfax County, Virginia; Chicago; and Los Angeles, over 100 languages are spoken.

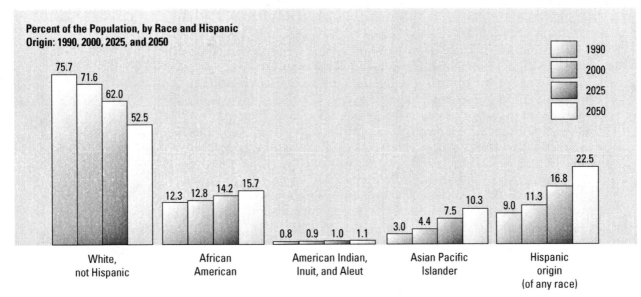

FIGURE 1.7

The Faces of the Nation

This figure shows the percent of the population of the United States by race and Hispanic origin for the years 1990 and 2000 and the projections for the years 2025 and 2050 (U.S. Bureau of the Census, 2001). It's important to realize that within each group there are also wide cultural variations. Whites from Sweden are culturally quite different from whites from Greece or Russia and Asians from Japan are culturally quite different from those from China or Korea. And, to complicate matters even further, not all Japanese or all Chinese or all Koreans are culturally similar. There are wide variations within each country, just as there are cultural differences between whites from, say, Manhattan and those from rural Tennessee. Visit one of the population Web sites and examine the cultural makeup of your state or county. How do the figures for your state or county compare to those presented here for the country as a whole?

- Over 50 percent of the residents of cities such as Miami and Hialeah in Florida, Union City in New Jersey, and Huntington Park and Monterey Park in California are foreign born.

- The foreign-born population of the United States in 1990 totaled almost 20 million, approximately 8 percent of the total U.S. population; a 1997 update reports it as 25.8 million, or 9.7 percent of the population (Schmidley & Alvarado, 1997).

- Thirty percent of the U.S. Nobel prize winners since 1901 have been foreign born.

We're also living in a time of changing gender roles. Many men, for example, are doing a great deal more housekeeping chores and caring for their children. More obvious perhaps is that many women are becoming much more visible in fields once occupied exclusively by men—politics, law enforcement, the military, and the clergy are just some examples. And, of course, women are increasingly entering corporate executive ranks; the glass ceiling may not have disappeared, but it has cracked.

At this point, you may wish to take a closer look at your own cultural beliefs and values by taking the self-test, "What are your cultural beliefs and values?"

Test Yourself

What Are Your Cultural Beliefs and Values?

Instructions: Here the extremes of 10 cultural differences are identified. For each characteristic indicate your own values:

a. If you feel your values are "very similar" to the extreme statements on the left, select 1; if "very similar" to the extreme statements on the right, select 7.

b. If you feel your values are "quite similar" to the extreme statements on the left, select 2; if "quite similar" to the statements on the right, select 6.

c. If you feel your values are "fairly similar" to the extreme statements on the left, select 3; if "fairly similar" to the statements on the right, select 5.

d. If you feel your values are in the middle of these extreme statements, select 4.

Men and women are equal and are entitled to equality in all areas.	**Gender Equality** 1 2 3 4 5 6 7	Men and women are very different and should stick to the specific roles assigned to them by their cultures.
"Success" is measured by your contribution to the group.	**Group and Individual Orientation** 1 2 3 4 5 6 7	"Success" is measured by how far you outperform others.
You should enjoy yourself as much as possible.	**Hedonism** 1 2 3 4 5 6 7	You should work as much as possible.
Religion is the final arbiter of what is right and wrong; your first obligation is to abide by the rules and customs of your religion.	**Religion** 1 2 3 4 5 6 7	Religion is like any other social institution; it's not inherently moral or right just because it's a religion.

	Family	
Your first obligation is to your family; each person is responsible for the welfare of his or her family.	1 2 3 4 5 6 7	Your first obligation is to yourself; each person is responsible for himself or herself.
	Time Orientation	
Work hard now for a better future.	1 2 3 4 5 6 7	Live in the present; the future may never come.
	Relationship Permanency	
Romantic relationships, once made, are forever.	1 2 3 4 5 6 7	Romantic relationships should be maintained as long as they're more rewarding than punishing and dissolved when they're more punishing than rewarding.
	Emotional Expression	
People should express their emotions openly and freely.	1 2 3 4 5 6 7	People should not reveal their emotions, especially those that may reflect negatively on them or others or make others feel uncomfortable.
	Money	
Money is extremely important and should be a major consideration in just about any decision you make.	1 2 3 4 5 6 7	Money is relatively unimportant and should not enter into life's really important decisions, such as what relationship to enter or what career to pursue.
	Belief in a Just World	
The world is a just place; bad things happen to bad people and good things happen to good people; what goes around comes around.	1 2 3 4 5 6 7	The world is random; bad and good things happen to people without any reference to whether they're good or bad people.

■ **HOW DID YOU DO?** This test was designed to help you explore the possible influence of your cultural beliefs and values on communication. If you visualize communication as involving choices, these beliefs will influence the choices you make and therefore how you communicate and how you listen and respond to the communications of others. For example, your beliefs and values about gender equality will influence the way you communicate with and about the opposite sex. Your group and individual orientation will influence how you perform in work teams and how you deal with your peers at school and at work. Your degree of hedonism will influence the kinds of communications you engage in, the books you read, the television programs you watch. Your religious beliefs will influence the ethical system you follow in communicating.

■ **WHAT WILL YOU DO?** Review the entire list of 10 characteristics and try to identify one *specific* way in which each characteristic influences your communication. As you do this, try to consider what you might do to increase your awareness of how your beliefs influence your communications.

The Importance of Culture

There are lots of reasons for the cultural emphasis you'll find in this book. Most obviously, perhaps, are the vast demographic changes taking place throughout the United States. Whereas at one time the United States was largely a country populated by Europeans, it's now a country greatly influenced by the enormous number of new citizens from Latin and South America, Africa, and Asia. This is especially true on college and university campuses throughout the United States. With these changes have come different customs and the need to understand and adapt to new ways of looking at communication. For example, health care workers and patients need to understand how each other communicates about illness, sees ways to prevent health problems, and views taking medication. Police officers and civilians need to understand how each other views "disorderly conduct," "the right of assembly," and "free speech."

As a people, we've become increasingly sensitive to cultural differences. U.S. society has moved from an assimilationist perspective (people should leave their native culture behind and adapt to their new culture) to one that values cultural diversity (people should retain their native cultural ways). And, with some notable exceptions—hate speech, racism, sexism, homophobia, and classism come quickly to mind—we're more concerned with saying the right thing and ultimately with developing a society in which all cultures can coexist and enrich each other. At the same time, the ability to interact effectively with members of other cultures often translates into financial gain and increased employment opportunities and advancement prospects.

Today, most countries are economically dependent on each other. Our economic lives depend on our ability to communicate effectively across cultures. Similarly, our political well-being depends in great part on that of other cultures. Political unrest in any part of the world—South Africa, Eastern Europe, or the Middle East, to take a few examples—affects our own security. Intercultural communication and understanding now seem more crucial than ever.

The rapid spread of communication technology has brought foreign and sometimes very different cultures right into your living room. News from foreign countries is commonplace. You see nightly—in vivid color— what is going on in remote countries. Technology has made intercultural communication easy, practical, and inevitable. Daily, the media bombard you with evidence of racial tensions, religious disagreements, sexual bias, and, in general, the problems caused when intercultural communication fails. And, of course, the Internet has made intercultural communication as easy as writing a note on your computer. You can now communicate by e-mail just as easily with someone in Europe or Asia, for example, as with someone in another city or state.

The Aim of a Cultural Perspective

Because culture permeates all forms of communication, it's necessary to understand its influences if you're to understand how communication works and master its skills. As illustrated throughout this text, culture influences communications of all types (Moon, 1996). It influences what you say to yourself and how you talk with friends, lovers, and family in everyday conversation. It influences how you interact in groups and how much importance you place on the group versus the individual. It influences the topics you talk about and the strategies you use in communicating information or in persuading. And it influences how you use the media and how much credibility you attribute to them.

A cultural emphasis helps distinguish what is universal (true for all people) from what is relative (true for people in one culture and not true for people in other cultures) (Matsumoto, 1991). The principles for communicating information and for changing listeners' attitudes, for example, will vary from one culture to another. If you're to understand communication, you need to know how its principles vary and how they must be qualified and adjusted on the basis of cultural differences. Success in communication—on your job and in your social life—will depend on your ability to communicate effectively with others who are culturally different from yourself.

This emphasis on culture does not imply that you should accept all cultural practices or that all cultural practices are equal (Hatfield & Rapson, 1996). For example, cock fighting, fox hunting, and bull fighting are parts of the cultures of some Latin American countries, England, and Spain, but you need not find these activities acceptable or equal to a cultural practice in which animals are treated kindly. Further, a cultural emphasis does not imply that you have to accept or follow even the practices of your own culture. For example, even if the majority in your culture find cock fighting acceptable, you need not agree with or follow the practice. Similarly, you can reject your culture's values and beliefs, its religion or political system, or its attitudes toward the homeless, the disabled, or the culturally different. Of course, going against your culture's traditions and values is often very difficult. Still, it's important to realize that culture influences but does not determine your values or behavior. Often, for example, personality factors (your degree of assertiveness, extroversion, or optimism, for example) will prove more influential than culture (Hatfield & Rapson, 1996).

As shown throughout this text, cultural differences exist throughout the communication spectrum—from the way you use eye contact to the way you develop or dissolve a relationship (Chang & Holt, 1996). But these differences should not blind you to the great number of similarities among even the most widely separated cultures. Close interpersonal relationships, for example, are common in all cultures, although they may be entered into for very different reasons by members of different cultures. Further, when reading about these differences, remember that they are usually matters of degree. Thus, for example, most cultures value honesty, but not all value it to the same degree. The advances in media and technology and the widespread use of the Internet, for example, are influencing cultures and cultural change and are perhaps homogenizing the different cultures, lessening the differences and increasing the similarities. They're also Americanizing the different cultures because the dominant values and customs evidenced in the media and on the Internet are in large part American, a product of America's current dominance in both media and technology.

Ethnocentrism

One of the problems that hinders cultural awareness and sensitivity is **ethnocentrism,** the tendency to see others and their behaviors through your own cultural filters and to evaluate the values, beliefs, and behaviors of your own culture as being more positive, logical, and natural than those of other cultures. Ideally, you should see both yourself and others as different but equal, with neither being inferior nor superior.

Ethnocentrism exists on a continuum (Table 1.3). People are not either ethnocentric or not ethnocentric; rather, most are somewhere between these

TABLE 1.3   The Ethnocentrism Continuum

This table, drawing from a number of researchers (Gudykunst, 1991; Gudykunst & Kim, 1984; Lukens, 1978), summarizes some of the interconnections between ethnocentrism and communication. In this table, five degrees of ethnocentrism are identified; in reality, of course, there are as many degrees as there are people. The "communication distances" are general terms that highlight the dominant attitude at each level of ethnocentrism. Under "Communications" are some of the major ways people might interact given their particular degree of ethnocentrism.

DEGREE OF ETHNOCENTRISM	COMMUNICATION DISTANCE	COMMUNICATIONS
Low	Equality	Treat others as equals; view different customs and ways of behaving as equal to your own
	Sensitivity	Want to decrease distance between self and others
	Indifference	Lack concern for others; prefer to interact in a world of similar others
	Avoidance	Avoid and limit communications, especially intimate ones, with interculturally different others
High	Disparagement	Engage in hostile behavior; belittle others; view different cultures and ways of behaving as inferior to your own

polar opposites. And, of course, your degree of ethnocentrism varies depending on the group on which you focus. For example, if you're Greek American, you may have a low degree of ethnocentrism when dealing with Italian Americans but a high degree when dealing with Turkish Americans or Japanese Americans. Your degree of ethnocentrism (and we're all ethnocentric to at least some degree) influences your interpersonal, group, public, and mass communication behaviors.

Thinking Critically About HUMAN COMMUNICATION

Suggestions for beginning your study of communication and for using your skills in a wide variety of contexts are provided in this chapter's critical thinking section.

Approaching the Study of Communication

In approaching the study of human communication, keep the following in mind. Realize, first, that the study of human communication involves both theory and research *and* practical skills for increasing communication effectiveness. A knowledge of theory will help you better understand the skills and a knowledge of skills will help you better understand theory.

The concepts and principles discussed throughout this book and this course directly relate to your everyday communications. Try, for example, to recall examples from your own communications that illustrate the ideas considered here. This will help to make the material more personal and easier to assimilate.

Analyze yourself as a critical thinker and communicator. Self-understanding is essential if you're to use this material in any meaningful sense, say, to change some of your own behaviors. Be open to new ideas, even those that may contradict your existing beliefs. Be willing to change your ways of communicating and even your ways of thinking. Carefully assess what you should and should not change, what you should strengthen or revise, and what you should leave as is.

Transferring Skills

Throughout this text, a wide variety of skills for improving interpersonal, small group, and public speaking are presented. Try not to limit these skills to the situations described here, but instead apply them to other situations. You will find that skills learned here will transfer to other areas of your life if you do three things (Sternberg, 1987):

1. Think about the principles flexibly and recognize exceptions to the rule. Consider where the principles seem useful and where they need to be adjusted. Recognize especially that the principles discussed here are largely the result of research conducted on college students in the United States. Ask yourself if they apply to other groups and other cultures.

2. Seek analogies between current situations and your earlier experiences. What are the similarities? What are the differences? For example, most people repeat relationship problems because they fail to see the similarities (and sometimes the differences) between the old and destructive relationship and the new and soon-to-be equally destructive relationship.

3. Look for situations at home, work, and school where you could apply the skills discussed here. For instance, how can active listening skills improve your family communications? How can brainstorming and problem-solving skills help you deal with challenges at work?

This chapter considered the nature of communication, its major components, and some major communication principles.

1. Communication is transactional. Communication is a process of interrelated parts.
2. Communication is the act, by one or more persons, of sending and receiving messages that are distorted by noise, occur within a context, have some effect (and some ethical dimension), and provide some opportunity for feedback.
3. The essentials of communication—the elements present in every communication act—are: context (physical, cultural, social-psychological, and temporal), source-receiver, competence, field of experience, message, channel, noise (physical, psychological, and semantic), sending or encoding processes, receiving or decoding processes, feedback and feedforward, effect, and ethics.
4. Communication messages may vary in form and may be sent and received through any combination of sensory organs. Communication messages may also metacommunicate—communicate about other messages. The communication channel is the medium through which the messages are sent.
5. *Feedback* refers to messages or information that is sent back to the source. It may come from the source itself or from the receiver. *Feedforward* refers to messages that preface other messages.
6. Noise is anything that distorts the message; it is present to some degree in every communication.
7. Communication ethics refers to the moral rightness or wrongness of a message and is an integral part of every effort to communicate.
8. Communication is a process of adjustment in which each person must adjust his or her signals to the understanding of the other if meaning is to be transmitted from one person to another. In fact, communication accommodation theory holds that people imitate the speaking style of the other person as a way of gaining social approval.
9. Normally, communication is a package of signals, each reinforcing the other. When these signals oppose each other, contradictory messages are sent.
10. Communication involves both content and relationship dimensions.
11. Communication sequences are punctuated for processing. Individuals divide the communication sequence into stimuli and responses in different ways.
12. Communication is purposeful. Through communication, you learn, relate, help, influence, and play.
13. In any interactional situation, communication is inevitable (you cannot not communicate, nor can you not respond to communication), irreversible (you cannot take back message), and unrepeatable (you cannot exactly repeat message).
14. Culture permeates all forms of communication and intercultural communication is becoming more and more frequent as the United States becomes home and business partner to a variety of cultures.
15. Ethnocentrism, existing on a continuum, is the tendency to evaluate the beliefs, attitudes, and values of one's own culture positively and those of other cultures negatively.

Several important communication skills, emphasized in this chapter, are presented here in summary form (as they are in every chapter). These skill checklists don't include all the skills covered in the chapter but rather are representative of the most important skills. Check your ability to apply these skills. You will gain the most from this brief experience if you think carefully about each skill and try to identify instances from your recent communications in which you did or did not act on the basis of the specific skill. Use the following rating scale: 1 = almost always, 2 = often, 3 = sometimes, 4 = rarely, 5 = hardly ever.

_____ 1. I'm sensitive to contexts of communication. I recognize that changes in the physical, cultural, social-psychological, and temporal contexts will alter meaning.

_____ 2. I look for meaning not only in words, but also in nonverbal behaviors.

_____ 3. I am sensitive to the feedback that I give to others and that others give to me.

_____ 4. I combat the effects of physical, psychological, and semantic noise that distort messages.

_____ 5. Because communication is a package of signals, I use my verbal and nonverbal messages to reinforce rather than to contradict each other and I respond to contradictory messages by identifying and openly discussing the dual meanings communicated.

6. I listen to the relational messages that I and others send and respond to the relational messages of others to increase meaningful interaction.

7. I actively look for the punctuation pattern that I and others use in order to better understand the meanings communicated.

8. Because communication is transactional, I recognize the mutual influence of all elements and that messages are sent and received simultaneously by each speaker/listener.

9. Because communication is purposeful, I look carefully at both the speaker's and the listener's purposes.

10. Because communication is inevitable, irreversible, and unrepeatable, I look carefully for hidden meanings, am cautious in communicating messages that I may later wish to withdraw, and am aware that any communication act occurs but once.

11. I am sensitive to cultural variation and differences and I see my own culture's teachings and those of other cultures without undue bias.

Key Word Quiz

Write T for those statements that are true and F for those that are false. For those that are false, replace the italicized term with the correct term.

1. *Intrapersonal communication* refers to communication with oneself.

2. The tendency to see others and their behaviors through your own cultural filters and to evaluate your cultural values and beliefs as more positive than those of other cultures is known as *ethnocentrism*.

3. The process of putting ideas into a code—for example, thinking of an idea and then describing it in words—is known as *decoding*.

4. The knowledge of how communication works and the ability to use communication effectively is called *communication competence*.

5. Messages that refer to other messages are called *metamessages*.

6. The messages you get back from your own messages and from the responses of others to what you communicate are known as *feedforward*.

7. Communication that refers to matters external to both speaker and listener is known as the *relationship dimension* of communication.

8. The ways in which the sequence of communication is divided up into, say, causes and effects or stimuli and responses is known as *punctuation*.

9. The view of communication that sees each person as taking both speaker and listener roles simultaneously is an *interactional* one.

10. Interpersonal communication is *inevitable, reversible,* and *unrepeatable*.

Answers: TRUE: 1, 2, 4, 5, 8; FALSE: 3 (*encoding*), 6 (*feedback*), 7 (*content communication*), 9 (*transactional*), 10 (*irreversible*)

Skill Development Experiences

1.1 Models of Human Communication

The model presented in this chapter is only one possible representation of how communication takes place. And, because it was introduced to explain certain foundation concepts, it was simplified to focus on two people in conversation. Either alone or in groups, construct your own diagrammatic model of the essential elements and processes involved in any one of the following situations. Your model's primary function should be to describe what elements are involved and what processes operate in the specific situation chosen. You may find it useful to define the situation in more specific terms before you begin constructing your model.

1. Sitting silently on the bus trying to decide what you should say in your job interview.
2. Using the phone to ask someone you've only communicated with on the Internet for a date.
3. Participating in a small work group to decide how to reduce operating costs.
4. Talking with someone who speaks a language you don't know and who comes from a culture very different from your own.
5. Delivering a lecture to a class of college students.
6. Performing in a movie.
7. Calling someone to try to get him or her to sign up with your telephone service.
8. Persuading an angry crowd to disband.
9. Writing a speech for a political candidate.
10. Watching television.

Thinking Critically About Modeling Human Communication. How adequately does your model explain the process of human communication? Would it help someone new to the field to get a clear picture of what communication is and how it operates? On the basis of this model, how might you revise the model presented in Figure 1.4 on page 7?

1.2 What's Happening?

How would you use the principles of human communication to *describe* what is happening in each of the following situations? Note that these scenarios are extremely brief and are intended only to stimulate you to think more concretely about the axioms. The objective is not to select the one correct principle (each scenario can probably be described by reference to several), but to think about how the principles can be applied to specific situations.

1. A couple, together for 20 years, argues constantly about the seemingly most insignificant things—who takes the dog out, who does the shopping, who decides where to go to dinner, and so on. It has gotten to the point where they rarely have a day without an argument and both are seriously considering separating.
2. Tanya and her grandmother can't seem to agree on what Tanya should or should not do. Tanya, for example, wants to go away for the weekend with her friends from college. But her grandmother fears she will get in with a bad crowd and end up in trouble and refuses to allow her to go.

3. In the heat of an argument, Harry says that he doesn't ever want to see Peggy's family again. "They don't like me and I don't like them," he says. Peggy reciprocates and says she feels the same way about his family. Now, weeks later, there remains a great deal of tension between them, especially when they find themselves with one or both families.
4. Grace and Mark are engaged and are currently senior executives at a large advertising agency. Recently, Grace made a presentation that was not received positively by the other members of the team. Grace feels that Mark—in not defending her proposal—created a negative attitude and actually encouraged others to reject her ideas. Mark says that he felt he could not defend her proposal because others in the room would have felt his defense was motivated by their relationship and not by his positive evaluation of her proposal. So he felt it was best to say nothing.
5. Pat and Chris have been online friends for the last two years, communicating with each other at least once a day. Recently, Pat wrote a number of things that Chris interpreted as insulting and as ridiculing Chris's feelings and dreams. Chris wrote back that these last messages were greatly resented and then stopped writing. Pat has written every day for the last two weeks to try to patch things up, but Chris won't respond.
6. Margo has just taken over as vice-president in charge of sales for a manufacturing company. She is extremely organized and refuses to waste time on nonessentials. In her staff meetings, she is business only. Several top sales representatives have requested to be assigned to other VPs because they feel she works them too hard and doesn't care about them as people.

Thinking Critically About the Principles of Human Communication. Although the purpose of this exercise is to describe what is happening, many people have a tendency to evaluate why things are going wrong and to suggest what should be done about it. Did you? If so, do you also do this when listening to someone talk about personal problems? Can you apply any of these principles to the questions that appear in an advice column?

1.3 The Sources of Your Cultural Beliefs

This exercise is designed to increase your awareness of your cultural beliefs and how you acquired them. For each of the beliefs noted below, try to answer these six questions:

What were you taught? Phrase it as specifically as possible, for example: I was taught to believe that . . .

Who taught you? Parents? Teachers? Television? Peers? Coaches?

How were you taught? By example? Explicit teaching?

When were you taught this? As a child? As a high school student? As an adult?

Where were you taught this? In your home? Around the dinner table? At school? On the playground?

Why do you suppose you were taught this? What motives led your parents or teachers to teach you this belief?

Beliefs

1. the nature of God (for example, belief in the existence of, organized religion, atheism, an afterlife)
2. the importance of family (respect for elders, interconnectedness, responsibilities to other family members)
3. the meaning of and means to success (the qualities that make for success, financial and relational "success")
4. the rules for sexual appropriateness (sex outside of committed relationships, same-sex and opposite-sex relationships)
5. the role of education (the role of education in defining success, the obligation to become educated, education as a way of earning a living)
6. male-female differences (recognizing differences, feminism)
7. intercultural interactions (friendship and romance with those of other religions, races, nationalities; importance of ingroup versus outgroup)
8. the importance of money (amount that's realistic or desirable, at what price, and professional goal, relative importance compared to relationships, job satisfaction)
9. the meaning of life (major goal in life, this life versus an afterlife)
10. time (the importance of being on time, the value of time, wasting time, adherence to the social timetable of your peers—doing what they do at about the same age)

Thinking Critically About the Sources of Cultural Beliefs. In what one way does each of these beliefs influence your communication style? If you have the opportunity to interact in small groups, a good way to gain added insight into cultural beliefs is for volunteers to talk about the belief they selected, how they answered each of the six questions, and how the belief influences their way of communicating. If you follow the principles for effective interpersonal communication, this simple interchange should give you some significant communication insights.

CHAPTER 2

The Communication Process

No records system can operate without clearly communicated policies, directives, and procedures. Nor can any police agency or officer carry out a mission or survive without clear communications. Communication involves more than shouting "Halt, police officer!" or ordering a patrol officer to respond to an emergency call.

This chapter examines the basic parameters of interpersonal and organization communication in a law enforcement agency. Other chapters will review special situations which involve communication issues. Communication is defined as a process involving several steps, among two or more persons, for the primary purpose of exchanging information. The dynamics of communication, or how we react to information, is an important aspect of the communication cycle. The next section reviews the interaction between a person who sends a message and the way in which the receiver processes that information.

THE JOHARI WINDOW

The preceding section pointed out how important effective communication is to a law enforcement agency generally, and a police officer, as a member of that organization, specifically. This section examines one model law enforcement officers can use to evaluate their communication skills. One of the simplest and most common communication models within law enforcement, it is known as the Johari window.

The Four Regions of Knowledge

Joseph Left and Harry Night created a communication model and named it after themselves. They combined their names and called the model the Johari window. This model has four regions or areas that represent basic areas of knowledge or information held by the manager and others. The Johari window is illustrated here:

	Known to self	Not known to self
Known to others	Free area I	Blind area II
Not known to others	Hidden area III	Unknown area IV

The four panes or windows represent relevant information about the manager's ability to interact with other persons effectively. The Johari window has two basic aspects of communication: exposure and feedback. The exposure area concerns the ability of the police administrator to express feelings and ideas in an open method. This is basically the manager's ability to transmit information. The feedback area involves the ability of the administrator to receive information from others.

The Johari window's panes are distinct regions that encompass the following characteristics:

Area I: This pane is known as the free area or arena. It is that portion of a manager's communication ability that allows one to freely share and receive information with and from others. This ability is the key to a successful interpersonal relationship in an organization. Therefore, the larger this pane or region is in relationship to the other panes, the more effective the manager becomes in dealing with superiors and subordinates.

Area II: This pane is known as the blind area or blindspot. We have all heard or used the term, "I was blindsided!" This area represents information known by others—superiors, peers, or subordinates—that is not known to the administrator. In many bureaucracies, individuals take the position that knowledge or information is power. In some ways this is true. Police officers cannot make a valid decision if information is hidden from them. The larger this pane, the more information is being withheld from the manager.

Area III: This pane is known as the hidden area or the facade. It is the area in which an officer keeps information private. Many of us make conscious or unconscious decisions to withhold certain information from others. This information may relate to personal habits or professional knowledge. When an officer withholds information, Area I, the free area or arena, is prevented from expanding. All of us withhold a portion of ourselves from others. This is only normal and healthy. The problem arises when an individual withholds information to the extent that it prevents a free, honest interchange of knowledge.

Area IV: This pane is known as the unknown area. It is the area that contains information that is unknown to both the manager and superiors, as well as subordinates. As the free area or arena grows through effective communication, the unknown area shrinks.

These four areas will expand or contract depending on the type of interpersonal communication patterns the manager adopts.

The Four Basic Types of Communication Patterns

The Johari window establishes four basic types of communication patterns in relation to the process of exposure and feedback. To understand how the Johari model functions, we will briefly examine each of these types.

Type A With this officer there is very little feedback or exposure. The person who is typified by this alternative does not communicate with subordinates or superiors. We have all interacted with the type of individual who withdraws from the decision-making process and is not willing to take a risk by making a decision. This officer is more concerned with self-protection than with functioning effectively. The unknown area is the dominating factor with this type of manager, while the free area or arena is correspondingly smaller.

Free Area	Blind Area	
	Unknown Area	**Type A**
Hidden Area		

Type B This officer does not transmit information to superiors, subordinates, or peers, but will accept some interaction and feedback from them. This individual does not trust fellow officers, but must receive information from them as a survival technique. We have all encountered individuals who constantly ask for our opinions or thoughts, but are hesitant to reciprocate by telling us what they believe or feel. This officer has a large hidden area or facade in the model.

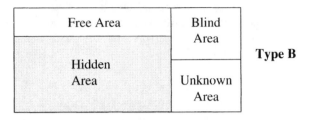

Type B

Type C This officer is characterized by continual self-expression and refusal to accept feedback from others. In this situation, the model shows an increase in exposure with a corresponding decrease in feedback. These are the individuals whose egos are so large that they believe they have all the right answers and strive to emphasize their authority and dominance over other officers. Friends and colleagues soon come to believe that they do not value the opinions of others or will only tolerate feedback that confirms their own beliefs or position. This officer is characterized by a large blindspot in the Johari window.

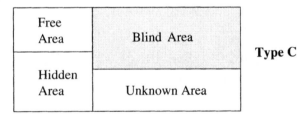

Type C

Type D This officer is considered the type of individual who shows outstanding leadership. He or she emphasizes open lines of communication, with feedback from superiors and subordinates alike. Unfortunately, many police officers are not used to dealing with this type of person and may distrust such communication techniques at first. This officer has a large free area or arena displayed in the model.

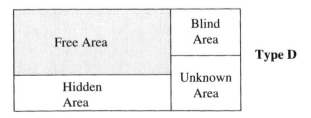

Type D

It should be obvious from the preceding discussion that the most effective law enforcement officer is Type D. This officer's relationships are characterized by trust, open lines of communication, and candor with superiors, peers, and subordinates. Open lines of communication result in a high quality of work from all the parties who interact with this type of police administrator.

The Johari window is an abstract concept that illustrates certain principles regarding the quality and style of interpersonal relationships. Its principles can be applied to any relationship; however, it is particularly applicable to law enforcement agencies. By studying and understanding the dynamics of the Johari window, we can enhance our ability to become effective law enforcement officers.

OTHER COMMUNICATION MODELS

Several other models deal with the dynamics of communication. All of these models or theories seek to explain how the communication process works. Each of these models has its advocates. It is important to understand that different respected theories examine the same process from different perspectives. Schramm and Lasswell were two of the early pioneers in the field of communications. Both of these leaders established models of communication that are still viable today.

Schramm's Model

Wilbur Schramm (1907–1987) introduced a model which illustrated the importance of interpersonal communication. He is considered by many to be the father of the study of communications, and he played a critical role in the development of this research. He was the first academic professional to identify himself as a communications scholar, he created the first degree in communications, and he trained the first generation of communications scholars. He founded research institutes at the University of Iowa, the University of Illinois, and Stanford, and he published numerous texts and articles dealing with the dynamics of communications.

From 1948 to 1977, Schramm produced almost a book a year dealing with the study of communications, in addition to the articles, conference papers, and high-quality academic reports that he turned out during this period. Schramm also wrote several very influential texts, including *Mass Media and National Development*. This book was an international best seller, studied by people throughout the world.

Schramm established a model of communication that attempts to explain the problems inherent in human communication. His models evolved in stages. They proceeded from a relatively simple individual form of communication to a complex model involving interaction between two parties.

In Schramm's first model, the source sends a message via an *encoder*, which is received by a decoder and transmitted to its designation. The *source* is the brain of the person starting the communications process. The *encoder* is the process by which ideas are converted to symbols for transmission to the other person. The *decoder* is the process by which the symbols

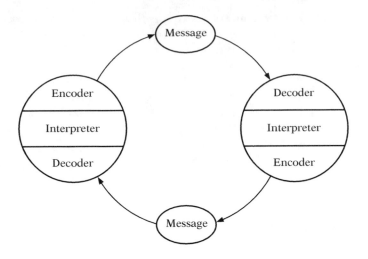

are received and converted into ideas by the person receiving the information. The *signal* indicates that the symbols are produced and transmitted.

Schramm slowly modified this first model to include the concept *that only that information which is shared in the respective parties' fields of experience is actually communicated.* This is the only portion of the information that is communicated, because it is the only shared portion of the signal that is understood by both parties. Schramm's contribution to communications theory included the concept that each person has a field of experience that controls both the encoding and decoding of information and determines the meaning of that information.

Schramm's third model viewed communication as an interaction with both parties actively encoding, interpreting, decoding, transmitting, and receiving signals. He included the feedback of continuously shared information.

Schramm will be remembered as the father of communications and a remarkable scholar who formalized the study of this very important discipline. During the time period when Schramm was developing his theories, another leader in the field was perfecting a different perspective on communications. Harold Lasswell studied propaganda and created the content analysis method of communications research.

Lasswell's Model

Harold Lasswell (1902–1978) published over six million words during his lifetime. His doctoral dissertation, *Propaganda Techniques* in the World War, studied the effect of propaganda on people during World War I. Lasswell defined propaganda *as the management of collective attitudes by the manipulation of significant symbols.* He did not necessarily consider propaganda bad or good; to him that determination depended on the sender's and receiver's points of view and whether the messages were truthful.

Harold Lasswell is best known for one sentence: "Who says what in which channel to who with what effects?" In one of the early classics, Lasswell identifies five common variables in the communication process. He states that one way to analyze the act of communication is to answer the following questions:

- **Who?** When scholars analyze the who component they look at factors that initiate and guide the act of communication. This is called control analysis.

- *Says what?* Scholars who examine this aspect of the communications process engage in content analysis.

- *In which channel?* Scholars who look at the method or ways information travels engage in data analysis. They look at radio, press, film, and other channels of communication.

- *To whom?* Scholars who investigate the persons reached by the media engage in audience analysis.

- *With what effect?* Scholars who are concerned about the impact of the information on audiences study effect analysis.

Despite both being in Washington, D.C., during the war years of 1942 to 1945, Lasswell and Schramm did not meet until 1954, at Stanford. Like Schramm, Lasswell was a prolific scholar. He authored or coauthored over 300 articles and 52 books. Harold Lasswell pioneered content analysis methods and invented the qualitative and quantitative measurement of communications messages. He also introduced psychoanalytic theory into political science. Lasswell will be remembered as one of the giants in the study of communication.

GROUP VERSUS INDIVIDUAL COMMUNICATION

Up to this point we have been discussing the communication cycle without making any distinction between whether the process involves a one-on-one relationship or a situation among more than two people. Most of the information that has been presented applies to an interpersonal relationship. That is, a relationship between two persons. This might include a sergeant talking to a patrol officer or a lieutenant responding to a question from a captain. Many of the communication principles described in this chapter also apply to group communication. For example, feedback can occur at roll call when one patrol officer asks for clarification from the shift sergeant regarding the description of a rape suspect. For purposes of clarification, interpersonal communication may be defined as *the sharing of information between two persons.* Group communication involves interaction among three or more individuals in a face-to-face situation. The three people share a common need that is satisfied by the exchange of information.

The Size of the Group

The term group has been defined as *a number of persons gathered or classified together.* The definition of group communication does not set limits on the ultimate size of the group. However, practical considerations inherent in the definition do define a maximum number of people that would be able to interact effectively. Individuals attending a professional sporting event may have a commonality of interest, but they may not have an opportunity to become involved in a face-to-face situation where they can exchange information that satisfies a common need. If we compare the Super Bowl, with an attendance of 100,000 people, to a group of 5 fans planning a tailgate party before the game, it is easy to see that the size of the group can be a factor in determining the ability of individuals to communicate with each other.

Numerous scholars have examined the dynamics of group communications.[11] Various research has determined that the range between 3 and 20 is a natural size for purposes of defining group interactions. Once the size of the group exceeds 20 people, the ability of individual members to influence each other diminishes. The nature of the gathering takes on more of the characteristics of a mass meeting or conference in which one person may influence the group but the ability of individual members within the group to influence each other is limited. The size of the group has a direct bearing on the nature and type of communication involved. Therefore, we will limit our discussion of communication to groups that do not exceed 20 individuals.

Once the size of the group involved in the communication process has been determined, group interaction must be addressed.

Group Interaction

It is generally accepted by leading scholars, such as Fisher, that there are four phases in group interaction: (1) orientation, (2) conflict, (3) emergence, and (4) reinforcement.

In the *orientation* phase, group members attempt to get to know each other and discover the problems that face the group. This may occur as strangers meet in a group for the first time, or it may happen with people who know each other and attend periodic meetings, such as roll call before the beginning of patrol shifts. In the latter situation, group members already know each other and the orientation is aimed at common problems facing the group. These problems could range from new shift hours to planning a social gathering after the shift.

The second phase, *conflict*, involves disagreement among the members of the group. This phase is characterized by an atmosphere of polarization and controversy. Using the previous two examples, patrol officers may be sharply divided concerning the benefits of the new shift hours or have strong feelings regarding the location of the social gathering.

During the *emergence* phase of group interaction, there is more emphasis on positive statements. This phase allows dissenting members to save face by moving toward the majority's position. Officers who oppose the new shift hours may begin to find other benefits that were not previously discussed. In a similar vein, the location for the party may be a third alternative that is acceptable to all members.

The final phase is *reinforcement*. This phase is the period when group members comment on the positive aspects of the group and its problem-solving ability.

The preceding discussion focused on the dynamics that normally occur in a problem-solving group; however, this interaction in one form or another will usually be present in most groups. A police officer may determine what phase a group is in by listening to the types of comments being made by members of the group, then use that information to express personal views in the most effective manner. Group interaction is an important aspect of any organization. Law enforcement officers need to understand these group dynamics in order to carry out their duties effectively.

Communication Patterns

Anyone who has observed a group of people discussing a topic has observed that not everyone in the group spends the same amount of time talking. Information flows according to status or power. Generally, persons with high status or actual or perceived power send and receive more messages than other members of the group. These persons serve as the hub for group communications. They will receive and send more messages than any other member of the group.

Once a group has been established, certain communication dynamics begin to emerge. A *communications network* is the pattern of information that flows among members of a group. After a group has been in existence and functioning for a period of time, certain members will repeatedly talk with other members. This forms a network over which information flows within the group.

Another communication dynamic that takes place in group communication concerns the *centrality of communication*. *Centrality* is the degree of centralization of the message flow and decision making. In a more centralized group's communication pattern, information is funneled to one or two persons with high status or power, who then transmit the same message to other members of the group.

The classic studies of Leavitt and Bavelas established that more decentralized communication networks are faster in solving complex problems, and centralized networks are more efficient in dealing with less complex issues. However, efficiency in problem solving should not be the only factor considered by the officer. Studies indicate that members of decentralized communication networks experience a greater degree of satisfaction with their participation in the group.

Communication patterns within a group are an important part of the communication process. An intelligent police officer will take the time to understand these patterns and ensure that they are used to the advantage of the department.

The group and individual communication cycle is a dynamic and changing environment. While it is difficult to communicate on an individual basis, a law enforcement officer should not despair at having to communicate with a group. Careful study and persistence will allow one to communicate effectively and thus become a leader within the department.

SUMMARY

Communication plays an important role in our personal and professional life. Up to 70 percent of our work time is spent communicating with others. Communication is a process involving several steps, between two or more persons, for the primary purpose of exchanging information. This process requires sending an idea, receipt of that idea by the other party, an understanding of the idea, and feedback to the sender of the message.

The Johari window is a communication model that allows police officers to examine their ability to communicate with subordinates and superiors effectively. The window is divided into four panes that represent basic areas of knowledge. The Johari window establishes four basic types of communication patterns: Type A has very little feedback or exposure, Type B does not transmit information to subordinates, Type C is characterized by constantly expressing opinions and refusing to accept feedback from others, and Type D emphasizes open lines of communication with feedback from all parties. Schramm and Lasswell are considered to be early pioneers in the field of communications. They also established models of communication. These models further explain this complex interchange of information.

While most of the principles of the communication process apply to both groups and individuals, certain interpersonal dynamics occur in a group setting. The police officer should understand these interactions so as to be able to communicate in any situation.

REVIEW QUESTIONS

1. Describe the concept behind the Johari window. What is the purpose of this concept?

2. How can use of the Johari window make you a better communicator?

3. Since police officers work in a quasi-military organization whose members follow orders, why should they understand the concepts involved in group communication?

CHAPTER 3

Perception in Interpersonal Communication

THE STAGES OF PERCEPTION

Perception is the process by which you become aware of objects, events, and, especially, people through your senses: sight, smell, taste, touch, and hearing. Perception is an active, not a passive, process. Your perceptions result from what exists in the outside world *and* from your own experiences, desires, needs and wants, loves and hatreds. Among the reasons why perception is so important in interpersonal communication is that it influences your communication choices. The messages you send and listen to will depend on how you see the world, on how you size up specific situations, on what you think of the people with whom you interact.

Interpersonal perception is a continuous series of processes that blend into one another. *For convenience of discussion* we can separate them into five stages: (1) you sense, you pick up some kind of stimulation; (2) you organize the stimuli in some way; (3) you interpret and evaluate what you perceive; (4) you store it in memory; and (5) you retrieve it when needed.

Stage One: Stimulation create it

At this first stage, your sense organs are stimulated—you hear a new CD, you see a friend, you smell someone's perfume, you taste an orange, you feel another's sweaty palm. Naturally, you don't perceive everything; rather, you engage in *selective perception,* which includes selective attention and selective exposure. In *selective attention,* you attend to those things that you anticipate will fulfill your needs or will prove enjoyable. For instance, when daydreaming in class, you don't hear what the instructor is saying until your name is called. Your selective attention mechanism focuses your senses on your name.

Through **selective exposure,** you expose yourself to people or messages that will confirm your existing beliefs, that will contribute to your objectives, or that will prove satisfying in some way. For example, after you buy a car, you're more apt to read and listen to advertisements for the car you just bought because these messages tell you that you made the right decision. At the same time, you would avoid advertisements for the cars that you considered but eventually rejected because these messages would tell you that you made the wrong decision.

You're also more likely to perceive stimuli that are greater in intensity than surrounding stimuli and those that have novelty value. For example, television commercials normally play at a greater intensity than regular programming to ensure that you take special notice. You're also more likely to notice the coworker who dresses in a novel way than you are to notice the one who dresses like everyone else. You will quickly perceive someone who shows up in class wearing a tuxedo or at a formal party in shorts.

Stage Two: Organization

At the second stage, you organize the information your senses pick up. Three interesting ways in which people organize their perceptions are by rules, by schemata, and by scripts. Let's look at each briefly.

Organization by Rules   One frequently used rule is that of **proximity,** or physical closeness. The rule, simply stated, says that things that are physically close together constitute a unit. Thus, using this rule, you would perceive people who are often together, or messages spoken one right after the other, as units, as belonging together. You also assume that the verbal and nonverbal signals sent at about the same time are related and constitute a unified whole: you assume they follow a *temporal rule* that says that things occurring together in time belong together.

Another rule is **similarity:** Things that are physically similar, things that look alike, belong together and form a unit. This principle of similarity would lead you to see people who dress alike as belonging together. Similarly, you might assume that people who work at the same jobs, who are of the same religion, who live in the same building, or who talk with the same accent belong together.

You use the principle of *contrast* when you note that some items (people or messages, for example) don't belong together because they are too different from each other to be part of the same perceptual organization. So, for example, in a conversation or a public speech, listeners will focus their attention on changes in intensity or rate because these contrast with the rest of the message.

Organization by Schemata   Another way you organize material is by creating **schemata,** mental templates or structures that help you organize the millions of items of information you come into contact with every day as well as those you already have in memory. Schemata may thus be viewed as general ideas about people (Pat and Chris, Japanese, Baptists, New Yorkers), about yourself (your qualities, abilities, and even liabilities), or about social roles (what's a police officer, professor, or multibillionaire CEO like). (*Schemata,* by the way, is the plural of *schema* and is preferred to the more logical plural *schemas*.)

You develop schemata from your own experience—actual as well as from vicarious experience gained from television, reading, and hearsay. Thus, for example, you might have a schema for college athletes, and this might include that they're strong, ambitious, academically weak, and egocentric. And, of course, you've probably developed schemata for different religious, racial, and national groups, for men and women, and for people of different affectional orientations. Each group that you have some familiarity with will be represented in your mind in some kind of schema. Schemata help you organize your perceptions by allowing you to classify millions of people into a manageable number of categories or classes. As you'll see below, however, schemata can also create problems and influence you to see what is not there or to miss seeing what is there.

Organization by Scripts   A **script** is really a type of schema. Like a schema, a script is an organized body of information about some action, event, or procedure. It's a general idea of how some event should play out or unfold; it's the rules governing events and their sequence. For example, you probably have a script for eating in a restaurant with the actions organized into a pattern something like this: enter, take a seat, review the menu, order from the menu, eat your food, ask for the bill, leave a tip, pay the bill, exit the restaurant. Similarly, you probably have scripts for how you do laundry,

[handwritten note: Once the uniform goes on. You have No Racism.]

how an interview is to be conducted, the stages you go through in introducing someone to someone else, and the way you ask for a date.

Stage Three: Interpretation-Evaluation

The interpretation-evaluation (hyphenated because the two processes cannot be separated) step is inevitably subjective and is greatly influenced by your experiences, needs, wants, values, beliefs about the way things are or should be, expectations, physical and emotional state, and so on. Your interpretation-evaluation will be influenced by your rules, schemata, and scripts as well as by your gender; for example, women have been found to view others more positively than men (Winquist, Mohr, & Kenny, 1998).

For example, upon meeting a new person who is introduced to you as a college football player, you would apply your schema to this person and view him as strong, ambitious, academically weak, and egocentric. You would, in other words, see this person through the filter of your schema and evaluate him according to your schema for college athletes. Similarly, when viewing someone performing some series of actions (say, eating in a restaurant), you apply your script to this event and view the event through the script. You would interpret the actions of the diner as appropriate or inappropriate depending on the script you had for this behavior and the ways in which the diner performed the sequence of actions.

Stage Four: Memory

Your perceptions and their interpretations-evaluations are put into memory; they're stored so that you may ultimately retrieve them at some later time. So, for example, you have in memory your schema for college athletes and you know that Ben Williams is a football player. Ben Williams is then stored in memory with "cognitive tags" that tell you that he's strong, ambitious, academically weak, and egocentric. Now, despite the fact that you've not witnessed Ben's strength or ambitions and have no idea of his academic record or his psychological profile, you still may store your memory of Ben along with the qualities that make up your script for "college athletes."

Now, let's say that at different times you hear that Ben failed Spanish I, normally an A or B course at your school, that Ben got an A in Chemistry (normally a tough course), and that Ben is transferring to Harvard as a theoretical physics major. Schemata act as filters or gatekeepers; they allow certain information to be stored in relatively objective form, much as you heard or read it, and may distort or prevent other information from being stored. As a result, these three items of information about Ben may get stored very differently in your memory along with your schema for college athletes.

For example, you might readily store the information that Ben failed Spanish because it's consis-tent with your schema; it fits neatly into the template that you have of college athletes. Information that's consistent with your schema—as in this example—will strengthen your schema and make it more resistant to change (Aronson, Wilson, & Akert, 1997). Depending on the strength of your schema, you might also store in memory (even though you didn't hear it) that Ben did poorly in other courses as well. The information that Ben got an A in Chemistry, because it contradicts your schema (it just doesn't seem right), might easily be distorted or lost. The information that Ben is transferring to Harvard, however, is a bit different. This information is also inconsistent with your schema, but it is so drastically inconsistent that you begin to look at this mindfully and may even begin to question your schema of athletes, or perhaps view Ben as an exception to the general rule. In either case, you're going to etch Ben's transferring to Harvard very clearly in your mind.

Stage Five: Recall

At some later date, you may want to recall or access the information you have stored in memory. Let's say you want to retrieve your information about Ben because he's the topic of discussion among you and a few friends. As you'll see in the discussion of listening in the next chapter, memory isn't reproductive; you don't simply reproduce what you've heard or seen. Rather, you reconstruct what you've heard or seen into a whole that is meaningful to you—depending in great part on your schemata and scripts—and it's this reconstruction that you store in memory. Now, when you want to retrieve this information from memory, you may recall it with a variety of inaccuracies. You're likely to

- recall information that is consistent with your schema; in fact, you may not even recall the specific information you're looking for (say about Ben) but actually just your schema (which contains the information about college athletes and, because he is one, also about Ben)

- fail to recall information that is inconsistent with your schema; you have no place to put that information, so you easily lose it or forget it

- recall information that drastically contradicts your schema because it forces you to think (and perhaps rethink) about your schema and its accuracy; it may even force you to revise your schema in general

Before moving on to the more specific processes involved in interpersonal perception, let's spell out some of the implications of this five-stage model for your own interpersonal perceptions.

1. Everyone relies on shortcuts—rules, schemata, and scripts, for example, are all useful shortcuts to simplify understanding, remembering, and recalling information about people and events. If you didn't have these shortcuts, you'd have to treat each person, role, or action differently from each other person, role, or action. This would make every experience a new one, totally unrelated to anything you already know. If you didn't use these shortcuts, you'd be unable to generalize, draw connections, and otherwise profit from previously acquired knowledge.

2. Shortcuts, however, may mislead you; they may contribute to your remembering things that are consistent with your schemata (even if they didn't occur) and distorting or forgetting information that is inconsistent.

3. What you remember about a person or an event isn't an objective recollection but is more likely heavily influenced by your preconceptions or your schemata about what belongs and what doesn't belong, what fits neatly into the templates in your brain and what doesn't fit. Your reconstruction of an event or person contains a lot of information that

was not in the original experience and may omit a lot that was in this experience.

4. Judgments about others are invariably ethnocentric; because your schemata and scripts are created on the basis of your own cultural experiences, you invariably apply these to members of other cultures. From this, it's easy to infer that when members of other cultures do things that conform to your scripts they're right and when they do things that contradict your scripts they're wrong—a classic example of ethnocentric thinking. As you can appreciate, this tendency can easily contribute to intercultural misunderstandings.

5. Memory is especially unreliable when the information can be interpreted in different ways, that is, when it's ambiguous. For example, consider the statement "Ben didn't do as well in his other courses as he would have liked." If your schema of Ben was "brilliant," you might "remember" that Ben got B's. But if, as in our example, your schema was of the academically weak athlete, you might "remember" that Ben got D's. Conveniently, but unreliably, schemata reduce ambiguity.

⚓ PERCEPTUAL PROCESSES

Before reading about the specific processes that you use in perceiving other people, examine your own perception strategies by taking the self-test, "How accurate are you at people perception?"

Test Yourself

How Accurate Are You at People Perception?

Instructions: Respond to each of the following statements with T (true) if the statement is usually accurate in describing your behavior or with F (false) if the statement is usually inaccurate. Resist the temptation to give the "preferred" or "desirable" answers; respond, instead, as you actually behave.

_____ 1. I base most of my impressions of people on the first few minutes of our meeting.

_____ 2. When I know some things about another person, I fill in what I don't know.

_____ 3. I make predictions about people's behaviors that generally prove to be true.

_____ 4. I have clear ideas of what people of different national, racial, and religious groups are really like.

_____ 5. I reserve making judgments about people until I learn a great deal about them and see them in a variety of situations.

_____ 6. On the basis of my observations of people, I formulate guesses (that I am willing to revise), rather than firmly held conclusions.

_____ 7. I pay special attention to people's behaviors that might contradict my initial impressions.

_____ 8. I delay formulating conclusions about people until I have lots of evidence.

_____ 9. I avoid making assumptions about what is going on in someone else's head on the basis of their behaviors.

_____ 10. I recognize that people are different and don't assume that everyone is like me.

■ **HOW DID YOU DO?**   This brief perception test was designed to raise questions to be considered in this chapter and not to provide you with a specific perception score. The first four questions refer to tendencies to judge others on the basis of first impressions (question 1), implicit personality theories (2), prophecies (3), and stereotypes (4). Ideally, you would have responded "false" to these four statements since they represent sources of distortion. Questions 5 through 10 refer to specific guidelines for increasing accuracy in people perception: looking for a variety of cues (5), formulating hypotheses rather than conclusions (6), being especially alert to contradictory cues (7), delaying conclusions until more evidence is in (8), avoiding the tendency to mind read (9), and recognizing the diversity in people (10). Ideally, you would have responded "true" to these six statements since they represent suggestions for increased accuracy in perception.

■ **WHAT WILL YOU DO?**   As you read this chapter, think about these principles and consider how you might use them more accurately and not allow them to get in the way of accurate and reasonable people perception. Do recognize, however, that situations vary widely and that these principles will prove useful only most of the time. You may want to identify situations in which these principles would be violated.

Implicit Personality Theory

Each person has a subconscious, or implicit, system of rules that says which characteristics of an individual go with other characteristics. Consider, for example, the following brief statements. Note the word in parentheses that you think best completes each sentence:

Carlo is energetic, eager, and (intelligent, stupid).

Kim is bold, defiant, and (extroverted, introverted).

Joe is bright, lively, and (thin, heavy).

Ava is attractive, intelligent, and (likable, unlikable).

Susan is cheerful, positive, and (outgoing, shy).

Angel is handsome, tall, and (friendly, unfriendly).

What makes some of these choices seem right and others seem wrong is your **implicit personality theory,** the system of rules that tells you which characteristics go with which other characteristics. Your theory may, for example, have told you that a person who is energetic and eager is also intelligent, not stupid, although there is no logical reason why a stupid person could not be energetic and eager. Similarly, you may find yourself hired for a job on the basis of your demonstrated competitiveness because the personnel director has the implicit personality theory that along with competitiveness comes the willingness to work hard and the determination to succeed.

The widely documented **halo effect** is a function of the implicit personality theory (Dion, Berscheid, & Walster, 1972; Riggio, 1987). If you believe a person has some positive qualities, you're likely to infer that she or he also possesses other positive qualities. There is also a *reverse halo effect:* if you know a person possesses several negative qualities, you're likely to infer that the person also has other negative qualities.

When using implicit personality theories, apply them carefully and critically so as to avoid perceiving qualities that your theory tells you should be present in an individual when they actually are not. For example, you see "goodwill" in a friend's "charitable" acts when a tax deduction may have been the real motive.

Similarly, be careful of ignoring or distorting qualities that don't conform to your theory but that are actually present in the individual. For example, you may ignore negative qualities in your friends that you would easily perceive in your enemies.

As you might expect, the implicit personality theories that people hold differ from culture to culture, group to group, and even person to person. For example, the Chinese have a concept called *shi gu*, which refers to "someone who is worldly, devoted to his or her family, socially skillful, and somewhat reserved" (Aronson, Wilson, & Akert, 1997, p. 190). This concept isn't easily encoded in English, as you can tell by trying to find a general concept that covers this type of person. In English, on the other hand, we have a concept of the "artistic type," a generalization that seems absent in the Chinese languages. Thus, although it is easy for speakers of English or Chinese to refer to specific concepts—such as socially skilled or creative—each language creates its own generalized categories. Thus, in Chinese languages, the qualities that make up *shi gu* are more easily seen as going together than they might be for an English speaker; they're part of the implicit personality theory of more Chinese speakers than of, say, English speakers.

Similarly, consider the different personality theories that "graduate students" and "blue-collar high-school dropouts" might have for "college students." Likewise, one person may have had great experiences with doctors and so may have a very positive personality theory of doctors whereas another person may have had negative experiences with doctors and might thus have developed a very negative personality theory.

The Self-Fulfilling Prophecy

A **self-fulfilling prophecy** occurs when you make a prediction that comes true because you act on it as if it were true (Merton, 1957). Put differently, a self-fulfilling prophecy occurs when you act on your schema as if it were true and in doing so make it true. There are four basic steps in the self-fulfilling prophecy:

1. You make a prediction or formulate a belief about a person or a situation. For example, you predict that Pat is friendly in interpersonal encounters.
2. You act toward that person or situation as if that prediction or belief were true. For example, you act as if Pat were a friendly person.

3. Because you act as if the belief were true, it becomes true. For example, because of the way you act toward Pat, Pat becomes comfortable and friendly.

4. You observe *your* effect on the person or the resulting situation, and what you see strengthens your beliefs. For example, you observe Pat's friendliness, and this reinforces your belief that Pat is in fact friendly.

The self-fulfilling prophecy can also be seen when you make predictions about yourself and fulfill them. For example, you might enter a group situation convinced that the other members will dislike you. Almost invariably you'll be proved right; the other members will appear to you to dislike you. What you may be doing is acting in a way that encourages the group to respond to you negatively. In this way, you fulfill your prophecies about yourself.

A widely known example of the self-fulfilling prophecy is the **Pygmalion effect.** In one study, teachers were told that certain pupils were expected to do exceptionally well, that they were late bloomers. The names of these students were actually selected at random by the experimenters. The results, however, were not random. The students whose names were given to the teachers actually performed at a higher level than the others. In fact, these students' IQ scores even improved more than did the other students'. The teachers' expectations probably prompted them to give extra attention to the selected students, thereby positively affecting their performance (Rosenthal & Jacobson, 1968; Insel & Jacobson, 1975).

Self-fulfilling prophecies can short-circuit critical thinking and influence another's behavior (or your own) so that it conforms to your prophecy. As a result, it can lead you to see what you predicted rather than what is really there (for example, to perceive yourself as a failure because you have predicted it rather than because of any actual failures).

Primacy-Recency

Assume for a moment that you're enrolled in a course in which half the classes are extremely dull and half extremely exciting. At the end of the semester, you evaluate the course and the instructor. Would your evaluation be more favorable if the dull classes occurred in the first half of the semester and the exciting classes in the second? Or, would it be more favorable if the order were reversed? If what comes first exerts the most influence, you have a **primacy effect.** If what comes last (or most recently) exerts the most influence, you have a **recency effect.**

In the classic study on the effects of primacy-recency in interpersonal perception, college students perceived a person who was described as "intelligent, industrious, impulsive, critical, stubborn, and envious" more positively than a person described as "envious, stubborn, critical, impulsive, industrious, and intelligent" (Asch, 1946). Clearly, there's a tendency to use early information to get a general idea about a person and to use later information to make this impression more specific. The initial information helps you form a schema for the person. Once that schema is formed, you're likely to resist information that contradicts it.

COMMUNICATING WITH POWER

Exerting Power Through Self-Presentation

One way to exert power and influence others is to use the strategies of self-presentation—to present yourself in ways that will encourage others to think or do as you wish. Here are four such strategies and the potential pitfalls of each (Jones & Pittman, 1982; Jones, 1990):

- Use *ingratiation*. Express lots of agreement with the opinions of the other person, compliment the other, or do favors for this person. However, you run the risk of being seen as a sycophant, someone who will stop at nothing to be liked.
- Use *self-promotion*. Present yourself as competent so that the other person will respect you. Be careful, however, that you're not perceived as incompetent on the theory that competent people *demonstrate* competence rather than talk about it.
- Use *exemplification*. Present yourself as worthy, moral, and virtuous. The downside is that you may appear sanctimonious, or "holier than thou," a quality that most people dislike.
- Use *supplication*. Present yourself as helpless and in need of assistance: "Can you type my paper? I'm such a bad typist." As a supplicant you run the risk of being seen as incompetent or perhaps lazy.

How would you explain it?

Which strategy do you think would prove most helpful in an employment interview situation? How might it play out?

One interesting practical implication of primacy-recency is that the first impression you make is likely to be the most important. The reason for this is that the schema that others form of you functions as a filter to admit or block additional information about you. If the initial impression or schema is positive, others are likely to remember additional positive information because it confirms their schema and to forget or distort negative information because it contradicts their schema. They are also more likely to interpret as positive information that is actually ambiguous. You win in all three ways—if the initial impression is positive.

The tendency to give greater weight to early information and to interpret later information in light of early impressions can lead you to formulate a total picture of an individual on the basis of initial impressions that may not be typical or accurate. For example, if you judge a job applicant as generally nervous when he or she may simply be showing normal nervousness at being interviewed for a much-needed job, you will have misperceived this individual.

Similarly, this tendency can lead you to discount or distort subsequent perceptions so as not to disrupt your initial impression or upset your original schema. For example, you may fail to see signs of deceit in someone you like because of your early impressions that this person is a good and honest individual.

Stereotyping

One of the most common shortcuts in interpersonal perception is stereotyping. A sociological or psychological **stereotype** is a fixed impression of a group of people; it's a schema. We all have attitudinal stereotypes—of national, religious, sexual, or racial groups, or perhaps of criminals, prostitutes, teachers, or plumbers. If you have these fixed impressions, you will, on meeting a member of a particular group, often see that person primarily as a member of that group and apply to him or her all the characteristics you assign to that group. If you meet someone who is a prostitute, for example, there is a host of characteristics for prostitutes that you may apply to this one person. To complicate matters further, you will often "see" in this person's behavior the manifestation of characteristics that you would not "see" if you didn't know that this person was a prostitute. Stereotypes can easily distort accurate perception and prevent you from seeing an individual as an individual rather than as a member of a group.

"It's all according to your point of view. To me, *you're* a monster."
© J. B. Handelsman

The tendency to group people and to respond to individuals primarily as members of groups can lead you to perceive an individual as possessing those qualities (usually negative) that you believe characterize his or her group (for example, "all Mexicans are . . . ," or "all Baptists are . . .") and, therefore, fail to appreciate the multifaceted nature of all individuals and groups. Stereotyping can also lead you to ignore each person's unique characteristics and, therefore, to fail to benefit from the special contributions each individual can bring to an encounter.

Attribution

Attribution is a process by which we try to explain the motivation for a person's behavior. One way to do this is to ask if the person was in control of the behavior. For example, say you invited your friend Desmond to dinner for 7 p.m. and he arrives at 9. Consider how you would respond to each of these reasons:

Reason 1: I just couldn't tear myself away from the beach. I really wanted to get a great tan.

Reason 2: I was driving here when I saw some young kids mugging an old couple. I broke it up and took the couple home. They were so frightened that I had to stay with them until their children arrived. Their phone was out of order, so I had no way of calling to tell you I'd be late.

Reason 3: I got in a car accident and was taken to the hospital.

Assuming you believe all three explanations, you would attribute very different motives to Desmond's behavior. With reasons 1 and 2, you would conclude that Desmond was in control of his behavior; with reason 3, that he was not. Further, you would probably respond negatively to reason 1 (Desmond was selfish and inconsiderate) and positively to reason 2 (Desmond was a Good Samaritan). Because Desmond was not in control of his behavior in reason 3, you would probably not attribute either positive or negative motivation to his behavior. Instead, you would probably feel sorry that he got into an accident.

You probably make similar judgments based on controllability in numerous situations. Consider, for example, how you would respond to the following situations:

- Doris fails her history midterm exam.
- Sidney's car is repossessed because he failed to keep up the payments.
- Margie is 150 pounds overweight and is complaining that she feels awful.
- Thomas's wife has just filed for divorce and he is feeling depressed.

You would most likely be sympathetic to each of these people if you feel that he or she was not in control of what happened, for example, if the examination was unfair, if Sidney lost his job because of employee discrimination, if Margie has a glandular problem, and if Thomas's wife wants to leave him for a wealthy drug dealer. On the other hand, you probably would not be sympathetic toward these people if you felt they were in control of what happened, for example, if Doris partied instead of studied, if Sidney gambled his payments away, if Margie ate nothing but junk food and refused to exercise, and if Thomas had been repeatedly unfaithful and his wife finally gave up trying to reform him.

COMMUNICATING WITH POWER

Referent Power

How you perceive a person will influence the kind and degree of **referent power** this person has over you. For example, if you perceive your older brother as someone you want to be like and identify with, your older brother has referent power over you. A seasoned and successful stockbroker on Wall Street may have referent power over the college interns because they want to be like the broker. The assumption made by the interns is that they will be more like the broker if they behave and believe as the broker does. Generally, your referent power increases when you're well liked and well respected, when you're perceived as attractive and prestigious, when you're the same sex as the other person, and when you have similar attitudes and experiences as the person perceiving you.

How would you explain it?

How would you explain the way referent power operates in your own everyday interactions? Can you identify those who have referent power over you? Over whom do you have referent power?

In perceiving, and especially in evaluating, other people's behavior, we frequently ask if they were in control of the behavior. Generally, research shows that if we feel a person was in control of negative behaviors, we will come to dislike him or her. If we believe the person was not in control of negative behaviors, we will come to feel sorry for and not blame the person.

Attribution Errors   Attribution of causality can lead to several potential errors.

The **self-serving bias** is an error usually made to preserve your self-esteem. You commit the self-serving bias when you take credit for the positive and deny responsibility for the negative. For example, you're more likely to attribute your positive behaviors (say, you get an A on an exam) to internal and controllable factors—to your personality, intelligence, or hard work (Bernstein, Stephan, & Davis, 1979). And you're more likely to attribute your negative behaviors (say, you get a D) to external and uncontrollable factors—to the exam being exceptionally difficult or unfair.

Another potential error is **overattribution,** the tendency to single out one or two obvious characteristics of a person and attribute everything that person does to this one or these two characteristics, which is exactly what the scientists are doing in the cartoon below. For example, if a person had exceptionally loving parents or is blind or was born into great wealth, there's often a tendency to attribute everything that person does to such factors. And so you might say, "Sally has little difficulty forming meaningful relationships because she grew up in a home of loving parents," "Alex overeats because he's blind," and "Lillian is irresponsible because she never had to work for her money." To prevent overattribution, recognize that most behaviors and personality characteristics result from lots of factors. You almost always make a mistake when you select one factor and attribute everything to it. So when you make a judgment, ask yourself if other factors might be operating here: Are there other factors that might be influencing Sally's relationships, Alex's eating habits, and Lillian's irresponsible behavior?

A third error is called the **fundamental attribution error,** which occurs when you overvalue the contribution of internal factors (for example, the

person's personality) and undervalue the influence of external factors (for example, the context or situation the person is in). It's the tendency to conclude that people do what they do because that's the kind of people they are, not because of the situation they're in. When Pat is late for an appointment, you're more likely to conclude that Pat is inconsiderate or irresponsible than to attribute the lateness to the bus breaking down or a traffic accident.

When you explain your own behavior, you also favor internal explanations—although not to as great an extent as when explaining the behaviors of others. One reason you give greater weight to internal factors in explaining your own behavior than in explaining the behavior of others is that you know the situation surrounding your own behavior. You know, for example, what's going on in your love life and your financial situation, so you naturally see the influence of these factors. But you rarely know as much about others. You're therefore likely to give less weight to the external factors in their cases.

This fundamental attribution error is at least in part culturally influenced. For example, in the United States, people are more likely to explain behavior by saying that people did what they did because of who they are. But when Hindus in India were asked to explain why their friends behaved as they did, they gave greater weight to external factors than did Americans in the United States (Miller, 1984; Aronson, Wilson, & Akert, 1997). Generally, Americans have little hesitation in offering causal explanations of a person's behavior ("Pat did this because . . ."); Hindus, on the other hand, are generally reluctant to explain a person's behavior in causal terms (Matsumoto, 1994). A similar difference has been found between Americans and Koreans. For example, in one study, American and Korean students were presented with a speech endorsing a particular position and told that the writer had been instructed to write this and really had no choice (Goode, 2000). Americans were more likely to believe that the speaker believed in the position endorsed; they believed that what the speaker was saying was due to what the speaker believed (and not to the external circumstances of being forced to write the speech). Korean students, on the other hand, were much less likely to believe in the sincerity of the speaker and gave greater weight to the external factors, that is, that the speaker was forced to write the speech.

Thinking Critically About
INTERPERSONAL PERCEPTION

Successful interpersonal communication depends largely on the accuracy of your interpersonal perception. You already know the barriers that can arise with each of the perceptual processes, for example, the self-serving bias, overattribution, and the fundamental attribution error in attribution. There are, however, additional ways to think more critically about your perceptions and thereby to increase your perceptual accuracy.

Analyze Your Perceptions

When you become aware of your perceptions, you'll be able to subject them to logical analysis, to critical thinking. Here are a few suggestions:

- Recognize your own role in perception. Your emotional and physiological state will influence the meaning you give to your perceptions. A movie may seem hysterically funny when you're in a good mood but just plain stupid when you're in a bad mood or when you're preoccupied with family problems. Beware of your own biases. Know when your perceptual evaluations are unduly influenced by your own biases—for example, perceiving only the positive in people you like and only the negative in people you don't like.

- Avoid early conclusions. On the basis of your observations of behaviors, formulate hypotheses to test against additional information and evidence rather than draw conclusions you then look to confirm. Delay formulating conclusions until you have had a chance to process a wide variety of cues.

- Avoid the one-cue conclusion. Look for a variety of cues pointing in the same direction. The more cues pointing to the same conclusion, the more likely your conclusion will be correct. Be especially alert to contradictory cues, ones that refute your initial hypotheses. It's relatively easy to perceive cues that confirm your hypotheses but more difficult to acknowledge contradictory evidence. At the same time, seek validation from others. Do others see things the same way you do? If not, ask yourself if your perceptions may be in some way distorted.

- Avoid mind reading; avoid trying to read the thoughts and feelings of other people just from observing their behaviors. Regardless of how many behaviors you observe and how carefully you examine them, you can only *guess* what is going on in someone's mind. A person's motives are not open to outside inspection; you can only make assumptions based on overt behaviors.

Check Your Perceptions

Perception checking is another way to reduce uncertainty and to make your perceptions more accurate. The goal of perception checking is to further explore the thoughts and feelings of the other person, not to prove that your initial perception is correct. With this simple technique, you lessen your chances of misinterpreting another's feelings. At the same time, you give the other person an opportunity to elaborate on his or her thoughts and feelings. In its most basic form, perception checking consists of two steps:

1. Describe what you see or hear, recognizing that even descriptions are not really objective, but heavily influenced by who you are, your emotional state, and so on. At the same time, you may wish to describe what you think is happening. Again, try to do this as descriptively (not evaluatively) as you can. Sometimes you may wish to offer several possibilities. Here are some examples:

   - "You've called me from work a lot this week. You seem concerned that everything is all right at home."

   - "You've not wanted to talk with me all week. You say that my work is fine, but you don't seem to want to give me the same responsibilities that other editorial assistants have."

2. Ask the other person for confirmation. Be careful that your request for confirmation does not sound as though you already know the answer: avoid phrasing your questions defensively. Avoid saying, for example, "You really don't want to go out, do you? I knew you didn't when you turned on that lousy television." Instead, ask for confirmation in as supportive a way as possible:

- "Would you rather watch TV?"
- "Are you worried about me or the kids?"
- "Are you pleased with my work? Is there anything I can do to improve my job performance?"

COMMUNICATING ETHICALLY

Making Ethical Choices

Your 16-year-old son has been diagnosed with a rare blood disease and given only a month or two to live. The doctors say that there is no need to tell him about the severity of his illness because it will only depress him and may even hasten his death. But, they say, the decision is up to you.

One approach to ethics revolves around this notion of choice and argues that people have the right to information relevant to the choices they make. In this view, communications are ethical when they facilitate people's freedom of choice by presenting them with accurate information, with the kind of information that is helpful in making their own choices. Communications are unethical when they interfere with people's freedom of choice by preventing them from securing information that will help them make those choices or by giving them false or misleading information that will lead them to make choices they would not make if they had accurate and truthful information. According to this approach, then, your child has the right to learn about his true condition because this information bears directly on the choices he may wish to make.

In this ethical system, you have the right to information about yourself that others possess and that influences the choices you will make. Thus, for example, you have the right to face your accusers, to know the witnesses who will be called to testify against you, to see your credit ratings, and to know

what Social Security benefits you'll receive. On the other hand, you do not have the right to information that is none of your business, such as information about whether your neighbors are happy or argue a lot or receive food stamps.

You also have the right to remain silent and to withhold information that has no bearing on the matter at hand. For example, your previous relationship history, affectional orientation, or religion is usually irrelevant to your ability to function as a doctor or police officer and may thus be kept private in most job-related situations. If these issues become relevant—say, you're about to enter a new relationship—then there *may* be an obligation to reveal your relationship history, affectional orientation, or religion, for example.

What would you do?

Your best friend's husband is currently having an extramarital affair with a 17-year-old girl. Your friend suspects this is going on and asks you if you know anything. Would it be ethical for you to lie and say you know nothing, or are you obligated to tell your friend what you know? Are you obligated to tell the police?

What would you do if you were the parent in the example opening this ethics box?

Reduce Your Uncertainty

We all have a tendency to reduce uncertainty, a process that enables us to achieve greater accuracy in perception. In large part, we learn about uncertainty and how to deal with it from our culture.

Culture and Uncertainty   People from different cultures differ greatly in their attitudes toward uncertainty and how to deal with it, attitudes that affect perceptual accuracy. In some cultures, people do little to avoid uncertainty and have little anxiety about not knowing what will happen next. Uncertainty to them is a normal part of life and is accepted as it comes. Members of these cultures don't feel threatened by unknown situations. Examples of such low-anxiety cultures include Singapore, Jamaica, Denmark, Sweden, Hong Kong, Ireland, Great Britain, Malaysia, India, Philippines, and the United States. Other cultures do much to avoid uncertainty and are anxious about not knowing what will happen next; uncertainty is seen as threatening and something that must be counteracted. Examples of such high-anxiety cultures include Greece, Portugal, Guatemala, Uruguay, Belgium, El Salvador, Japan, Yugoslavia, Peru, France, Chile, Spain, and Costa Rica (Hofstede, 1997).

The potential for communication problems can be great when people come from cultures with different attitudes toward uncertainty. For example, managers from cultures with weak uncertainty avoidance will accept workers who work only when they have to and will not get too upset when workers are late. Managers from cultures with strong uncertainty avoidance will expect workers to be busy at all times and will have little tolerance for lateness.

Because weak uncertainty avoidance cultures have great tolerance for ambiguity and uncertainty, they minimize the rules governing communication and relationships (Hofstede, 1997; Lustig & Koester, 1996). People who don't follow the same rules as the cultural majority are readily tolerated. Different approaches and perspectives may even be encouraged in cultures with weak uncertainty avoidance. Strong uncertainty avoidance cultures create clear-cut rules for communication. It's considered unacceptable for people to break these rules.

Students from weak uncertainty avoidance cultures appreciate freedom in education and prefer vague assignments without specific timetables. These students will want to be rewarded for creativity and will easily accept the instructor's (sometimes) lack of knowledge. Students from strong uncertainty avoidance cultures prefer highly structured experiences where there is little ambiguity; they prefer specific objectives, detailed instructions, and definite timetables. These students expect to be judged on the basis of the right answers and expect the instructor to have all the answers all the time (Hofstede, 1997).

Strategies for Reducing Uncertainty   A variety of strategies can help reduce uncertainty (Berger & Bradac, 1982; Gudykunst, 1991). For instance, observing another person while he or she is engaged in an active task, preferably interacting with others in more informal social situations, will often reveal a great deal about the person because people are less apt to monitor their behaviors and more likely to reveal their true selves in informal situations.

Listening to Others' Perceptions

"Galileo and the Ghosts" is a technique for seeing how a particular group of people perceives a problem, person, or situation (DeVito, 1996). It involves setting up a mental "ghost-thinking team," much as corporations and research institutes maintain think tanks. In this ghost-thinking technique, you select a team of four to eight "people" you admire, for example, historical figures such as Aristotle or Picasso, fictional figures such as Wonder Woman or Captain Picard, public figures such as Oprah Winfrey or Ralph Nader, or people from other cultures or of a different sex or affectional orientation.

You pose a question or problem and then listen to how this team of ghosts perceives and ultimately solves your problem. Of course, you are really listening to yourself, but yourself acting in the roles of other people. The technique forces you to step outside your normal role and to consider the perceptions of someone totally different from you. If you wish, visualize yourself and your ghost-thinking team seated around a conference table, in a restaurant having lunch, or even jogging in the park. Choose the team members and the settings in any way you would like.

In the ghost-thinking technique, each team member views your problem from his or her unique perspective. As a result, your perception of the problem will change. Your team members then view this new perception and perhaps analyze it again. As a result, your perception of the problem changes again. The process continues until you achieve a solution or decide that this technique has yielded all the insight it's going to yield.

In interpersonal communication and relationships, this technique might be used to see an issue or problem from the point of view of your romantic partner, parent, or child. In a small group setting, you might use it to help you to see an issue from management's or the employees' point of view. And in public speaking, it could help you visualize your topic or purpose from the perspective of different audiences.

Suggestions?

Try setting up a ghost-thinking team to help you become a more responsive and supportive friend, more popular at work, or a better student. Who would you select? What specific questions would you ask? What might each member say?

You can also manipulate the situation in such a way that you observe the person in more specific and more revealing contexts. Employment interviews, theatrical auditions, and student teaching are some of the ways situations can be created to observe how the person might act and react and hence to reduce uncertainty about the person.

When you log on to an Internet chat group for the first time and lurk, reading the exchanges between the other group members before saying anything yourself, you're learning about the people in the group and about the group itself and thus reducing uncertainty. When uncertainty is reduced, you're more likely to make contributions that will be appropriate to the group and less likely to violate any of the group's norms; in short, you're more likely to communicate effectively. Another common situation in which you'd seek to reduce uncertainty is when you have two or three job offers. In an effort to select the best offer, you'd seek to reduce your uncertainty about the potential for advancement, the benefits package, the likelihood that the company will expand, and so on.

Another way to reduce uncertainty, this time about a particular person, is to collect information about the person through asking others. You might inquire of a colleague whether another colleague finds you interesting and might like to have dinner with you.

And, of course, you can interact with the individual. For example, you can ask questions: "Do you enjoy sports?" "What did you think of that computer science course?" "What would you do if you got fired?" You also gain knowledge of another by disclosing information about yourself. Your disclosures will help to create an environment that encourages disclosures from the person you wish to know better.

Increase Your Cultural Sensitivity

Recognizing and being sensitive to cultural differences will help increase your accuracy in perception. For example, Russian or Chinese artists such as ballet dancers will often applaud their audiences by clapping. Americans seeing this may easily interpret it as egotistical. Similarly, a German man will enter a restaurant before a woman in order to see if the place is respectable enough for the woman to enter. This simple custom can easily be interpreted as rude when viewed by those who come from cultures in which it's considered courteous for the woman to enter first (Axtell, 1991).

Within every cultural group, there are wide and important differences. As all Americans are not alike, neither are all Indonesians, Greeks, Mexicans, and so on. When you make assumptions that all people of a certain culture are alike, you are using stereotypes. Recognizing differences between another culture and your own and recognizing differences among members of a particular culture will help you perceive the situation more accurately.

Summary of Concepts and Skills

In this chapter, we explored the way we receive messages through perception, how perception works, the processes that influence it, and how to make your perceptions more accurate.

1. Perception refers to the process by which you become aware of the many stimuli impinging on your senses. It occurs in five stages: sensory stimulation occurs, sensory stimulation is organized, sensory stimulation is interpreted-evaluated, sensory stimulation is held in memory, and sensory stimulation is recalled.
2. The following processes influence perception: (1) implicit personality theory, (2) self-fulfilling prophecy, (3) primacy-recency, (4) stereotyping, and (5) attribution.
3. *Implicit personality theory* refers to the private personality theory that you hold and that influences how you perceive other people.
4. A self-fulfilling prophecy occurs when you make a prediction or formulate a belief that comes true because you have made the prediction and acted as if it were true.

5. *Primacy-recency* refers to the relative influence of stimuli as a result of their order. If what occurs first exerts greater influence, you have a primacy effect. If what occurs last exerts greater influence, you have a recency effect.
6. Stereotyping is the tendency to develop and maintain fixed, unchanging perceptions of groups of people and to use these perceptions to evaluate individual members of these groups, ignoring their individual, unique characteristics.
7. Attribution, the process through which you try to understand the behaviors of others (and your own, in self-attribution), particularly the reasons or motivations for these behaviors, is made on the basis of consensus, consistency, distinctiveness, and controllability. Errors of attribution include the self-serving bias, overattribution, and the fundamental attribution error.
8. Increase the accuracy of your interpersonal perceptions by (1) perceiving critically, for example, recognizing your role in perception, formulating hypotheses rather than conclusions, looking for a

variety of cues (especially contradictory ones), avoiding mind reading, and being aware of your own biases; (2) perception checking, that is, describing what you see or hear and asking for confirmation; (3) reducing uncertainty by, for example, lurking before joining a group, collecting information about the person or situation, and interacting and observing the interaction; and (4) being culturally sensitive, recognizing the differences between you and others as well as the differences among members of the culturally different group.

Throughout this discussion of perception, a variety of skills were identified. Check your ability to apply these skills, using the following scale: 1 = almost always, 2 = often, 3 = sometimes, 4 = rarely, 5 = hardly ever.

_____ 1. I think mindfully when I use perceptual shortcuts so that they don't mislead me and result in inaccurate perceptions.

_____ 2. I guard against ethnocentric thinking by viewing the behavior and customs of others from a multicultural view rather than from just my cultural view.

_____ 3. I bring to consciousness my implicit personality theories.

_____ 4. To guard against the self-fulfilling prophecy, I take a second look at my perceptions when they conform too closely to my expectations.

_____ 5. To prevent distortions from perceptual accentuation, I consciously search for information that may contradict what I expect or want to see.

_____ 6. Recognizing how primacy-recency works, I actively guard against first impressions that might prevent accurate perceptions of future events; I formulate hypotheses rather than conclusions.

_____ 7. I recognize stereotyping in the messages of others and avoid it in my own.

_____ 8. I am aware of and am careful to avoid the self-serving bias, overattribution, and the fundamental attribution error when trying to account for another person's behavior.

_____ 9. I think critically about perception, analyzing my perceptions, checking my perceptions for accuracy, using uncertainty reduction strategies, and acting with cultural sensitivity.

Key Word Quiz

Write T for those statements that are true and F for those that are false. For those that are false, replace the italicized term with the correct term.

_____ 1. The mental templates or structures that help you organize new information as well as the information you already have in memory are called *schemata*.

_____ 2. Concluding that a person has positive qualities because you know that he or she has other positive qualities is known as *mind reading*.

_____ 3. The process by which we try to explain the motivation for a person's behavior is known as *attribution*.

_____ 4. A fixed impression of a group of people is known as a *stereotype*.

_____ 5. An organization of information about some action, event, or procedure is called a *script*.

_____ 6. Selective attention and selective exposure are examples of *perceptual organization by rules*.

_____ 7. Taking credit for the positive things you do and attributing your negative actions to external uncontrollable factors is often the result of the *self-serving bias*.

_____ 8. When what comes first exerts the most influence, you have a *recency effect*.

_____ 9. When you make a prediction and it comes true because you made the prediction and acted as if it were true, the process is called the *self-fulfilling prophecy*.

_____ 10. Attributing just about everything a person does to one or two obvious characteristics is known as *personality theory*.

Answers: TRUE: 1, 3, 4, 5, 7, 9; FALSE: 2 (the *halo effect*), 6 (*selective perception*), 8 (*primacy effect*), 10 (*overattribution*)

3.1 Perceptual Differences

This exercise is designed to give you some practice in appreciating the different perceptions that people are likely to have depending on who they are and their connection with the person involved or the event taking place. For each of these three situations, indicate what you think might be the likely perceptions of each person identified.

> *Pat, a single parent, has two small children (ages 7 and 12) who often lack some of the important things children their age should have—for example, school supplies, sneakers, and toys—because Pat can't afford them. Yet, Pat smokes two packs of cigarettes a day.*

Pat sees . . .

The 12-year-old daughter sees . . .

Pat's parents (who also smoke two packs a day) see . . .

The children's teacher sees . . .

> *Pat has extremely high standards and feels that getting all A's in college is an absolute necessity and would be devastated with even one B. In fear of earning that first B (after three and a half years of college), Pat cheats on an exam in a Family Communication course and gets caught by the instructor.*

Pat sees . . .

The instructor sees . . .

The average B-student sees . . .

> *Pat, a supervisor in an automobile factory, was ordered to increase production or be fired. In desperation, Pat gave a really tough message to the workers—many of whom were greatly insulted and as a result slowed down rather than increased their efforts.*

Pat sees . . .

The average worker sees . . .

Pat's supervisor sees . . .

The average stockholder sees . . .

Thinking Critically About Perceptual Differences. What one general principle of interpersonal perception can you formulate from this experience? Can you identify occasions when you have failed to apply this principle? What happened?

3.2 Perspective Taking

Taking the perspective of the other person and looking at the world through this perspective, this point of view, rather than through your own is crucial in achieving mutual understanding. For each of the specific behaviors listed below, identify specific circumstances that might lead to a *positive perception* and specific circumstances that might lead to a *negative perception*. The first one is done for you.

1. Giving a beggar in the street a $20 bill.

   Positive perception: *Grace once had to beg to get money for food. She now shares all she has with those who are like she once was.*

   Negative perception: *Grace is a first-class snob. She just wants to impress her friends, to show them that she has so much money she can afford to give $20 to a total stranger.*

2. Ignoring a homeless person who asks for money.
3. A middle-aged man walking down the street with his arms around a teenage girl.
4. A mother refusing to admit her teenage son back into her house.

Thinking Critically About Perspective Taking. The following should have been clear from this experience. Often, in perceiving a person, you may assume a specific set of circumstances and, on this basis, evaluate specific behaviors as positive or negative. Also, you may evaluate the very same specific behavior positively or negatively depending on the circumstances that you infer to be related to the behavior. Clearly, if you're to understand the perspectives of other people, you need to understand the reasons for their behaviors and to resist defining circumstances from your own perspective.

3.3 Barriers to Accurate Perception

This exercise is designed to reinforce an understanding of the processes of perception. Read the following dialogue and identify the processes of perception that may be at work here.

> **Pat:** All I had to do was to spend two seconds with him to know he's an idiot. I said I went to

Graceland and he asked what that was. Can you believe it? Graceland! The more I got to know him, the more I realized how stupid he was. A real loser; I mean, really.

Chris: Yeah, I know what you mean. Well, he is a jock, you know.

Pat: Jocks! The worst. And I bet I can guess who he goes out with. I'll bet it's Lucy.

Chris: Why do you say that?

Pat: Well, I figure that the two people I dislike would like each other. And I figure you must dislike them, too.

Chris: Definitely.

Pat: By the way, have you ever met Marie? She's a computer science major, so you know she's bright. And attractive—really attractive.

Chris: Yes, I went out of my way to meet her, because she sounded like she'd be a nice person to know.

Pat: You're right. I knew she'd be nice as soon as I saw her.

Chris: We talked at yesterday's meeting. She's really complex, you know. I mean really complex. Really.

Pat: Whenever I think of Marie, I think of the time she helped that homeless man. There was this homeless guy—real dirty—and he fell, running across the street. Well, Marie ran right into the street and picked this guy up and practically carried him to the other side.

Chris: And you know what I think of when I think of Lucy? The time she refused to visit her grandmother in the hospital. Remember? She said she had too many other things to do.

Pat: I remember that—a real selfish egomaniac. I mean really.

Thinking Critically About the Barriers to Perception. Seeing the processes of perception and especially the barriers to accurate perception operate in ourselves and in others with whom we interact is a lot more difficult. For the next several days, record all personal examples of the five barriers to accurate perception. Record also the specific context in which they occurred. Consider such questions as: What barrier seems most frequent? What problems did the barrier cause? What advantages do you gain when you avoid making first impressions? When you avoid using implicit theories? When you avoid making prophecies? When you avoid stereotyping? What disadvantages are there in avoiding these shortcuts to people perception?

CHAPTER 4

Verbal Messages

THE NATURE OF LANGUAGE

In communication, you use two major signal systems—verbal and nonverbal. This chapter focuses on the verbal system: language as a system for communicating meaning, how it can be used effectively, and how it creates problems when it isn't. The next chapter focuses on the nonverbal communication system.

Language Is Both Denotative and Connotative

You speak both denotatively and connotatively. **Denotation** refers to the objective meaning of a term, the meaning you would find in a dictionary. It's the meaning that people who share a common language assign to a word. **Connotation** refers to the subjective or emotional meaning that specific speakers or listeners give to a word. Take as an example the word *death*. To a doctor, this word might mean (or denote) the time when the heart stops. This is an objective description of a particular event. On the other hand, to the dead person's mother (upon being informed of her son's death), the word means (or connotes) much more. It recalls her son's youth, ambition, family, illness, and so on. To her, it is a highly emotional, subjective, and personal word. These emotional, subjective, or personal reactions are the word's connotative meaning.

Semanticist S. I. Hayakawa (Hayakawa & Hayakawa, 1990) coined the terms **snarl words** and **purr words** to clarify further the distinction between denotation and connotation. Snarl words are highly negative: "She's an idiot." "He's a pig." "They're a bunch of losers." Purr words are highly positive: "She's a real sweetheart." "He's a dream." "They're the greatest." Snarl and purr words, although they may sometimes seem to have denotative meaning and to refer to the "real world," are actually connotative in meaning. These terms do not describe people or events in the real world, but rather the speaker's feelings about these people or events.

Language Varies in Abstraction

Consider the following list of terms:

> entertainment
> film
> American film
> recent American film
> *The Gladiator*

At the top is the general or abstract *entertainment*. Note that *entertainment* includes all the other items on the list plus various other items—*television, novels, drama, comics,* and so on. *Film* is more specific and concrete. It includes all of the items below it as well as various other items such as *Indian film* or *Russian film*. It excludes, however, all entertainment that is not film. *American film* is again more specific than *film* and excludes all films that are not American. *Recent American film* further limits *American film* to a time period. *The Gladiator* specifies concretely the one item to which reference is made.

Effective verbal messages include words from a wide range of abstractions. At times, a general term may suit your needs best; at other times, a more specific term may serve better. Generally, however, the specific term will prove the better choice. As you get more specific—less abstract—you more effectively guide the images that come to your listeners' minds.

Language Varies in Directness

Think about how you would respond to someone saying the following sentences:

1A. I'm so bored; I have nothing to do tonight.

2A. I'd like to go to the movies. Would you like to come?

1B. Would you feel like hamburgers tonight?

2B. I'd like hamburgers tonight. How about you?

The statements numbered 1 are relatively indirect; they are attempts to get the listener to say or do something without committing the speaker. The statements numbered 2 are more direct—they more clearly state the speaker's preferences and then ask listeners whether they agree. A more obvious example of an indirect (nonverbal) message occurs when you glance at your watch to communicate that it is late and that you had better be going. Indirect messages have both advantages and disadvantages.

Indirect messages allow you to express a desire without insulting or offending anyone; they allow you to observe the rules of polite interaction. So instead of saying, "I'm bored with this conversation," you say, "It's getting late and I have to get up early tomorrow," or you look at your watch and pretend to be surprised by the time. In this way, you are stating a preference but are saying it indirectly so as to avoid offending someone. Not all direct requests, however, should be considered impolite. In one study of Spanish and English speakers, for example, no evidence was found to support the assumption that politeness and directness were incompatible (Mir, 1993).

Sometimes indirect messages allow you to ask for compliments in a socially acceptable manner, such as when you say, "I was thinking of getting a nose job." You hope to get the desired compliment: "A nose job? You? Your nose is perfect."

Indirect messages, however, can also create problems. Consider the following dialogue in which an indirect request is made:

Pat: You wouldn't like to have my parents over for dinner this weekend, would you?

Chris: I really wanted to go to the shore and just relax.

Pat: Well, if you feel you have to go to the shore, I'll make the dinner myself. You go to the shore. I really hate having them over and doing all the work myself. It's such a drag shopping, cooking, and cleaning all by myself.

Given this situation, Chris has two basic alternatives. One is to stick with the plans to go to the shore and relax. In this case, Pat is going to be upset and Chris is going to be made to feel guilty for not helping with the dinner. A second alternative is to give in to Pat, help with the dinner, and not go to the shore. In this case, Chris is going to have to give up a much-desired plan and is likely to resent Pat's "manipulative" tactics. Regardless of which decision is made, one person wins and one person loses. This win-lose situation creates resentment, competition, and often an "I'll get even" attitude. With direct requests, this type of situation is much less likely to develop. Consider:

Pat: I'd like to have my parents over for dinner this weekend. What do you think?

Chris: Well, I really wanted to go to the shore and just relax.

Regardless of what develops next, both individuals are starting out on relatively equal footing. Each has clearly and directly stated a preference. Although at first these preferences seem mutually exclusive, it might be possible to meet both persons' needs. For example, Chris might say, "How about going to the shore this weekend and having your parents over next weekend? I'm really exhausted; I could use the rest." Here is a direct response to a direct request. Unless there is some pressing need to have Pat's parents over for dinner this weekend, this response may enable each to meet the other's needs.

Gender and Cultural Differences in Directness

The popular stereotype in much of the United States holds that women are indirect in making requests and in giving orders. This indirectness communicates a powerlessness and discomfort with their own authority. Men, the stereotype continues, are direct, sometimes to the point of being blunt or rude. This directness communicates power and comfort with one's own authority.

Deborah Tannen (1994a) provides an interesting perspective on these stereotypes. Women are, it seems, more indirect in giving orders and are more likely to say, for example, "It would be great if these letters could go out today" than "Have these letters out by 3." But Tannen (1994a, p. 84) argues that "issuing orders indirectly can be the prerogative of those in power" and does in no way show powerlessness. Power, to Tannen, is the ability to choose your own style of communication.

Men are also indirect, but in different situations. For example, men are more likely to use indirectness when they express weakness, reveal a problem, or admit an error (Rundquist, 1992; Tannen, 1994a, 1994b). Men are more likely to speak indirectly when expressing emotions other than anger. They are also more indirect when they refuse expressions of increased romantic intimacy. Men are thus indirect, the theory goes, when they are saying something that goes against the masculine stereotype.

Many Asian and Latin American cultures stress the values of indirectness largely because it prevents overt criticism and losing face. A somewhat different kind of indirectness is seen in the greater use of third parties or mediators to resolve conflict among the Chinese than among North Americans (Ma, 1992). In most of the United States, however, directness is the preferred style. "Be up front" and "tell it like it is" are commonly heard communication guidelines. Contrast these with the following two principles of indirectness found in the Japanese language (Tannen, 1994a):

[O]moiyari, close to empathy, says that listeners need to understand the speaker without the speaker being specific or direct. This style places a much greater demand on the listener than would a direct speaking style.

COMMUNICATING WITH POWER

Avoiding Sexual Harassment Messages

Here are three suggestions for avoiding messages that might be considered sexually harassing (Bravo & Cassedy, 1992):

- Begin with the assumption that others at work are not interested in your sexual advances, sexual stories and jokes, or sexual gestures.
- Listen and watch for negative reactions to any sex-related discussion. Use the suggestions and techniques discussed throughout this book (for example, perception checking, critical listening) to become aware of such reactions. When in doubt, find out; ask questions, for example.
- Avoid saying or doing what you think your parent, partner, or child would find offensive in the behavior of someone with whom she or he worked.

How would you explain it?

If you were manager of an office, what specific recommendations would you give workers for avoiding sexual harassment? Would your recommendations be the same for opposite-sex harassment as for same-sex harassment?

[S]assuru advises listeners to anticipate a speaker's meanings and use subtle cues from the speaker to infer his or her total meaning.

In thinking about direct and indirect messages, it is important to realize how easy it is for misunderstandings to occur. For example, a person from a culture that values an indirect style of speech may be speaking indirectly to be polite. If, however, you are from a culture that values a more direct style of speech, you may assume that the person is using indirectness to be manipulative, because this is how your culture regards indirectness.

Language Is Rule Based

Language is based on a wide variety of rules, and the two most important types are grammatical and cultural rules. You learned the grammatical rules—the rules for combining words into sentences (the rules of syntax), the rules for using words meaningfully (semantics), and the rules for combining sounds (phonology)—as you were growing up, by exposure to a particular language. If you grew up in a Cantonese-speaking environment, you would learn the rules for Cantonese; if you grew up in an English-speaking environment, you would learn the rules for English.

Cultural rules, on the other hand, focus on the principles that your culture considers important. When you follow these principles, you're seen as a properly functioning member of the culture. When you violate these principles, you risk being seen as deviant or perhaps insulting.

Each culture has its own style of communication, its own principles or maxims governing communication. For example, in much of the United States, we operate with the maxim of quality (communication must be truthful); that is, we expect that what the other person says will be the truth and we follow that maxim by telling the truth ourselves. Similarly, we operate with the maxim of relevance: What we talk about should be relevant to the conversation. Thus, if you are talking about A, B, and C and someone brings up D, you would assume that there is a connection between A, B, and C on the one hand and D on the other. Of course, not all of the maxims followed in the United States are given equal importance throughout the rest of the world, or vice versa. Here are four maxims that are not common in much of the United States.

The Maxim of Peaceful Relations   Research on Japanese conversations and group discussions uncovered a maxim of keeping peaceful relationships with others (Midooka, 1990). The ways in which such peaceful relationships may be maintained will vary with the person with whom you are interacting. For example, in Japan, your status or position in the hierarchy will influence the amount of self-expression you are expected to engage in. Similarly, there is a great distinction made between public and private conversations. In public, this maxim is much more important than it is in private conversations, where it is at times violated.

The Maxim of Politeness   The maxim of politeness is probably universal across all cultures (Brown & Levinson, 1987). Cultures differ, however, in how they define politeness and in how important politeness is compared with, say, openness or honesty. Cultures also differ in the rules for expressing politeness or impoliteness and in the punishments for violating the accepted rules of politeness (Mao, 1994; Strecker, 1993). You may wish to examine your own level of politeness by taking the self-test, "How polite is your conversation?"

Test Yourself

How Polite Is Your Conversation?

Instructions: This is a first approximation to a conversational politeness scale, a device for measuring politeness in conversation. Try estimating your own level of politeness. For each of the statements below, indicate how closely it describes your *typical* communication in conversations with peers. Avoid giving responses that you feel might be considered "socially acceptable"; instead, give responses that accurately represent your typical conversational behaviors. Use a 10-point scale with 10 being "very accurate description of my typical communications in conversations" and 1 being "very inaccurate description of my typical communications in conversations."

_____ 1. I make jokes at the expense of another nationality, race, religion, or affectional orientation.

_____ 2. I say "please" when asking someone to do something.

_____ 3. When talking with guests in my home, I leave the television on.

_____ 4. I make an effort to make sure that other people are not embarrassed.

_____ 5. I use body adaptors when in conversation—for example, touching my hair or face or playing with a pen, Styrofoam cup, or the clothing of the other person.

_____ 6. I ask people I call whether it's a good time to talk.

_____ 7. I will raise my voice to take charge of the conversation.

_____ 8. I give the speaker cues to show that I'm listening and interested.

_____ 9. I avoid using terms that may prove offensive to people with whom I'm talking, terms that might be considered sexist, racist, or heterosexist.

_____ 10. I interrupt the speaker when I think I have something important to say.

■ **HOW DID YOU DO?**   This scale was developed to encourage you to consider some of the ways in which politeness is signaled in conversations and to encourage you to examine your own politeness behaviors. Nevertheless, you may want to compile a general politeness score that you can compare with others. To compile your politeness score, follow these steps:

- ■ Step 1. Add up your scores for items 2, 4, 6, 8, and 9.
- ■ Step 2. Reverse your scores for items 1, 3, 5, 7, and 10. For example, if you ranked a statement 10, it becomes 1; if you ranked a statement 9, it becomes 2; 8 becomes 3; 7 becomes 4; 6 becomes 5; 5 becomes 6; 4 becomes 7; 3 becomes 8; 2 becomes 9; and 1 becomes 10.
- ■ Step 3. Add the scores for Steps 1 and 2 (using the reverse numbers, of course, for the six items noted in Step 2).
- ■ Your score should range from 20 (extremely impolite) to 100 (extremely polite).

■ **WHAT WILL YOU DO?**   Realize that this "scale" is only a pedagogical tool; it's not a scientifically valid research instrument. So use it to stimulate thinking about your own interpersonal politeness behaviors rather than to give yourself a label.

Notice that this score indicates your evaluation of your own conversational behaviors and so may be very different from the scores others would assign to you. Generally, do you think you see yourself as more (or less) polite than your peers see you?

Are there some statements in this scale that you feel are not indicative of politeness as you see it? Are there indicators that are more important than those mentioned here and that should be included in a scale measuring politeness? Are there some statements that members of some cultures would see very differently? For example, might some cultures see interrupting, raising one's voice, or bending the truth as having different implications for politeness?

Using this scale, your modification of it, or a totally new measuring instrument, do you find that women and men are equally polite or that one sex is more polite than the other? Does politeness increase with age? For example, do teenagers score dramatically different from those in their 50s or 60s? Does the level of politeness depend on the people with whom you're talking? For example, are people more polite when talking with supervisors than with subordinates? Are people more polite with old friends than with new acquaintances? Are they more polite to business associates than to family members?

In Asian, especially Chinese and Japanese, cultures, politeness is especially important and violators of this maxim meet with harsher social punishments than they would in most of the United States or western Europe (Fraser, 1990). In Asian cultures, this maxim may overshadow other maxims. For example, the maxim of politeness may require that you not tell the truth, a situation that would violate the maxim of quality.

There are also large gender differences (and some similarities) in the expression of politeness (Holmes, 1995). Generally, studies from a number of different cultures show that women use more polite forms than men (Brown, 1980; Wetzel, 1988; Holmes, 1995). For example, in informal conversation and in conflict situations, women tend to seek areas of agreement more than men. Young girls are more apt to try to modify disagreements, while young boys are more apt to express "bald disagreements" (Holmes, 1995). There are also similarities. For example, both men and women in the United States and New Zealand seem to pay compliments in similar ways (Manes & Wolfson, 1981; Holmes, 1986, 1995) and both men and women use politeness strategies when communicating bad news in an organization (Lee, 1993).

Politeness also varies with the type of relationship. One researcher, for example, has proposed that politeness is greatest with friends and considerably less with strangers and intimates and depicts this relationship as shown in Figure 4.1 (Wolfson, 1988; Holmes, 1995).

In Internet communication, politeness is covered very specifically in **netiquette,** rules that are very clearly stated in most computer books. Some of these rules are: find out what a group is talking about before breaking in with your own comment, be tolerant of newbies (those who are new to newsgroups or chat groups), don't send duplicate messages, and don't attack other people.

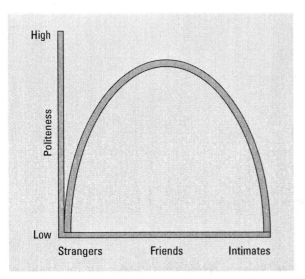

FIGURE 4.1
Wolfson's Bulge Model of Politeness
Do you find this model a generally accurate representation of your own level of politeness in different types of relationships? Can you build a case for an inverted U theory (in which politeness would be high for both strangers and intimates and low for friends)?

The Maxim of Saving Face   This maxim, extremely important in collectivist cultures, though not absent in individualist cultures, holds that you do nothing in conversation to embarrass another person and cause him or her to lose face. This often involves avoiding the truth, as when you tell someone he or she did a fine job when it was actually poorly executed.

The Maxim of Self-Denigration   This maxim, observed in the conversations of Chinese people and seen in other cultures as well, requires that a speaker make little of an ability or talent or avoid taking credit for accomplishments (Gu, 1997). In this case, putting yourself down is a form of politeness because downplaying your own abilities and strengths works to elevate the person to whom you're speaking.

COMMUNICATING ETHICALLY

Lying

Lying occurs when you intend to mislead someone deliberately and without warning when you have not been asked to do so by this person (Ekman, 1985, p. 28). You can lie by commission (making explicitly false statements) or by omission (omitting relevant information, thereby allowing others to draw incorrect inferences). Similarly, you can lie verbally (in speech or writing) or nonverbally (with an innocent facial expression despite the commission of some wrong or a knowing nod instead of an honest expression of ignorance) (O'Hair, Cody, & McLaughlin, 1981). Lies may range from the "white lie" and truth stretching to lies that form the basis of infidelity in a relationship, libel, and perjury. Not surprisingly, lies have ethical implications.

Some lies are considered innocent, acceptable, and ethical (for example, lying to a child to protect a fantasy belief in Santa Claus or the Tooth Fairy or publicly agreeing with someone to enable the person to save face). Other lies are considered unacceptable and unethical (for example, lying to defraud investors or to falsely accuse someone of a crime). Other lies, however, are not so easy to classify as ethical or unethical. (You may wish to take the self-test "Is lying unethical?"; it examines a variety of situations in which many people would lie. An interesting exercise on lying, "Must-Lie Situations," examines those situations in which lying may be expected and considered ethical.)

What would you do?

You've been asked to serve as a witness in a robbery of a local grocery store. You really don't want to get involved; in fact, you're afraid to get involved. Yet you wonder if you can ethically refuse and say you didn't see anything (although you did). There are other witnesses and your testimony is not likely to make a significant difference. What would you do?

Language Meanings Are in People

To discover the meanings people try to communicate, look into the people in addition to the words. An example of the confusion that can result when this relatively simple fact is not taken into consideration is provided by Ronald D. Laing, H. Phillipson, and A. Russell Lee (1966) and analyzed with insight by Paul Watzlawick (1977). A couple on the second night of their honeymoon are sitting at a hotel bar. The woman strikes up a conversation with the couple next to her. The husband refuses to communicate with the couple and becomes antagonistic toward his wife and the couple. The wife then grows angry because he has created such an awkward and unpleasant situation. Each becomes increasingly disturbed, and the evening ends in a bitter conflict, with each convinced of the other's lack of consideration. Eight years later, they analyze this argument. Apparently *honeymoon* had meant different things to each. To the husband, it was a "golden opportunity to ignore the rest of the world and simply explore each other." He felt his wife's interaction with

Peter Steiner from cartoonbank.com. All rights reserved.

the other couple implied there was something lacking in him. To the wife, *honeymoon* meant an opportunity to try out her new role as wife. "I had never had a conversation with another couple as a wife before," she said. "Previous to this I had always been a 'girlfriend' or 'fiancée' or 'daughter' or 'sister.'"

Also recognize that as you change, you also change the meanings you created out of past messages. Thus, although the message sent may not have changed, the meanings you created from it yesterday and the meanings you create today may be quite different. Yesterday, when a special someone said, "I love you," you created certain meanings. But today, when you learn that the same "I love you" was said to three other people or when you fall in love with someone else, you drastically change the meanings you perceive from those three words.

DISCONFIRMATION AND CONFIRMATION

A useful way to introduce disconfirmation and its alternatives, confirmation and rejection, is to consider a specific situation: Pat arrives home late one night. Chris is angry and complains about Pat's coming home so late. Consider some responses Pat might make:

1. Stop screaming. I'm not interested in what you're babbling about. I'll do what I want, when I want. I'm going to bed.

2. What are you so angry about? Didn't you come home three hours late without calling two weeks ago? So knock it off.

3. You have a right to be angry. I should have called when I was going to be late, but I got involved in an argument at work and I couldn't leave until it was resolved.

In 1, Pat dismisses Chris's anger and even indicates a dismissal of Chris as a person. In 2, Pat rejects the validity of Chris's reasons for being angry but does not dismiss Chris's feelings of anger or Chris as a person. In 3, Pat acknowledges Chris's anger and the reasons for being angry. In addition, Pat provides some kind of explanation and, in doing so, shows that Chris's feelings and Chris as a person are important and that Chris deserves to know what happened. The first response is an example of disconfirmation, the second of rejection, and the third of confirmation.

Psychologist William James once observed that "No more fiendish punishment could be devised, even were such a thing physically possible, than that one should be turned loose in society and remain absolutely unnoticed by all the members thereof." In this often-quoted observation, James identifies the essence of disconfirmation (Watzlawick, Beavin, & Jackson, 1967; Veenendall & Feinstein, 1996).

Disconfirmation is a communication pattern in which we ignore someone's presence as well as that person's communications. We say, in effect, that this person and what this person has to say are not worth serious attention or effort—that this person and this person's contributions are so unimportant or insignificant that there is no reason to concern ourselves with her or him.

Note that disconfirmation is not the same as **rejection.** In rejection, you disagree with the person; you indicate your unwillingness to accept something the other person says or does. In disconfirming someone, however, you deny that person's significance; you claim that what this person says or does simply does not count.

Confirmation is the opposite communication pattern. In confirmation, you not only acknowledge the presence of the other person, but you also indicate your acceptance of this person, of this person's definition of self, and of your relationship as defined or viewed by this other person.

Disconfirmation and confirmation may be communicated in a wide variety of ways. Table 4.1 shows just a few examples.

You can gain insight into a wide variety of offensive language practices by viewing them as types of disconfirmation, as language that alienates and separates and prevents effective communication. Three common practices are sexism, heterosexism, and racism.

Sexism

Sexist language is language that puts down someone because of her or his gender. Usually, the term refers to language that denigrates women, but it can

TABLE 4.1 Confirmation and Disconfirmation

As you review this table, try to imagine a specific illustration for each of the ways of communicating disconfirmation and confirmation (Pearson, 1993; Galvin & Brommel, 2000).

CONFIRMATION	DISCONFIRMATION
1. Acknowledge the presence and the contributions of the other by either supporting or taking issue with what the other says.	1. Ignore the presence and the messages of the other person; ignore or express (nonverbally and verbally) indifference to anything the other says.
2. Make nonverbal contact by maintaining direct eye contact, touching, hugging, kissing, or otherwise demonstrating acknowledgment of the other; engage in dialogue—communication in which both persons are speakers and listeners, both are involved, and both are concerned with each other.	2. Make no nonverbal contact; avoid direct eye contact; avoid touching the other person; engage in monologue—communication in which one person speaks and one person listens, there is no real interaction, and there is no real concern or respect for each other.
3. Demonstrate understanding of what the other says and means and reflect these feelings to demonstrate your understanding.	3. Jump to interpretation or evaluation rather than working at understanding what the other means; express your own feelings, ignore the feelings of the other, or give abstract, intellectualized responses.
4. Ask questions of the other concerning both thoughts and feelings and acknowledge the questions of the other, return phone calls, and answer e-mails and letters.	4. Make statements about yourself; ignore any lack of clarity in the other's remarks; ignore the other's requests; and fail to answer questions, return phone calls, or answer e-mails and letters.
5. Encourage the other to express thoughts and feelings and respond directly and exclusively to what the other says.	5. Interrupt or otherwise make it difficult for the other to express him- or herself; respond only tangentially or by shifting the focus in another direction.

also legitimately refer to language that denigrates men. Usually, sexist language is used by one sex against the other, but it need not be limited to these cases; women can be sexist against women and men can be sexist against men. The National Council of Teachers of English has proposed guidelines for non-sexist (gender-free, gender-neutral, or sex-fair) language. These concern the use of generic *man,* the use of generic *he* and *his,* and sex-role stereotyping (Penfield, 1987).

Generic Man   The word *man* refers most clearly to an adult male. To use the term to refer to both men and women emphasizes "maleness" at the expense of "femaleness." Similarly, the terms *mankind* and *the common man* and even *cavemen* imply a primary focus on adult males. Gender-neutral terms can easily be substituted. Instead of *mankind,* you can say *humanity, people,* or *human beings.* Instead of *the common man,* you can say *the average person* or *ordinary people.* Instead of *cavemen,* you can say *prehistoric people* or *cave dwellers.*

Similarly, the use of terms such as *policeman* and *fireman* and other terms that presume maleness as the norm and femaleness as a deviation from this norm are clear and common examples of sexist language. Using non-sexist alternatives for these and similar terms and making these alternatives (for example, *police officer* and *firefighter* instead of *policeman* and *fireman*) a part of your active vocabulary will include the female sex as "normal" in such professions. Similarly, using "female forms" such as *actress* or *stewardess* is considered sexist because these are derivations of *actor* and *steward* which, again, emphasize that the male form is the norm and the female is the deviation from the norm.

Generic He and His   The use of the masculine pronoun to refer to any individual regardless of sex is certainly declining. But it was only as far back as 1975 that all college textbooks, for example, used the masculine pronoun as generic. There is no legitimate reason why the feminine pronoun can't alternate with the masculine pronoun in referring to hypothetical individuals or why terms such as *he and she* or *her and him* can't be used instead of just *he* or *him.* Perhaps the best solution is to restructure your sentences to eliminate any reference to gender. Here are a few examples from the NCTE Guidelines (Penfield, 1987):

Sexist	**Gender-Free**
The average student is worried about his grades.	The average student is worried about grades.
Ask the student to hand in his work as soon as he is finished.	Ask students to hand in their work as soon as they are finished.

Sex-Role Stereotyping   The words we use often reflect a sex-role bias, the assumption that certain roles or professions belong to men and others belong to women. In eliminating sex-role stereotyping, avoid, for example, making the hypothetical elementary school teacher female and the college professor male. Avoid referring to doctors as male and nurses as female. Avoid noting the sex of a professional with terms such as *female doctor* or *male nurse.* When you are referring to a specific doctor or nurse, the person's

COMMUNICATING WITH POWER

Responding to Sexual Harassment Messages

What should you do if you think you're being sexually harassed? Here are a few suggestions (Petrocelli & Repa, 1992; Bravo & Cassedy, 1992; Rubenstein, 1993):

- Talk to the harasser. Tell this person, assertively, that you do not welcome the behavior and that you find it offensive. If this doesn't solve the problem, consider the next suggestion.
- Collect evidence—this may mean, for example, seeking corroboration from others who have experienced similar harassment or keeping a log of the offensive behaviors.
- Use the channels within the organization to deal with such grievances. If this doesn't stop the harassment, consider going further.
- File a complaint with an organization or governmental agency.
- Don't blame yourself. Like many who are abused, you may blame yourself, feeling that you're responsible for being harassed. You aren't; however, you may need to seek emotional support from friends or perhaps from trained professionals.

How would you explain it?

A colleague at work persists in talking about the XXX-rated videos he's just seen, sometimes going into graphic description. You really don't want to hear this and want him to stop. What steps might you take to put an end to this unwanted behavior?

---

sex will become clear when you use the appropriate pronoun: "Dr. Smith wrote the prescription for her new patient" or "The nurse recorded the patient's temperature himself."

Heterosexism

A close relative of sexism is heterosexism, a relatively new addition to our list of linguistic prejudices. As the term implies, **heterosexist language** refers to language used to disparage gay men and lesbians. As with racist language, we see heterosexism in the derogatory terms used for lesbians and gay men as well as in more subtle forms of language usage. For example, when you qualify a profession—as in *gay athlete* or *lesbian doctor,* you are in effect stating that athletes and doctors are not normally gay or lesbian. Further, you are highlighting the affectional orientation of the athlete and the doctor in a context in which it may have no relevance, in the same way that gender or racial distinctions often have no relevance to the issue at hand.

Still another instance of heterosexism—and perhaps the most difficult to deal with—is the presumption of heterosexuality. Usually, people assume that the person they are talking to or about is heterosexual. They are usually correct because the majority of the population is heterosexual. At the same time, however, this assumption denies the lesbian and gay identity a certain legitimacy. The practice is similar to the presumptions of whiteness and maleness that we have made significant inroads in eliminating. Here are a few suggestions for avoiding heterosexist, or what some call homophobic, language.

- Avoid offensive nonverbal mannerisms that parody stereotypes when talking about gays and lesbians.
- Avoid "complimenting" gay men and lesbians because "they don't look it." To gays and lesbians, it's not a compliment. Similarly, expressing disappointment that a person is gay—often thought to be a compliment when said in comments such as "What a waste!"—is not a compliment.
- Avoid the assumption that every gay or lesbian knows what every other gay or lesbian is thinking. It's very similar to asking a Japanese person why Sony is investing heavily in the United States or, as one comic put it, asking an African American, "What do you think Jesse Jackson meant by that last speech?"
- Avoid denying individual differences. Saying things such as "Lesbians are so loyal," or, "Gay men are so open with their feelings," which ignore the reality of wide differences within any group, are potentially insulting to all groups.
- Avoid overattribution, the tendency—in this case—to attribute just about everything a person does, says, and believes to his or her being gay or lesbian. This tendency helps to recall and perpetuate stereotypes.
- Remember that relationship milestones are important to all people. Ignoring anniversaries or birthdays of, say, a relative's partner is resented by everyone.

Racism

According to Andrea Rich (1974), "any language that, through a conscious or unconscious attempt by the user, places a particular racial or ethnic group in an inferior position is racist." **Racist language** expresses racist attitudes. It also contributes to the development of racist attitudes in those who use or hear the language. This, of course, is similar to sexist and heterosexist language perpetuating sexist and heterosexist attitudes.

Racist terms are used by members of one culture to disparage members of other cultures, their customs, or their accomplishments and to establish and maintain power over other groups. Racist language emphasizes differences rather than similarities and separates rather than unites members of different cultures. The social consequences of racist language in terms of employment, education, housing opportunities, and general community acceptance are well known.

It has often been pointed out (Bosmajian, 1974; Davis, 1973) that there are aspects of language that may be inherently racist. For example, one examination of English found 134 synonyms for *white*. Of these, 44 had positive connotations (for example, *clean, chaste,* and *unblemished*) and only 10 had negative connotations (for example, *whitewash* and *pale*). The remaining were rela-

Listening Without Bias or Prejudice

Just as racist, sexist, and heterosexist attitudes will influence your language, they can also influence your listening. In this type of listening, you hear what the speaker is saying through the stereotypes you hold. You assume that what the speaker is saying is influenced by the speaker's gender, affectional orientation, or race.

Sexist, racist, and heterosexist listening occur in a wide variety of situations. For example, when you dismiss a valid argument or attribute validity to an invalid argument because the speaker is of a particular sex, race, or affectional orientation, you're practicing sexist, racist, or heterosexist listening. Put differently, sexist, racist, or heterosexist listening occurs when you listen differently to a person because of his or her sex, race, or affectional orientation when these characteristics are irrelevant to the message.

But there are many instances where these characteristics are relevant and pertinent to your evaluation of the message. For example, the sex of the speaker talking on pregnancy, fathering a child, birth control, or surrogate fatherhood is, most would agree, probably relevant to the message. So in these cases it is not sexist listening to take the sex of the speaker into consideration. It is, however, sexist listening to assume that only one sex can be an authority on a particular topic or that one sex's opinions are without value. The same is true when listening through a person's race or affectional orientation.

Suggestions?

Your friend Maria refuses to listen to men when they voice their opinions on any "woman's issue"— whether it's abortion, women in religion, the glass ceiling, adoption rights, or divorce settlements. What would you say to Maria?

---

tively neutral. Of the 120 synonyms for *black*, 60 had unfavorable connotations (*unclean*, *foreboding*, and *deadly*) and none had positive connotations.

Consider the following terms:

- the Korean doctor
- the Chicano prodigy
- the African American mathematician
- the white nurse

In some cases, of course, the racial identifier may be relevant, as in, say, "The Korean doctor argued for hours with the French [doctors] while the Mexicans tried to secure a compromise." Here, the aim might be to identify the nationality of the doctor or the specific doctor (as you would if you forgot her or his name).

Cultural Identifiers

Perhaps the best way to develop nonsexist, nonheterosexist, and nonracist language is to examine the preferred cultural identifiers to use in talking to and about members of different cultures. Remember, however, that preferred terms frequently change over time, so keep in touch with the most currently preferred language. The preferences and many of the specific examples identified here are drawn largely from the findings of the Task Force on Bias-Free Language of the Association of American University Presses (Schwartz, 1995).

Generally, the term *girl* should be used only to refer to very young females and is equivalent to *boy*. Neither term should be used for people older than say 13 or 14. *Girl* is never used to refer to a grown woman, nor is *boy* used to refer to people in blue-collar positions, as it once was. *Lady* is negatively evaluated by many because it connotes the stereotype of the prim and proper woman. *Woman* or *young woman* is preferred. *Older person* is preferred to *elder, elderly, senior,* or *senior citizen* (which technically refers to someone older than 65).

Generally, *gay* is the preferred term to refer to a man who has an affectional preference for other men and *lesbian* is the preferred term for a woman who has an affectional preference for other women (Lever, 1995). (*Lesbian* means "homosexual woman," so the term *lesbian woman* is redundant.) *Homosexual* refers to both gays and lesbians, but more often to a sexual orientation to members of one's own sex. *Gay* and *lesbian* refer to a lifestyle and not just to sexual orientation. *Gay* as a noun, although widely used, may prove offensive in some contexts, for example, "We have two gays on the team." Because most scientific thinking holds that sexuality is not a matter of choice, the term *sexual orientation*, rather than *sexual preference* or *sexual status* (which is also vague), is preferred.

Generally, most African Americans prefer *African American* to *black* (Hecht, Collier, & Ribeau, 1993), although *black* is often used with *white*, as well as in a variety of other contexts (for example, Department of Black and Puerto Rican Studies, the *Journal of Black History,* and Black History Month). The American Psychological Association recommends that both terms be capitalized, but the *Chicago Manual of Style* (the manual used by most newspapers and publishing houses) recommends using lowercase. The terms *negro* and *colored,* although used in the names of some organizations (for example, the United Negro College Fund and the National Association for the Advancement of Colored People), are not used outside these contexts.

White is generally used to refer to those whose roots are in European cultures and usually does not include Hispanics. Analogous to *African American* (which itself is based on a long tradition of terms such as *Irish American* and *Italian American*) is the phrase *European American.* Few European Americans, however, call themselves that; most prefer their national origins emphasized, as in, for example, *German American* or *Greek American.* This preference may well change as Europe moves toward becoming a more cohesive and united entity. *People of color*—a more literary-sounding term appropriate perhaps to public speaking but awkward in most conversations—is preferred to *nonwhite,* which implies that whiteness is the norm and nonwhiteness is a deviation from that norm. The same is true of the term *non-Christian:* it implies that people who have other beliefs deviate from the norm.

Generally, *Hispanic* is used to refer to anyone who identifies him- or herself as belonging to a Spanish-speaking culture. *Latina* (female) and *Latino* (male) refer to those whose roots are in one of the Latin American countries, for example, Haiti, the Dominican Republic, Nicaragua, or Guatemala. *Hispanic American* refers to those United States residents whose ancestry is in a Spanish culture; the term includes Mexican, Caribbean, and Central and South Americans. In emphasizing a Spanish heritage, the term is inadequate in that it leaves out those large numbers of people in the Caribbean and in South America whose origins are African, Native American, French, or Portuguese. *Chicana* (female) and *Chicano* (male) refer to those with roots in

Mexico, although it often connotes a nationalist attitude (Jandt, 1995) and is considered offensive by many Mexican Americans. *Mexican American* is generally preferred.

Inuk (the plural is *Inuit*), also spelled with two *n*s (*Innuk* and *Innuit*) is preferred to *Eskimo* (a term the United States Census Bureau uses), which was applied to the indigenous peoples of Alaska and Canada by Europeans and literally means "raw meat eaters."

Indian refers only to someone from India and is incorrectly used when applied to members of other Asian countries or to the indigenous peoples of North America. *American Indian* or *Native American* are preferred, even though many Native Americans refer to themselves as *Indians* and *Indian people*. In Canada, indigenous people are called *first people*. The term *native American* (with a lowercase *n*) is most often used to refer to persons born in the United States. Although technically the term could refer to anyone born in North or South America, people outside the United States generally prefer more specific designations such as *Argentinean, Cuban,* or *Canadian.* The term *native* means an indigenous inhabitant; it is not used to mean "someone having a less developed culture."

Muslim is the preferred form (rather than the older *Moslem*) to refer to a person who adheres to the religious teachings of Islam. *Quran* (rather than *Koran*) is the preferred term for the scriptures of Islam. *Jewish people* is preferred to *Jews*, and *Jewess* (a Jewish female) is considered derogatory.

When history was being written from a European perspective, Europe was taken as the focal point and the rest of the world was defined in terms of its location from Europe. Thus, Asia became the east or the orient and Asians became *Orientals*—a term that is today considered inappropriate or "Eurocentric." Thus, people from Asia are *Asians,* just as people from Africa are *Africans* and people from Europe are *Europeans.*

Thinking Critically About VERBAL MESSAGES

Four general principles will help you think more critically about verbal messages: (1) language *symbolizes* reality, but it is not the reality itself; (2) language can express both facts and inferences yet often obscures the important distinction between the two; (3) language is relatively static and unchanging, but the world and the people it describes are changing all the time; and (4) language can obscure important distinctions between people. These four principles all concern what critical thinking theorists call "conceptual distortions," or thinking errors.

Language Symbolizes Reality (Partially)

Language describes the objects, people, and events in the world with varying degrees of accuracy. But words and sentences are not objects, people, or events even though we sometimes act as if they are. Two ways in which we sometimes act as if words and things are the same is when we think and speak intensionally or with an allness attitude.

Thinking Intensionally   Have you ever reacted to the way something was labeled or described rather than to the actual item? Have you ever bought something because of its name rather than because of the actual object? If so, you were probably responding intensionally.

Intensional orientation (the *s* in *intensional* is intentional) refers to the tendency to view people, objects, and events in the way they are talked about—the way they are labeled. For example, if Sally is labeled "uninteresting," if you responded intensionally, you would evaluate her as uninteresting before listening to what she had to say. You would see Sally through a filter imposed by the label "uninteresting." The opposite tendency, **extensional orientation,** is the tendency to look first at the actual people, objects, and events and only afterward at their labels. In this case, it would mean looking at Sally without any preconceived labels, guided by what she says and does, not by the words used to label her.

The way to avoid intensional orientation is to extensionalize. You can do this by focusing your attention on the people, things, and events in the world as you see them and not as they are presented in the words of others. For example, when you meet Jack and Jill, observe and interact with them. Then form your impressions. Don't respond to them as "greedy, money-grubbing landlords" because Harry labeled them this way. Don't respond to Carmen as "lazy and inconsiderate" because Elaine told you she was.

Thinking in Allness Terms   No one can know all or say all about anything. The parable of the six blind men and the elephant is an excellent example of an "allness" orientation and its problems. You may recall the John Saxe poem that tells of six blind men of Indostan who examine an elephant, an animal they had only heard about. The first blind man touched the elephant's side and concluded the elephant was like a wall. The second felt the tusk and said the elephant must be like a spear. The third held the trunk and concluded the elephant was like a snake. The fourth touched the knee and knew the elephant was like a tree. The fifth felt the ear and said the elephant was like a fan. And the sixth grabbed the tail and said the elephant was like a rope.

Each reached his own conclusion; each argued that he was correct and that the others were wrong. Each was correct and, at the same time, wrong. We are all in the position of the six blind men. We never see all of anything. We never experience anything fully. We see a part, then conclude what the whole is like. We have to draw conclusions on the basis of insufficient evidence (and we always have insufficient evidence). We must recognize that when we make judgments based only on a part, we are making inferences that can later prove wrong once we have more complete information.

A useful device to help you remember the nonallness orientation is to end each statement, verbally or mentally, with *etc.*—a reminder that there is more to learn, more to know, and more to say—that every statement is inevitably incomplete. Be careful, however, that you do not use the *etc.* as a substitute for being specific.

Language Expresses Both Facts and Inferences

Often, when we listen or speak, we don't distinguish between statements of fact and those of inference. Yet there are great differences between the two. Barriers to clear thinking can be created when inferences are treated as facts.

For example, you can say, "She is wearing a blue jacket," as well as, "He is harboring an illogical hatred." Although the sentences have similar structures, they are different. You can observe the jacket and the blue color, but how do you observe "illogical hatred"? Obviously, this is not a descriptive, but an inferential, statement. It is one you make on the basis not only of what you observe, but also on what you infer. For a statement to be considered factual, it must be made by the observer after observation and must be limited to what is observed (Weinberg, 1959).

There is nothing wrong with making inferential statements. You must make them to talk about much that is meaningful to you. The problem arises when you act as if those inferential statements are factual. Consider the following anecdote (Maynard, 1963): A woman went for a walk one day and met a friend whom she had not seen, heard from, or heard of in 10 years. After an exchange of greetings, the woman said: "Is this your little boy?" and her friend replied, "Yes, I got married about six years ago." The woman then asked the child, "What is your name?" and the little boy replied, "Same as my father's." "Oh," said the woman, "then it must be Peter."

How did the woman know the boy's father's name when she had had no contact with her friend in the last 10 years? The answer is obvious, but only after we recognize that in reading this short passage we have made an unconscious inference. Specifically, we have inferred that the woman's friend is a woman. Actually, the friend is a man named Peter.

You may test your ability to distinguish facts from inferences by taking the self-test, "Can you distinguish facts from inferences?" (based on the tests constructed by William Haney [1973]).

Test Yourself

Can You Distinguish Facts from Inferences?

Instructions: Carefully read the following report and the observations based on it. Indicate whether you think the observations are true, false, or doubtful on the basis of the information presented in the report. Write T if the observation is definitely true, F if the observation is definitely false, and ? if the observation may be either true or false. Judge each observation in order. Do not reread the observations after you have indicated your judgment, and do not change any of your answers.

A well-liked college teacher had just completed making up the final examinations and had turned off the lights in the office. Just then a tall, broad figure with dark glasses appeared and demanded the examination. The professor opened the drawer. Everything in the drawer was picked up and the individual ran down the corridor. The dean was notified immediately.

_____ 1. The thief was tall, broad, and wore dark glasses.

_____ 2. The professor turned off the lights.

_____ 3. A tall figure demanded the examination.

_____ 4. The examination was picked up by someone.

_____ 5. The examination was picked up by the professor.

_____ 6. A tall, broad figure appeared after the professor turned off the lights in the office.

_____ 7. The man who opened the drawer was the professor.

_____ 8. The professor ran down the corridor.

_____ 9. The drawer was never actually opened.

_____ 10. Three persons are referred to in this report.

■ **HOW DID YOU DO?** After you answer all 10 questions, form small groups of five or six and discuss the answers. Look at each statement from each member's point of view. For each statement, ask yourself, "How can you be absolutely certain that the statement is true or false?" You should find that only one statement can be clearly identified as true and only one as false; eight should be marked ?.

■ **WHAT WILL YOU DO?** As you read this chapter, try to formulate specific guidelines that will help you distinguish facts from inferences.

Make your inferential statements tentatively. When you make an inferential statement, leave open the possibility of being wrong. If, for example, you treat the statement "Our biology teacher was fired for poor teaching" as factual, you eliminate alternative explanations. When making inferential statements, be psychologically prepared to be proved wrong. In this way, you'll be less hurt if you're shown to be wrong.

Be especially sensitive to this distinction when you're listening. Most talk is inferential. Beware of the speaker (whether in interpersonal, group, or public speaking) who presents everything as fact. Analyze closely and you'll uncover a world of inferences.

Language Is Relatively Static

Static evaluation is a conceptual distortion in which we retain evaluations without change while the reality to which they refer is constantly changing. Often, a verbal statement we make about an event or person remains static while the event or person may change enormously. Consider this example (Korzybski, 1933). In a tank, we have a large fish and many small fish, the natural food for the large fish. Given freedom in the tank, the large fish will eat the small fish. If we partition the tank, separating the large fish from the small fish by a clear piece of glass, the large fish will continue to attempt to eat the small fish but will fail, knocking instead into the glass partition.

Eventually, the large fish will "learn" the futility of attempting to eat the small fish. If we now remove the partition, the small fish will swim all around the large fish, but the large fish will not eat them. In fact, the large fish will die of starvation while its natural food swims all around. The large fish has learned a pattern of behavior, and even though the actual territory has changed, the map remains static.

While you would probably agree that everything is in a constant state of flux, do you act as if you know this? Do you act in accordance with the notion of change, or do you just accept it intellectually? Do you realize, for example, that because you have failed at something once, you need not fail again? Your evaluations of yourself and of others must keep pace with the rapidly changing real world; otherwise, your attitudes and beliefs will be about a world that no longer exists.

To guard against static evaluation, date your statements and especially your evaluations. Remember that Pat Smith$_{1987}$ is not Pat Smith$_{2001}$; academic abilities$_{1999}$ are not academic abilities$_{2001}$. In listening, look carefully at messages that claim that what was once true still is. It may or may not be. Look for change.

Language Can Obscure Distinctions

Language can obscure distinctions between people or events that are covered by the same label but are really quite different (indiscrimination) and can also make it easy to focus on extremes rather than on the vast middle ground between opposites (polarization).

Indiscrimination   **Indiscrimination** refers to the failure to distinguish between similar but different people, objects, or events. It occurs when we focus on classes of things and fail to see that each is unique and needs to be looked at individually.

Our language, however, provides us with common nouns, such as *teacher, student, friend, enemy, war, politician,* and *liberal.* These lead us to focus on similarities—to group together all teachers, all students, and all politicians. At the same time, the terms divert attention away from the uniqueness of each person, each object, and each event.

This misevaluation is at the heart of stereotyping on the basis of nationality, race, religion, sex, and affectional orientation. A stereotype is a fixed mental picture of a group that is applied to each individual in the group without regard to his or her unique qualities.

Whether the stereotypes are positive or negative, they create the same problem. They provide us with shortcuts that are often inappropriate. For instance, when you meet a particular person, your first reaction may be to pigeonhole him or her into some category—perhaps religious, national, or academic. Then you assign to this person all the qualities that are part of your stereotype. Regardless of the category you use or the specific qualities you are ready to assign, you fail to give sufficient attention to the individual's unique characteristics. Two people may both be Christian, Asian, and lesbian, for example, but each will be different from the other. Indiscrimination is a denial of another's uniqueness.

A useful antidote to indiscrimination is the **index.** This verbal or mental subscript identifies each individual as an individual, even though a group of these individuals may be covered by the same label. Thus, politician$_1$ is not politician$_2$, teacher$_1$ is not teacher$_2$. The index helps us to discriminate between without discriminating against.

Polarization   **Polarization** is the tendency to look at the world in terms of opposites and to describe it in extremes—good or bad, positive or negative, healthy or sick, intelligent or stupid. It is often referred to as the fallacy of "either-or" or "black and white." Most people exist somewhere between the extremes. Yet we have a strong tendency to view only the extremes and to categorize people, objects, and events in terms of these polar opposites.

We create problems when we use the absolute form in inappropriate situations. Consider this example: "The politician is either for us or against us." These options do not include all possibilities. The politician may be for us in some things and against us in other things or may be neutral.

To correct this tendency to polarize, beware of implying (and believing) that all individuals and events must fit into one extreme or the other, with no alternatives in between. Most people, events, and qualities exist between polar extremes. When others imply that there are only two sides or alternatives, look for the middle ground.

Summary of Concepts and Skills

In this chapter, we considered verbal messages. We looked at the nature of language and identified several major ways in which language works, and we looked at the concept of disconfirmation, especially as it relates to sexist, heterosexist, and racist language.

1. Language is both denotative (objective and generally easily agreed upon) and connotative (subjective and generally highly individual in meaning).
2. Language varies in abstraction; language can vary from extremely general to extremely specific.
3. Language varies in directness; language can state exactly what you mean, or it can hedge and state your meaning very indirectly.
4. Language is rule based; grammatical and cultural rules guide performance.
5. Language meanings are in people, not simply in words.
6. *Disconfirmation* refers to the process of ignoring the presence and the communications of others. *Confirmation* refers to accepting, supporting, and acknowledging the importance of the other person.
7. Racist, sexist, and heterosexist language disconfirms, puts down, and negatively evaluates various cultural groups.
8. Thinking critically about verbal messages involves realizing that language symbolizes reality and is not the reality itself; that language can express

both facts and inferences but doesn't indicate this grammatically; that language is relatively static but people and events are forever changing; and that language can obscure distinctions, as when it provides lots of extreme terms but few terms to describe the middle ground.

The study of verbal messages and how meaning is communicated from one person to another has important implications for developing the skills of effective communication. Check your ability to apply these skills, using the following rating scale: 1 = almost always, 2 = often, 3 = sometimes, 4 = rarely, 5 = hardly ever.

_____ 1. I try to understand not only the objective, denotative meanings, but also the subjective, connotative meanings.

_____ 2. I recognize that snarl and purr words describe the speaker's feelings and not objective reality.

_____ 3. I take special care to make spoken messages clear and unambiguous, especially when using terms for which people will have very different connotative meanings.

_____ 4. I recognize the gender and cultural differences in directness and can adjust my style of speaking and listening as appropriate.

5. I communicate with a clear recognition of the grammatical and cultural rules (and maxims, especially that of politeness) of the language.

6. I focus attention not only on words, but also on the person communicating, recognizing that meanings are largely in the person.

7. I avoid disconfirmation and instead use responses that confirm the other person.

8. I avoid sexist, heterosexist, and racist language and, in general, language that puts down other groups.

9. I use the cultural identifiers that facilitate communication and avoid those that set up barriers to effective interaction.

10. I avoid responding intensionally to labels as if they are objects; instead, I respond extensionally and look first at the reality and secondarily at the words.

11. I end my statements with an implicit *etc.* in recognition that there is always more to be known or said.

12. I distinguish facts from inferences and respond to inferences with tentativeness.

13. I mentally date my statements and thus avoid static evaluation.

14. I avoid indiscrimination by viewing the uniqueness in each person and situation.

15. I avoid polarization by using "middle ground" terms and qualifiers in describing the world, especially people.

Key Word Quiz

Write T for those statements that are true and F for those that are false. In addition, for those that are false, replace the italicized term with the correct term.

1. The meaning of a word that you would find in a dictionary is the word's *connotative meaning*.

2. The emotional meaning that speakers and listeners give to a word is known as the word's *denotative meaning*.

3. The word *magazine* differs from *Time* magazine in *abstraction*.

4. A pattern of communication in which you ignore someone's presence as well as that person's communication is known as *confirmation*.

5. A pattern of communication in which you acknowledge the presence of the other person as well as your acceptance of that person is known as *disconfirmation*.

6. Language that puts down members of either sex is known as *sexist language*.

7. The tendency to look at the world in terms of opposites and to describe it in extremes —good or bad, positive or negative, young or old—is known as *static evaluation*.

8. The tendency to look first at the actual person, object, or event and only afterwards at its label or the way it is talked about is known as *intensional orientation*.

9. The failure to distinguish between similar but different people, objects, or events is known as *discrimination*.

10. A useful antidote to allness is the *index*.

Answers: TRUE: 3, 6; FALSE: 1 (*denotative meaning*), 2 (*connotative meaning*), 4 (*disconfirmation*), 5 (*confirmation*), 7 (*polarization*), 8 (*extensional orientation*), 9 (*indiscrimination*), 10 (*etc.*)

Skill Development Experiences

4.1 Thinking with E-Prime

The expression *E-prime* (*E'*) refers here to the mathematical equation E – e = E' where E = the English language and e = the verb *to be*. E', therefore, stands for

normal English without the verb *to be*. D. David Bourland, Jr. (1965–1966; Wilson, 1989) argued that if you wrote and spoke without the verb *to be*, you would describe events more accurately. The verb *to be* often suggests that qualities are in the person or thing rather than in the observer making the statement, and this makes it easy to forget that these statements are evaluative rather than purely descriptive. For example, when you say, "Johnny is a failure," you imply that failure is somehow within Johnny instead of a part of someone's evaluation of Johnny. This type of thinking is especially important in making statements about yourself. When you say, for example, "I'm not good at mathematics," or, "I'm unpopular," or, "I'm lazy," you imply that these qualities are *in* you. But these are simply evaluations that may be incorrect or, if at least partly accurate, may change. The verb *to be* implies a permanence that is simply not true of the world in which we live. (A symposium of 18 articles on E-prime appears in the Summer 1992 issue of *ETC.: A Review of General Semantics.*)

To further appreciate the difference between statements that use the verb *to be* and those that do not, try to rewrite the following sentences without using the verb *to be* in any of its forms—*is, are, am, was,* etc. What differences do you observe in the meaning these sentences communicate?

1. I'm a poor student.
2. They are inconsiderate.
3. What is meaningful communication?
4. Is this valuable?
5. Happiness is a dry nose.
6. Love is a useless abstraction.
7. Is this book meaningful?
8. Was the movie any good?
9. Dick and Jane are no longer children.
10. This class is boring.

4.2 Confirming, Rejecting, and Disconfirming

Classify the following responses as confirmation, rejection, or disconfirmation, and develop original responses to illustrate all three types of responses.

1. Enrique receives this semester's grades in the mail; they are a lot better than previous semesters' grades but are still not great. After opening the letter, Enrique says, "I really tried hard to get my grades up this semester." Enrique's parents respond:

_____ "Going out every night hardly seems like trying very hard."

_____ "What should we have for dinner?"

_____ "Keep up the good work."

_____ "I can't believe you've really tried your best. How can you study with the stereo blasting in your ears?"

_____ "I'm sure you've tried real hard."

_____ "That's great."

_____ "What a rotten day I had at the office."

_____ "I can remember when I was in school; got all B's without ever opening a book."

2. Pat, who has been out of work for the past several weeks, says, "I feel like such a failure; I just can't seem to find a job. I've been pounding the pavement for the last five weeks and still nothing." Pat's friend responds:

_____ "I know you've been trying real hard."

_____ "You really should get more training so you'd be able to sell yourself more effectively."

_____ "I told you a hundred times; you need that college degree."

_____ "I've got to go to the dentist on Friday. Boy, do I hate that."

_____ "The employment picture is pretty bleak this time of the year but your qualifications are really impressive. Something will come up soon."

_____ "You are not a failure. You just can't find a job."

_____ "What do you need a job for? Stay home and keep house. After all, Chris makes more than enough money to live in style."

_____ "What's five weeks?"

_____ "Well, you'll just have to try harder."

4.3 Recognizing Gender Differences

The best way to start thinking about gender differences in language is to think about your own beliefs. Here are 10 statements about the "differences" between the speech of women and men. For each of the following statements, indicate whether you think the statement describes women's speech (W), men's speech (M), or women's and men's speech equally (=).

_____ 1. This speech is logical rather than emotional.

_____ 2. This speech is vague.

_____ 3. This speech is endless, less concise, and jumps from one idea to another.

_____ 4. This speech is highly businesslike.

_____ 5. This speech is more polite.

_____ 6. This speech uses weaker forms (for example, weak intensifiers such as *so* and *such*) and fewer exclamations.

_____ 7. This speech contains more tag questions (for example, questions appended to statements that ask for agreement, such as "Let's meet at ten o'clock, *okay?*").

_____ 8. This speech is more euphemistic (contains more polite words as substitutes for some taboo or potentially offensive terms) and uses fewer swear terms.

_____ 9. This speech is generally more effective.

_____ 10. This speech is less forceful and less in control.

Thinking Critically About Gender Differences After responding to all 10 statements, consider the following: (1) On what evidence did you base your answers? (2) How strongly do you believe that your answers are correct? (3) What do you think might account for sex differences in verbal behavior? That is, how did the language differences that might distinguish the sexes come into existence? (4) What effect might these language differences (individually or as a group) have on communication (and relationships generally) between the sexes? *Do not read any further* until you have responded to the above statements and questions.

The 10 statements were drawn from the research of Cheris Kramarae (1974a, 1974b, 1977, 1981; also see Coates & Cameron, 1989), who argues that these "differences"—with the exception of statements 5 and 8 (research shows that women's speech is often more "polite")—are actually stereotypes of women's and men's speech that are not confirmed in analyses of actual speech. According to Kramarae, then, you should have answered "Women's and Men's Speech Equally" (=) for statements 1, 2, 3, 4, 6, 7, 9, and 10 and "Women's Speech" (W) for statements 5 and 8. Perhaps we see these "differences" in the media and believe that it accurately reflects real speech.

Reexamine your answers to the above 10 statements. Were your answers based on your actual experience with the speech of women and men, or might they have been based on popular beliefs (or myths) about women's and men's speech?

CHAPTER 5

Nonverbal Messages

Nonverbal communication is communication without words; it is the communication that takes place through bodily gestures, facial expressions, eye movements, spatial relationships, clothing and color, touch, vocal rate and volume, and even the way you treat time.

What would your life be like if you were able to read a person's nonverbal behavior and tell what the person was thinking and feeling? What would it be like with your friends? Your coworkers? Your family? And what if others could do the same with you? What would your interpersonal and professional lives be like if everyone could read your thoughts and feelings from simply observing your nonverbal messages? This kind of mind reading is obviously impossible. Yet we do know a great deal about nonverbal messages and how they are used in communication.

BODY MESSAGES

The body communicates with movements and gestures and just with its general appearance.

Body Movements

Nonverbal researchers identify five major types of body movements: emblems, illustrators, affect displays, regulators, and adaptors (Ekman & Friesen, 1969; Knapp & Hall, 1997).

Emblems are body gestures that directly translate into words or phrases—for example, the OK sign, the thumbs up for "good job," and the V for victory. You use these consciously and purposely to communicate the same meaning as the words. Emblems are culture-specific, so be careful when using your culture's emblems in other cultures (see Figure 1.5 on page 18). For example, when President Richard Nixon visited Latin America and gestured with the OK sign, which he thought communicated something positive, he was quickly informed that this gesture was not universal. In Latin America, the gesture has a far more negative meaning. Here are a few differences in meaning across cultures of the emblems you may commonly use (Axtell, 1991):

- In the United States, you wave with your whole hand moving from side to side to say "hello," but in a large part of Europe, that same signal means "no." In Greece, however, this signal would be considered insulting to the person to whom you are waving.

- The V for victory common throughout much of the world—if used with the palm facing your face—is as insulting in England as the raised middle finger in the United States.

- In Texas, the raised fist with raised little finger and index finger is a positive expression of support because it represents the Texas longhorn steer. But in Italy, it is an insult that means "cuckold." In parts of South America, it is a gesture used to ward off evil. In parts of Africa, it is a curse: "May you experience bad times."

- In the United States and much of Asia, hugs are rarely exchanged among acquaintances, but among Latin Americans and southern Europeans,

COMMUNICATING WITH POWER

Signaling Power Nonverbally I

If you want to signal your power nonverbally, try these suggestions (Lewis, 1989; Burgoon, Buller, & Woodall, 1995).

- Avoid self-manipulations (playing with your hair or touching your face, for example) and leaning backward; these will damage your persuasiveness by communicating a lack of comfort and an ill-at-ease feeling.
- Engage in affirmative nodding; it shows others you're paying attention and establishes your position in the interaction.
- Walk slowly and deliberately. To appear hurried is to appear without power, as if you were rushing to meet the expectations of those who have power over you.
- Use facial expressions and gestures as appropriate; these help you express your concern for the other person and for the interaction and help you communicate your comfort and control of the situation.

How would you explain it?

How would you explain the nonverbal power signals of media personalities such as Barbara Walters, Katie Couric, Geraldo Rivera, Jerry Springer, and Oprah Winfrey?

hugging is a common greeting gesture which, if withheld, may communicate unfriendliness.

Illustrators enhance (literally "illustrate") the verbal messages they accompany. For example, when referring to something to the left, you might gesture toward the left. Most often, you illustrate with your hands, but you can also illustrate with head and general body movements. You might, for example, turn your head or your entire body toward the left. You might also use illustrators to communicate the shape or size of objects you're talking about.

Affect displays are movements of the face (smiling or frowning, for example) but also of the hands and general body (body tenseness or relaxed posture, for example) that communicate emotional meaning. You use affect displays to accompany and reinforce your verbal messages, but also as substitutes for words: For example, you might smile while saying how happy you are to see your friend or you might just smile. Affect displays are primarily centered in the facial area, and are covered in more detail in the next section.

Regulators are behaviors that monitor, control, coordinate, or maintain another individual's speaking. When you nod your head, for example, you tell the speaker to keep on speaking; when you lean forward and open your mouth, you tell the speaker that you would like to say something.

Adaptors are gestures that satisfy some personal need, for example, scratching to relieve an itch or moving your hair out of your eyes. **Self-adaptors** are self-touching movements (for example, rubbing your nose). **Alter-adaptors** are movements directed at the person with whom you're speaking—for example, removing lint from a person's jacket or straightening his or her tie or folding your arms in front of you to keep others a comfortable distance from you. **Object-adaptors** are those gestures focused on objects—for example, doodling on or shredding a Styrofoam coffee cup. Table 5.1 below summarizes these five movements.

Body Appearance

Your general body appearance also communicates. Height, for example, has been shown to be significant in a wide variety of situations. Tall presidential candidates have a much better record of winning the election than do their shorter opponents. Tall people seem to be paid more and are favored by interviewers over shorter applicants (Keyes, 1980; DeVito & Hecht, 1990; Knapp & Hall, 1997).

Your body also reveals your race through skin color and tone and may also give clues as to your nationality. Your weight in proportion to your height will also communicate messages to others, as will the length, color, and style of your hair.

Your general attractiveness is also a part of body communication. Attractive people have the advantage in just about every activity you can name. They get better grades in school, are more valued as friends and lovers, and are preferred as coworkers (Burgoon, Buller, & Woodall, 1995). Although we normally think that attractiveness is culturally determined—and to some degree it is—some research seems to show that definitions of attractiveness are becoming universal (*New York Times*, March 21, 1994, p. A14). A person rated as attractive in one culture is likely to be rated as attractive in other cultures—even cultures in which people are generally quite different in appearance from people in the first culture.

TABLE 5.1 Five Body Movements

What other examples can you think of for these five movements?

	NAME AND FUNCTION	EXAMPLES
	EMBLEMS directly translate words or phrases; they are especially culture-specific.	"OK" sign, "come here" wave, hitchhiker's sign
	ILLUSTRATORS accompany and literally "illustrate" verbal messages.	Circular hand movements when talking of a circle; hands far apart when talking of something large
	AFFECT DISPLAYS communicate emotional meaning.	Expressions of happiness, surprise, fear, anger, sadness, disgust/contempt
	REGULATORS monitor, maintain, or control the speaking of another.	Facial expressions and hand gestures indicating "keep going," "slow down," or "what else happened?"
	ADAPTORS satisfy some need.	Scratching your head

The facial area, including the eyes, is probably the single most important source of nonverbal messages.

Facial Communication

Throughout your interpersonal interactions, your face communicates, especially your emotions. In fact, facial movements alone seem to communicate the degree of pleasantness, agreement, and sympathy felt; the rest of the body doesn't provide any additional information. But for other aspects—for example, the intensity with which an emotion is felt—both facial and bodily cues are used (Graham, Bitti, & Argyle, 1975; Graham & Argyle, 1975). These cues are so important in communicating your full meaning that graphic representations are now commonly used in Internet communication. In some Internet Relay Chat groups (those that use GUI, Graphic User Interface), buttons are available to help you encode your emotions graphically. Table 5.2 identifies some of the more common "emoticons," icons that communicate emotions.

Some nonverbal research claims that facial movements may communicate at least the following eight emotions: happiness, surprise, fear, anger, sadness, disgust, contempt, and interest (Ekman, Friesen, & Ellsworth, 1972). Other research proposes that facial movements may also communicate bewilderment and determination (Leathers, 1997).

Try to communicate surprise using only facial movements. Do this in front of a mirror and try to describe the specific movements of the face that make

TABLE 5.2   Some Popular Emotico

These are some of the popular emoticons used in computer communication. The first six are popular in the United States; the last three are popular in Japan and illustrate how culture influences such symbols. Because Japanese culture considers it impolite for women to show their teeth when smiling, the emoticon for a woman's smile shows a dot signifying a closed mouth.

EMOTICON	MEANING
:-)	Smile; I'm kidding
:-(	Frown; I'm feeling down
;-)	Wink
*	Kiss
{ }	Hug
{*****}	Hugs and kisses
^ . ^	Woman's smile
^ _ ^	Man's smile
^ o ^	Happy

up surprise in as much detail as possible. If you signal surprise like most people, you probably use raised and curved eyebrows, long horizontal forehead wrinkles, wide-open eyes, a dropped-open mouth, and lips parted with no tension. Even if there were differences—and clearly there would be from one person to another—you could probably recognize the movements listed here as indicative of surprise.

Of course, some emotions are easier to communicate and to decode than others. For example, in one study, happiness was judged with an accuracy ranging from 55 to 100 percent, surprise from 38 to 86 percent, and sadness from 19 to 88 percent (Ekman, Friesen, & Ellsworth, 1972). Research finds that women and girls are more accurate judges of facial emotional expression than men and boys (Hall, 1984; Argyle, 1988).

Facial Management Techniques   As you learned the nonverbal system of communication, you also learned certain facial management techniques—for example, to hide certain emotions and to emphasize others. Here are four types of facial management techniques that are frequently and widely used:

- Intensifying to exaggerate a feeling, for example, exaggerating surprise when friends throw you a party or pleasure in getting a birthday gift

- Deintensifying to underplay a feeling—for example, if you place first in a race and your friend barely finishes, you'd minimize your own joy in winning in the presence of your friend's poor showing

- Neutralizing to hide a feeling—for example, covering up your sadness so as not to depress others

- Masking to replace or substitute the expression of one emotion for another—for example, expressing happiness to cover up disappointment or, as in the cartoon below, substituting an expression of confidence for worry

You probably learned these facial management techniques along with the display rules that dictate what emotions to express when; these are the rules of appropriate behavior. For example, when your boss tells you that she is resigning, you may be ready to jump for joy because you never liked her, but the display rule dictates that you frown and otherwise nonverbally signal your displeasure. If you violate these display rules, you will be judged insensitive.

"Look at me. Do I look worried?"

The Facial Feedback Hypothesis   According to the **facial feedback hypothesis,** your facial expression influences your level of physiological arousal. People who exaggerate their facial expressions show higher physiological arousal than those who suppress these expressions. In research studies, those who neither exaggerated nor suppressed their expressions had arousal levels between these two extremes (Lanzetta, Cartwright-Smith, & Kleck, 1976; Zuckerman, Klorman, Larrance, & Spiegel, 1981). In one interesting study, subjects held a pen in their teeth in such a way as to simulate a sad expression. They were then asked to rate photographs. Results showed that mimicking sad expressions actually increased the degree of sadness the subjects reported feeling when viewing the photographs (Larsen, Kasimatis, & Frey, 1992). So not only does your facial expression influence the judgments and impressions others have of you, it also influences your own level of emotional arousal (Cappella, 1993).

The Influence of Context and Culture   The wide variations in facial communication that we observe in different cultures seem to reflect which reactions are publicly permissible rather than a difference in the way emotions are facially expressed. For example, Japanese and American students watched a film of an operation (Ekman, 1985). The students were videotaped in both an interview situation about the film and alone while watching the film. When alone, the students showed very similar reactions, but in the interview, the American students displayed facial expressions indicating displeasure, whereas the Japanese students did not show any great emotion. Similarly, it is considered "forward" or inappropriate for Japanese women to reveal broad smiles, so they will hide their smiles, sometimes with their hands (Ma, 1996). Women in the United States, on the other hand, have no such restrictions and so are more likely to smile openly. Thus, the difference may not be in the way different cultures express emotions but rather in the cultural rules for displaying emotions in public (Matsumoto, 1991).

Similarly, cultural differences exist in decoding the meaning of a facial expression. For example, in one study American and Japanese students were asked to judge the meaning of a smiling and of a neutral facial expression. The Americans rated the smiling face as more attractive, more intelligent, and more sociable than the neutral face. The Japanese, however, rated the smiling face as more sociable, but not as more attractive. They did, however, rate the neutral face as the more intelligent one (Matsumoto & Kudoh, 1993).

Eye Communication

From Ben Jonson's poetic observation "Drink to me only with thine eyes, and I will pledge with mine" to the scientific observations of contemporary researchers (Hess, 1975; Marshall, 1983), the eyes are regarded as the seat of the most important nonverbal message system.

The messages communicated by the eyes vary depending on the duration, direction, and quality of the eye behavior. For example, there are rather strict, though unstated, rules for the proper duration of eye contact in every culture. In one study conducted in England, the average length of gaze is 2.95 seconds. The average length of mutual gaze (two persons gazing at each other) is 1.18 seconds (Argyle & Ingham, 1972; Argyle, 1988). When eye contact falls short of this amount, members of some cultures may think the person is uninterested, shy, or preoccupied. When the appropriate amount of time is exceeded, they may perceive the person as showing unusually high interest or even hostility.

The direction of the gaze also communicates. In the United States, it is considered appropriate to glance alternatively at the other person's face, then away, then again at the face, and so on. The rule for public speakers is to scan the entire audience, not focusing on one area for too long or ignoring any one area of the audience. When you break these directional rules, you communicate different meanings—abnormally high or low interest, self-consciousness, nervousness over the interaction, and so on. How wide or narrow your eyes get during an interaction also communicates meaning, especially interest level and emotions such as surprise, fear, and disgust.

The Functions of Eye Movements   With eye movements, you communicate a variety of messages. For example, you can seek feedback. In talking with someone, you might look at her or him intently, as if to say, "Well, what do you think?"

You can also inform the other person that the channel of communication is open and that he or she should now speak. You see this in college classrooms when the instructor asks a question and then locks eyes with a student. Without saying anything, the instructor expects that student to answer the question and the student knows it.

Eye movements may also signal the nature of a relationship, whether positive (an attentive glance) or negative (avoidance). You can also signal your power through "visual dominance behavior" (Exline, Ellyson, & Long, 1975). The average speaker, for example, maintains a high level of eye contact while listening and a lower level while speaking. When people want to signal dominance, they may reverse this pattern—maintaining a high level of eye contact while talking but a lower level while listening.

Eye contact can also change the psychological distance between yourself and another person. When you catch someone's eye at a party, for example, you become psychologically close even though physically far apart. By avoiding eye contact—even when physically close, as in a crowded elevator—you increase the psychological distance between you.

Because these messages vary from one culture to another, you risk breaking important rules when you communicate with eye movements. Americans, for example, consider direct eye contact an expression of honesty and forthrightness, but the Japanese often view this as a lack of respect. A Japanese person will glance at the other person's face rarely, and then only for very short periods (Axtell, 1990).

Women make eye contact more and maintain it longer (both in speaking and in listening) than men. This holds true whether the woman is interacting with other women or with men. This difference in eye behavior may result from women's greater tendency to display their emotions (Wood, 1994).

When you avoid eye contact or avert your glance, you help others maintain their privacy. You might engage in this **civil inattention** when you see a couple arguing in public (Goffman, 1967). You turn your eyes away (although your eyes may be wide open) as if to say, "I don't mean to intrude; I respect your privacy."

Eye avoidance can also signal lack of interest—in a person, a conversation, or some visual stimulus. At times, you might hide your eyes to block off unpleasant stimuli or close your eyes to block out visual stimuli and thus heighten other senses. For example, you might listen to music with your eyes closed. Lovers often close their eyes while kissing, and many prefer to make love in a dark or dimly lit room.

SPATIAL AND TERRITORIAL COMMUNICATION

Your use of space speaks as surely and loudly as words and sentences. Speakers who stand close to their listener, with their hands on the listener's shoulders and their eyes focused directly on those of the listener, communicate something very different from speakers who stand in a corner with arms folded and eyes downcast. Similarly, the executive office suite on the top floor with huge windows, private bar, and plush carpeting communicates something totally different from the 6-foot-by-6-foot cubicle occupied by the rest of the workers.

Spatial Distances

The way in which you treat space, a field of study called **proxemics,** communicates a wide variety of messages. Edward Hall (1959, 1966) distinguishes four distances that define the type of relationship between people and identifies the various messages that each distance communicates.

In **intimate distance,** ranging from actual touching to 18 inches, the presence of the other individual is unmistakable. Each person experiences the sound, smell, and feel of the other's breath. You use intimate distance for love-making and wrestling, for comforting and protecting. This distance is so short that most people do not consider it proper in public.

Personal distance refers to the protective "bubble" that defines your personal space, which measures from 18 inches to 4 feet. This imaginary bubble keeps you protected and untouched by others. You can still hold or grasp another person at this distance—but only by extending your arms—allowing you to take certain individuals such as loved ones into your protective bubble. At the outer limit of personal distance, you can touch another person only if both of you extend your arms.

At **social distance,** ranging from 4 to 12 feet, you lose the visual detail you have at personal distance. You conduct impersonal business and interact at a social gathering at this social distance. The more distance you maintain in your interactions, the more formal they appear. Many people in executive and management positions place their desks so that they are assured of at least this distance from employees.

Public distance, measuring from 12 to more than 25 feet, protects you. At this distance, you could take defensive action if threatened. On a public bus or train, for example, you might keep at least this distance from a drunkard. Although you lose fine details of the face and eyes at this distance, you are still close enough to see what is happening. These four distances are summarized in Table 5.3 on page 101.

Influences on Space Communication

Several factors influence the way we relate to and use space in communicating. Here are a few examples of how status, culture, context, subject matter, sex, and age influence space communication (Burgoon, Buller, & Woodall, 1995).

People of equal **status** maintain shorter distances between themselves than do people of unequal status. When status is unequal, the higher-status person may approach the lower-status person more closely than the lower-status person would approach the higher-status person.

Members of different cultures treat space differently. For example, those from northern European cultures and many Americans stand fairly far apart when conversing when compared with those from southern European and Middle Eastern cultures, who stand much closer. It's easy to see how those who normally stand far apart may interpret the close distances of others as pushy and overly intimate. It's equally easy to appreciate how those who normally stand close may interpret the far distances of others as cold and unfriendly.

TABLE 5.3 Relationships and Prox

Note that these four distances can be further divided into close and far phases and that the far phase of one level (say, personal) blends into the close phase of the next level (social). Do your relationships also blend into one another or are your personal relationships totally separate from your social relationships?

RELATIONSHIP	DISTANCE
Intimate Relationship	Intimate Distance 0 _____ 18 inches Close phase Far phase
Personal Relationship	Personal Distance 1½ _____ 4 feet Close phase Far phase
Social Relationship	Social Distance 4 _____ 12 feet Close phase Far phase
Public Relationship	Public Distance 12 _____ 25+ feet Close phase Far phase

If you live next door to someone in the United States, you are almost automatically expected to be friendly and to interact with that person. It seems so natural that we probably don't even consider that this is a cultural expectation not shared by all cultures. In Japan, for instance, the fact that your house is next to another's does not imply that you should become close or visit each other. Consider, then, what happens when a Japanese buys a house next to an American. The Japanese may well see the American as overly familiar and as taking friendship for granted. The American may see the Japanese as distant, unfriendly, and unneighborly. Yet each person is merely acting according to the expectations of his or her own culture (Hall & Hall, 1987).

When discussing personal *subject matter,* you maintain shorter distances than when discussing impersonal subjects. Also, you stand closer to someone praising you than to someone criticizing you.

Your *sex* also influences your spatial relationships: Women generally stand closer than men. And as people *age* there is a tendency for spaces between them to become larger: Children stand much closer than do adults. There is some evidence that keeping these distances is a learned behavior.

Territoriality

Another aspect of communication having to do with space is **territoriality,** a term that comes to us from ethology (the study of animals in their natural habitat). *Territoriality* refers to an ownership-like reaction toward a particular space or object. The size and location of human territory also say something about status (Mehrabian, 1976; Sommer, 1969). An apartment or office in midtown Manhattan or downtown Tokyo is extremely high-status territory because its cost restricts it to the wealthy.

"We're moving you to a cubicle, Harrison."
© Charles Barsotti

Status is also indicated by the unwritten law granting the right of invasion. In some cultures and in some organizations, higher-status individuals have more right to invade the territory of others than vice versa. The president of a large company can invade the territory of a junior executive by barging into her or his office, but the reverse would be unthinkable.

Many animals mark their territory. Humans do too. We make use of three types of markers: central, boundary, and ear markers (Hickson & Stacks, 1989). **Central markers** signify that the territory is reserved. When you place a drink on a bar, books on your desk, or a sweater over a chair, you let others know that this territory belongs to you.

Boundary markers distinguish your territory from that belonging to others. The divider in the supermarket checkout line, the armrests separating your chair from those on either side, the fence around your house, and the door to your apartment are examples.

Ear markers identify your possessions. Trademarks, nameplates, and initials on a shirt or attaché case specify that this particular object belongs to you.

ARTIFACTUAL COMMUNICATION

Artifactual messages are those made or arranged by human hands. Color, the clothing or jewelry you wear, the way you decorate space, and even bodily scents communicate a wide variety of meanings.

Color Communication

When you're in debt, you speak of being "in the red"; when you make a profit, you're "in the black." When you're sad, you're "blue"; when you're healthy, you're "in the pink"; when you're jealous, you're "green with envy." To be a coward is to be "yellow" and to be inexperienced is to be "green." When you talk a great deal, you talk "a blue streak"; when you are angry, you "see red." As revealed through these clichés, color symbolism abounds in language.

Colors vary greatly in their meanings from one culture to another. Some of these cultural differences are illustrated in Table 5.4, but before looking at

TABLE 5.   Some Cultural Meanings of Color

This table, constructed from the research reported by Henry Dreyfuss (1971), Nancy Hoft (1995), and Norine Dresser (1996), illustrates some of the different meanings that colors may communicate and how they are viewed in different cultures. As you read this table, consider the meanings you give to these colors and where your meanings came from.

COLOR	CULTURAL MEANINGS AND COMMENTS
Red	Red signifies prosperity and rebirth in China and is used for festive and joyous occasions. It signifies masculinity in France and the United Kingdom, blasphemy or death in many African countries, and anger and danger in Japan. Red ink is used by Korean Buddhists only to write a person's name at the time of death or on the anniversary of the person's death; it therefore creates problems when American teachers use red ink to mark homework.
Green	Green signifies capitalism, go ahead, and envy in the United States; patriotism in Ireland; femininity among some Native Americans; fertility and strength in Egypt; and youth and energy in Japan.
Black	Black signifies old age in Thailand, courage in parts of Malaysia, and death in much of Europe and North America.
White	White signifies purity in Thailand, purity and peace in many Muslim and Hindu cultures, and death and mourning in Japan and other Asian countries.
Blue	Blue signifies something negative in Iran, virtue and truth in Egypt, joy in Ghana, and defeat among the Cherokee.
Yellow	Yellow signifies wealth and authority in China, caution and cowardice in the United States, happiness and prosperity in Egypt; and femininity in many countries throughout the world.
Purple	Purple signifies death in Latin America, royalty in Europe, virtue and faith in Egypt, grace and nobility in Japan, and barbarism in China.

the table, think about the meanings your own culture(s) gives to colors such as red, green, black, white, blue, yellow, and purple.

There is some evidence that colors affect us physiologically. For example, respiration rates increase in the presence of red light and decrease in the presence of blue light. Similarly, eye blinks increase in frequency when eyes are exposed to red light and decrease when exposed to blue. This seems consistent with our intuitive feelings that blue is more soothing and red more provocative. After the administration changed a school's walls from orange and white to blue, the students' blood pressure levels decreased and their academic performance improved (Ketcham, 1958; Malandro, Barker, & Barker, 1989).

Colors surely influence our perceptions and behaviors (Kanner, 1989). People's acceptance of a product, for example, is largely determined by its package. For example, consumers in the United States described the very same coffee taken from a yellow can as weak, from a dark brown can as too strong, from a red can as rich, and from a blue can as mild. Even our acceptance of a person may depend on the colors that person wears. Consider, for example, the comments of one color expert (Kanner, 1989 p. 23): "If you have to pick the wardrobe for your defense lawyer heading into court and choose anything but blue, you deserve to lose the case. . . ." Black is so powerful that it can work against the lawyer with the jury. Brown lacks sufficient authority. Green will probably elicit a negative response.

Clothing and Body Adornment

People make inferences about who you are—in part—by the way you dress. Whether these inferences are accurate or not, they will influence what people think of you and how they react to you. Your social class, seriousness, attitudes (for example, whether you are conservative or liberal), concern for convention, sense of style, and perhaps even your creativity will all be judged—in part at least—by the way you dress. For instance, college students will perceive an instructor dressed informally as friendly, fair, enthusiastic, and flexible and the same instructor dressed formally as prepared, knowledgeable, and organized (Malandro, Barker, & Barker, 1989).

Your jewelry also communicates messages about you. Wedding and engagement rings are obvious examples that communicate specific messages. College rings and political buttons likewise communicate specific messages. If you wear a Rolex watch or large precious stones, for example, others are likely to infer that you are rich. Men who wear earrings will be judged differently from men who don't. Body piercing and tattoos likewise communicate something about the individual.

The way you wear your hair communicates something about who you are—from caring about being up-to-date to a desire to shock, to perhaps a

COMMUNICATING WITH **POWER**

Signaling Power Nonverbally II

Here are some additional suggestions for signaling power nonverbally.

- Consider standing relatively close to your listeners (even in public speaking); it will create greater immediacy and is likely to be more persuasive.
- Other things being equal, dress relatively conservatively if you want to influence others; conservative clothing is associated with power and status.
- Select chairs you can get in and out of easily; avoid deep plush chairs that you sink into and have trouble getting out of.
- Communicate dominance with your handshake by exerting more pressure than usual and holding the grip a bit longer than normal.
- Use consistent packaging; be careful that your verbal and nonverbal messages do not contradict each other, which can signal uncertainty and a lack of conviction.

How would you explain it?

How would you explain the power signals that you see in the behaviors of managers and supervisors at your workplace that you don't see from those at lower levels of the organizational hierarchy?

lack of concern for appearances. Men with long hair, to take just one example, will generally be judged as less conservative than those with shorter hair. And in a study of male baldness, a man with a full head of hair was rated as younger and more dominant, masculine, and dynamic than the same man without hair (Butler, Pryor, & Grieder, 1998).

Space Decoration

The way you decorate your private spaces also tells a lot about you. The office with the mahogany desk and bookcase set and oriental rugs communicates your importance and status within the organization, just as the metal desk and bare floors indicate an entry-level employee much further down in the company hierarchy.

Similarly, people will make inferences about you based on the way you decorate your home. The expensiveness of the furnishings may communicate your status and wealth; their coordination, your sense of style. The magazines on your coffee table may reflect your interests, while the arrangement of chairs around a television set may reveal how important watching television is to you. Bookcases lining the walls reveal the importance of reading. In fact, there is probably little in your home that would not send messages that others could use in making inferences about you. Computers, wide-screen televisions, well-equipped kitchens, and oil paintings of great-grandparents, for example, all say something about the people who live in a home.

Similarly, the lack of certain items will communicate something about you. Consider what messages you would get from a home where there is no television, no phone, or no books.

Smell Communication

Smell communication, or **olfactics,** is extremely important in a wide variety of situations and is now "big business" (Kleinfeld, 1992). There is some evidence (although clearly not very conclusive evidence), for example, that the smell of lemon contributes to a perception of health, the smell of lavender and eucalyptus seems to increase alertness, and the smell of rose oil seems to reduce blood pressure. Findings such as these have contributed to the growth of aromatherapy and to a new profession of aromatherapists (Furlow, 1996). Because humans possess "denser skin concentrations of scent glands than almost any other mammal," it has been argued that it only remains for us to discover how we use scent to communicate a wide variety of messages (Furlow, 1996, p. 41). Two particularly important messages scent communicates are those of attraction and identification.

Attraction Messages   In many animal species, the female gives off a scent that draws males, often from far distances, and thus ensures the continuation of the species. Humans use perfumes, colognes, aftershave lotions, powders, and the like to (perhaps similarly) enhance attractiveness. You also use odors to make yourself feel better; after all, you also smell yourself. When the smells are pleasant, you feel better about yourself; when the smells are unpleasant, you feel less good about yourself and probably shower and perhaps put on some cologne.

Identification Messages Smell is often used to create an image or an identity for a product. Advertisers and manufacturers spend millions of dollars each year creating scents for cleaning products and toothpastes, for example, that have nothing to do with their cleaning power. Instead, they function solely to create an image for the product. There is also evidence that we can identify specific significant others by smell. For example, young children were able to identify the T-shirts of their brothers and sisters solely on the basis of smell (Porter & Moore, 1981). And one researcher goes so far as to advise, "If your man's odor reminds you of Dad or your brother, you may want genetic tests before trying to conceive a child" (Furlow, 1996, p. 41).

TOUCH COMMUNICATION

Touch communication (also called **haptics**) is perhaps the most primitive form of nonverbal communication (Montagu, 1971). Touch develops before the other senses; a child is stimulated by touch even in the womb. Soon after birth, the child is fondled, caressed, patted, and stroked. In turn, the child explores its world through touch and quickly learns to communicate a variety of meanings through touch.

Touching varies greatly from one culture to another. For example, African Americans touch each other more than European Americans, and touching declines from kindergarten to the sixth grade for European Americans but not for African American children (Burgoon, Buller, & Woodall, 1995). Japanese people touch each other much less than Anglo-Saxons, who in turn touch much less than southern Europeans (Morris, 1977; Burgoon, Buller, & Woodall, 1995).

The Meanings of Touch

Researchers studying nonverbal communication have identified the major meanings of touch (Jones & Yarbrough, 1985). Here are five of the most important.

- Touch may communicate such *positive emotions* as support, appreciation, inclusion, sexual interest or intent, and affection.
- Touch often communicates *playfulness*, affectionately or aggressively.
- Touch may also *control* or direct the behaviors, attitudes, or feelings of another person. In attention getting, for example, you touch the person to gain his or her attention, as if to say, "Look at me," or, "Look over here."
- *Ritual* touching centers on greetings and departures, for example, shaking hands to say hello or goodbye or hugging, kissing, or putting your arm around another's shoulder when greeting or saying farewell.
- *Task-related* touching occurs while you are performing some function—for example, removing a speck of dust from another person's face or helping someone out of a car.

Cultural Differences and Touch

The several functions and examples of touching discussed above were based on studies conducted in North America; in other cultures, these functions are served differently. In some cultures, for example, some task-related touching is viewed negatively and is to be avoided. Among Koreans, it is considered disrespectful for a store owner to touch a customer when, say, handing back change; doing so is considered too intimate a gesture. Members of other cultures who are used to such touching may consider the Korean's behavior cold and aloof. Muslim children are socialized not to touch members of the opposite sex, a practice that can easily be interpreted as unfriendly by American children who are used to touching each other (Dresser, 1996).

In one study on touch, college students in Japan and the United States were surveyed (Barnlund, 1975). Students from the United States reported being touched twice as often as did the Japanese students. In Japan, there is a strong taboo against strangers touching, and the Japanese are therefore especially careful to maintain sufficient distance.

Some cultures—such as southern European and Middle Eastern—are contact cultures and others—such as northern European and Japanese—are noncontact cultures. Members of contact cultures maintain close distances, touch each other in conversation, face each other more directly, and maintain longer and more focused eye contact. Members of noncontact cultures maintain greater distance in their interactions, touch each other rarely if at all, avoid facing each other directly, and maintain much less direct eye contact. As a result, northern Europeans and Japanese may be perceived as cold, distant, and uninvolved by southern Europeans, who may in turn be perceived as pushy, aggressive, and inappropriately intimate.

Touch Avoidance

Much as we have a tendency to touch and be touched, we also have a tendency to avoid touch from certain people or in certain circumstances. Researchers in nonverbal communication have found some interesting relationships between touch avoidance and other significant communication variables (Andersen & Leibowitz, 1978).

Touch avoidance is positively related to communication apprehension: Those who fear oral communication also score high on touch avoidance. Touch avoidance is also high in those who self-disclose little. Both touch and self-disclosure are intimate forms of communication; people who are reluctant to get close to another person by self-disclosing also seem reluctant to get close by touching.

Touch avoidance is also affected by age and gender. Older people have higher touch-avoidance scores for opposite-sex persons than do younger people. As we get older, we are touched less by members of the opposite sex, and this decreased frequency may lead us to further avoid touching. Males score higher on same-sex touch avoidance than do females, which matches our stereotypes. Men avoid touching other men, but women may and do touch other women. On the other hand, women have higher touch-avoidance scores for opposite-sex touching than do men.

PARALANGUAGE AND SILENCE

Paralanguage refers to the vocal (but nonverbal) dimension of speech. It refers to *how* you say something rather than to what you say. While silence is the absence of sound, it is not the absence of communication.

Paralanguage

An old exercise teachers used to increase a student's ability to express different emotions, feelings, and attitudes was to have the student repeat a sentence while accenting or stressing different words each time. Placing the stress on different words easily communicates significant differences in meaning. Consider the following variations of the sentence "Is this the face that launched a thousand ships?"

1. *Is* this the face that launched a thousand ships?
2. Is *this* the face that launched a thousand ships?
3. Is this *the face* that launched a thousand ships?
4. Is this the face that *launched* a thousand ships?
5. Is this the face that launched *a thousand ships?*

Each sentence communicates something different—in fact, each asks a different question even though the words are the same. All that differentiates the sentences is the words stressed, one aspect of paralanguage.

In addition to stress, paralanguage includes such vocal characteristics as rate, volume, and rhythm. It also includes vocalizations you make in crying, whispering, moaning, belching, yawning, and yelling (Trager, 1958, 1961; Argyle, 1988). A variation in any of these vocal features communicates. When you speak quickly, for example, you communicate something different from when you speak slowly. Even though the words are the same, if the speed (or volume, rhythm, or pitch) differs, the meanings people receive will also differ.

Judgments About People   Do you make judgments about people's personalities on the basis of their paralinguistic cues? For example, do you conclude that your colleague, who speaks softly when presenting ideas at a department meeting, isn't sure of the ideas' usefulness and believes that no one really wants to listen to them? Do you assume that people who speak loudly have overinflated egos? Do those who speak with no variation, in a complete monotone, seem uninterested in what they are saying? Might you then assume that they have a lack of interest in life in general? All these conclusions are based on little evidence, yet they persist in much popular talk.

Research has found that people can accurately judge the status (whether high, middle, or low) of speakers from 60-second voice samples (Davitz, 1964). Many listeners in this study made their judgments in fewer than 15 seconds. Speakers judged to be of high status were also given higher credibility than speakers rated middle and low.

Listeners can also accurately judge the emotional states of speakers from vocal expression alone. In these studies, speakers recite the alphabet or numbers while expressing emotions. Some emotions are easier to identify than others; it is easy to distinguish between hate and sympathy but more difficult to distinguish between fear and anxiety. And, of course, listeners vary in their ability to decode, and speakers in their ability to encode, emotions (Scherer, 1986).

Judgments About Communication Effectiveness   Speech rate is an important component of paralanguage. In one-way communication (when one person is doing all or most of the speaking and the other person is doing all or most of the listening), those who talk fast (about 50 percent faster than normal) are more persuasive. People agree more with a fast speaker than with a slow speaker and find the fast speaker more intelligent and objective (MacLachlan, 1979).

When we look at comprehension, rapid speech shows an interesting effect. When the speaking rate is increased by 50 percent, the comprehension level drops by only 5 percent. When the rate is doubled, the comprehension level drops only 10 percent. These 5 and 10 percent losses are more than offset by the increased speed; faster speech rates are thus much more efficient in communicating information. If the speeds are more than twice that of normal speech, however, the comprehension level begins to fall dramatically.

Using Electronic Communication Ethically

The principles of free and responsible communication have long been a hallmark of communication study. Since 1963, the National Communication Association has included among its core documents a Credo for Free and Responsible Communication in a Democratic Society. Recognizing the advent of electronic means of global communication that are accessible to the general public, we members of the National Communication Association endorse the following statement of principles relating to electronic communication:

We take the concept of "free speech" literally: There is limited freedom of expression if access to the means of expression is limited by financial ability. We, therefore, urge the development of free and low-cost means of accessing the means for processing and distributing information in electronic forms.

We realize that access is limited if specialized expertise is required to take advantage of the necessary technology. We, therefore, urge the development of hardware and software that requires minimal training but that still allows wide use of worldwide electronic resources.

We support freedom of expression and condemn attempts to constrain information processing or electronic communication, especially expressions that are offensive to some or even most of the populace. Likewise, we support a right to privacy, both in the ability to maintain the integrity of individual message exchanges and in the ability to shield oneself from unwanted messages.

While supporting free expression, we nevertheless consider the maintenance of intellectual property

rights to be crucial to the encouragement of creativity and originality. We, therefore, urge the designers and regulators of electronic forms of communication to use special vigilance to insure that the works of individuals or groups are protected from unfair use by others.

We encourage communication researchers to produce findings that will guide policy decisions concerning the social impact of electronic communication and to make those findings available widely. Likewise, we encourage the designers and regulators of electronic forms of communication to take credible findings about the social impact of their work into account as they implement new products and services.

We accept the need to teach students not only how to use electronic forms of communication but how to use them both wisely and well.

Finally, we call upon users of information processing and distribution networks to do so responsibly, with respect for language, culture, gender, sexuality, ethnicity, and generational and economic differences they may encounter in others.

Source: "Credo for Free and Responsible Use of Electronic Communication Networks" by the National Communication Association, adopted 1994.

What would you do?

You discover that your college roommate is constructing a right wing website that advocates white supremacy and separation of the races. What is your ethical obligation? What would you do?

Exercise caution in applying this research to all forms of communication (MacLachlan, 1979). While the speaker is speaking, the listener is generating, or framing, a reply. If the speaker talks too rapidly, there may not be enough time to compose this reply and the listener may become resentful. Furthermore, the increased rate may seem so unnatural that the listener may focus on the speed rather than on the message being communicated.

Silence

"Speech," wrote Thomas Mann, "is civilization itself. The word, even the most contradictory word, preserves contact; it is silence which isolates." Philosopher Karl Jaspers, on the other hand, observed that "the ultimate in thinking as in communication is silence," and philosopher Max Picard noted that "silence is nothing merely negative; it is not the mere absence of speech. It is a positive, a complete world in itself." The one thing on which these contradictory observations agree is that silence communicates. Your silence communicates just as intensely as anything you verbalize (see Jaworski, 1993).

Functions of Silence   Silence allows the speaker and the listener *time to think,* time to formulate and organize the meaning of the message. For example, a lawyer may have many sophisticated points to make during closing arguments to the jury and will use silence not only to give her- or himself time to present these issues in an organized way, but also to give the jury time to digest the information presented. Before messages indicative of intense conflict, as well as those confessing undying love, there is often silence. Again, silence seems to prepare the receiver for the importance of these future messages.

Some people use silence as a weapon *to hurt* others. We often speak of giving someone "the silent treatment." After a conflict, for example, one or both individuals may remain silent as a kind of punishment. Silence used to hurt others may also take the form of refusing to acknowledge the presence of another person, as in disconfirmation; in this case, silence is a dramatic demonstration of the total indifference one person feels toward the other.

People sometimes use silence because of *personal anxiety* or shyness, or in response to threats. You may feel anxious or shy among new people and prefer to remain silent. By remaining silent, you preclude the chance of rejection. Only when the silence is broken and an attempt to communicate with another person is made do you risk rejection.

People may also use silence *to prevent communication* of certain messages. In conflict situations, silence is sometimes used to prevent certain topics from surfacing and to prevent one or both parties from saying things they may later regret. In such situations, silence often allows people time to cool off before expressing hatred, severe criticism, or personal attacks, which are irreversible.

Like the eyes, face, or hands, silence can also be used *to communicate emotional responses* (Ehrenhaus, 1988). Silence sometimes communicates a determination to be uncooperative or defiant: By refusing to engage in verbal communication, you defy the authority or the legitimacy of the other person's position. Silence is often used to communicate annoyance; in this case, it is usually accompanied by a pouting expression, arms crossed in front of the

Listening Ineffectively

Poet Walt Whitman once said, "To have great poets, there must be great audiences too." The same is true of conversation: To have great conversation, there must be great listeners as well as great talkers. So much of ineffective listening is communicated nonverbally that it seems appropriate to identify some general types of listeners who make conversation difficult.

Suggestions?

What steps can you take to prevent yourself from falling into one of these difficult listener traps?

Listener Type	Listening Behavior	(Mis)interpreting Thoughts
The static listener	Gives no feedback, remains relatively motionless and expressionless	Why isn't she reacting? Can't she hear me?
The monotonous feedback giver	Seems responsive, but the responses never vary; regardless of what you say, the response is the same	Am I making sense? Why is he still smiling? I'm being dead serious.
The overly expressive listener	Reacts to just about everything with extreme responses	Why is she so expressive? I didn't say anything that provocative. She'll have a heart attack when I get to the punch line.
The eye avoider	Looks all around the room and at others but never at you	Why isn't he looking at me? Do I have spinach on my teeth?
The preoccupied listener	Listens to other things at the same time, often with headphones with the sound so loud that it interferes with your own thinking	When is she going to shut that music off and really listen? Am I so boring that my talk needs background music?
The waiting listener	Listens for a cue to take over the speaking turn	Is he listening to me or rehearsing his next interruption?
The thought-completing listener	Listens a little and then finishes your thought	Am I that predictable? Why do I bother saying anything? He already knows what I'm going to say.

chest, and nostrils flared. Silence may also express affection or love, especially when coupled with long and longing stares into another's eyes.

Of course, you may also use silence when you simply have *nothing to say,* when nothing occurs to you or when you do not want to say anything. James Russell Lowell expressed this well: "Blessed are they who have nothing to say, and who cannot be persuaded to say it."

Cultural Differences and Silence   Not all cultures view silence as functioning in the same way. In the United States, for example, silence is often interpreted negatively. At a business meeting or even in informal social groups, the silent member may be seen as not listening, having nothing interesting to add, not understanding the issues, being insensitive, or being too self-absorbed to focus on the messages of others. Other cultures, however, view silence more positively. In many situations in Japan, for example, silence is considered a more appropriate response than speech (Haga, 1988).

The traditional Apache, for example, regard silence very differently from European Americans (Basso, 1972). Among the Apache, mutual friends do not feel the need to introduce strangers who may be working in the same area or on the same project. The strangers may remain silent for several days. This period enables them to observe others in the area and come to a judgment about them. Once this assessment is made, the individuals talk. When courting, especially during the initial stages, the Apache remain silent for hours; if they do talk, they generally talk very little. Only after a couple has been dating for several months will they have lengthy conversations. The use of silence is explicitly taught to Apache women, who are especially discouraged from engaging in long discussions with their dates. Silence during courtship is a sign of modesty to many Apache.

TIME COMMUNICATION

Temporal communication (or **chronemics**) concerns the use of time—how you organize it and react to it and the messages it communicates (Bruneau, 1985, 1990). Cultural and psychological time are two aspects of particular interest in human communication.

Cultural Time

Two types of cultural time are especially important: formal and informal time. In the United States and in most of the world, *formal time* is divided into seconds, minutes, hours, days, weeks, months, and years. Some cultures, however, may use phases of the moon or the seasons to delineate time periods. In the United States, if your college is on the semester system, your courses are divided into 50- or 75-minute periods that meet two or three times a week for 14-week periods. Eight semesters of 15 or 16 50-minute periods per week equal a college education. As these examples illustrate, formal time units are arbitrary. The culture establishes them for convenience.

Informal time refers to the use of general time terms—for example, *forever, immediately, soon, right away,* and *as soon as possible.* This type of time creates the most communication problems because the terms have different meanings for different people.

Attitudes toward time vary from one culture to another. In one study, for example, the accuracy of clocks was measured in six cultures—Japan, Indonesia, Italy, England, Taiwan, and the United States. Japan had the most accurate and Indonesia the least accurate clocks. The speed at which people in these six cultures walked was also measured, and results showed that the Japanese walked the fastest, the Indonesians the slowest (LeVine & Bartlett, 1984).

Monochronism and Polychronism Another important distinction is that between **monochronic** and **polychronic time orientations** (Hall 1959, 1976; Hall & Hall, 1987). Monochronic people or cultures such as the United States, Germany, Scandinavia, and Switzerland schedule one thing at a time. In these cultures, time is compartmentalized and there is a time for everything. Polychronic people or cultures such as Latin Americans, Mediterranean people, and Arabs, on the other hand, schedule a number of things at the same time. Eating, conducting business with several different people, and taking care of family matters may all be conducted at the same time. No culture is entirely monochronic or polychronic; rather, these are general tendencies that are found across a large part of the culture. Some cultures combine both time orientations; Japanese and parts of American culture are examples in which both orientations are found. Table 5.5, based on Hall and Hall (1987), identifies some of the distinctions between these two time orientations.

The Social Clock An especially interesting aspect of cultural time is your "social clock" (Neugarten, 1979). Your culture and your specific society within that culture maintain a time schedule that dictates the right time to do a variety of important things—for example, the right time to start dating, to finish college, to buy your own home, and to have a child. You may also feel that you should be making a certain salary and working at a particular level of management by a certain age. Most people are taught about this clock as they grow up and internalize these lessons. You evaluate your own social and professional development on the basis of this social clock. If you are on time with the rest of your peers—for example, you all started dating at around the same age or you're all finishing college at around the same age—you will feel well adjusted, competent, and a part of the group. If you are late, you will probably experience feelings of dissatisfaction and inadequacy.

TABLE 5.5   Monochronic and Polychronic

As you read down this table, note the potential for miscommunication that these differences might create when monochronic time and polychronic time people interact. Have any of these differences ever created interpersonal misunderstandings for you?

THE MONOCHRONIC TIME PERSON	THE POLYCHRONIC TIME PERSON
does one thing at a time.	does several things at once.
treats time schedules and plans very seriously and feels they may only be broken for the most serious of reasons.	treats time schedules and plans as useful (not sacred) and feels they may be broken for a variety of reasons.
considers the job the most important part of his or her life, ahead of even family.	considers the family and interpersonal relationships more important than the job.
considers privacy extremely important, seldom borrows or lends to others, and works independently.	is actively involved with others and works in the presence of and with lots of people at the same time.

Psychological Time

Psychological time refers to the importance we place on the past, present, and future. With a past orientation, we have a particular reverence for the past. We relive old times and regard the old methods as the best. We see events as circular and recurring and find that the wisdom of yesterday is applicable also to today and tomorrow. With a present orientation, we live in the present—for now—without planning for tomorrow. With a future orientation, we look toward and live for the future. We save today, work hard in college, and deny ourselves luxuries because we are preparing for the future. Before reading about some of the consequences of the way we view time, take the self-test, "What time do you have?" to assess your own psychological time orientation.

Test Yourself

What Time Do You Have?

Instructions: For each statement, indicate whether the statement is true (T) or untrue (F) of your general attitude and behavior. A few statements are repeated; this is to facilitate interpreting your score.

_____ 1. Meeting tomorrow's deadlines and doing other necessary work comes before tonight's partying.

_____ 2. I meet my obligations to friends and authorities on time.

_____ 3. I complete projects on time by making steady progress.

_____ 4. I am able to resist temptations when I know there is work to be done.

_____ 5. I keep working at a difficult, uninteresting task if it will help me get ahead.

_____ 6. If things don't get done on time, I don't worry about it.

_____ 7. I think that it's useless to plan too far ahead because things hardly ever come out the way you planned anyway.

_____ 8. I try to live one day at a time.

_____ 9. I live to make better what is rather than to be concerned about what will be.

_____ 10. It seems to me that it doesn't make sense to worry about the future, since fate determines that whatever will be, will be.

_____ 11. I believe that getting together with friends to party is one of life's important pleasures.

_____ 12. I do things impulsively, making decisions on the spur of the moment.

_____ 13. I take risks to put excitement in my life.

_____ 14. I get drunk at parties.

_____ 15. It's fun to gamble.

_____ 16. Thinking about the future is pleasant to me.

_____ 17. When I want to achieve something, I set subgoals and consider specific means for reaching those goals.

_____ 18. It seems to me that my career path is pretty well laid out.

_____ 19. It upsets me to be late for appointments.

_____ 20. I meet my obligations to friends and authorities on time.

_____ 21. I get irritated at people who keep me waiting when we've agreed to meet at a given time.

_____ 22. It makes sense to invest a substantial part of my income in insurance premiums.

_____ 23. I believe that "A stitch in time saves nine."

_____ 24. I believe that "A bird in the hand is worth two in the bush."

_____ 25. I believe it is important to save for a rainy day.

_____ 26. I believe a person's day should be planned each morning.

_____ 27. I make lists of things I must do.

_____ 28. When I want to achieve something, I set subgoals and consider specific means for reaching those goals.

_____ 29. I believe that "A stitch in time saves nine."

■ **HOW DID YOU DO?** This time test measures seven different factors. If you selected true (T) for all or most of the questions within any given factor, you are probably high on that factor. If you selected untrue (F) for all or most of the questions within any given factor, you are probably low on that factor.

The first factor, measured by questions 1 through 5, is a future, work motivation, perseverance orientation. People high in this factor have a strong work ethic and are committed to completing a task despite difficulties and temptations. The second factor (questions 6 through 10) is a present, fatalistic, worry-free orientation. High scorers on this factor live one day at a time, not necessarily to enjoy the day but to avoid planning for the next day or anxiety about the future. The third factor (questions 11 through 15) is a present, pleasure-seeking, partying orientation. People high in this factor enjoy the present, take risks, and engage in a variety of impulsive actions. The fourth factor (questions 16 through 18) is a future, goal-seeking, and planning orientation. High scorers on this factor derive special pleasure from planning and achieving a variety of goals.

The fifth factor (questions 19 through 21) is a time-sensitivity orientation. People who score high are especially sensitive to time and its role in social obligations. The sixth factor (questions 22 through 25) is a future, practical action orientation. People high in this factor do what they have to do—take practical actions—to achieve the future they want. The seventh factor (questions 26 through 29) is a future, somewhat obsessive daily planning orientation. High scorers on this factor make daily "to do" lists and devote great attention to specific details.

■ **WHAT WILL YOU DO?** Now that you have some idea of how you treat the different types of time, consider how these attitudes and behaviors work for you. For example, will your time orientations help you achieve your social and professional goals? If not, what might you do about changing these attitudes and behaviors?

Source: From "Time in Perspective" by Alexander Gonzalez and Philip G. Zimbardo. Reprinted with permission from _Psychology Today_ magazine. Copyright © 1985 (Sussex Publishers, Inc.).

Consider some of the findings on psychological time (Gonzalez & Zimbardo, 1985). Future income is positively related to future orientation; the more future oriented you are, the greater your income is likely to be. Present orientation is strongest among lowest-income males.

The time orientation you develop depends on your socioeconomic class and your personal experiences. The researchers who developed the scale in the self-test and on whose research these findings are based observe, "A child with parents in unskilled and semiskilled occupations is usually socialized in a way that promotes a present-oriented fatalism and hedonism. A child of parents who are managers, teachers, or other professionals learns future-oriented values and strategies designed to promote achievement" (Gonzalez & Zimbardo, 1985). Similarly, the future-oriented person who works for tomorrow's goals will frequently look down on the present-oriented person as lazy and poorly motivated for enjoying today and not planning for tomorrow. In turn, the present-oriented person may see those with strong future orientations as obsessed with amassing wealth or rising in status.

Different time perspectives also account for much intercultural misunderstanding because different cultures often teach their members drastically different time orientations. For example, members of some Latin cultures would rather be late for an appointment than end a conversation abruptly. While the Latin person sees this behavior as politeness toward the person with whom he or she is conversing, others may see this as impolite to the person with whom he or she had the appointment (Hall & Hall, 1987).

Thinking Critically About NONVERBAL MESSAGES

When thinking critically about nonverbal communication, try following these suggestions.

Analyze your own nonverbal communication patterns. If you are to use this material in any meaningful way—for example, to change some of your behaviors—self-analysis is essential.

Observe. Observe. Observe. Observe the behaviors of those around you as well as your own. See in everyday behavior what you read about here and discuss in class.

Resist the temptation to draw conclusions from nonverbal behaviors. Instead, develop hypotheses or educated guesses about what is going on and test their correctness on the basis of other evidence.

Connect and relate. Although the areas of nonverbal communication are presented separately in textbooks and in many class lectures, all of these areas work together in actual communication situations. And, of course, they work with the verbal message system. Remember that messages occur in packages; see the package, the whole.

Recognize the vast cultural differences in the meanings of nonverbal behaviors. The very same gesture, for example, can be a compliment in one culture and an insult in another.

In this chapter, we explored nonverbal communication—communication without words—and looked at the ways in which messages are communicated by body movements, facial and eye movements, space and territoriality, artifacts, touch, paralanguage and silence, and time.

1. Five types of body movements are especially important: emblems (nonverbal behaviors that directly translate words or phrases), illustrators (nonverbal behaviors that accompany and literally "illustrate" the verbal messages), affect displays (nonverbal movements that communicate emotional meaning), regulators (nonverbal movements that coordinate, monitor, maintain, or control the speaking of another individual), and adaptors (nonverbal behaviors that are emitted without conscious awareness and that usually serve some kind of need, as in scratching an itch).

2. Facial movements may communicate a wide variety of emotions. The most frequently studied are happiness, surprise, fear, anger, sadness, and disgust/contempt. Facial management techniques enable you to control revealing the emotions you feel.

3. The facial feedback hypothesis claims that facial display of an emotion can lead to physiological and psychological changes.

4. Eye movements may seek feedback, tell others to speak, signal the nature of a relationship, and compensate for increased physical distance.

5. *Proxemics* refers to the communicative function of space and spatial relationships. Four major proxemic distances are: (1) intimate distance, ranging from actual touching to 18 inches; (2) personal distance, ranging from 18 inches to 4 feet; (3) social distance, ranging from 4 to 12 feet; and (4) public distance, ranging from 12 to more than 25 feet.

6. Your treatment of space is influenced by factors such as status, culture, context, subject matter, sex, age, and positive or negative evaluation of the other person.

7. *Territoriality* refers to our possessive reaction to an area of space or to particular objects. Markers are devices that identify a territory as ours; these include central, boundary, and ear markers.

8. *Artifactual communication* refers to messages that are human made—for example, the use of color, clothing and body adornment, smell, and space decoration.

9. Touch communication (or haptics) may communicate a variety of meanings, the most important being positive affect, playfulness, control, ritual, and task relatedness. *Touch avoidance* refers to our desire to avoid touching and being touched by others.

10. *Paralanguage* refers to the vocal but nonverbal dimension of speech. It includes rate, pitch, volume, resonance, and vocal quality as well as pauses and hesitations. On the basis of paralanguage, we make judgments about people, conversational turns, and believability.

11. *Time communication* (chronemics) refers to the messages communicated by our treatment of time. Cultural time is how a culture defines and teaches time; difficulties may be created by the different meanings people give to informal time terms. *Psychological time* refers to time orientations, whether past, present, or future.

The text discussion covered a wide variety of communication skills. Check your ability to apply these skills, using the following rating scale: 1 = almost always, 2 = often, 3 = sometimes, 4 = rarely, 5 = hardly ever.

_____ 1. I recognize messages communicated by body gestures and facial and eye movements.

_____ 2. I take into consideration the interaction of emotional feelings and nonverbal expressions of the emotion; each influences the other.

_____ 3. I recognize that what I perceive is only a part of the total nonverbal expression.

_____ 4. I use my eyes to seek feedback, to tell others to speak, to signal the nature of my relationship with others, and to compensate for increased physical distance.

_____ 5. I give others the space they need, giving more space to those who are angry or disturbed, for example.

_____ 6. I am sensitive to the markers (central, boundary, and ear) of others and use these markers to define my own territories.

_____ 7. I use artifacts to communicate desired messages.

_____ 8. I am sensitive to the touching behaviors of others and distinguish among those touches that communicate positive emotion, playfulness, control, ritual, and task relatedness.

_____ 9. I recognize and respect each person's touch-avoidance tendency. I am especially sensitive to cultural and gender differences in touching preferences and in touch-avoidance tendencies.

_____ 10. I vary paralinguistic features (rate, pausing, quality, tempo, and volume) to communicate my intended meanings.

_____ 11. I specify what I mean when I use informal time terms.

_____ 12. I interpret time cues from the cultural perspective of the person with whom I am interacting.

_____ 13. I balance my psychological time orientation and don't ignore the past, present, or future.

Key Word Quiz

Write T for those statements that are true and F for those that are false. In addition, for those that are false, replace the italicized term with the correct term.

_____ 1. The nonverbal OK sign and the head nod that signals agreement are examples of *illustrators*.

_____ 2. Emotional expressions are called *affect displays*.

_____ 3. Facial and hand expressions that try to control the other person's speaking (for example, nonverbal movements that tell the speaker to speed up or clarify something) are known as *adaptors*.

_____ 4. The assumption that your facial expression influences your level of positive and negative physiological arousal is known as the *facial feedback hypothesis*.

_____ 5. The act of avoiding eye contact or averting your glance to help others maintain their privacy is called *civil inattention*.

_____ 6. The study of the way people use space when relating to each other and even to the layout of their towns and cities is known as *territoriality*.

_____ 7. Messages sent through the use of color, clothing, jewelry, and the decoration of space are known as *artificial messages*.

_____ 8. The study of communication through touch is known as *haptics*.

_____ 9. The vocal but nonverbal aspect of speech is called *paralanguage*.

_____ 10. Communication by the way you treat time is known as *chronemics*.

Answers: TRUE: 2, 4, 5, 8, 9, 10. FALSE: 1 (*emblems*), 3 (*regulators*), 6 (*proxemics*), 7 (*artifactual messages*)

Skill Development Experiences

5.1 Integrating Verbal and Nonverbal Messages

Think about how you integrate verbal and nonverbal messages in your own everyday communications. Try reading each of the following statements and describing (rather than acting out) the nonverbal messages that you would use in making these statements in normal conversation.

1. I couldn't agree with you more.
2. Absolutely not, I don't agree.
3. Hurry up; we're an hour late already.

4. You look really depressed. What happened?
5. I'm so depressed I can't stand it.
6. Life is great, isn't it? I just got the job of a lifetime.
7. I feel so relaxed and satisfied.
8. I'm feeling sick; I feel I have to throw up.
9. You look fantastic; what did you do to yourself?
10. Did you see that accident yesterday?

This experience was probably a lot more difficult than it seemed at first. The reason is that we're generally unaware of the nonverbal movements we make; they often function below the level of conscious awareness. What value might there be to bringing these processes to consciousness? Can you identify any problems with bringing these processes to consciousness?

5.2 Sitting at the Company Meeting

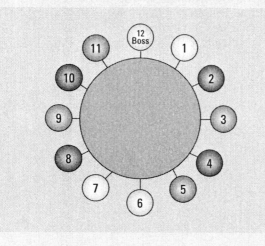

Where would you sit in each of the four situations identified below? What would be your first choice? Your second choice?

1. You want to polish the apple and ingratiate yourself with your boss.
2. You aren't prepared and want to be ignored.
3. You want to challenge your boss on a certain policy that will come up for a vote.
4. You want to be accepted as a new (but important) member of the company.

Thinking Critically About Seating. Why did you make the choices you made? Do you normally make choices based on such factors as these? What interpersonal factors—for example, the desire to talk to or the desire to get a closer look at someone—influence your day-to-day seating behavior?

5.3 Coloring Meanings

This exercise is designed to raise questions about the meanings that colors communicate and focuses on the ways advertisers and marketers use colors to influence our perceptions of a particular product. The color spectrum is presented below with numbers from 1 to 25 to facilitate identifying the colors that you select for the objects noted below.

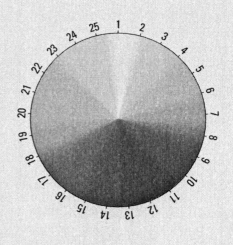

Assume that you are working for an advertising agency and that your task is to select colors for the various objects listed below. For each object, select the major color as well as the secondary colors you would use in its packaging. Record these in the spaces provided by selecting the numbers corresponding to the colors of the spectrum.

Objects	Major Color	Secondary Colors
Especially rich ice cream	_____	_____

Objects	Major Color	Secondary Colors
Low-calorie ice cream	_____	_____
Inexpensive puppy food	_____	_____
Packaging for upscale jewelry store	_____	_____
An exercise machine for people over 60	_____	_____
A textbook in human communication	_____	_____

Thinking Critically About Color Communication. After each person has recorded his or her decisions, discuss them in small groups of five or six or with the class as a whole. You may find it helpful to consider the following:

1. What meanings did you wish to communicate for each of the objects?
2. How much agreement is there among the group members that these meanings are the appropriate ones for these products?

3. How much agreement is there among group members on the colors selected?
4. How effectively do the various colors communicate the desired meanings?
5. Pool the insights of all group members and re-color the products. Are these group designs superior to those developed individually? If a number of groups are working on this project at the same time, it may be interesting to compare the final group colors for each of the products.

5.4 Praising and Criticizing

Consider how paralanguage variations can communicate praise and criticism by reading each of the following 10 statements aloud, the first time to communicate praise and the second to communicate criticism. Then consider which paralanguage cues you used to communicate the praise and criticism. Although this exercise focused on paralanguage, did you also read the statements with different facial expressions, eye movements, and body postures?

1. Now that looks good on you.
2. You lost weight.
3. You look younger than that.
4. You're gonna make it.
5. That was some meal.
6. You really know yourself.
7. You're an expert.
8. You're so sensitive. I'm amazed.
9. Your parents are really something.
10. Are you ready? Already?

CHAPTER 6

Conversation and Conflict

Interpersonal communication is communication that occurs between two people who have a clearly defined relationship. It thus includes what takes place between a waiter and a customer, a son and his father, two people in an interview, and so on. This definition makes it almost impossible for communication between two people not to be considered interpersonal—inevitably, some relationship exists. Even a stranger asking directions from a local resident has established a clearly defined relationship as soon as the first message is sent. Sometimes this "relational" or "dyadic" definition is extended to include small groups of people, such as family members, groups of three or four friends, or work colleagues.

The first part of this chapter examines conversation, its stages, and the qualities that make it effective (Bochner & Kelly, 1974; Ruben, 1988; Rubin, 1982; Spitzberg & Cupach, 1984, 1989; Spitzberg & Hecht, 1984; Wiemann, 1977; Wiemann & Backlund, 1980). The second part of the chapter explores interpersonal conflict, how it works, and how you can manage it for greater interpersonal effectiveness.

CONVERSATION

Conversation takes place in five steps: opening, feedforward, business, feedback, and closing, as shown in Figure 6.1. These five stages of conversation are discussed as they relate to both face-to-face and computer-mediated communication.

E-mail is especially similar to interpersonal conversation. (Internet Relay Chat groups, in some situations resembling interpersonal communication, have more in common with small group communication. And newsgroups are in many ways the electronic equivalent of public speaking. A few features of e-mail that people are often unaware of are worthy of mention.

First, unlike face-to-face communication, e-mail does not take place in real time: You may send your letter today, but the receiver may not read it for a week and may take another week to respond. By the time the receiver gets your e-mail, the situation that prompted you to send it may have changed. And

FIGURE 6.1

The Conversation Process
This model of the stages of conversation is best seen as a way of talking about conversation, not as a map of unvarying stages that all conversations follow. Can you use this diagram to explain the structure of a recent conversation? How would you diagram a model of communication by e-mail?

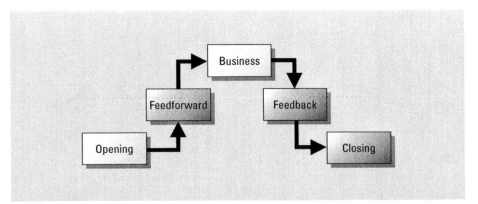

e-mail is more like a postcard than a letter: It can be read by others along the route to its intended receiver. In addition, it is virtually unerasable. Especially in large organizations, employees' e-mails are stored on hard disk or on backup tapes and may be retrieved for a variety of reasons. Currently, for example, large corporations are being sued because of sexist and racist e-mail written by their employees; plaintiffs' lawyers have retrieved these e-mails from archives long thought destroyed. Your e-mail can also be easily forwarded to other people by anyone who receives it or has access to your files. Although this practice is considered unethical, it's unfortunately relatively common. All these features add up to the principle that communication is irreversible, especially when it comes to e-mail. Don't send anything in e-mail that you wouldn't want made public.

Opening

Your first step is to open the conversation; you usually do this with some kind of greeting: "Hi." "How are you?" "Hello, this is Joe." In face-to-face conversation, greetings can be verbal or nonverbal but are usually both (Krivonos & Knapp, 1975; Knapp, 1984). In e-mail (and in most computer communication today), the greetings are verbal with perhaps an emoticon or two thrown in (see Table 6.2). As video and sound are added to your Internet connections, this difference from face-to-face conversation will be practically obliterated. Verbal greetings include, for example, verbal salutes ("Hi," "Hello"), initiation of the topic ("The reason I called . . ."), making reference to the other ("Hey, Joe, what's up?"), and personal inquiries ("What's new?" "How are you doing?"). Nonverbal greetings include waving, smiling, shaking hands, and winking (and their emoticon equivalents).

In your greeting, you can accomplish several purposes (Krivonos & Knapp, 1975; Knapp & Vangelisti, 1996). For example, you can *signal a stage of access;* you can indicate that the channels of communication are open for more meaningful interaction, a good example of **phatic communication,** or "small talk" opening the way for "big talk." Or, you can *reveal important information about the relationship between the two of you.* For example, a big smile and a warm "Hi, it's been a long time" signals that your relationship is still a friendly one. With greetings, you can also *help maintain the relationship.* You see this function served between colleagues who frequently pass by each other in the workplace. This greeting-in-passing assures you that even though you do not stop and talk, you still have access to each other.

Feedforward

In the second step of conversation, you usually give some kind of feedforward in which you might seek to accomplish a variety of functions. One function is to *open the channels of communication,* usually with some phatic message—a message that signals that communication will take place rather than communicates any significant denotative information. An example would be "Haven't we met before?" or "Nice day, isn't it?" In e-mail, this is done simply by sending the message—it tells the other person that you want to communicate.

Another function of feedforward is to *preview future messages,* for example, "I'm afraid I have bad news for you" or "Listen to this before you make a move" or "I'll tell you all the gory details." In office memos and e-mail, this function is served—in part—with headers that indicate the subject of your message, the recipients, and those who'll receive courtesy copies.

Feedforward can also help to **altercast,** to place the receiver in a specific role and request that the receiver respond to you in terms of this assumed role (Weinstein & Deutschberger, 1963; McLaughlin, 1984). Examples of altercasting are, "But you're my best friend, you have to help me" and "As an advertising executive, what do you think of advertising directed at children?"

You can also use a **disclaimer,** a statement used to persuade the listener to hear your message as you wish it to be heard (Hewitt & Stokes, 1975). Examples include, "Don't get me wrong, I'm not sexist," "I didn't read the entire report, but . . . ," and "Don't say anything until you hear my side." In e-mail and other forms of computer communication, you can use emoticons to indicate that you're only joking and thereby disclaim any negative intent.

Business

The third step is the business, or the substance and focus, of the conversation. *Business* is a good term to use for this stage because it emphasizes that most conversations are directed at achieving some goal. You converse to fulfill one or several of the general purposes of interpersonal communication: to learn, relate, influence, play, or help. The business is conducted through an exchange of speaker and listener roles—you talk about the new supervisor, what happened in class, or your vacation plans. This is obviously the longest part of the conversation; both the opening and feedforward support and foreshadow this part of the conversation.

The defining feature of face-to-face conversation is that the participants exchange the roles of speaker and listener frequently throughout the interaction. Usually, brief (rather than long) speaking turns characterize mutually satisfying conversations. This is where e-mail differs greatly from most face-to-face communication. In e-mail, you send a message without any interruptions or feedback from the receiver. Then the receiver responds. Then you respond. E-mail communication thus better resembles the linear model of communication, in which either speaker or listener, never both at once, sends messages. Face-to-face conversation is better described with the transactional model, in which each person sends and receives messages simultaneously and is more closely represented in, for example, instant messaging systems. Here are just a few suggestions for sending and receiving messages in both face-to-face and computer-mediated communication.

Ask questions of clarification and extension to show that you're listening and that you're interested. Ask for opinions and ideas to draw the person into the conversation and to initiate an exchange of thoughts. Paraphrase important ideas to make sure you understand what the sender is thinking and feeling and give her or him an opportunity to correct or modify your paraphrase ("Does this mean you're going to quit your job?").

Strive for a balance between sending and receiving at least most of the time. Be sure to have good reasons if your speaking time or e-mail sending is greatly different from your listening time or your e-mail responses.

Beware of detouring—taking a word or idea from a message and then going off on a tangent. Too many of these tangents can cause you to lose the opportunity to achieve any conversational depth. Keep the main subject of the conversation clearly in mind as you talk and as you listen.

Interruptions are only possible in face-to-face conversation; you can't interrupt someone's e-mail writing. In face-to-face situations, it is best to avoid interruptions. Generally, interruptions that take the speaking turn away from the speaker damage a conversation by preventing each person from saying what he or she wants to say. Excessive interruptions may result in monologues rather than dialogues. Remember, however, to use **backchanneling cues**, signals that you send back to the speaker that do not take away the speaker's turn (Burgoon, Buller, & Woodall, 1995; Kennedy & Camden, 1988; Pearson & Spitzberg, 1990). Backchanneling cues include, for example, indicating agreement or disagreement through smiles or frowns, gestures of approval or disapproval, or brief comments such as "right" or "never." They also include displaying *involvement* or *boredom* with the speaker through attentive or inattentive posture, forward or backward leaning, and focused or no eye contact. You can also give the speaker *pacing* cues, for example, indicating by raising your hand near your ear and leaning forward that he or she should slow down. And you can ask for *clarification* with a puzzled facial expression, perhaps coupled with a forward lean.

Pay attention to turn-taking cues. In face-to-face conversation, look for verbal and nonverbal cues that the speaker wants to maintain or give up a turn as speaker or that a listener wants to say something (or simply remain a listener). Also, pay attention to **leave-taking cues**, signals that the other person wants to end the conversation or the e-mail relationship. See the discussion of ways of closing a conversation below.

The absence of the nonverbal dimension in most current e-mail systems makes misunderstanding more likely, so be sure to explain anything you suspect may not be clear. Use emoticons to show that you are being sarcastic or making a joke, for example. Also, don't be disturbed when the formalities customary in traditional letter writing are omitted in e-mail. E-mail is often viewed more like a memo, with the *to, from, subject, date,* and *courtesy copy recipients* in the preformatted heading. Still, it's important to remember that different organizations will have different standards for what is considered acceptable e-mail style. Generally, the more formal the organization, the more likely it is that e-mail style will be expected to resemble that of printed business correspondence. For example, emoticons would probably be avoided in a formal organization.

Feedback

The fourth step of conversation, feedback, is the reverse of the second. In feedback, you reflect back on the conversation to signal that as far as you're concerned the business is completed. You normally do this immediately in face-to-face conversation and in your response to a previous e-mail. You say, for example, "So, you may want to send Jack a get well card," or, "Wasn't that the dullest meeting you ever went to?"

Feedback can be viewed in terms of five important dimensions: positive–negative, person focused–message focused, immediate–delayed, low monitoring–high monitoring, and critical–supportive. To give effective feedback, you need to make educated choices along each dimension (see Figure 6.2).

Positive feedback (applause, smiles, head nods signifying approval, or a "thank you" e-mail) tells the speaker or e-mail sender that the message is well-received and that he or she should continue communicating in the same

FIGURE 6.2

**Five Dimensions of
Feedback**

It may be argued that, generally at least, your interpersonal relationships would be characterized by the labels on the left side of the figure. This "feedback model of relationships" would characterize close or intimate personal relationships as involving feedback that is strongly positive, person focused, immediate, low in monitoring, and supportive. Acquaintance relationships might involve feedback somewhere in the middle of these scales. Relationships with those you dislike would involve feedback close to the right side of the scales, such as negative, message focused, delayed, highly monitored, and critical. Do you find this generally true?

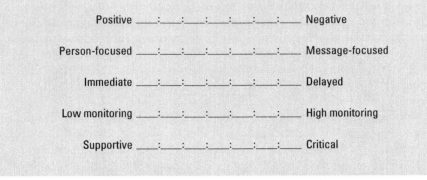

general mode. **Negative feedback** (boos, puzzled looks, or verbal criticism) tells the sender that something is wrong and that some adjustment needs to be made to the communication.

Feedback may be *person focused* or *message focused;* it may center on the person ("You're sweet," "You have a great smile") or on the message ("Can you repeat that phone number?" "Your argument is a good one"). In some situations (for example, giving criticism in a public speaking class), it's especially important to make clear that your feedback is message focused—that you are critical of the speech's organization and not of the speaker as a person.

Feedback may be *immediate* or *delayed.* In interpersonal situations, feedback is most often sent immediately after the message is received. In other communication situations, however, feedback may be delayed. Instructor evaluation questionnaires completed at the end of the course provide feedback long after the class began. When you applaud or ask questions of a public speaker or compliment the message in the previous e-mail, the feedback is more immediate. In interview situations, the feedback may come weeks afterwards. In media situations, some feedback comes immediately through, as with Nielsen ratings, while other feedback comes much later through examination of viewing and buying patterns.

Another dimension of feedback is the variation from the spontaneous and totally honest reaction (*low-monitored feedback*) to the carefully constructed response designed to serve a specific purpose (*high-monitored feedback*). In most interpersonal situations, you probably give feedback spontaneously; you allow your responses to show without any monitoring. At other times, however, you may be more guarded, as when your boss asks you what you think of the new direction the company is taking or when someone sends you an e-mail message asking for a big favor.

Critical feedback is evaluative. When you give critical feedback, you judge another's performance, as when, for example, you evaluate a speech or coach someone learning a new skill. Feedback can also be *supportive,* as when you console someone, simply encourage someone to talk, or affirm someone's self-definition.

Closing

The fifth and last step of the conversation process, the opposite of the first step, is the closing, the good-bye (Knapp, Hart, Friedrich, & Shulman, 1973;

Knapp & Vangelisti, 1996). Like the opening, the closing may be verbal or non-verbal but is usually a combination of both. Just as the opening signals access, the closing signals the intention to end access. The closing usually also signals some degree of supportiveness—for example, you express your pleasure in interacting ("Well, it was good talking with you."). The closing may also summarize the interaction to offer more of a conclusion to the conversation.

Thinking About the Five Stages of Conversation

Not all conversations will be easily divided into these five steps. Often, the opening and the feedforward are combined, as when you see someone on campus, for example, and say, "Hey, listen to this," or when someone in a work situation says, "Well, folks, let's get the meeting going." In a similar way, the feedback and the closing may be combined: "Look, I've got to think more about this commitment, okay?"

As noted, the business is the longest part of the conversation. The opening and the closing are usually about the same length as the feedforward and feedback stages. When these relative lengths are severely distorted, you may feel that something is wrong. For example, when someone uses a long feedforward or too short an opening, you may suspect that what is to follow is extremely serious.

Different cultures, however, vary the basic steps of conversation. In some cultures, the openings are especially short, whereas the openings are elaborate, lengthy, and, in some cases, highly ritualized in others. It is easy to violate another culture's conversational rules in intercultural communication situations. Being overly friendly, too formal, or too forward may hinder the remainder of the conversation. Such violations may have significant consequences in conversation because, if you are not aware of these cultural differences, you may interpret these "violations" as aggressiveness, stuffiness, or pushiness, take an immediate dislike to the person you're talking with, and put a negative cast on future communications.

The five-stage model may help you to identify skill weaknesses and distinguish effective and satisfying conversations from those that are ineffective and unsatisfying. Consider, for example, the following violations and how they can damage an entire conversation:

- The use of openings that are insensitive, for example, "Wow, you've gained a few pounds."
- The use of overly long feedforwards that make you wonder if the speaker will ever get to the business at hand
- The omission of feedforward before a truly shocking message (for example, the death or illness of a friend or relative) that leads you to judge the other person as insensitive or uncaring
- Conducting business without the normally expected greeting, as when, for example, you go to a doctor who begins the conversation by saying, "Well, what's wrong?"
- The omission of feedback, which leads you to wonder whether the speaker heard or read what you said
- The omission of an appropriate closing, which makes you wonder whether the other person is disturbed or angry with you

Skill in conversation depends on your ability to make adjustments along a number of dimensions. Your listening effectiveness depends on your ability to make adjustments between, for example, empathic and objective listening. In a similar way, your effectiveness in conversation depends on your ability to make adjustments along seven dimensions: openness, empathy, positiveness, immediacy, interaction management, expressiveness, and other orientation (see Figure 6.3).

As you read the discussions of these concepts, keep in mind that the most effective communicator in conversation and (as you'll see later in the chapter) in conflict is the person who (1) is flexible and adapts to the individual situation, (2) is mindful and aware of the situation and of the available communication choices, and (3) uses metacommunication to avoid any real or potential ambiguity. These concepts are discussed in greater detail in the section Thinking Critically About Conversation and Conflict at the end of the chapter.

Openness

Openness refers to your willingness to self-disclose, to reveal information about yourself, and also to your openness to listening to another person. Openness also involves the degree to which you "own" your own feelings and thoughts, the degree to which you acknowledge responsibility for your thoughts and feelings. Consider the difference between these responses:

1. Why did you say that? It was really inconsiderate.
2. Everyone thought your behavior was inconsiderate.
3. I was really disturbed when you told my father he was an old man.

Comments 1 and 2 do not show ownership of feelings. In 1, the speaker accuses the listener of being inconsiderate without assuming any of the responsibility for the judgment. In 2, the speaker assigns responsibility to the

FIGURE 6.3

The Dimensions of Interpersonal Effectiveness

After you read this section, return to this figure and rate yourself on all seven qualities. What specific steps can you take to improve your interpersonal effectiveness?

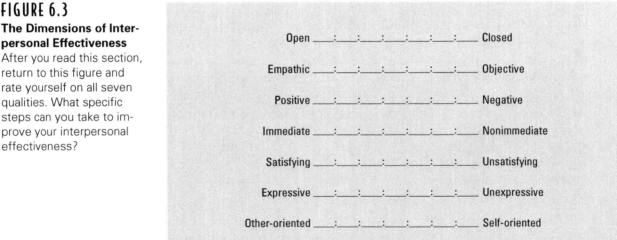

Open ____:____:____:____:____:____ Closed

Empathic ____:____:____:____:____:____ Objective

Positive ____:____:____:____:____:____ Negative

Immediate ____:____:____:____:____:____ Nonimmediate

Satisfying ____:____:____:____:____:____ Unsatisfying

Expressive ____:____:____:____:____:____ Unexpressive

Other-oriented ____:____:____:____:____:____ Self-oriented

COMMUNICATING ETHICALLY

Gossiping

Gossip seems universal among cultures, and it's a commonly accepted ritual among some cultures (Hall, 1993; Laing, 1993). Gossip—third party talk about another person—is an inevitable part of daily interactions; to advise anyone not to gossip would be absurd. Not gossiping would eliminate one of the most frequent and enjoyable forms of communication.

In some instances, however, gossip is considered unethical. Ethicist Sissela Bok (1983) argues that gossip is unethical (1) when it invades the privacy that everyone has a right to—for example, when it concerns matters that are no one else's business; (2) when it can hurt the individuals involved; or (3) when it is known to be false.

What would you do?

Laura and Linda have been friends ever since high school and are now working in the same com-

pany and competing for the position of sales manager. Laura, Linda knows, has lied on her résumé, claiming much more experience than she really has. This experience is likely to land Laura the position over Linda. Laura's lying has not bothered Linda until now, when it's likely to work against her own promotion. Linda wonders whether it would be ethical to let it be known, through informal gossip channels, that Laura doesn't really have all the experience she claims to have. After all, Linda reasons, each person should be judged on the basis of actual accomplishments and experience and not on fabrication. If you were Linda, what would you do?

convenient but elusive "everyone" and again assumes no responsibility. Comment 3, however, is drastically different. Note that the speaker takes responsibility for his or her own feelings ("*I* was really disturbed").

When you own your own messages, you use **I-messages** instead of **you-messages.** Instead of saying, "You make me feel so stupid when you ask what everyone else thinks but don't ask my opinion," the person who owns his or her feelings says, "I feel stupid when you ask everyone else what they think but don't ask me." When you own your feelings and thoughts, when you use I-messages, you say in effect, "This is how *I* feel," "This is how *I* see the situation," "This is what *I* think," with the *I* always paramount. Instead of saying, "This discussion is useless," you would say, "*I'm* bored by this discussion," or "*I* want to talk more about myself," or any other such statement that includes a reference to the fact that *I* am making an evaluation and not describing objective reality. By doing so, you make it explicit that your feelings are the result of the interaction between what is going on in the world outside yourself (what others say, for example) and what is going on inside yourself (your perceptions, preconceptions, attitudes, and prejudices, for example).

Empathy

To *empathize* with someone is to feel as that person feels. When you feel **empathy** for another, you are able to experience what the other is experiencing from that person's point of view. Empathy does *not* mean that you agree with

Research shows that negative gossip is passed on more than positive gossip (Walker & Blaine, 1991). Do you find this to be true? Try to recall the last five or six pieces of gossip you've heard. How many of these were positive? How many were negative?

what the other person says or does. You never lose your own identity or your attitudes and beliefs. To *sympathize*, on the other hand, is to feel *for* the individual—to feel sorry for the person, for example. Empathy allows you to understand, emotionally and intellectually, what another person is experiencing. The other half of this aspect of communication is objectivity, remaining objective and viewing what the speaker says and feels as a totally disinterested third-party observer would.

Empathy is important in just about every type of communication you can think of. It's important for parents to empathize with their children so they can experience, at least to some degree, the problems of growing up today. Conversely, children need to be able to empathize with their parents. Teachers need to see the students' point of view, and students need to see the teachers' perspective. It's important for those in managerial roles to show empathy when listening to the various issues and concerns of their employees. While there may be nothing that you can do about a particular situation, your empathic attitude toward the other person will help the person feel important and valued and will demonstrate that someone really is listening and caring.

Most people find it easier to communicate empathy in response to positive statements (Heiskell & Rychiak, 1986). So perhaps you will have to exert special effort to communicate empathy for negative statements. When you experience empathy and wish to communicate it to the speaker, try the following suggestions.

Confront mixed messages, messages that are communicated simultaneously but contradict each other. You might say, for example, "You say that it doesn't bother you, but I seem to hear a lot of anger coming through." In doing so, be especially careful to avoid judgmental and evaluative (nonempathic) responses. Avoid "should" and "ought" statements that tell the other person how he or she *should* feel. For example, avoid expressions such as "Don't feel so bad," "Don't cry," "Cheer up," "In time you'll forget all about this," and "You should start dating others; by next month you won't even remember her name."

Use reinforcing comments. Let the speaker know that you understand what he or she is saying and encourage the speaker to continue talking about this issue. For example, use comments such as "I see," "I get it," "I understand," "Yes," and "Right."

Demonstrate interest by maintaining eye contact. Avoid scanning the room or focusing on objects or persons other than the person with whom you are interacting. Maintain physical closeness (avoid large spaces between yourself and the other person), lean toward (not away from) the other person, and communicate your interest and agreement nonverbally, with your facial expressions, head nods, and eye movements.

Positiveness

In most situations, you strive to increase positiveness. (We should not ignore the importance of communicating negatively, though. If you communicated your criticism to one of your work assistants in too positive a tone, you would defeat the very purpose of criticism. And people who smile while giving criticism are believed less than those who use more negative facial expressions.) To communicate positiveness, you can state positive attitudes and you can "stroke" the person with whom you interact. Positiveness in attitudes also demonstrates a positive feeling for the general communication situation and makes participants feel a welcomed part of the conversation. Negativeness, on the other hand, may make participants feel unwelcomed and that communication breakdown will come soon.

Positiveness can be seen most clearly in the way you phrase statements. Consider these two sentences:

1. You look horrible in stripes.
2. You look your best, I think, in solid colors.

The first sentence is critical and will almost surely provoke an argument. The second sentence, on the other hand, expresses the speaker's thought clearly and positively and should encourage responses that are cooperative.

"Clemson here. How may I disappoint you?"

In communicating positiveness, don't exaggerate; positive comments and compliments work best when they are realistic and not blown out of proportion. Try to be specific; instead of saying, "I liked your speech," say why you liked the speech: "Your introduction really got my attention; I especially liked the anecdote about your first day on the job." Throughout this positive exchange, own your own messages; say, "I liked your report," instead of, "Your report was well received."

Finally, make sure your verbal and nonverbal messages are consistent; if your comments are genuinely felt, your verbal and nonverbal messages are likely to be consistent; if you are only pretending to be positive, your nonverbals may betray your real feelings.

Immediacy

Immediacy refers to the degree to which the speaker and listener are connected or joined. *High immediacy* refers to extreme closeness and connection; *low immediacy* to distance and a lack of togetherness. The communicator who demonstrates high immediacy conveys a sense of interest and attention, a liking for and an attraction to the other person. People generally respond favorably to high immediacy.

You can communicate immediacy in many ways. Nonverbally, you can maintain appropriate eye contact, limit looking around at others, maintain a physical closeness that suggests a psychological closeness, and use a direct and open body posture by, for example, arranging your body to keep others out of "your private conversation."

Use the other person's name—for example, say, "*Joe,* what do *you* think?" instead of, "What do you think?" Let the speaker know that you have heard and understood what was said and will base your feedback on it. Using questions that ask for clarification or elaboration as well as referring to the speaker's previous remarks will help you to achieve immediacy.

Reinforce, reward, or compliment the other person. Make use of expressions such as "I like your new outfit" or "Your comments were really to the point." Smile and otherwise express that you are interested in and care about the other person and what he or she is saying.

There are, however, times when you may want to communicate a lack of immediacy, in discouraging romantic advances, for example, criticizing a subordinate, or registering a complaint. Obviously, in these situations, you would avoid using the suggestions offered above.

Interaction Management

The effective communicator *manages the interaction to the satisfaction of both parties*. In most cases, you would manage the interaction so that the other person doesn't feel ignored or on stage, so that each of you can contribute to the total communication interchange. Maintaining your role as speaker or listener and passing back and forth the opportunity to speak are **interaction management** skills. If one person speaks all the time while the other listens, effective conversation becomes difficult, if not impossible. Here are two suggestions for effective interaction management.

First, avoid interrupting the other person; interruption signals that what you have to say is more important than what the other person is saying and puts him or her in an inferior position. The result is dissatisfaction with the conversation. Second, keep the conversation flowing and fluent to avoid long and awkward pauses that make everyone uncomfortable.

Expressiveness

Expressiveness refers to the degree to which you display involvement in the interpersonal interaction. The expressive speaker plays the game instead of just watching it as a spectator. Expressiveness is similar to openness in its concern with involvement. It includes taking responsibility for your thoughts and feelings, encouraging expressiveness or openness in others, and providing direct and honest feedback.

This quality also includes taking responsibility for both talking and listening and in this way is similar to interaction management. In conflict situations, discussed later in this chapter, expressiveness involves fighting actively and stating disagreement directly. Expressiveness means using I-messages in which you accept responsibility for your thoughts and feelings (for example, "I'm bored when I don't get to talk" or "I want to talk more") rather than you-messages ("you ignore me," "you don't ask my opinion"). It is the opposite of fighting passively, withdrawing from the encounter, or attributing responsibility to others.

When you want to communicate expressiveness, use I-messages to signal personal involvement and a willingness to share your feelings. Instead of saying, "You never give me a chance to make any decisions," say, "I'd like to contribute to the decisions that affect both of us." Avoid clichés and trite expressions that signal a lack of personal involvement and originality. Use appropriate variations in both voice and body. Vary your vocal rate, pitch, volume, and rhythm to convey involvement and interest and allow your facial muscles to reflect and echo this inner involvement. Use gestures appropriately; too few gestures may signal lack of interest, while too many may communicate discomfort, uneasiness, and awkwardness.

Other-Orientation

Other-orientation is the opposite of self-orientation and is the generally desired mode of communication. It involves the ability to communicate attentiveness and interest in the other person and in what is being said. Without other-orientation, each person pursues his or her own goal; cooperation and working together to achieve a common goal are absent.

Other-orientation demonstrates consideration and respect—for example, asking whether it's all right to dump your troubles on someone before doing so or asking whether your phone call comes at an inconvenient time before launching into your conversation. Other-orientation involves acknowledging others' feelings as legitimate: "I can understand why you're so angry; I would be, too."

You can communicate other-orientation with, for example, eye contact, smiles, and head nods. Leaning toward the other person and revealing feelings and emotions through appropriate facial expressions also communicate a concern for the other person. Focus on the person to whom you're speaking rather than on yourself (avoid primping or preening, for example) or any third person (through frequent or prolonged eye contact or body orientation).

Use minimal responses to encourage the other person to express him- or herself. Minimal responses are brief expressions that encourage other people to continue talking without your intruding on their thoughts and feelings or directing them to go in any particular direction. For example, "Yes," "I see," or even "A-ha" or "Hmm" are minimal responses that tell the other person you are interested in learning what he or she has to say. Express agreement when appropriate. Comments such as "You're right" or "That's interesting" help to focus the interaction on the other person, which encourages greater openness.

Use positive affect statements to refer to the other person and to his or her contributions to the conversation; for example, "I really enjoy talking with you" or "That was a clever way of looking at things" are positive affect statements that are often felt but rarely expressed. Ask the other person for suggestions, opinions, and clarification as appropriate. Statements such as "How do you feel about it?" or "What do you think?" will focus the communication on the other person.

There are times when you may want to be more self-oriented and self-focused. For example, in employment interview situations, the interviewee is expected to talk about him- or herself and to do more of the speaking than the listening. If you are being interviewed because of something you accomplished, you obviously don't want to focus the conversation on the interviewer; rather, you're expected to focus the conversation on yourself. In this situation, you would obviously not ask the interviewer for suggestions or opinions or use minimal responses to encourage the interviewer to express him- or herself. But you would be positive, use focused eye contact, lean toward the other person, and so on.

CONFLICT

Tom wants to go to the movies and Sara wants to stay home. Tom's insisting on going to the movies interferes with Sara's staying home, and Sara's determination to stay home interferes with Tom's going to the movies. Randy and

Grace have been dating for several years. Randy wants to get married; Grace wants to continue dating. Each couple is experiencing **interpersonal conflict,** a situation in which the people involved

- are interdependent. What one person does has an effect on the other person.
- perceive their goals to be incompatible. If one person's goal is achieved, the other's cannot be.
- see each other as interfering with the other person's achieving his or her goal (Hocker & Wilmot, 1985; Folger, Poole, & Stutman, 1997).

We can further describe the types and nature of **conflict** in reference to the concepts of content and relationship.

Content and Relationship Conflicts

Content conflict centers on objects, events, and people that are usually, but not always, external to the parties involved in the conflict. These include the millions of issues that we argue and fight about every day—the value of a particular movie, what to watch on television, the fairness of the last exam or job promotion, and how to spend our savings.

Relationship conflicts are equally numerous and include situations such as a younger brother who does not obey his older brother, partners who each want an equal say in making vacation plans, and a mother and daughter who each want to have the final word concerning the daughter's lifestyle. Relationship conflicts do not arise as much from an external object as from relationships between individuals, focusing on issues such as who is in charge, the equality of a primary relationship, and who has the right to establish rules of behavior.

Like many such concepts, content and relationship conflicts are easier to separate in a textbook than they are in real life, where many conflicts contain elements of both. But in understanding and effectively managing conflict, it helps if you can recognize which issues pertain to content (primarily) and which to relationship (primarily).

What beliefs do you have about conflict? How do these beliefs influence the way you engage in conflict?

Myths About Conflict

One of the problems in dealing with interpersonal conflict is that you may be operating with false assumptions about what conflict is and what it means. For example, do you think the following are true or false?

If two people in a relationship fight, it means their relationship is a bad one.

Fighting hurts an interpersonal relationship.

Fighting is bad because it reveals our negative selves, for example, our pettiness, our need to control, our unreasonable expectations.

COMMUNICATING WITH POWER

Understanding Conversational Power Plays

Power is often used unfairly in conversations, whether at home or in the workplace. Here are three examples of **power plays,** consistent patterns of behavior designed to control another person (Steiner, 1981).

In *Nobody Upstairs,* the person refuses to acknowledge your request. Sometimes, the "nobody upstairs" player ignores socially and commonly accepted (but unspoken) rules such as not opening your mail or not going through your wallet. The power play takes the form of expressing ignorance of the rules: "I didn't know you didn't want me to look in your wallet."

In *You Owe Me,* a person, often a friend or coworker, does something for you and then asks for something in return: "But, I lent you money when you needed it."

In *Thought Stoppers,* someone literally stops you from thinking and expressing your thoughts. The interruption is probably the most common. Before you can finish your thought, the other person interrupts and either completes it or goes off on another topic. Other thought stoppers include using profanity and the other person raising his or her voice to drown you out.

How would you explain it?

What specific interactions have you witnessed in which someone used one of these power plays?

As with most things, simple answers are usually wrong. The three assumptions above may all be true or all be false. It depends. In and of itself, conflict is neither good nor bad. Conflict is a part of every interpersonal relationship, between parents and children, brothers and sisters, friends, lovers, coworkers. If it isn't, the relationship is probably dull, irrelevant, or insignificant. It is not so much the conflict that creates a problem as the way in which the individuals approach and deal with it. This is why the major portion of this chapter focuses on ways of managing conflict rather than ways of avoiding it.

The Negatives and Positives of Conflict

Conflict can lead to both negative and positive effects. Among the potential negative effects is that it may lead to increased negative feelings for your "opponent" (who may be your best friend or lover). It may cause a depletion of energy better spent on other areas, or it may lead you to close yourself off from the other person. When you hide your true self from an intimate, you prevent meaningful communication.

The major positive value of interpersonal conflict is that it forces you to closely examine a problem that you might otherwise avoid and work toward a potential solution. If productive conflict strategies are used, a stronger, healthier, and more satisfying relationship may well emerge from the encounter. The very fact that you are trying to resolve a conflict means that you feel the relationship is worth the effort; otherwise, you would walk away from such a conflict. Through conflict, you learn more about each other; with that knowledge comes understanding.

Cultural Context

The cultural context is important in understanding and effectively managing conflict. Culture not only influences the issues people fight about, but also what is considered appropriate and inappropriate when dealing with conflict. For example, cohabitating 18-year-olds are more likely to experience conflict with their parents about their living style if they live in the United States than if they live in Sweden, where cohabitation is much more accepted. Similarly, male infidelity is more likely to cause conflict among American couples than among southern European couples. Students from the United States are more likely to engage in conflict with another U.S. student than with someone from another culture. Chinese students, on the other hand, are more likely to engage in conflict with a non-Chinese student than with another Chinese student (Leung, 1988).

When American and Chinese students were asked to analyze a conflict episode, say between a mother and her daughter, they saw it quite differently (Goode, 2000). The American students were more likely to decide in favor of the mother or the daughter—one side was seen as right and one side as wrong. The Chinese students, however, were more likely to see the validity of both sides; both mother and daughter were right, but both were also wrong. This finding is consistent with the Chinese preference for proverbs that contain a contradiction (for example, "too modest is half boastful") and the American view that these proverbs are "irritating" (Goode, 2000).

The ways in which members of different cultures express conflict also differ. In Japan, for example, it's especially important that you not embarrass the person with whom you are in conflict, especially if the conflict occurs in public. This face-saving principle prohibits the use of strategies such as personal rejection or verbal aggressiveness. In the United States, men and women, ideally at least, are both expected to express their desires and complaints openly and directly. Many Middle Eastern and Pacific Rim cultures would discourage women from such expressions. Rather, a more agreeable and permissive posture would be expected.

Even within a given general culture, more specific cultures differ from each other in their methods of conflict management. African American men and women and European American men and women, for example, engage in conflict in very different ways (Kochman, 1981). The issues that cause and aggravate conflict, the conflict strategies expected and accepted, and the entire attitude toward conflict vary from one group to the other.

For example, one study found that African American men prefer to manage conflict with clear arguments and a focus on problem solving. African American women, however, deal with conflict through expressing assertiveness and respect (Collier, 1991). In another study, African American females were found to use more direct controlling strategies (for example, assuming control over the conflict and arguing persistently for their point of view) than

European American females. European American females used more problem-solution–oriented conflict management styles than African American women. Interestingly, African American and European American men were very similar in their conflict management strategies: Both tended to avoid or withdraw from relationship conflict. They preferred to keep quiet about their differences or downplay their significance (Ting-Toomey, 1986).

Among Mexican Americans, men preferred to achieve mutual understanding through discussing the reasons for the conflict while women focused on being supportive of the relationship. Among Anglo Americans, men preferred direct and rational argument while women preferred flexibility (Collier, 1991). These, of course, are merely examples, but the underlying principle is that techniques for dealing with interpersonal conflict will be viewed differently by different cultures.

Conflict on the Net

Even in cyberspace, you can experience conflict. Conflict occurs there for the same reasons and deals with the same topics as in face-to-face interactions. So the suggestions for dealing with conflict remain essentially the same for computer-mediated and face-to-face encounters. There is one source of conflict that is unique to cyberspace, and that is the conflict created when the rules of netiquette, the rules for communicating politely over the Internet, are violated or ignored. You can avoid this source of conflict by following these rules of netiquette:

- Read the Frequently Asked Questions (FAQs). Before asking questions about the system, go to the FAQ page and see if you can find an answer to your question. Chances are your question has probably been asked before. This way, you'll put less strain on the system and be less likely to annoy other users.

- Don't shout. WRITING IN ALL CAPS IS PERCEIVED AS SHOUTING. While it's acceptable to use caps occasionally to achieve emphasis, it's better to underline, _like this_, or use asterisks *like this*.

- Lurk before speaking. Lurking is reading the posted notices and conversations without contributing. In computer communication, lurking is good, not bad. Lurking will educate you about the rules of a particular group and help you avoid saying things you'd like to take back.

- Be brief. Follow the "maxim of quantity" by communicating only the information that is needed; follow the "maxim of manner" by communicating clearly, briefly, and in an organized way.

- Be especially kind when talking to newbies; remember that you were once one yourself.

- Don't send commercial messages to those who didn't request them. Junk mail is junk mail; but on the Internet, the receiver has to pay for the time it takes to read and delete these unwanted messages.

- Don't spam. Spamming is sending someone unsolicited mail, repeatedly sending the same mail, or posting the same message on lots of bulletin boards, mailing lists, or newsgroups, especially when the message is irrelevant to the group's focus. Like electronic junk mail, spamming is frowned upon because it costs people money, in addition to wasting time. Because

Listening to Conflict Starters

Usually, conflicts develop over a long period of time; they begin with a word here and a disagreement there and, eventually, a fully developed conflict blows up in your face. Recognizing the beginnings of conflict can help you diffuse it or bring it into the open before it explodes. The skill, of course, is to be able to hear these beginnings in your own speech and in that of others. Here are a few types of potential conflict starters:

- I can't bear another weekend sitting home watching television. I'm not going to do it.
- You think I'm fat, don't you?
- Just leave me alone.

- You never think I contribute anything to these department meetings, do you?
- You should have been more available when he needed us. I was always at work.
- You shouldn't have said that. I hate when you do that.

Suggestions?

What suggestions would you give to someone confronted with each of these statements? What suggestions would you give to the person making these statements?

you're paying to read your e-mail, for example, you're paying to read something you didn't want in the first place. Another reason it is received negatively, of course, is that it clogs the system, slowing it down for everyone and wasting everyone's time.

- Don't flame. Flaming is personally attacking another user. Personal attacks are best avoided on the Internet, as they are in face-to-face conflicts. So avoid flaming and participating in flame wars.

- Don't troll. Trolling is posting information you know to be false just so you can watch other people try to correct you. It's a waste of others' time and of the system's resources.

Before and After the Conflict

If you are to make conflict truly productive, you'll need to consider a few suggestions for preparing for the conflict and for using the conflict as a means to relational growth.

Before the Conflict   Try to fight in private. In front of others, you may not be willing to be totally honest; you may feel you have to save face and therefore must win the fight at all costs. You also run the risk of incurring resentment and hostility by embarrassing your partner in front of others. For example, you may find yourself extremely annoyed about your supervisor taking credit for your ideas in a company meeting. Yet it may be best not to confront your boss during the meeting but to wait instead for the right time (after the meeting) to discuss your feelings.

Although conflicts typically arise at the most inopportune times, you can choose the time when you will try to resolve them. Confronting your partner

COMMUNICATING WITH POWER

when she or he comes home after a hard day of work may not be the right time for resolving a conflict. Make sure you are both relatively free of other problems and ready to deal with the conflict at hand.

Know what you're fighting about. Only when you define your differences in specific terms can you begin to understand them and, hence, resolve them. Fight about problems that can be solved. Fighting about past behaviors or about family members or situations over which you have no control is usually counterproductive.

After the Conflict   Learn from the conflict and from the process you went through in trying to resolve it. For example, can you identify the fight strategies that aggravated the situation? Does your partner need a cooling off period? Do you need extra space when upset? Can you tell when minor issues are going to escalate into major arguments? Does avoidance make matters worse? What issues are particularly disturbing and likely to cause difficulties? Can these be avoided?

Keep the conflict in perspective. Be careful not to blow it out of proportion to the point where you begin to define your relationship in terms of conflict. Avoid the tendency to see disagreement as inevitably leading to major blowups. Conflicts in most relationships actually occupy a very small percentage of the couple's time, yet in the couple's recollection, they often loom extremely large.

Attack your negative feelings. Negative feelings frequently arise because unfair fight strategies were used to undermine the other person—for example, personal rejection, manipulation, or force. Resolve to avoid such unfair tactics in the future, but at the same time let go of guilt, of blame, for yourself and your partner. If you think it would help, discuss these feelings with your partner or even a therapist.

Increase the exchange of rewards and cherishing behaviors to demonstrate your positive feelings and that you are over the conflict. It's a good way of saying you want the relationship to survive and flourish.

EFFECTIVE CONFLICT MANAGEMENT

Throughout the process of resolving conflict, avoid the common but damaging strategies that can destroy a relationship. At the same time, consciously apply the strategies that will help resolve the conflict and even improve the relationship. Here we consider seven general strategies, each of which has a destructive and a productive dimension: win-lose and win-win strategies, avoidance and fair fighting, force and talk, gunnysacking and present focus, face-enhancing and face-detracting strategies, attack and acceptance, and verbal aggressiveness and argumentativeness.

Win-Lose and Win-Win Strategies

In any interpersonal conflict, you have a choice. You can look for solutions in which one person wins—usually you—and the other person loses (win-lose solutions). Or you can look for solutions in which you and the other person both win (win-win solutions). Obviously, win-win solutions are more desirable, at least when the conflict is interpersonal. Too often, however, we fail to even consider the possibility of win-win solutions and what they might be.

For example, let's say that I want to spend our money on a new car (my old one is unreliable) and you want to spend it on a vacation (you are exhausted and feel the need for a rest). In the best circumstances, we learn what each of us really wants through our conflict and its resolution. We may then be able to figure out a way for each of us to get what we want. I might accept a good used car, and you might accept a less expensive vacation. Or we might buy a used car and take an inexpensive road trip. Each of these solutions will satisfy both of us—they are win-win solutions. Skill Development Experience 6.3 provides practice in developing win-win strategies.

Avoidance and Fighting Actively

Avoidance is physical or psychological withdrawal from the conflict situation. Sometimes, it involves physical flight: you leave the scene of the conflict (walk out of the apartment or go to another part of the office or shop). Sometimes, it involves setting up a physical barrier, such as blasting the stereo to drown out all conversation. Sometimes, it takes the form of emotional or intellectual avoidance. In this case, you leave the conflict psychologically by not dealing with any of the arguments or problems raised.

Instead of avoiding the issues, take an active role in your interpersonal conflicts. Don't close your ears or mind. This is not to say that a cooling-off period is not at times desirable. It is to say, instead, that if you wish to resolve conflicts, you need to confront them actively.

Another part of active fighting involves taking responsibility for your thoughts and feelings. For example, when you disagree with your partner or find fault with her or his behavior, take responsibility for these feelings, use I-messages as described earlier in this chapter. Say, for example, "I disagree with . . . " or, "I don't like it when you. . . ." Avoid statements that deny your responsibility—for example, "Everybody thinks you're wrong about . . ." or, "Chris thinks you shouldn't. . . ."

Force and Talk

When confronted with conflict, many people prefer not to deal with the issues but rather to force their position on the other person. The force may be emotional or physical. In either case, however, the conflict at hand is avoided and the person who "wins" is the one who exerts the most force. This technique is commonly used by warring nations, children, and even some normally sensible and mature adults. This is surely one of the most serious problems confronting relationships today, but many approach it as if it were of only minor importance or even something humorous, as in the cartoon below.

Over 50 percent of both single and married couples in many studies report that they have experienced physical violence in their relationship. If we add symbolic violence (for example, threatening to hit the other person or throwing something), the percentages are above 60 percent for singles and above 70 percent for marrieds (Marshall & Rose, 1987). In another study, 47 percent of a sample of 410 college students reported some experience with violence in a dating relationship. In most cases, the violence was reciprocal—each person in the relationship used violence. In cases in which only one person was violent, the research results are conflicting. For example, Deal and Wampler (1986) found that in cases in which one partner was violent, the aggressor was significantly more often the female partner. Earlier research found a similar sex difference (e.g., Cate, Koval, Christopher, & Lloyd, 1982). Other research, however, has found that the popular conception of men being more likely than women to use force is indeed true (DeTurck, 1987): Men are more apt than women to use violent methods to achieve compliance.

One of the most puzzling findings is that many victims of violence interpret it as a sign of love. For some reason, they see being beaten, verbally abused, or raped as a sign that their partner is fully in love with them. Many victims, in fact, accept the blame for

"What's amazing to me is that this late in the game we *still* have to settle our differences with rocks."

The New Yorker Collection 1993 Jack Ziegler from cartoonbank.com. All Rights Reserved.

contributing to the violence instead of blaming their partners (Gelles & Cornell, 1985).

The only real alternative to force is talk. Instead of using force, we need to talk and listen. The qualities of openness, empathy, and positiveness discussed earlier, for example, are suitable starting points.

Gunnysacking and Present Focus

A gunnysack is a large bag, usually made of burlap. As a conflict strategy, **gunnysacking** refers to the practice of storing up grievances so we may unload them at another time. The immediate occasion may be relatively simple (or so it might seem at first), such as someone's coming home late without calling. Instead of arguing about this, the gunnysacker unloads all past grievances: the birthday you forgot two years ago, the time you arrived late for dinner last month, the hotel reservations you forgot to make. As you probably know from experience, gunnysacking begets gunnysacking. When one person gunnysacks, the other person often reciprocates. As a result, two people end up dumping their stored up grievances on one another. Frequently, the original problem never gets addressed. Instead, resentment and hostility escalate.

A present focus is far more constructive than gunnysacking. Focus your conflict on the here and now rather than on issues that occurred in the past. Similarly, focus your conflict on the person with whom you are fighting, not on the person's mother, child, or friends.

Face-Enhancing and Face-Detracting Strategies

Another dimension of conflict strategies is that of face orientation. Face-detracting or face-attacking strategies involve treating the other person as incompetent or untrustworthy, as unable or bad (Donahue & Kolt, 1992). Such attacks can vary from mildly embarrassing the other person to severely damaging his or her ego or reputation. When such attacks become extreme, they may be similar to verbal aggressiveness—a tactic explained in the next section.

Face-enhancing techniques involve helping the other person maintain a positive image, one that is competent and trustworthy, able and good. There is some evidence to show that even when you get what you want, say at bargaining, it is wise to help the other person retain positive face. This makes it less likely that future conflicts will arise (Donahue & Kolt, 1992). Not surprisingly, people are more likely to make a greater effort to support the listener's "face" if they like the listener than if they don't (Meyer, 1994). Confirming the other person's definition of self, avoiding attack and blame, and using excuses and apologies as appropriate are some generally useful face-enhancing strategies.

Attack and Acceptance

An attack can come in many forms. In **personal rejection,** for example, one party to a conflict withholds love and affection. He or she seeks to win the argument by getting the other person to break down in the face of this withdrawal. In withdrawing affection, the individual hopes to make the other person question his or her own self-worth. Once the other is demoralized and feels less than worthy, it is relatively easy for the "rejector" to get his or her way. The "rejector," in other words, holds out the renewal of love and affection as a reward for resolving the conflict in his or her favor.

Much like fighters in a ring, each of us has a "beltline." When you attack someone by hitting below the belt, a tactic called **beltlining,** you can inflict serious injury. When you hit above the belt, however, the person is able to absorb the blow. With most interpersonal relationships, especially those of long standing, we know where the beltline is. You know, for example, that to hit Pat with the inability to have children is to hit below the belt. You know that to hit Chris with the failure to get a permanent job is to hit below the belt. Hitting below the beltline causes added problems for all persons involved. So keep blows to areas your opponent can absorb and handle.

Express positive feelings for the other person and for the relationship between the two of you. In fact, recent research shows that positiveness is a crucial factor in the survival of a relationship (Gottman, 1994). Throughout any conflict, many harsh words will probably be exchanged, and later regretted. Communication is irreversible; the words cannot be unsaid or uncommunicated, but they can be partially offset by the expression of positive statements. If you are engaged in combat with someone you love, remember that you are fighting with a loved one and express that feeling: "I love you very much, but I still don't want your mother on vacation with us. I want to be alone with you."

Verbal Aggressiveness and Argumentativeness

An especially interesting perspective on conflict has emerged from work on verbal aggressiveness and argumentativeness (Infante & Rancer, 1982; Infante, 1988; Infante & Wigley, 1986).

Verbal aggressiveness is a method of winning an argument by inflicting psychological pain—by attacking the other person's self-concept. It is a type of disconfirmation in that it seeks to discredit the person's view of him- or herself. This talk often leads to physical force (Infante & Wigley, 1986; Infante, Sabourin, Rudd, & Shannon, 1990; Infante, Riddle, Horvath, & Tumlin, 1992).

Argumentativeness, on the other hand and contrary to popular usage, refers to a quality that is productive in conflict resolution. It refers to your willingness to argue for a point of view, your tendency to speak your mind on significant issues. It is the preferred alternative to verbal aggressiveness for dealing with disagreements. Before reading about ways to increase your argumentativeness, take the self-test "How argumentative are you?"

Test Yourself

How Argumentative Are You?

Instructions: This questionnaire contains statements about controversial issues. Indicate how often each statement is true for you personally using the following scale: 1 = almost never true, 2 = rarely true, 3 = occasionally true, 4 = often true, 5 = almost always true.

_____ 1. While in an argument, I worry that the person I am arguing with will form a negative impression of me.

_____ 2. Arguing over controversial issues improves my intelligence.

_____ 3. I enjoy avoiding arguments.

_____ 4. I am energetic and enthusiastic when I argue.

_____ 5. Once I finish an argument, I promise myself that I will not get into another.

_____ 6. Arguing with a person creates more problems for me than it solves.

_____ 7. I have a pleasant, good feeling when I win a point in an argument.

_____ 8. When I finish arguing with anyone, I feel nervous and upset.

_____ 9. I enjoy a good argument over a controversial issue.

_____ 10. I get an unpleasant feeling when I realize I am about to get into an argument.

_____ 11. I enjoy defending my point of view on an issue.

_____ 12. I am happy when I keep an argument from happening.

_____ 13. I do not like to miss the opportunity to argue a controversial issue.

_____ 14. I prefer being with people who rarely disagree with me.

_____ 15. I consider an argument an exciting intellectual challenge.

_____ 16. I find myself unable to think of effective points during an argument.

_____ 17. I feel refreshed and satisfied after an argument on a controversial issue.

_____ 18. I have the ability to do well in an argument.

_____ 19. I try to avoid getting into arguments.

_____ 20. I feel excitement when I expect that a conversation I am in is leading to an argument.

■ **HOW DID YOU DO?**   To compute your argumentativeness score, follow these steps:

1. Add your scores on items 2, 4, 7, 9, 11, 13, 15, 17, 18, and 20.
2. Add 60 to the sum obtained in Step 1.
3. Add your scores on items 1, 3, 5, 6, 8, 10, 12, 14, 16, 19.
4. To compute your argumentativeness score, subtract the total obtained in Step 3 from the total obtained in Step 2.

The following guidelines will help you interpret your score:

Scores between 73 and 100 indicate high argumentativeness.

Scores between 56 and 72 indicate moderate argumentativeness.

Scores between 20 and 55 indicate low argumentativeness.

Generally, those who score high in argumentativeness have a strong tendency to state their position on controversial issues and argue against the positions of others. A high scorer sees arguing as exciting, intellectually challenging, and an opportunity to win a kind of contest.

The moderately argumentative person possesses some of the qualities of the high-argumentative person and some of the qualities of the low-argumentative person. The person who scores low in argumentativeness tries to prevent arguments. This person experiences satisfaction not from arguing, but from avoiding arguments. The low-argumentative person sees arguing as unpleasant and unsatisfying. Not surprisingly, this person has little confidence in his or her ability to argue effectively.

■ **WHAT WILL YOU DO?**   The researchers who developed this test note that both high and low argumentatives may experience communication difficulties. The high-argumentative person, for example, may argue needlessly, too often,

To cultivate argumentativeness and prevent it from degenerating into aggressiveness, treat disagreements as objectively as possible; avoid assuming that because someone takes issue with your position or your interpretation, they are attacking you as a person (Infante, 1988). Avoid attacking the other person (rather than the person's arguments), even if this would give you a tactical advantage; it will probably backfire at some later time and make your relationship more difficult. Center your arguments on issues rather than people.

Reaffirm the other person's sense of competence; compliment the other person as appropriate. Allow the other person to save face; never humiliate the other person. Avoid interrupting; allow the other person to state her or his position fully before you respond. Stress equality and the similarities that you share; stress your areas of agreement before attacking the disagreements. Throughout the conflict episode, express interest in the other person's position, attitude, and point of view. Be especially careful to avoid disconfirmation.

Thinking Critically About
CONVERSATION AND CONFLICT

Because each conversation and each conflict is unique, the qualities of interpersonal effectiveness cannot be applied indiscriminately. You need to know how the skills themselves should be applied. We suggest that you be mindful, be flexible, use metacommunication skills as appropriate, and be culturally sensitive.

Mindfulness

After you have learned a skill or rule, you may have a tendency to apply it without thinking or "mindlessly," without, for example, considering the unique aspects of a situation. This may cause problems, especially in intercultural situations, which may be drastically different from your more frequently experienced encounters. For instance, after learning the skills of active listening, many people use them in all situations. Some of these responses will be appropriate, but others will prove inappropriate and ineffective.

The opposite of mindlessness is **mindfulness,** a state in which you are aware of the logic and rationality of your behaviors and of the logical connections existing among elements. In interpersonal, small group, and public speaking situations, apply your conversation and conflict skills mindfully (Elmes & Gemmill, 1990; Langer, 1989).

Langer (1989) offers several suggestions for increasing mindfulness:

- Create and recreate categories. See an object, event, or person as belonging to a wide variety of categories. Avoid storing an image of a person, for example, with only one specific label in memory; it will be difficult to recategorize later.

- Be open to new information even if it contradicts your most firmly held stereotypes.

- Be open to different points of view. This will help you avoid the tendency to blame outside forces for your negative behaviors ("That test was unfair") and internal forces for the negative behaviors of others ("Pat didn't study," "Pat isn't very bright"). Be willing to see your own and others' behaviors from a variety of perspectives.

- Try not to rely too heavily on first impressions, what is sometimes called "premature cognitive commitment" (Chanowitz & Langer, 1981; Langer, 1989). Treat your first impressions as tentative, as hypotheses.

Flexibility

Before reading about flexibility, take the self-test, "How flexible are you in communication?"

Test Yourself
How Flexible Are You in Communication?

Instructions: Here are some situations that illustrate how people sometimes act when communicating with others. The first part of each situation asks you to imagine that you are in the situation. Then, a course of action is identified and you are asked to determine how much your own behavior would be like the action described in the scenario. If it is *exactly* like you, mark a 5; if it is *a lot* like you, mark a 4; if it is *somewhat* like you, mark a 3; if it is *not much* like you, mark a 2; and if it is *not at all* like you, mark a 1. Imagine:

_____ 1. Last week, as you were discussing your strained finances with your family, family members came up with several possible solutions. Even though you had already decided on one solution, you decided to spend more time considering all the possibilities before making a final decision.

_____ 2. You were invited to a Halloween party and, assuming it was a costume party, you dressed as a pumpkin. When you arrived at the party and found everyone else dressed in formal attire, you laughed and joked about the misunderstanding and decided to stay and enjoy the party.

_____ 3. You have always enjoyed being with your friend Chris but do not enjoy Chris's habit of always interrupting you. The last time you met, every time Chris interrupted you, you then interrupted Chris to teach Chris a lesson.

_____ 4. Your daily schedule is very structured, and your calendar is full of appointments and commitments. When asked to make a change in your schedule, you reply that changes are impossible before even considering the change.

_____ 5. You went to a party that over 50 people attended. You had a good time but spent most of the evening talking to one close friend rather than meeting new people.

_____ 6. When discussing a personal problem with a group of friends, you noticed that many different solutions were offered. Although several of the solutions seemed feasible, you already had your opinion and did not listen to any of the alternative solutions.

_____ 7. You and a friend are planning a fun evening, and you're dressed and ready ahead of time. You find that you are unable to do anything else until your friend arrives.

_____ 8. When you found your seat at the ball game, you realized you did not know anyone sitting nearby. However, you introduced yourself to the people sitting next to you and attempted to strike up a conversation.

_____ 9. You had lunch with your friend Chris, and Chris told you about a too-personal family problem. You quickly finished your lunch and stated that you had to leave because you had a lot to do that afternoon.

_____ 10. You were involved in a discussion about international politics with a group of acquaintances, and you assumed that the members of the group were as knowledgeable as you on the topic. But, as the discussion progressed, you learned that most of the group knew little about the subject. Instead of explaining your point of view, you decided to withdraw from the discussion.

_____ 11. You and a group of friends got into a discussion about gun control and, after a while, it became obvious that your opinions differed greatly from the rest of the group. You explained your position once again, but you agreed to respect the group's opinion.

_____ 12. You were asked to speak to a group you belong to, so you worked hard preparing a 30-minute presentation. But at the meeting, the organizer asked you to lead a question-and-answer session instead of giving your presentation. You agreed and answered the group's questions as candidly and fully as possible.

_____ 13. You were offered a managerial position in which you would face new tasks and challenges every day and a changing day-to-day routine. You decided to accept this position instead of one that has a stable daily routine.

_____ 14. You were asked to give a speech at a Chamber of Commerce breakfast. Because you did not know anyone at the breakfast and would feel uncomfortable not knowing anyone in the audience, you declined the invitation.

■ **HOW DID YOU DO?**   To compute your score:

1. Reverse the scoring for items 4, 5, 6, 7, 9, 10, and 14. That is, for each of these questions, substitute as follows:
   a. If you answered 5, reverse it to 1.
   b. If you answered 4, reverse it to 2.
   c. If you answered 3, keep it as 3.
   d. If you answered 2, reverse it to 4.
   e. If you answered 1, reverse it to 5.

2. Add the scores for all 14 items. Be sure to use the reversed scores for items 4, 5, 6, 7, 9, 10, and 14 instead of your original responses. Use your original scores for items 1, 2, 3, 8, 11, 12, and 13.

In general, you can interpret your score as follows:

65–70 = much more flexible than average
57–64 = more flexible than average
44–56 = about average
37–43 = less flexible than average
14–36 = much less flexible than average

■ **WHAT WILL YOU DO?** Are you satisfied with your level of flexibility? What might you do to cultivate flexibility in general and communication flexibility in particular?

Source: From "Development of a Communication Flexibility Measure" by Matthew M. Martin and Rebecca B. Rubin, *The Southern Communication Journal* 59 (Winter 1994) pp. 171–178. Reprinted by permission of the Southern States Communication Association.

As you gathered from the self-test, **flexibility** is the ability to respond differently depending on the specific situation, to be open to new and different alternatives, to adapt to the situation as it unfolds. Here are a few suggestions for cultivating flexibility:

■ Recall the principle of indiscrimination—no two things or situations are exactly alike. When faced with a particular problem, ask yourself what is different about this situation.

■ Remember that communication always takes place in a context. Ask yourself: What is unique about this specific context that might alter my communications? Will cultural differences play a role in this communication? The physical distance you maintain between yourself and colleagues in the United States, for example, may prove too distant for Arabs and southern Europeans, who may perceive you as cold and uninterested.

■ Realize that everything is in a constant state of change so that responses that were appropriate yesterday may therefore not be appropriate today. Responding protectively when your child is 5 might be appropriate; the same response may be inappropriate when your child is 18. Also, recognize that sudden changes may also greatly influence communication; the death of a lover, the knowledge of a fatal illness, the birth of a child, and a promotion are just a few examples of such changes.

■ Remember that everyone is different. Thus, you may openly express empathy to your American friends but may want to tone it down when expressing it to a Korean, who may feel uncomfortable with obvious expressions of empathy (Yun, 1976).

Metacommunicational Ability

Much talk concerns people, objects, and events in the world. But you can also talk about your talk; this is called **metacommunication.** Your interpersonal effectiveness often hinges on your ability to metacommunicate. Let's say that someone says something positive, but in a negative way; for example, the person says, "At last! You've finally completed that report. Good job!" You are faced with several alternatives. Your first two alternatives are to respond to the message positively or negatively.

A third alternative, however, is to talk about the message and say something like, "I'm not sure I understand whether you're complimenting or criticizing me." In this way, you may avoid lots of misunderstandings. Talking about your talk will prove an especially useful tool in intercultural situations, in which the chances for misunderstanding are often considerable.

Here are a few suggestions for increasing your metacommunicational effectiveness:

- Give clear feedforward. This will help the other person get a general picture of the message that will follow; it will provide a kind of schema that makes information processing and learning easier.
- Confront contradictory or inconsistent messages. At the same time, explain your own messages that may appear inconsistent to your listener.
- Explain the feelings that go with the thoughts. People often communicate only the thinking part of their message, with the result that listeners are not able to appreciate the other parts of their meaning.
- Paraphrase your own complex messages. Similarly, to check on your own understanding of another's message, paraphrase what you think the other person means and ask if you are accurate.
- Ask questions. If you have doubts about another's meaning, don't assume; instead, ask.
- When you do talk about your talk, do so only to gain an understanding of the other person's thoughts and feelings. Avoid substituting talk about talk for talk about a specific problem.

Cultural Sensitivity

This text stresses the variations between and among cultures. You need to keep the customs, rules, and meanings of different cultures clearly in mind when you think about both conversation and conflict. A distinction that is especially important in both conversation and conflict is the difference between high- and low-context cultures.

A **high-context culture** is one in which much of the information in communication is in the context or in the person—for example, information that was shared through previous communications, through assumptions about each other, and through shared experiences. The information is thus known by all participants, but it isn't explicitly stated in their verbal messages. A **low-context culture** is one in which most of the information is explicitly stated in verbal messages. In formal transactions, it would be stated in written (or contract) form.

To further appreciate the distinction between high and low context, consider giving directions ("Where's the voter registration center?") to someone who knows the neighborhood and to a newcomer to your city. If someone knows the neighborhood (a high-context situation), you can assume that she or he knows the local landmarks. So you can give directions such as "next to the laundromat on Main Street" or "the corner of Albany and Elm." With a newcomer (a low-context situation), you can't assume that she or he shares any information with you. So you would have to use only those directions that a stranger would understand—for example, "make a left at the next stop sign" or "go two blocks and then turn right."

High-context cultures are also **collectivist cultures** (Gudykunst & Kim, 1992; Gudykunst, Ting-Toomey, & Chua, 1988). These cultures (Japanese, Arabic, Latin American, Thai, Korean, Apache, and Mexican are examples) place great emphasis on personal relationships and oral agreements (Victor, 1992). Low-context cultures, on the other hand, are **individualistic cultures.** These cultures (German, Swedish, Norwegian, and American are examples) place less emphasis on personal relationships and more emphasis on the verbalized, explicit explanation and on the written contract in business transactions.

This difference between high- and low-context orientation is partly responsible for the differences observed in Japanese and American business groups. The Japanese spend lots of time getting to know each other before conducting actual business, whereas Americans get down to business very quickly. The Japanese (and other high-context cultures) want to get to know each other because important information isn't made explicit. They have to know you so they can read your nonverbals, for example (Sanders, Wiseman, & Matz, 1991). Americans can get right down to business because all important information will be stated explicitly.

To a high-context culture member, what is omitted or assumed is a vital part of the communication transaction. Silence, for example, is highly valued (Basso, 1972). To a low-context culture member, what is omitted creates ambiguity. And to this person, this ambiguity is simply something that will be eliminated by explicit and direct communication. To a high-context culture member, ambiguity is something to be avoided; it's a sign that the interpersonal and social interactions have not proved sufficient to establish a shared base of information (Gudykunst, 1983).

When this simple difference isn't understood, intercultural misunderstandings can easily result. For example, the directness characteristic of the low-context culture may prove insulting, insensitive, or unnecessary to the high-context culture member. Conversely, to the low-context member, the high-context culture member may appear vague, underhanded, or dishonest in his or her reluctance to be explicit or engage in communication that a low-context member would consider open and direct.

Another frequent source of intercultural conflict that can be traced to the differences between high and low context can be seen in face saving (Hall & Hall, 1987). High-context cultures place much more emphasis on face saving. For example, they're more likely to avoid argument for fear of causing others to lose face; low-context members (with their individualistic orientation), on the other hand, will use argument to win a point. Similarly, in high-context cultures, criticism should take place only in private. Low-context cultures may not make this public-private distinction. Low-context managers who criticize high-context workers in public will find that their criticism causes interpersonal problems and does little to resolve the difficulty that led to the criticism in the first place (Victor, 1992). Members of high-context cultures are reluctant to say no for fear of offending and causing the person asking to lose face. And so, for example, it's necessary to be able to read in the Japanese executive's "yes" when it means yes and when it means no. The difference isn't in the words used, but in the way they're used.

Keeping this distinction—as well as the various other cultural differences discussed throughout this text—in mind when thinking about conversation and conflict will help to heighten your cultural sensitivity and to make both intercultural conversation and intercultural conflict more productive and constructive.

Summary of Concepts and Skills

In this chapter, we looked at the nature of interpersonal communication, especially the qualities that make for effectiveness in interpersonal communication (in general) and in interpersonal conflict.

1. The conversation process consists of at least five steps: opening, feedforward, business, feedback, and closing.
2. The qualities of interpersonal communication effectiveness are openness, empathy, positiveness, immediacy, interaction management, expressiveness, and other-orientation.
3. Interpersonal conflict is a situation in which two or a few people are interdependent, perceive their goals to be incompatible, and see each other as interfering with their own goal achievement.
4. Conflicts (in face-to-face situations and in cyberspace) can be content or relationship oriented but are usually a combination of both, can have both negative and positive benefits, and always occur within a cultural context.
5. Useful guides to fair fighting are: look for win-win strategies, fight actively, use talk instead of force, focus on the present rather than gunnysacking, use face-enhancing instead of face-detracting strategies, express acceptance rather than attacking the other person, and use your skills in argumentation, not in verbal aggressiveness.
6. When thinking critically about both interpersonal effectiveness and interpersonal conflict, do so with mindfulness, flexibility, and metacommunication as appropriate.

The skills covered in this chapter are vital to effective interpersonal interactions and relationships. Check your ability to apply these skills, using the following rating scale: 1 = almost always, 2 = often, 3 = sometimes, 4 = rarely, 5 = hardly ever.

_____ 1. I open conversations with comfort and confidence.

_____ 2. I use feedforward that is appropriate to my message and purpose.

_____ 3. I exchange roles as speaker and listener to maintain mutual conversational satisfaction.

_____ 4. I vary my feedback as appropriate on the basis of positiveness, focus (person or message), immediacy, degree of monitoring, and supportiveness.

_____ 5. I close conversations at the appropriate time and with the appropriate parting signals.

_____ 6. I practice an appropriate degree of openness.

_____ 7. I communicate empathy to others.

_____ 8. I express supportiveness.

_____ 9. I communicate positiveness in attitudes and through stroking others.

_____ 10. I express equality in my interpersonal interactions.

_____ 11. I communicate confidence in voice and bodily actions.

_____ 12. I express immediacy both verbally and nonverbally.

_____ 13. I manage interpersonal interactions to the satisfaction of both parties.

_____ 14. I self-monitor my verbal and nonverbal behaviors in order to communicate the desired impression.

_____ 15. I communicate expressiveness verbally and nonverbally.

_____ 16. I communicate other-orientation in my interactions.

_____ 17. I avoid using unproductive methods of conflict resolution.

_____ 18. I make active use of fair fighting guides.

_____ 19. I approach communication situations with an appropriate degree of mindfulness.

20. I am flexible in the way I communicate and adjust my communications on the basis of the unique situation.

21. I use metacommunication to clarify ambiguous meanings.

22. I am sensitive to the cultural differences that influence the ways conversation and conflict are pursued.

Key Word Quiz

Write T for those statements that are true and F for those that are false. For those that are false, replace the italicized term with the correct term.

_____ 1. The small talk that paves the way for the big talk is known as *phatic communication*.

_____ 2. Positive-negative, person focused-message focused, immediate-delayed, low monitoring-high monitoring, and supportive-critical are dimensions of *feedforward*.

_____ 3. To feel as another person feels is known as *sympathy*.

_____ 4. The degree to which the speaker and the listener are connected or joined is known as *interaction management*.

_____ 5. The manipulation of the image that you present to others in your interpersonal interactions is referred to as *expressiveness*.

_____ 6. The process of storing up grievances so that you can unload them at another time (usually during an interpersonal conflict) is known as *beltlining*.

_____ 7. Your willingness to defend a point of view, to speak your mind on significant issues, is called *argumentativeness*.

_____ 8. Creating and recreating categories, being open to new information and to different points of view, and not relying too heavily on first impressions are ways to achieve *flexibility*.

_____ 9. Communication about communication is called *metacommunication*.

_____ 10. Nobody Upstairs, You Owe Me, and Thought Stoppers are examples of *ingratiation strategies*.

Answers: TRUE: 1, 7, 9; FALSE: 2 (*feedback*), 3 (*empathy*), 4 (*immediacy*), 5 (*interaction management*), 6 (*gunnysacking*), 8 (*mindfulness*), 10 (*power plays*)

Skill Development Experiences

6.1 Opening and Closing a Conversation

Think about how you might open a conversation with the people described in each of these situations. What general approaches would meet with a favorable response? What general approaches might be frowned on?

1. On the first day of class, you and another student are the first to come into the classroom and are seated in the room alone.
2. You are a guest at a friend's party. You are one of the first guests to arrive and are now there with several other people to whom you have only just been introduced. Your friend, the host, is busy with other matters.

3. You have just started a new job in a large office, where you are one of several computer operators. It seems as if most of the other people know each other.
4. You're in the college cafeteria eating alone. You see a student from your English Literature class who is also eating alone. You're not sure whether this person has noticed you in class.

Think about how you might go about closing each of the following conversations. Which types of closing seem most effective? Which seem least effective?

1. You and a friend have been talking on the phone for the last hour, but not much new is being said.

You have a great deal of work to get to and would like to close the conversation. Your friend just doesn't seem to hear your subtle cues.

2. You are at a party and are anxious to meet a person with whom you have exchanged eye contact for the last 10 minutes. The problem is that a friendly and talkative former teacher of yours is demanding all your attention. You don't want to insult the instructor but at the same time want to make contact with this other person.

3. You have had a conference with a supervisor and have learned what you needed to know. This supervisor, however, doesn't seem to know how to end the conversation, seems very ill at ease, and just continues to go over what has already been said. You have to get back to your desk and must close the conversation.

4. You are at a party and notice a person you would like to get to know. You initiate the conversation but after a few minutes realize that this person is not the kind of person with whom you would care to spend any more time. You want to close this conversation as soon as possible.

6.2 Formulating Excuses

Although excuses are not always appropriate, they are often helpful in lessening possible negative effects of mishaps. Try formulating an appropriate excuse for each of the five situations listed below, and explain why you assume each excuse will lessen any negative consequences. Three types of excuses that you might use as starting points are: (1) *I didn't do it* or *I did do what I'm accused of not doing* ("I didn't say that." "I wasn't even near the place." "I did try to get in touch with you to tell you I'd be late."); (2) *It wasn't so bad* ("Sure I pushed him, but I didn't kill him."); and (3) *Yes, but* ("It was just my jealousy making those accusations.").

1. Because of some e-mail glitch, colleagues all receive a recent personal letter you sent to a friend in which you admit to having racist feelings. You even gave several examples. As you enter work, you see a group of colleagues discussing your letter. They aren't pleased.

2. Your boss accuses you of making lots of personal long distance phone calls from work, a practice explicitly forbidden.

3. In a discussion with your supervisor, you tell a joke that puts down lesbians and gay men. She tells you she finds the joke homophobic and offensive to everyone and, she adds, she has a gay son and is proud of it. Because you just started

the job, you're still on probation, and this supervisor's recommendation will count heavily.

4. Your friend tells you that he thinks you hurt Joe's feelings when you criticized his presentation.

5. Your history instructor is walking behind you and hears you and another student discussing your class. Your instructor clearly hears you say, "That last lecture was a total waste of time," but says nothing.

Can you identify specific situations in which excuses would be inappropriate? What effects does repeated excuse making have on a romantic relationship? Do you have stereotypes of people who consistently make excuses for just about everything they do?

6.3 Generating Win-Win Solutions

To get into the habit of looking for win-win solutions, consider the following conflict situations, either alone or in groups of five or six. Try generating as many possible win-win solutions as you can for each of these six situations. Give yourself one minute for each case. Write down all win-win solutions that you (or the group) think of; don't censor yourself or any other members of the group. For the purposes of this exercise, the conflict situations are identified only briefly.

1. Pat and Chris plan to take a two-week vacation in August. Pat wants to go to the shore and relax by the water. Chris wants to go hiking and camping in the mountains.

2. Pat and Chris have recently adopted a young child. Pat thinks the child should be raised with strict rules; Chris favors an extremely permissive atmosphere.

3. Logan owns an apartment building and must paint the apartments every three years to comply with city laws. Because the building actually runs at a loss, due to changing real estate conditions, Logan has hired only the most inept (and least expensive) painters and uses the cheapest paint. The tenants have confronted Logan to demand better service.

4. Pat hangs around the house wearing only underwear. Chris really hates this, and they argue about it frequently.

5. Philip has recently come out as gay to his parents. He wants them to accept him and his lifestyle (which includes a committed relationship with another man). His parents refuse to accept him and want him to seek religious counseling to change.

6. Workers at the local accounting office want a 20-percent raise to bring them into line with the salaries of accountants at similar firms. The owner has repeatedly turned down their requests.

If possible, share and compare your win-win solutions with those of other individuals or groups. From this experience, it should be clear that win-win solutions exist for most conflict situations, but not necessarily all. And, of course, some situations allow for the easy generation of a lot more win-win solutions than others. Not all conflicts are equal.

CHAPTER 7

Monitoring Your Attitude

A POSITIVE ATTITUDE

Monitoring your attitude each day is one of the best ways to communicate effectively. The ability to maintain a positive outlook despite the ups and downs of life and work will do much to help you maintain good relationships with the important people in your life.

It is likely that you chose a criminal justice career because you want to make a significant contribution to society. That desire can keep you motivated during discouraging moments—but it also makes you a candidate for stress and burnout. Keep your motivation high by focusing on the present moment. Give yourself credit for each small accomplishment, and take pride in performing routine tasks well. Remember that an incident that seems minor to you may be remembered for a long time by the citizens you deal with. Years after a brief encounter with an officer, many citizens continue to be grateful for a small extra effort or additional courtesy. Take pride in each opportunity to be a positive force in your community.

TELLING THE TRUTH

Honesty is the first principle taught in 12-step programs, and it's an effective communication tool as well. Besides helping your mind and body deal more effectively with stress, it builds bonds with other people, both on and off the job.

Do not deny facts and feelings. Don't smother them with food, drown them in alcohol, project them onto your family or fellow officers, or blast them away with macho street talk. Allow yourself to acknowledge the inevitable fears and frustrations of your job. Develop relationships with others who deal honestly with their feelings. "Stress debriefings" can be lifesaving.

Avoid the "John Wayne syndrome"—pretending you're a lone crusader for justice, untroubled by doubts or fears. Modern law enforcement is less concerned with toughness than it used to be. There is much more emphasis on problem solving, communication, and sensitivity. Don't be afraid to face your emotions honestly.

Spend a few minutes talking over each day's events with a trusted friend before you return home. Look for someone with a high level of commitment to law enforcement. A cynical officer may increase your stress level instead of easing it.

When negative feelings are defused this way, they don't have a chance to build up. But when negative feelings are denied, they turn into monsters whose destructive power can ruin your health, family life, and career.

Honest talk with other officers can empower you to work for needed changes in law enforcement. If you're frustrated by the constraints you face in carrying out your duties, seek power in numbers. Get involved in a professional organization, and work with other officers for change.

GET INVOLVED WITH THE LARGER WORLD

An important strategy for maintaining a positive attitude is to forge strong connections with the larger world outside law enforcement. The criminal justice field often focuses on people at their worst. If you spend most of your time with lawbreakers and officers, you may rapidly lose your perspective. Good alternatives include family time, health clubs, community organizations, church activities, and socializing with friends in other professions. Resist the "I don't have time" excuse. Exploring new ways to spend your leisure time will benefit you much more than sitting in front of the TV—or in a lounge. Your morale will improve, you'll win friends for your agency, and you'll be sharing your gifts and knowledge with an ever-widening circle of people.

MAINTAINING YOUR PERSPECTIVE

If you have been involved in law enforcement for several years, you may have noticed negative changes in some of the officers you know. Often the deterioration is slow and gradual—the result of a buildup of small annoyances. Try to eliminate some of the daily irritants that cause headaches and frayed tempers. For example, don't allow yourself to be overwhelmed by minor tasks during your time off—unless you truly enjoy puttering around the house. Alternatives include delegating jobs to other family members, hiring someone else to do them, or simplifying your lifestyle to minimize home and automobile maintenance. Schedule a family meeting to plan strategies that will make your time off more enjoyable. To ensure that the meeting will be positive and productive, assure your spouse and children that you're concerned about their stress levels too.

Make a realistic assessment of yourself, your time, and your abilities. Don't burden yourself by expecting to do the impossible, and don't berate yourself for mistakes. Many idealists increase their stress by clinging to overblown expectations of themselves.

Remind yourself often that your career allows you to reach out to people in need during the critical moments in their lives. Your words and gestures can have a lasting effect on those around you. Never underestimate the importance of what you are doing. Frequently remind yourself that you are providing a vital service to your community.

ENRICHING YOUR LIFE

Research suggests that one of the best weapons against negativism is an activity you do regularly for enjoyment. You will know you have found the right activity if you lose track of time when you're focused on doing it.

Unfortunately, many people talk themselves out of activities they enjoy because they feel tired and drained after working. The result is increased fatigue, boredom, depression, and emptiness. Missed opportunities for fun can lead to a rapid deterioration in a love relationship. You are at high risk for disease or divorce if your life gives you nothing to look forward to but a glass of liquor at the end of your shift.

Recreation—preferably with family and friends outside of law enforcement—is not a luxury. It's a necessity for anyone who works hard. Clear a space for your favorite activities, and enjoy them as much as you can. They are true lifesavers.

QUESTIONS FOR DISCUSSION

1. Why might officers be tempted not to "tell the truth" about their own stress factors?
2. What communication skills might encourage officers to "tell the truth"?
3. Why might some officers lose contact with the world outside of law enforcement?

SUMMARY

1. Honest communication with trusted friends can help officers maintain a positive attitude.
2. Small irritants can gradually erode an officer's morale and effectiveness.
2. Recreation is vital to physical health and personal relationships.

CHAPTER 8

Special Communication Issues

Previous chapters examined the process of communication and its impact on criminal justice personnel. The principles described in those chapters apply to the operations of any police department as well as many other government entities and private businesses. This chapter reviews communications issues that are especially important to law enforcement departments. The focus of this chapter is on those communication skills needed by the officer on the street, whether that person is a patrol officer working traffic or a homicide investigator. By the very nature of its mission, a law enforcement agency has unique issues that are not found in any other organization. No other bureaucracy in the free world holds the power of life and death over other human beings. The duties and requirements of police officers are distinct from those of any other job. With these different job requirements comes the need for special communication skills in a variety of situations.

Communicating with other cultures or encountering a foreign language during a routine patrol is becoming more and more common. Our cities, counties, and states are becoming more populated and the number of different cultures within any given area is increasing. In many of our major metropolitan cities, there are areas completely occupied by specific groups of people from different cultures. An officer must be prepared to communicate effectively in this environment. As persons with hearing impairments continue to enter the mainstream of life, they need the assistance of law enforcement personnel. The person with a hearing impairment is one of the most misunderstood individuals in modern society.

COMMUNICATION WITH OTHER CULTURES

This is an area in law enforcement that is still evolving. The United States is a melting pot for other races and cultures. With the increase of Southeast Asian refugees and the increasing Hispanic population, the problem of communicating with persons who do not speak English as a primary language is critical within the law enforcement community.

Survival Spanish

Hispanics constitute the fastest growing minority group in the United States. Population experts predict that this group will outnumber African-Americans by the end of the first quarter of the 21st century.

Development of "Survival Spanish for Police Officers" began in mid-1986 at Sam Houston State University, in a cooperative effort between the police academy and a faculty member of the university's Spanish department. The cross-cultural training grew from a minor part of the language component when it became apparent that cultural barriers were just as important as the language barrier and had to be addressed in more detail.

Even with the awareness that minority populations continue to expand in the United States, the ability to communicate with them will continue to be a problem for most law enforcement agencies. Various departments are attempting to solve this problem in a number of ways. Some departments are hiring bilingual officers and offering additional compensation for their

Spanish Language Component (8 hours)

Curriculum: Instruction begins with a crash course in Spanish pronunciation that emphasizes eliminating problems with the most troublesome sounds for Anglos learning Spanish. To help with pronunciation, a list of the 50 most common Spanish names is used for practice. The gain is twofold: not only are officers given an opportunity to work with single-word units (names), but they also quickly perfect the pronunciation of the very names they will encounter on the street. The class then learns to read the *Miranda* warning in Spanish, thus moving to entire sentence units. This increases the officers' confidence and level of comfort with unfamiliar Spanish sounds.

The core of the day consists of four one-hour classes that include a total of 39 "survival" commands, questions, warnings, and exchanges. Some of the items included are "Sit down," "Shut up," "I'm a police officer," "Stop," "Get out of the car," and "Put the weapon down." The Spanish equivalents are taught as purely rote items to be mastered quickly through a variety of language techniques. The last session of the day is devoted to simulations and role playing in which officers act out a variety of scenarios using their newly acquired abilities.

Cross-Cultural Training Component (8 Hours)

Curriculum: This is a multifaceted treatment of the Hispanic community in this country and its relationship to law enforcement and the criminal justice system. Population trends, racial characteristics, Roman law versus English law, and alien documentation are studied. Numerous subtle but important cultural barriers are explored, including deception, eye contact, differing concepts of time and direction, the Hispanic surname system, personal space and touching, and the use of the body as a personal "bank."

More in-depth presentations and discussions cover such topics as machismo, Hispanic women (vis-à-vis spousal abuse, domestic disturbances, rape, and incest), Hispanics and vehicular law (bribes, driving without a license or insurance, speeding, and hit-and-run), and Anglo–Hispanic stereotypes. In addition, there is a cross-cultural simulation exercise designed especially for police officers that dramatizes the problem of cultural barriers.

services, others maintain lists of qualified interpreters, and many agencies are including cultural awareness programs in their roll-call training.

Methods of Responding to Language Differences

An officer who arrives at the scene of a crime and is confronted by a non-English-speaking citizen must attempt to gather information from that person. In some cases, this information must not only be gathered quickly, but it must be accurate. The citizen may be a victim of a crime or a witness who can provide a description of the suspect. One of the most obvious places to turn for assistance is family or neighbors who are bilingual. By using these individuals as on-the-scene interpreters, the officer can obtain the initial information quickly. The officer should ensure that not only the name of the witness, but also the name and address of the translator, are recorded. Follow-up investigations normally utilize the services of trained translators. In some cities, the courts, prosecutors, and police agencies maintain lists of interpreters to call on if the need arises. For example, in the main Los Angeles County Courthouse, interpreters are available for 78 different languages.

It is obvious that there are inherent problems with using family or neighbors as interpreters. They may have difficulty with English, and some terms may be outside their knowledge or vocabulary. In addition, they may be biased and want to help the victim or witness, to the detriment of others. Because of these issues, departments try to utilize bilingual officers. These are officers who are able to speak and write in both English and another language. In many cases, these officers not only speak a second language, but are members of that ethnic group and are familiar with the history, traditions, and customs of the culture.

Many departments offer additional compensation to bilingual officers. Those officers respond to situations where their language skill is needed. They provide an independent interpretation without such issues as friendship or bias.

Many departments encourage roll-call training that emphasizes the cultures of minorities within their jurisdiction. This is another method by which officers may learn basic phrases of a different language. Some agencies will reimburse officers if they take and pass conversational language courses that enable them to interact with minority groups.

Other Multicultural Issues

The term *culture* can be applied to various population categories. However, it is normally associated with race and ethnicity. It is this diversity that both enriches and obstructs a law enforcement officer's involvement and interaction with other persons, groups, and cultures.

Officers should remember that most minorities have developed a sharp sense for detecting condescension, manipulation, and insincerity. There is no substitute for compassion as the foundation, and sincerity as its expression, in carrying out law enforcement services equally and fairly.

Although it is not possible to feel the same compassion for all victims, it is the responsibility of law enforcement officers to provide the same compassionate service to every victim. The plight of undocumented residents or illegal aliens, for example, involves complex issues of personal prejudice and international policies. Many of these persons suffer financial exploitation and other criminal victimization once they enter the United States. Officers must make an effort to understand their situation and not let personal opinions affect their interaction with these individuals when they are victimized.

The first contact minorities have with law enforcement officers will either confirm or dispel suspicion as to how they will be treated. Proper pronunciation of a person's surname is an excellent place to begin contact with a person. Surnames have histories and meanings that allow for conversation beyond the introduction. In working with immigrant, refugee, or native populations, it is helpful to learn a few words of greeting from that culture. This willingness to go beyond what is comfortable and usual conveys the officer's intent to communicate.

Listening is fundamental to human relationships. The principles and manner of listening, however, differ among cultures. Asians and Pacific Islanders, for example, deflect direct eye contact in conversation as a sign of patient listening and deference. These groups therefore consider staring to be impolite and confrontational. Many Western cultures, on the other hand, value direct eye contact as a sign of sympathy or respect. Looking elsewhere is seen as disinterest or evasiveness. Misunderstanding in the communication process can occur if some allowance is not made for these differences. Multicultural issues must be understood by all law enforcement officers. Understanding that "different" does not mean "criminal" will assist officers attempting to communicate in an environment that continues to become more and more diverse.

 # COMMUNICATION WITH PERSONS WITH HEARING IMPAIRMENTS

Introduction

More than 21 million Americans suffer from some degree of hearing impairment. There is a serious problem when a law enforcement officer encounters a person who is completely deaf. The ability to communicate with such individuals is limited. Many persons with hearing impairments utilize movements of their hands, body, and face to communicate. This is known as *signing.* American Sign Language, also known as *Ameslan,* is the sign language used by some deaf people in America. Many colleges and universities across the United States offer Ameslan as a course to satisfy the foreign language requirement for graduation.

Basic Principles

The interpersonal and communication skills of a police officer who contacts a deaf person will be drawn on to their fullest extent. The first and most important rule in dealing with a deaf person is never to assume he or she understands what is being communicated until positive feedback is received, either through signing or other actions.

Basic principles that officers should utilize when dealing with deaf individuals include the following:

- *Recognize that the person is deaf.* When deaf persons are approached by an officer, most will usually indicate their condition by pointing to their ears or shaking their head. The deaf person may attempt to speak, but many times the officer will not be able to understand what the person is saying. On occasion, when a deaf person attempts to speak, the speech will sound distorted. The officer should understand that this is a sign of the individual's disability and not the result of alcohol or drugs.

Use of the following phrases and their American Sign Language counterparts should enable the police officer to establish a sound working relationship with the deaf victim, suspect, or witness. After initial communication has been made, the officer can write his questions and comments or, when available and appropriate, an interpreter can be used.

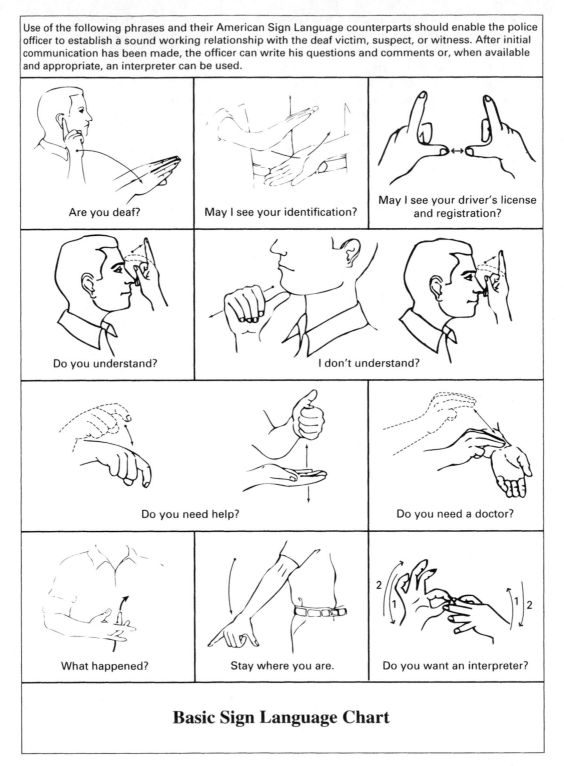

Are you deaf?

May I see your identification?

May I see your driver's license and registration?

Do you understand?

I don't understand?

Do you need help?

Do you need a doctor?

What happened?

Stay where you are.

Do you want an interpreter?

Basic Sign Language Chart

Source: "The Deaf and the Police," International Association of Chiefs of Police Training Key Series no. 244 (Alexandria, Va.).

- *Understand the disability.* Because many deaf people rely on written communication, they may reach for a pen and paper when stopped by an officer. In some situations, such an action might be viewed as reaching for a weapon. The officer should be alert to this and not interpret the action as threatening.

- *Attempt to establish communication through any available means.* In a perfect world, the officer would understand Ameslan and be able to communicate with the deaf person. However, this is not a perfect world. The second most acceptable method of communication is through written notes. Contrary to popular belief, most deaf people do not read lips. The written notes should be clear, concise, and legible.

The officer who comes into contact with a deaf person should treat that individual the same as any other person with a disability—respect, patience, and understanding will go a long way in opening lines of communication. Many officers may go a number of years without coming into contact with a deaf person; however, when they do, it is essential that they understand the disability and act accordingly.

The Americans with Disabilities Act requires organizations to take all reasonable steps to accommodate those persons who have disabilities. This act is very complex and does not need an expanded discussion here. However, some public safety agencies have been sued for failing to provide adequate sign language interpreters for persons with hearing impairments. This is another example of an issue in the area of special communications that impacts officers.

Police officers, administrators, and agencies face unique communication issues in the modern world. These issues range from dealing with different cultures and languages to communicating with deaf persons. By understanding these issues and addressing them in a training environment, law enforcement personnel will be able to more effectively carry out their mission of protecting the public.

SUMMARY

Police officers and administrators face unique communication issues as law enforcement officers. The mission of law enforcement is such that these issues are rarely encountered by any other group of professionals. Officers must be aware of these special situations and strive to communicate effectively when they encounter them.

Communicating with minorities and deaf persons poses special communication needs. By becoming more sensitive to these persons' needs and backgrounds, officers will be able to communicate with them more effectively.

Negotiating with hostage takers is an unusual event for the average law enforcement officer. It should be approached with caution, but not avoided. The next chapter reviews communication in such situations.

1. Is it realistic to expect police officers to learn a second language while attending roll-call training? Justify your answer and present any alternatives.

2. Should officers be required to learn a sign language? Why?

3. Some individuals argue that since people from other nations are in our country, they should speak our language. If you accept this principle then officers do not need to know how to communicate with other cultures. Do you agree or disagree with this position? Why?

CHAPTER 9

Ten Guidelines for Effective Communication

Anyone can communicate—when we merely speak we are communicating. But, exchanging words effectively is something that generally does not come naturally for most people. As policing in America becomes more complex, technically advanced, and sophisticated, good communication is essential for all law enforcement officials whether it be the foot patrol officer, the administrative executive or the Chief of Police. Previous chapters reviewed communications issues that were especially important to law enforcement departments and focused on the skills needed by the officer on the street. This challenge becomes particularly difficult for law enforcement officers because the communication process is not the same for everyone and one set of guide lines will not cover every situation.

There are many different tasks that must be accomplished before law enforcement officers can be effective in their communication efforts. These tasks can be broken down into two categories. The first category is that of establishing safety and the second is to decide what structure of communication is needed. The structure needed will depend upon the nature of the call and the type of citizen involved.

We will discuss ways to achieve the successful implementation of these special communication skills and the types of situations in which the skills may be needed.

SAFETY

- *Establish and/or maintain order*

  In order to properly investigate a situation the officer at the scene must establish and/or maintain order to provide for officer and citizen safety. Law enforcement is often viewed negatively and thought of as something that restricts freedom. However, policing in America is the necessary element of society that serves to establish and /or maintain order. Without authority and organization, the human nature will navigate toward mischief and chaos.

- *Safety*

  Law enforcement is a hazardous profession. Officers voluntarily put themselves into dangerous situations in order t protect and serve their communities. Consequently, officers must continually educate themselves about the dangers and how to minimize risks. When the scene of an incident is safe, communication becomes much easier.

- *Take risks*

  Officers face risks that range from volatile domestic disturbances to weapon carrying addicts. Over the years, a variety of criminals and citizens have accepted violence as a viable tactic to achieve their ends. They have also shown a willingness to direct that violence at law enforcement. Officers need to assess these risks at the scene of any situation and be able to communicate what needs to be done to minimize those risks.

- *Be honest*

  Open and honest communication by police to citizens at the scene of an incident helps citizens, and criminals, feel better about putting their physical and emotional safety into the hands of the officer. Honest communication instills trust.

- *Ask questions to learn more*

  Questions—questions—questions. An officer can never ask to many questions—the life and safety officer, as well as the citizen, can depend upon it. The officer will want to get as much information as possibleby asking probing or open-ended questions that draw attention to things that may be only implied and that cannot merely be answered with a simple "yes" or "no."

- *Listen*

  Unless Officers develop skills for listening, questions are useless. No other communication skill can impact officer rapport more than efficient listening. However, as important as it is, listening is the most neglected communication skill and is one of the most difficult for officers to learn. Mastering this skill can improve a volatile situation. Multifaceted learning of this skill should include training in the areas of:

  - Asking good questions to increase understanding;
  - Employing simple tools to identify others' needs and letting them know that you heard them completely;
  - Discovering the reasoning and feelings behind the words so that there is an understand of the unspoken message;
  - Incorporating simple techniques that will prevent formulating a response while others are still talking, interrupting others, or finishing their sentences.
  - Really listen rather than doing what most people do—wait for their turn to talk

- *Do what you do best*

  While the job of law enforcement officers is to fight crime, they must also be the information officers of the community. They are the "helping hands" for all citizens. The communication between the police and public creates this trust. Directing the general public away from crime scenes provides safety for those involved in the incident.

- *Identify why you're there*

- *Work to balance participation*

- *Close the gap*

- *Reach a resolution—good or bad*

Once these safeguards and communication preparation techniques have been established, law enforcement personnel will then become experts in communicating with the different types of groups or situations which may arise.

Elderly

Listening skills are essential when communicating with the elderly or with children. Some tips for effective communication might include:

1. Take more time with the elder person and be very patient with them.
2. Determine if the individual is capable of making his/her own decisions?
3. Often the elderly person will feel less afraid If there Is a friend or family member with them. Communicate face-to-face with the individual.
4. Ask the person If they are uncomfortable or need any assistance.
5. An older persons may not comply with your requests or demands The noncompliance is often unintentional and often due to a misunderstanding. Provide visual information such as clearly written instructions if possible.
6. Always tell the elderly person if you are going to be speaking to someone else regarding them.
7. Don't judge the elderly person or defensive. If you do, they will not trust you or listen to you.
8. Don't do all the talking. Let them know you are listening to them.
9. Be clear about your reasoning, goals, and procedures.
10. Don't expect a quick resolution, the elderly person will take much more time to process what is going on around them.

Children

Communicating with a child is very much like dealing with an elderly person. Some guidelines for talking with children are:

1. It is important to let children know that they are safe.
2. Talk to the child immediately and let them know what is happening.
3. Children need to know that what might be occurring is not their fault. Early discussions with the child are critical.
4. Talk to the adults outside the hearing range of the child.
5. Remove the child from the scene and quickly and safely as possible. Try to find a relative or friend who can help do this.
6. Be patient and listen to the child.

Hearing Impaired

When communicating with a hard of hearing person, there are several things you must remember.

- Talk to the person(s)—not about the person.
- Talk face to face to the person and making sure that your face is easy to see. Many hearing impaired persons can read lips and facial expressions and lip movements are very important.
- Speak clearly and do not shout or mumble.

- Move to a quiet location of the situation is noisy.
- Do not cover your mouth. This makes it impossible for the hard of hearing person to see your lips.
- Be patient and relax. The hard of hearing person is more nervous than you.
- Speak to only one person at a time.
- Ask the hearing impaired person how you can best communicate with them.
- If an interpreter is needed, get one as quickly as possible.

HAZARD/RISK OR CRISIS SITUATION COMMUNICATIONS

Law enforce personnel often face risks that range from volatile domestic disturbances to hazardous traffic situation to undercover drug stings. Over the years, more and more hate groups such as gang units, terrorists, and anti-government groups have shown a willingness to direct violence toward law enforcement. It is unknown exactly why this willingness is present; but, several ideas worth examining has surfaced.

- The officer is the figure of authority and many of these individuals and groups defy authority.
- It is the job of law enforcement to arrest criminals and to aid in preventing crime. Most people who break the law already think of law enforcement officers as the enemy.
- Many of these individuals believe that the police are deliberately stereotyping and targeting them because of their beliefs; their ideas, behaviors, and actions.

While members of hate groups are less common than spouse abusers, officers will routinely come into contact with them. Communicating with these type of groups in hazard/risk or crisis situations, is tense at best. As such, officers must be trained to recognize certain facts for the purpose of develop effective communication lines .

Facts

- Law enforcement officers are often the individuals who will be confronting these extreme types of groups.
- Criminals belonging to these groups often act differently than criminals motivated by more traditional motives such as anger and mischief.
- Members of these extreme groups off target law enforcement officers.
- It is the 'street cops' who will be most likely be the first to encounter the group members.
- Local police departments with limited resources are likely to have to cope with large, well-organized groups.
- Groups are often much more cause-oriented rather than self-oriented.
- Groups are often more likely to be attack-oriented than defense-oriented. Typical criminals are much more like to run.

SUMMARY

Before communication can begin in any of the above situations, officers must establish authority, make sure the scene is secure and safe, and make sure order is restored if need be. Remembering that see is oftentimes more powerful than saying, law enforcement officers must always be aware of their surroundings and when possible should use calming, non-threatening mannerisms and professionalism.

PART TWO

Listening

CHAPTER 10

Listening and Responding

T hink of someone you know to whom you'd like to give an award as an outstanding communicator. Perhaps your nominee is a trusted friend, a close family member, or someone you've had a relationship with since elementary school. Picture him or her in your mind. What are the defining characteristics that make your friend or acquaintance an excellent communicator? If you're typical, we suspect that you've thought about how your friend listens carefully to what you have to say, and genuinely cares about what you have to offer the relationship. In addition, your outstanding communicator is also probably not a silent listener; he or she gives thoughtful reactions to you and your ideas.

Effective communicators listen to others and accurately interpret the verbal and nonverbal symbols of others; they are sensitive to what others are saying. One of the hallmarks of being an effective leader is to be a good listener. To be sensitive is to be aware of others and to be concerned about others. Sensitivity is derived from taking time to listen and observe. In the previous two chapters, we discussed the ways effective communicators use appropriate verbal and nonverbal symbols. Not only do effective communicators use and understand words and unspoken messages, they also accurately interpret messages they receive. They listen and respond actively, not passively, interpreting both verbal and nonverbal messages.

THE PRINCIPLE OF LISTENING AND RESPONDING

It shows up on every list of what effective communicators do: They listen. You spend more time listening to others than almost anything else you do. Americans spend more than 80 percent of a typical day communicating with people, and they spend 45 percent of that communication time listening to others. Increasing your skill in listening to others is one of the most productive ways to increase your communication sensitivity. As shown in Figure 10.1, if you're typical, you spend the least amount of your communication time writing, yet that is where you receive more training than any other communication skill. Most people have not had formal training in listening or responding. In this chapter we focus on the principle of increasing your sensitivity to others by listening. Becoming sensitive to others includes more than just understanding and interpreting the words, thoughts, and ideas of another—sensitivity also involves understanding the emotions of words and unspoken messages of others.

In addition to listening, as shown in our now familiar model of the communication principles for a lifetime in Figure 10.2, we also discuss strategies for responding thoughtfully to others. Effective communicators do more than absorb a message; they provide an appropriate response to the speaker. We'll address both listening and responding to others in this chapter.

Listening and responding to others is an important principle of communication, not only because you spend more time listening than any other communication activity, but also because of its importance in establishing and maintaining relationships with others. In interpersonal communication situations, your ability to listen and respond is at the heart of your ability to maintain a conversation with someone. A satisfying conversation occurs when all participants feel a comfortable level of give and take in listening

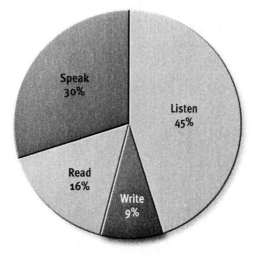

FIGURE 10.1
What You Do with Your Communication Time

and responding to others. The essence of being a good conversationalist is being a good listener. Rather than focusing only on what to say, a person skilled in the art of conversation listens and picks up on interests and themes of others.

Being a good listener is also an essential skill when communicating with others in small groups. Whether you are the appointed or emerging leader of a group, or are a stalwart group or team member, your ability to listen and connect to others will affect your value to other group members. Group members afflicted with bafflegab, those who verbally dominate group meetings, are not typically held in high esteem. Groups need people who can listen and connect conversational threads that often become tangled or dropped in group dialogue.

It may be less clear how being an effective listener can enhance a public speaker's ability to connect with an audience. Effective speakers, however,

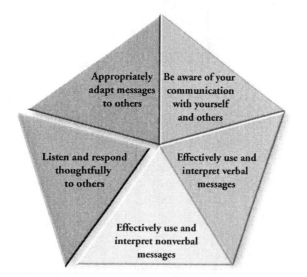

FIGURE 10.2
Fundamental Principles of Human Communication

are those who can relate to their listeners; good speakers know how to establish a relationship with the audience by listening to audience members one-on-one before a talk or lecture. Good public speakers are also audience-centered. They consider the needs of their listeners first. They understand what will hold listeners' attention.

HOW WE LISTEN

Do you know someone who is interpersonally inert? Interpersonally inert people are those who just don't "get it." You can drop hints that it's late and you'd rather they head home instead of playing another hand of cards, but they don't pick up on your verbal and nonverbal cues. They may *hear* you, but they certainly aren't listening; they are not making sense out of your symbols. **Hearing** is the physiological process of decoding sounds. You hear when the sound vibrations reach your eardrum and buzz the middle ear bones: the hammer, anvil, and stirrup. Eventually, the sound vibrations are translated into electrical impulses that reach your brain. In order to listen to something, you must first select that sound from competing sounds. **Listening** is a complex process we use to make sense out of what we hear. Listening involves five activities: (1) selecting, (2) attending, (3) understanding, (4) remembering, and—to confirm that listening has occurred—(5) responding.

"No, Douglas, I won't be drawn further into the subject of *listening*."

Selecting

To **select** a sound is to focus on one soundbite as you sort through the myriad of noises competing for your attention. Even now, as you are reading this book, there are probably countless sounds within earshot. Stop reading for a moment. What sounds surround you? Do you hear music? Is a TV on? Maybe there is the tick of a clock, a whir of a computer, or a whoosh of a furnace or an air conditioner. To listen—to be sensitive to another person—you must first select the sound or nonverbal behavior that symbolizes meaning. The interpersonally inert person does not pick up on the clues because he or she is oblivious to the information. To listen, you must select which of the sounds or behaviors will receive your attention.

Attending

After selecting a sound, you attend to it. To **attend** is to focus on a particular sound or message. When you change channels on your TV, you first select the channel and then you attend or focus on the program you've selected. Attention can be brief. You may attend to the program or commercial for a moment and then move on or return to other thoughts or other sounds. Just as you tune in to TV programs that reflect your taste in information while you channel surf, you attend to messages of others that satisfy your needs or whims.

What holds our attention? In general, conflict, humor, new ideas, and real or concrete things command your attention more easily than abstract theories or other topics that don't relate to you. Most people focus on their own needs. You are also more likely to tune someone in when you are specifically invited to listen and respond, than when someone speaks or behaves in ways that aren't other-oriented and don't take your needs into consideration. You become bored when your needs aren't met.

Understanding

To understand is to assign meaning to messages—to make sense out of what you hear. You can select and attend to sounds and nonverbal cues but not interpret what you see and hear. Seeing and hearing are physiological processes. Understanding occurs when we relate what we see and hear to our experiences or knowledge. There are several theories about how you assign meaning to words you hear, but there is no single theory that best explains how the process works. We know that you are more likely to understand messages if you can relate what you are hearing and seeing to something you already know.

Once we select the sounds we want to listen to, we need to attend to, or focus on those sounds, for communication to take place.

The more similar you are to others, the greater the likelihood that you will accurately understand them. People from different cultures who have substantially different religions, family lifestyles, values, or attitudes often have difficulty understanding each other, particularly in the early phases of a relationship.

You understand best that which you also experience; the more senses that are involved, the greater the chance of holding your attention and increasing your accuracy of interpretation. Perhaps you have heard the Montessori school philosophy: I hear, I forget; I see, I remember; I experience, I understand. Hearing alone does not provide us with understanding. It's been estimated that we hear over 1 billion words each year, but we understand a mere fraction of that number.

Remembering

Remembering information is included in the listening process because it's the primary way we determine whether a message was understood. To **remember** is to recall information. Some scholars speculate that you store every detail you have ever heard or wit-

ETHICAL PROBE

You've had a stress-filled day. As you come in your front door and sink down into your favorite chair, all you want to do is watch TV, fix dinner, and unwind. The phone rings. It's your mother. She too has had a difficult, stressful day and needs a listener. You could probably get away with just adding a few "uh-huhs" and "mm-hmms," and your Mom would think you are listening to everything she is saying. Is it ethical to fake attending to your mother's call? Is it ethical to fake attention to anyone who asks for your attention?

nessed; your mind operates like a computer's hard drive, recording each life experience. But you cannot retrieve or remember all of the bits of information. Sometimes, even though you were present, you have no recollection of what occurred in a particular situation. You can't consciously remember everything; your eye is not a camera; your ear is not a microphone; your mind is not a hard drive.

The first communication principle we presented in this book is to become self- aware. When we are not self-aware of our actions, thoughts, or what we are perceiving—when we are mindless—our ability to remember what occurs plummets. We increase our ability to remember what we hear by being not only physically present, but mentally present.

Our brains have both short-term and long-term memory storage. Short-term memory is where you store almost all the information you hear. You look up a phone number in the telephone book, mumble the number to yourself, then dial the number, only to discover that the line is busy. Three minutes later you have to look up the number again because it did not get stored in your long-term memory. Our short-term storage area is limited. Just as airports have only a relatively few short-term parking spaces, but lots of spaces for long-term parking, our brains can accommodate a few things of fleeting significance, but not vast amounts of information. Most of us forget hundreds of bits of insignificant information that pass though our cortical centers each day.

We tend to remember what is important to us, or something we try to remember or have practiced to remember (like the information in this book for your next communication test). We tend to remember dramatic information (like where you were when you heard about the April 19, 1999, tragic shooting at Columbine High School in Colorado) or vital information (such as your phone number or your mother's birthday).

Responding

Communication is a transactive process—not a one-way, linear interaction. Communication involves responding to others as well as simply articulating messages. You **respond** to people to let them know you understand their message. Your lack of response may signal that you didn't understand the message. As we learned in the previous chapter, our predominant response is unspoken; direct eye contact and head nods let our partner know we're tuned in. An unmoving, glassy-eyed, frozen stupor may tell our communication partner that we are physically present, yet mentally a thousand miles away.

▐▞ LISTENING GOALS

You listen to other people for a variety of reasons. Sometimes it's just fun to hear a story or watch a TV show. Or you listen because it's your job: Your job as a student is to listen and recall on a test what you heard. You also listen to sort out fact from fiction. When someone tells you something that doesn't quite sound right, you listen to evaluate. Other times you listen just because you care about the other person. The goals of listening are as varied as the listening situations in which we find ourselves. Yet we can group lis-

DEVELOPING YOUR SKILL
PUTTING PRINCIPLES INTO PRACTICE

Assessing Your Listening Skills

The purpose of this questionnaire is to assess your listening skills. Respond to each statement with a number as follows: 1 for always false, 2 for usually false, 3 for sometimes false, 4 for sometimes true and 5 for always true.

_____ 1. I have a difficult time separating important and unimportant ideas when I listen to others.

_____ 2. I check new information against what I already know when I listen to others.

_____ 3. I have an idea what others will say when I listen to them.

_____ 4. I am sensitive to others' feelings when I listen to them.

_____ 5. I think about what I am going to say next when I listen to others.

_____ 6. I focus on the process of communication that is occurring between me and others when I listen to them.

_____ 7. I cannot wait for others to finish talking so I can take my turn.

_____ 8. I try to understand the meanings that are being created when I communicate with others.

_____ 9. I focus on determining whether others understand what I said when they are talking.

_____ 10. I ask others to elaborate when I am not sure what they mean.

To find your score, first reverse your responses for the odd-numbered items (if you wrote 1, make it 5; if you wrote 2; make it 4; if you wrote 3, leave it as 3; if you wrote 4, make it 2; if you wrote 5, make it 1). Next, add the numbers next to each statement. Scores range from 10 to 50. The higher your score, the better your listening skill.

Source: William Gudykunst, Bridging Differences, 2d ed. (Thousand Oaks, CA: Sage Publications, 1998). Reprinted by permission of Sage Publications, Inc.

tening goals into four categories: to enjoy, to learn, to evaluate, and to empathize. Knowing your listening goal can increase your self-awareness of the listening process and subsequently increase your skill.

Listening to Enjoy

Sometimes we listen just because it's fun. It's so enjoyable that we stay up later than we should to watch a comedian on late-night television, or

To listen is very hard, because it asks of us so much interior stability that we no longer need to prove ourselves by speeches, arguments, statements, or declarations. True listeners no longer have an inner need to make their presence known. They are free to receive, to welcome, to accept.

Listening is much more than allowing another to talk while waiting for a chance to respond. Listening is paying full attention to others and welcoming them into our very beings. The beauty of listening is that those who are listened to start feeling accepted, start taking their words more seriously and discovering their true selves. Listening is a form of spiritual hospitality by which you invite strangers to become friends, to get to know their inner selves more fully, and even to dare to be silent with you.

—*Henri J. M. Nouwen*

Source: Henri J. M. Nouwen. *Bread for the Journey* (New York: Harper Collins, 1997).

pay $25 to listen to a comic at a comedy club. We like to be with our friends because we just like to listen to what they have to say. If you listened to your stereo, watched TV, went to a movie, or heard a friend talk about his weekend escapades, you listened because you simply wanted to listen.

Listening to Learn

Nothing snaps a class to attention more quickly than a professor's proclamation that "This next point will be covered on the test." Another key reason we listen is to learn. At some colleges and universities, tuition and room and board cost $1,000 a week! Even at state-supported public universities and community colleges, if you calculate not only what it costs you to attend college but also what you give up in additional income you could make if you were working full-time (or at a second job) instead of going to college, you could be investing close to a dollar a minute of class time to get your degree. Our society values knowledge, and you are willing to pay for it.

You don't have to be a college student to listen to learn. Phone calls from family and friends contain information that we want to remember. In interpersonal situations, you listen for such everyday information as who will pick up the kids after school and what to buy at the grocery store for tonight's dinner. You also listen to find out about the daily activities of others. It is through listening that we learn.

It is usually a challenge to remember the details of a lengthy speech, lecture, or even a phone message without taking notes. People who have mastered the art of listening for information are also good note takers. When your task is to listen to learn, consider the following suggestions for improving your note-taking skill:

1. Be prepared to take notes. Have a pencil and paper handy by the phone or with you when you think there is information that may not make it into your long-term memory.
2. Decide on a note-taking system. For some messages you may need to simply jot down facts. For other presentations you may need to sort facts and principles—one side of your paper for major ideas and the other side for facts and data that support the principles. An outline strategy works best if the speaker is following an outline pattern. Trying to outline the unoutlineable will not only expose a disorganized speaker, it will increase your note-taking frustration. Consider what information you need to retrieve before deciding how you will take notes.
3. Take the right number of notes. A Mozart critic, after listening to one of the great master's brilliant operas, said of the composition: "There are too many notes." Don't let the same criticism apply to your summary of lecture material or messages. If your goal is to transcribe the message,

you may miss it. One the other hand, scribbling brief snatches of words or terms may have you scratching your head a couple of days later, wondering, "What's this mean?"

Listening to Evaluate

When you listen to evaluate, you try to determine whether the information you hear is valid, reliable, believable, or useful. One problem you may have when you listen to evaluate is that you may become so preoccupied with your criticism that you often do not completely understand the message. When listening to a politician whose ideas are radically different from yours, you may miss the details of the message if you continually criticize the talk as it is occurring. Often the very process of evaluating and making judgments and decisions about information interferes with the capacity to understand and recall. To compensate for this tendency, it is important first to make sure that you understand what a speaker is saying before making a judgment about the value of the information.

We use critical-thinking skills to evaluate the messages of others. If we are adept at separating facts from inferences, identifying fallacies in reasoning, and analyzing evidence, then our evaluations of other's messages can be reasonably accurate. We will be discussing these important skills throughout this book. Critical listening and thinking are highly valued skills. For example, when we discuss how to persuade others, we will also describe how to spot invalid, illogical approaches to reasoning and structuring and argument. We'll also identify how to evaluate the facts, statistics, opinions, and examples other people offer as evidence to support their conclusions. Whether it is a telemarketer, politician, sales clerk, or even a friend or family member, people will seek your vote, money, and time; being able to evaluate the messages of others is an important skill that will serve you well.

Listening to Empathize

Your best friend tells you that it's been "one of those days." Everything seemed to go wrong. Life is unraveling at the seams. After a day like this, your friend needs to talk to someone—not for advice, wisdom or expertise, but just to have someone listen. Your job is not to take notes as if you were going to be tested over the information, nor do you need to evaluate what your friend is saying—just listen. Your friend needs someone who can empathize with his trauma.

The word **empathy** comes from a Greek word for "passion" and a translation of the German word *Einfuhling*, which means "to feel with." Empathy involves connecting with someone's emotions, not just the message content. To empathize with someone is to try to feel what he or she is feeling rather than just to think about or acknowledge the feelings. In effect, you act as a sounding board for the other person. Empathic listening serves an important therapeutic function. Just having an empathic listener may help someone out. No, we are not empowering you to be a therapist, but we are suggesting that simply listening and feeling with someone can help your communication partner sort things out for him- or herself. Empathic listeners don't judge or offer advice. They listen because the process of sharing and listening is soothing, and can often restore a person's perspective. We're

RECAP

Reasons for Listening

Why We Listen	Example
Listening for Enjoyment	Listening to your uncle tell stories
Listening to Learn	Getting instructions on how to make bread
Listening to Evaluate	Sorting through a telemarketer's sales pitch to switch phone service
Listening to Empathize	Listening to a good friend talk about the death of a cherished pet

also not suggesting that you only need to empathize with others when they've had a bad day. Being able to discern when your friends, family, and colleagues are having celebratory experiences and empathizing with their positive peak experiences, as well as with discouraging or disconfirming ones, is important in building supportive relationships with others.

Why is it important to determine whether you are listening to enjoy, learn, evaluate, or empathize? Because your listening goal often determines your listening strategy. If you're primarily listening to Aunt Delynn talk about her recent hunting trip to Northern Minnesota during her annual bear hunt, you need not worry about taking extensive notes and trying to remember all of the details of her expedition. But when your sociology professor tells a story to illustrate a sociological theory, you should be more attuned to the point he is making; the implications of his anecdote may be on a test about sociological theory. There are also times when you need to be on your guard to evaluate the spiel of a politician or salesperson. Being mindful or aware of your listening goal can help you more effectively achieve your communication goal. Be aware of your communication with yourself and others. Listen mindfully, not mindlessly.

LISTENING BARRIERS

Although we spend almost half of our communication time listening, some say we don't use that time well. Most people remember a day later only about half of what was said. It gets worse. An additional day later, our listening comprehension drops by another 50 percent. The result: most of us remember about 25 percent of what we hear two days after hearing a lecture or speech.

Our listening deteriorates not only when we listen to speeches or lectures, but when we interact interpersonally. Even in the most intimate relationships (or perhaps we should say especially in the most intimate relationships), we tune out what others are saying. One study reported that we sometimes pay more attention to strangers than to our close friends or spouses. Married couples tend to interrupt each other more often than non-married couples, and are usually less polite to one another than are strangers involved in a simple decision-making task.

COMMUNICATION AND DIVERSITY

Gender and Listening

Do men and women listen differently? One researcher says it's not so much that they listen differently as that they attend to information in different ways. When men listen, they may be looking for a new structure or organizational pattern, or to separate pieces of information they hear. The male attention style is to shape, form, observe, inquire, and direct effort toward a goal. Men's attention style also is reported to be more emotionally controlled than women's attention style. Women's attention style is more emotionally involved and tends to be more empathic and subjective. Women are more likely to search for relationships among parts of a pattern and to rely on more intuitive perceptions or feelings. These differences in attention styles and the way men and women process information can potentially affect listening, even though we do not have clear-cut research that links attention style to listening skills.

Research suggests that men tend to listen to solve a problem—to get to the bottom line when listening. Women are more likely to listen to seek new information to enhance understanding. Women also listen to establish personal relationships. It is not accurate to suggest that men listen better than women or vice versa. Emerging patterns in the research suggest there are listening differences. Perhaps men need to listen a bit more like women and women need to listen more like men. In any case, gender-based differences in attention style and information processing may explain some of the relational problems that husbands and wives, lovers, siblings, and men and women friends and colleagues experience. We caution you, however, in assuming that communicating with a member of the opposite sex is like interacting with someone from a different planet. Avoid making sweeping generalizations about the way others speak and listen.

There may also be gender differences in how we focus on message content. While all of us have thoughts and messages running through our minds as we listen, men have a greater tendency to focus not only on the "bottom line," but also on one message at a time; women may be able to focus on more things simultaneously. When a man is watching the news or a sports broadcast, he may seem lost in thought—oblivious to other voices around him. Women, on the other hand, are more likely to shift between competing messages. They are more likely to be carrying on a conversation with one person and also focus on a message they may hear nearby. No, it doesn't mean women are more likely to eavesdrop intentionally, but that women have greater potential to listen to two things at once. This means it is especially important for women to stop and become focused on the message of others, rather than on either internal or external competing messages. And men will need to concentrate on the conversation of others, rather than become fixated on their own internal message.

Research also suggests that women and men can be equally good listeners; but in addition to differences in how we focus on messages, we often listen for different reasons. Communication researcher Melanie Booth-Butterfield suggests that the sexes actually learn to listen for different reasons. Since men tend to view communication as serving the primary purpose of information exchange, they tend to listen to receive facts. They listen more for the "big picture" or major ideas than for details. They also listen so that they can give advice and solve problems, rather than listening to reflect understanding of the other person. Women tend to attend to the details of what is being said, as well as to the speaker's nonverbal behaviors (such as tone of voice, gestures, and facial expressions accompanying certain words). And they tend to listen primarily to detect the mood of the other person and to offer support. Obviously, this difference in approaches to listening can cause serious problems when a man and a woman attempt to converse.

So how can you use this information? It's not that women cannot listen for information and men cannot listen in support of others; it's more in how we prefer to listen, how we are taught and reinforced to listen. So we may have to re-teach ourselves or un-learn some listening habits. If the situation suggests that listening to gain information is warranted, men and women are equally capable of accomplishing that task. Women may have a harder time merely listening for facts, rather than reading into the conversation more than those

continued

facts or attempting to "take the emotional temperature" of the other person. What if, however, the information someone is relating doesn't seem to be the main reason for the conversation? What if you perceive that the person just needs you to listen—not to solve the problem or offer advice or disagree to show them the error in their thinking? In this circumstance, you should work to adapt your approach and offer support as a listener by listening with your ears and your eyes. The skill comes in detecting accurately what the situation requires (the principle of self-awareness), and then adapting your behavior so that you engage in the situation appropriately and communicate effectively.

What keeps us from listening well? The most critical elements viewed from the perspective of the model of communication we introduced in chapter 1 include three things: (1) self-barriers—personal habits that work against listening well; (2) information processing—the way we mentally manage information; and (3) context—the surroundings in which we listen.

Self-Barriers

"We have met the enemy and he is us" is the oft-quoted line from the comic strip Pogo. Evidence suggests we are our own worst enemy when it comes to listening to others—whether it's listening to enjoy, learn, evaluate, or empathize. We mentally comment on the words and sights that we see and hear. Our internal thoughts are like a play-by-play sports commentator describing the action of a sports contest. If our internal narration is focused on the message, then it may be useful. But we often attend to our own internal dialogues and diatribes instead of others' messages; when we do that, our listening effectiveness plummets.

Inattentive listening is like channel surfing when we watch TV—pushing the remote control button to switch from channel to channel, avoiding commercials, and focusing for brief periods on attention-grabbing program "bites." When we listen to others, we may tune in to the message for a moment, decide that it is boring or useless, and then focus on a personal thought. These personal competitions for listening to others stem from several habits and tendencies.

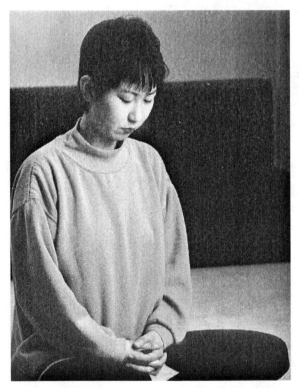

Some people find that yoga or quiet meditation can help them control the internal barriers that prevent them from listening effectively.

Self-Focus

That personal play-by-play commentary we may be carrying on in our minds is typically about us. "How long will I have to be here for this lecture?" "Wonder what's for dinner tonight?" "I've got to get that report finished." "She's still talking—will we be out of here in ten minutes?" "Do I have a school meeting tonight or is that tomorrow night?" Focusing on an internal message often keeps us from selecting and attending to the other person's message. If there is a competition between listening to what someone else may be droning on about and focusing on our own needs and agenda, our personal needs often bubble to the top of the list of priorities. Another symptom of self-focus is our tendency to think about what we are going to say while we look like we are listening to someone else.

What's the antidote for the self-focus we typically have when listening to others? The first and one of the most important actions is drawing on the first principle of communication; Become aware of your actions. Diagnosing the problem is the first step in managing the problem. Become consciously competent. Note consciously when you find yourself drifting off, thinking about your agenda or running commentary on what you see and hear, rather than concentrating on the speaker.

A second suggestion: Concentrate. When you become aware that your internal messages are distracting you from listening well, double your efforts to stay on task. If your internal "announcer" is telling you the message is boring, useless, or stupid, make sure you don't automatically tune out. Yes, some messages are boring, useless, and stupid. But the habit of quickly dismissing ideas and messages without effort will keep you from being nominated for the Listening Hall of Fame.

You can also improve your concentration by relating the speaker's topic to your own interests. Dig for information you can use. Search for connections between what you already know and information that is unfamiliar to you.

Here's another suggestion: Be actively involved in the communication process by taking notes and, when appropriate, providing feedback to the speaker; this strategy can also help you stay on track. Also, if the speaker is using words and phrases you don't understand, write down the words you don't understand so you can look them up later. The key to concentration is finding ways to be active rather than passive when words bombard your ears. Don't just sit there and "take it"; if you find your concentration waning, you'll more than likely "leave it."

Emotional Noise

Emotions are powerful. Your current body posture, facial expression, and even your blood pressure are affected by your emotional state. What we see and hear affects our emotions. **Emotional noise** occurs when our emotional arousal interferes with communication effectiveness. Certain words or phrases can arouse emotions very quickly; and, of course, the same word may arouse different emotions in different people. You respond emotionally because of your cultural background, religious convictions, or political philosophy. Words that reflect negatively on your nationality, ethnic origin, or religion can trigger strong emotional reactions. Cursing and obscene language may also reduce your listening efficiency. If you grew up in a home in which R-rated language was never used, then four-letter words may distract you.

Sometimes it's not just a word but a concept or idea that causes an emotional eruption. Third-trimester abortion and public school prayer, for example, are sure-fire ways to get radio talk show hosts' audiences involved in lively discussion. Whether you love him or hate him, TV talk show host Jerry Springer is a master at pushing emotional hot buttons for his talk show guests; and when emotions become heated, thoughtful listening is rare.

The emotional state of the speaker may also affect your ability to understand and evaluate what you hear. One researcher found that if you are listening to someone who is emotionally distraught, you will be more likely to focus on his or her emotions, than on the content of the message. Another researcher advises that when you are communicating with someone who is emotionally excited, you should remain calm and focused, and try simply to communicate your interest in the other person.

What are other strategies to keep your emotions from getting the best of you? It's not always easy, but research suggests there are ways of not letting your emotions run amok. Daniel Goleman offers several research-based strategies in his best-selling book *Emotional Intelligence*. For example, one simple yet powerful strategy to manage emotions when you find you may be ready to lose it is to take a deep breath. Yes, just breathe. Taking a deep, slow breath is a way of regaining control by calming us down. It helps makes us more conscious of our anger or frustration, much like the old technique of counting to ten. Another strategy for managing emotions is to use the power of self-talk. Tell yourself you won't get angry. Early detection of the emotions bubbling inside your can help you assess and then manage emotions before your nonrational, emotional impulses take control. As we've noted, we're not suggesting it's inappropriate to experience emotions; however, unchecked, intense emotional outbursts do not enhance your ability to listen, comprehend, or empathize with others.

Sometimes, of course, expressing your frustration is appropriate. We're not suggesting you go through life unrealistically serene or that you avoid experiencing emotions. Only the dead and mentally incompetent could follow the prescription of never becoming emotional. We do suggest that you become aware of the effect that emotions have upon your listening ability; this is a constructive first step to avoid being ruled by unchecked emotions. The principle of self-awareness gives you choice and control, rather than simply letting emotions go unchecked. Your listening challenge is to avoid emotional sidetracks and keep your attention focused on the message. When emotionally charged words or actions kick your internal dialogue into high gear, make an effort to quiet it down and steer back to the subject at hand. Becoming consciously aware of our emotions and then talking to ourselves about our feelings is a way of not letting emotions get out of hand.

Criticism

We usually associate the word "criticism" with negative judgments and attitudes. Although critiquing a message can provide positive as well as negative insights, most of us don't like to be criticized. Mother Teresa once said, "If you judge people, you have no time to love them." Being inappropriately critical of the speaker may distract us from focusing on the message.

Mother Teresa understood the value of open listening without pre-judging a person.

A person's appearance and speech characteristics can affect your ability to listen to him or her. Many a speaker's droning monotone, lack of eye contact, and distracting mannerisms have contributed to their ideas not being well received—even if the ideas are potentially life-changing for the listener. The goal of a sensitive communicator is to be conscious of when the delivery or other distracting features of the message or messenger are interfering with your ability simply to listen. In fact, now that you are studying principles of communication, you may find that this problem looms even larger, because you now pay more attention to nonverbal cues.

It would be unrealistic to suggest that you refrain from criticizing speakers and their messages. It is realistic, however, to monitor your internal critiques of speakers to make sure you are aware of your biases. Good listeners say to themselves, "While this speaker may be distracting, I am simply not going to let the appearance or mannerisms keep my attention from the message." For example, Stephen Hawking is a prize-winning physicist at Cambridge University in England; because of a debilitating illness, he is able to speak only with the aid of computer-synthesized sounds. He is unquestionably brilliant. If you let his speaking delivery overpower you, you'd miss his marvelous message. Avoid using your mental energy to criticize a speaker unnecessarily; the longer your mental critique, the less you'll remember.

Information-Processing Barriers

Processing Rate

An extension of the self-barriers of self-focus, emotions, and criticism is the manner in which we process information. One of the barriers that has long been documented is the difference between our ability to process information and the rate at which information comes to us. The barrier boils down to this: You can think faster than people speak. Most people speak 125 words per minute, give or take a few words. You have the tremendous ability, however, to process four to ten times that amount of information. Some people can listen to 600 to 800 words a minute and still make sense out of what the speaker is saying; another estimate puts the processing rate up to 1,200 words per minute. Yet another estimate claims that we think not just in words but also in images and sounds: we can process 2,000 bits of information a minute for short periods of time. This difference between your capacity to make sense out of words at the speed at which they register in your cortical centers can cause trouble. You have extra time on your hands to tune in to your own thoughts, rather than focus on the speaker.

You can use your information-processing rate to your advantage if you use the extra time to summarize mentally what a speaker is saying. By periodically sprinkling in mental summaries during a conversation, you can dramatically increase your listening ability and make the speech-rate/thought-rate difference work to your advantage.

Information Overload

Information abounds. We are constantly bombarded with sights and sound bites, and experts suggest that the amount of information competing for our attention is going to increase in the future. Incoming messages and information on computers, fax machines, e-mail, car phones, beepers, and other technological devices can interrupt conversations and distract us from listening to others.

The amount of information coming at us on any given day also wears us out. The one word to describe many a poor listener is "weary." We spend 45 percent of our communication time listening, and the pace at which the information zips toward us exhausts us. The billion words that we hear contribute to our fatigue.

Again we recommend self-awareness. Be on the alert for drifting attention due to information overload. And when the encroaching information dull our attentiveness to messages, either take a break or consider communication triage (determine what's urgent and what's not urgent) to sort through the information that is most important.

Receiver Apprehension

Just as some people are fearful of presenting a speech or speaking up during a meeting, research suggests that some people are fearful of receiving information. **Receiver apprehension** is being fearful of misunderstanding or misinterpreting the messages spoken by others or not being able to adjust

DEVELOPING YOUR SKILL
PUTTING PRINCIPLES INTO PRACTICE

Assessing Your Listening Skills

Receiver apprehension is the anxiety some people feel when they listen to others; this anxiety stems from a fear of misunderstanding messages or concern about psychologically adjusting to the information someone presents. Take the following test to assess your level of receiver apprehension. Scores range from 50 to 10. The higher your score, the more you're likely to experience some anxiety when you listen to others and the harder you'll have to work at developing strategies to improve your listening comprehension.

Receiver Anxiety Scale

Respond to each of these questions about how much this describes you, using a 5-point scale.
5 = Strongly Agree; 4 = Agree; 3 = Uncertain or Sometimes;
2 = Disagree; 1 = Strongly Disagree

_____ 1. When I am listening, I feel nervous about missing information.

_____ 2. I worry about being able to keep up with the material presented in lecture classes.

_____ 3. Sometimes I miss information in class because I am writing down the notes.

_____ 4. I feel tense and anxious when listening to important information.

_____ 5. I am concerned that I won't be able to remember information I've heard in lectures or discussions.

_____ 6. Although I try to concentrate, my thoughts sometimes become confused when I'm listening.

_____ 7. I worry that my listening skill isn't very good.

_____ 8. I regularly can't remember things that I have just been told.

_____ 9. I feel anxious and nervous when I am listening in class.

_____ 10. I prefer reading class material rather than listening to it, so I don't have to be stressed about catching all the information the first time.

SOURCE: L. Wheeless, "An Investigation of Receiver Apprehension and Social Context Dimensions of Communication Apprehension," *The Speech Teacher* 24 (1975): 261–268.

psychologically to messages expressed by others. Some people may just be fearful of receiving new information and being able to understand it. Or it may just be a characteristic or pattern in the way some people respond psychologically to information; they may not be able to make sense out of some of what they hear, which causes them to be anxious or fearful of listening to others. If you are fearful of receiving information, you'll remember less information.

What are the implications of these research studies for you? If you know that you are one of those people who is fearful of listening to new information, you'll have to work harder to understand the information presented. Using a tape recorder to record a lecture may help you feel more comfortable and less anxious about trying to remember every point.

Becoming actively involved in the listening experience by taking notes or mentally repeating information to yourself may also help.

Context Barriers

Barriers of Time and Place

Besides our own inadequacies and the way in which we process information, the communication situation can hinder effective listening. The time of day can interfere with your listening acuity. Are you a morning person or an evening person? Morning people are cheerfully and chirpily at their mental peak before lunch. An evening person prefers to tackle major projects after dark; they are at their worst when they arise in the morning. Use the skill development activity on page 206 to plot your ideal work time, the period when you are at your sharpest.

If you know you are sharper in the morning, whenever possible, schedule your key listening times then. Evening listeners should try to shift heavy listening to the evening hours. Of course, that's not always practical. If you can't change the time of listening, you can then increase your awareness of when you will need to listen with greater concentration.

Don't assume that because you are ready to talk, the other person is ready to listen. If your message is particularly sensitive or important, you may want to ask your listening partner, "Is this a good time to talk?" Even if he or she says yes, look for eye contact and a responsive facial expression to make sure the positive response is genuine.

Noise

You have undoubtedly noticed one obvious barrier to listening well: It is hard to concentrate on a friend's comments while the TV is blaring or when you are sitting in a noisy restaurant. Or have you tried to enjoy a concert or movie while the family in front of you uses the outing to provide their own narration of the action or catch up on family business? No matter how interesting or important a message is to you, if you can't hear or if other messages are noisily competing for your attention, your listening efficiency will suffer.

Noise can be in the form of sights or sounds. The best environment for listening for most people is one that offers as few audio and visual distractions as possible. When you want to talk to someone, pick a quiet time and place, especially if you know you will be discussing a potentially conflict-producing subject. In the context of a family, it may be a challenge to find a quiet time to talk. With one family member going to play ball, another going shopping, and a third coming home from an exhausting day and just wanting to relax, it is difficult to find moments when all are available for conversation.

Perhaps a good title for a listening text would be *How to Turn Off the TV.* It is difficult to listen with the ever-present background chatter of cartoons, comedies, music videos, news, and dramatic monologue in the background. Listening takes all the powers of concentration that you can muster. A good listener seeks a quiet time and place to maximize listening comprehension. Closing a door or window, turning off a radio, or even asking inappropriate offending talkers to converse more quietly or not at all are action steps that you may need to pursue to manage the listening noise barrier.

RECAP

Managing Listening Barriers

Listening Barriers	What to Do
Self-Barriers	
Self-Focus	■ Consciously become aware of the self-focus and shift attention back to the speaker.
	■ Concentrate: Find ways of becoming actively involved in the message, such as taking meaningful notes.
Emotional Noise	■ Act calm to remain calm.
	■ Use self-talk to stay focused on the message.
	■ Take a deep breath if you start to lose control.
Criticism	■ Focus on the message, not the messenger.
Information-Processing Barriers	
Processing Rate	■ Use the difference between speech rate and thought rate to mentally summarize the message.
Information Overload	■ Realize when you or your partner is tired or distracted and not ready to listen.
	■ Assess what is urgent and not urgent when listening.
Receiver Apprehension	■ If you are fearful or anxious about listening to new information, use a backup strategy such as a tape recorder to help you capture the message; review the tape later. Seek ways to become actively involved when listening, such as taking notes or making mental summaries of the information you hear.
Context Barriers	
Barriers of Time and Place	■ Note when your best and worse listening times are; if possible, shift difficult listening situations to when you're at your best.
Noise	■ When appropriate, modify the listening environment by eliminating distracting, competing noise.

IMPROVING LISTENING COMPETENCE

With appropriate knowledge and practice, all of us can become better listeners (refer to the nearby cartoon). First, we must recognize the importance of listening effectively. Second, we must think of listening as an active behavior that requires conscious participation. Third, we must recognize that a willingness to work and a desire to improve are essential to increasing listening effectiveness.

In some situations, we need not listen with full attention. For example, if we listen to a CD while conversing with a friend, we're not likely to create problems by attending closely to the friend and partially to the music. However, each listener must be able to identify when total energy and involvement in the listening process are crucial. Effective listening often requires both energy and concentration; listeners need to constantly remind themselves that listening is vital to communication. People call on different listening skills, depending on whether their goal is to comprehend information, critique and evaluate messages, show empathy for others, or appreciate a performance. According to the National Communication Association, competent listeners demonstrate (1) knowledge and understanding of the listening process, (2) the ability to use appropriate and effective listening skills for a given communication situation and setting, and (3) the ability to identify and manage barriers to listening, all of which we have covered in this chapter.

Competent listeners work at listening (see the Guidelines for Competent Listening). They are prepared to listen and know what they wish to gain from their listening experiences. Competent listeners also engage in appropriate listening behaviors. They realize that being a good listener is active and complex. They know that they must pay attention if they are to listen well. They do not interrupt others, they look at the speaker, they listen to ideas, and they concentrate on what is being said.

COMPETENT LISTENERS

1. Be prepared to listen. Learn to control internal and external distractions.

2. Behave like a good listener. Stop talking and let others have their say. Do not interrupt. Concentrate on what is being said, not who is saying it, or what the speaker is doing. Good listeners maintain eye contact with speakers, ask questions at appropriate times, and maintain flexibility as they carefully listen to the speaker's views.

3. Take good notes. Listen for main ideas and write down the most significant, most important points; don't attempt to write down every word. Good note taking helps listeners remember better and longer, and provides a written indication of ideas to remember. Brevity is usually best, so that you can carefully listen to the speaker and the speaker's intent. Write clearly to facilitate the review of your notes later. Review your notes as soon after the event as possible to help you recall them later. And, finally, reorganize or rearrange your notes if necessary for clarity before filing them for future reference. Do not get so involved in note taking that effective listening is lost. Note taking should be used as an aid to listening, not as a replacement for it. All six stages of the listening process are brought into play when we listen effectively. Never concentrate so hard on writing everything down that you fail to think about what is said.

LISTENING SKILLS

At the heart of listening is developing sensitivity to focus on the messages of others, rather than your own thoughts. To improve your listening involves a set of skills that can increase your sensitivity toward others. At first glance, these skills may look deceptively simple—as simple as the advice given to most elementary students about crossing the railroad tracks: (1) stop, (2) look, and (3) listen. Despite the appearance of simplicity, decades of research and insight about how to avoid being labeled "interpersonally inert" can be summarized around these three skills. Let's consider each separately.

Stop: Turn Off Competing Messages

Many of the barriers to improved listening skill relate to the focus we often place on ourselves and our own messages, rather than focusing on others. As we noted earlier, while you are "listening," you may also be "talking" to yourself—providing a commentary about the messages you hear. These internal, self-generated messages may distract you from giving your undivided attention to what others are saying. In order to select and attend to the messages of others, we need to become aware of our internal dialogue and stop our own running commentary about issues and ideas that are self-focused rather than other-focused.

Try a process called **decentering.** Decentering involves stepping away from your own thoughts and attempting to experience the thoughts of another. In essence, you're asking yourself this question: "If I were the other person, what would I be thinking?" To decenter is to practice the first principle of communication—self-awareness—to be aware that your own thoughts are keeping you from focusing on another's message so that you can focus on another person. Of course, we are not suggesting that your own ideas and internal dialogue should be forever repressed; that would be both impossible and inappropriate. We are suggesting, however, that to connect to another, you must place the focus on the other person rather than on yourself. To decenter requires conscious effort. Decentering is a mental or cognitive process that involves trying to guess what someone else may be thinking. In attempting to decenter, consider this question, "If I were my communication partner, what would I be thinking?"

The essence of the "stop" step is to become aware of whether you are listening or not listening to someone. You are either on task (focusing on another) or off task (oblivious to another and focusing on your own thoughts and emotions). The goal, of course, is to be on task—listening to others.

Look: Observe Nonverbal Cues

Nonverbal messages are powerful, especially in communicating feelings, attitudes, and emotions. Up to 93 percent of emotional information may be expressed by nonverbal cues. A person's facial expression, presence or lack of eye contact, posture, and use of gestures speaks volumes, even when no word is uttered. When words are spoken, the added meaning that comes from vocal cues provides yet another dimension to the emotion and nature of the relationship. When there is a contradiction between the verbal and nonverbal message, we will almost always believe the unspoken message; nonverbal cues are more difficult to fake.

Sensitive listeners are aware of nonverbal as well as verbal messages; they listen with their eyes as well as their ears. A person's body movement and posture, for example, communicate the intensity of his or her feelings, while the facial expression and vocal cues provide clues as to the specific

emotion being expressed. A competent listener notices these cues, and an incompetent listener attempts to decode a message based only on what is said rather than "listening between the lines."

Besides looking at someone to discern his or her emotions and relational cues, it is important to establish eye contact, which signals that you are focusing your attention on your partner. Even though mutual eye contact typically lasts only one to seven seconds, when we carry on an interpersonal conversation, it is important to establish and reestablish eye contact to signal that you are on task and listening. We usually have more eye contact with someone when we are listening than talking. Looking over your partner's head, peeking at your watch, or gazing into space will likely tell him or her you're not tuned in. Even though there are cultural variations in the advice to establish eye contact (for example some children in African-American homes have been taught to avoid eye contact with high-status people), generally, for most North Americans, eye contact signals that the communication channel is open and the communication is welcome.

Not only is eye contact important, but other nonverbal cues signal whether you are on task and responsive to the messages of others. If you look like you are listening, you will be more likely to listen. Maintaining eye contact, remaining focused, not fidgeting with your hands and feet, and even leaning forward slightly are nonverbal cues that communicate to someone that you are listening. Appropriate head nods and verbal responses also signal that you are attending to your partner's message.

Listen: Understand Both Details and Major Ideas

How do you improve your listening skill? First, stop the internal dialogue that may distract your attention from your partner. Look for nonverbal clues about emotions and the nature of the relationship. Here are several additional strategies that can improve your listening skill.

1. *Identify your listening goal.* As we noted earlier, you listen for several reasons—to learn, enjoy yourself, evaluate, or empathize. Of course, you may be listening for a variety of these reasons. Just make sure you know what your goal is. In some listening situations, you need to remember every detail (there is no final exam at the end of each day to test what we can recall). In other situations, your goal is simply to empathize—listen to "feel with" your partner—not to give advice, just support.
2. *Mentally summarize the details of the message.* This suggestion may seem to contradict the suggestion to avoid focusing only on facts, but it is important to have a grasp of the details your partner presents. To listen is to do more than focus on facts. Studies suggest that poor listeners are more likely to focus on only facts and data, rather than the overall point of the message. To listen is to connect the details of the message with the major points. You can process words quicker than a person speaks, so you can use the extra time to your advantage by periodically summa-

rizing the names, dates, and facts embedded in the message. If the speaker is disorganized and rambling, use your tremendous mental ability to organize the speaker's information into categories, or try to place events in chronological order. If you miss the details, you will likely miss the main point.

3. *Link message details with the major idea of the message.* Facts and data make the most sense when we can use them to support an idea or point. Mentally weave your summaries of the details into a focused major point or series of major ideas. So as you summarize, link the facts you have organized in your mind with key ideas and principles. Use facts to enhance your critical thinking as you analyze, synthesize, evaluate, and finally summarize the key points or ideas your partner makes.

4. *Practice by listening to difficult or challenging material.* You can also sharpen your listening skill by consciously developing your abilities to stop, look, and listen. You learn any skill with practice. Listening experts suggest that our listening skills deteriorate if we listen only to easy and entertaining material. Make an effort to listen to news or documentary programs. As you listen to material in a lecture that may seem chock full of content, make a conscious effort to stay focused, concentrate, and summarize facts and major ideas.

   While listening to someone give you directions to Centennial Hall, one of the oldest buildings on campus, you would listen differently than if your sister were telling you about her fears that her marriage was on the rocks. In the case of your sister, your job is to listen patiently and provide emotional support. In trying to get to Centennial Hall, you would be focusing on the specific details and making either mental or written notes.

5. *Transform listening barriers into listening goals.* If you can transform the listening barriers we presented earlier, you will be well on your way to improving your listening skill. Make it a deliberate goal not to be self-focused, let emotional noise distract you, or criticize a message before you've understood it. Watch out for information overload. And, when possible, take steps to minimize external noise and provide an ideal listening environment.

RECAP

How to Listen Well

What to do	How to Do It
STOP	■ Focus on your partner, not your own thoughts.
	■ Cease what you are doing; give your undivided attention to your partner.
LOOK	■ Observe the nonverbal messages of your listening partner.
	■ Make sure your nonverbal message communicates your interest in your partner.
LISTEN	■ Listen for both details and major ideas.
	■ Mentally summarize key ideas.

To respond is to provide feedback to another about his or her behavior or communication. Your response can be verbal or nonverbal, intentional or unintentional.

Your thoughtful response serves several purposes. First, it tells a speaker how well his or her message has been understood. Second, your response lets a speaker know how the message affects you. It indicates whether you agree or disagree. Third, it provides feedback to correct statements or assumptions that you find vague, confusing, or wrong. It helps an individual keep the communication on target and purposeful. Finally, your response signals to the speaker that you are still "with" him or her. Your verbal or nonverbal response lets the speaker know you are still ready to receive messages. To respond appropriately and effectively, consider the following strategies.

Be Descriptive

"I see that from a different point of view" sounds better than "You're wrong, I'm right." Effective feedback describes rather than evaluates what you hear. Although one type of listening is to evaluate and make critical judgments of messages, evaluate once you're sure you understand the speaker. We're not suggesting it's easy to listen from a nonevaluative perspective, or that you should refrain from ever evaluating messages and providing praise or negative comments. Remember: Feedback that first acts like a mirror to help the speaker understand what he or she has said is more useful than immediately providing a barrage of critical comments. Describing your own reactions to what your partner has said rather than pronouncing a quick judgment on his or her message is also more likely to keep communication flowing. If your partner thinks your prime purpose in listening is to take pot-shots at the message or messenger, the communication climate will cool quickly.

Be Timely

Feedback is usually most effective at the earliest opportunity after the behavior or message is presented, especially if the purpose is to teach. Waiting to provide a response after much time has elapsed invites confusion.

Now let us contradict our advice. Sometimes, especially if a person is already sensitive and upset about something, delaying feedback can be wise. Use your critical-thinking skills to analyze when feedback will do the most good. Rather than automatically offering immediate correction, use the just-in-time (JIT) approach. Provide feedback just before the person might make another mistake, just in time for the feedback to have the most benefit.

Be Brief

Less information can be more. Cutting down on the amount of your feedback can highlight the importance of what you do share. Don't overwhelm your listener with details that obscure the key point of your feedback. Brief is usually best.

Be Useful

Perhaps you've heard this advice: "Never try to teach a pig to sing. It wastes your time, it doesn't sound pretty, and it annoys the pig." When you provide feedback to someone, be certain that it is useful and relevant. Ask yourself, "If I were this person, how would I respond to this information? Is it information I can act on?" Immersing your partner in information that is irrelevant or that may be damaging to the relationship may make you feel better, but may not enhance the quality of your relationship or improve understanding.

RESPONDING WITH EMPATHY

The underlying premise of this chapter is: Effective communicators are sensitive to others. They listen and thoughtfully respond to confirm their understanding of the content and, when appropriate, the feelings of the communicator. A sensitive communicator is actively rather than passively involved in the message, whether it is listening to a friend's story about a flat tire, a professor's lecture, or your mother's request that you come home for the holidays.

Boyd likes to bring empathy to the task at hand.

Passive listeners sit with a blank stare or a frozen facial expression. Often they have not "stopped" their own thoughts and may be a thousand miles away, even though physically present. Active listeners, in contrast, respond mentally, verbally, and nonverbally to a speaker's message.

Responding is something we do for others that holds great benefits for us. It is the key to exchanging mutually understood, emotionally satisfying messages. Responding is especially critical if you are listening to provide support. Research suggests that some of us have a people-oriented listening style. People-oriented listeners are better at empathizing with others. Of course, listening to empathize is only one of the possible listening goals you may have. We are not suggesting that ferreting out someone's emotions is the goal of every listening encounter. That would be tedious for both you and your listening partners. But when you do want to listen and respond empathically, you must shift the focus to your partner and try to understand the message from his or her perspective. Here are four strategies to help respond to provide empathic support when you listen.

Understand Your Partner's Feelings

If your goal is to empathize or "feel with" your partner, you might begin by imagining how you would feel under the same circumstances. If your roommate comes home from a hassle-filled day at work or school, try to imagine what you might be thinking or feeling if you had had a stressful day. If a friend calls to tell you his mother died, consider how you would feel if the situation were reversed. Even if you've not yet experienced the loss of your mother, you can identify with what it would be like to suffer such a loss. Of course, your reaction to life events is unlikely Of course, your reaction to life events is unlikely to be exactly like someone else's response. Empathy is not telepathically trying to become your communication partner. But you do attempt to decenter—consider what someone may be thinking—by first projecting how you might feel, followed by appropriate questions and paraphrases to confirm the accuracy of your assumptions. Considering how others might feel has been called the Platinum Rule—even more valuable than the Golden Rule ("Do unto others as you would have others do unto you"). The Platinum Rule invites you to treat others as _they_ would like to be treated—not just as _you_ would like to be treated.

East and West Listening Styles

North American communication very often centers on the sender, and until recently the linear, one-way model from sender to receiver was the prevailing model of communication. Much emphasis has been placed on how senders can formulate better messages, improve source credibility, polish their delivery skills, and so forth. In contrast, the emphasis in East Asia has always been on listening and interpretation.

Communication researcher C. Y. Cheng has identified infinite interpretation as one of the main principles of Chinese communication. The process presumes that the emphasis is on the receiver and listening rather than the sender and speaking. According to T. S. Lebra, "anticipatory communication" is common in Japan—instead of the speaker's having to tell or ask for what he or she wants specifically, others guess and accommodate his or her needs, sparing him or her embarrassment in case the verbally expressed request cannot be met. In such cases, the burden of communication falls not on the message sender, but on the message receiver. A person who "hears one and understands ten" is regarded as an intelligent communicator. To catch on quickly and to adjust oneself to another's position before his or her position is clearly revealed is regarded as an important communication skill. One of the common puzzles expressed by foreign students from East Asia is why they are constantly being asked what they want when they are visiting in American homes. In their own countries, the host or hostess is supposed to know what is needed and serve accordingly. The difference occurs because in North America it is important to provide individual freedom of choice; in East Asia, it is important to practice anticipatory communication and to accommodate accordingly.

With the emphasis on indirect communication, the receiver's sensitivity and ability to capture the under-the-surface meaning and to understand implicit meaning becomes critical. In North America, an effort has been made to improve the effectiveness of senders through such formal training as debate and public speaking, whereas in East Asia, the effort has been on improving the receiver's sensitivity. The highest sensitivity is reached when one empties the mind of one's preconceptions and makes it as clear as a mirror.

Recently, there has been increased interest in listening in the United States. Both communication scholars and practitioners recognize that listening is necessary not only for the instrumental aspect of communication (comprehension) but, more importantly, for the affective aspect (satisfaction of being listened to).

SOURCE: June Ock Yum, "The Impact of Confucianism on Interpersonal Relationships and Communication Patterns in East Asia," in Larry A. Samovar and Richard E. Porter, eds. *Intercultural Communication: A Reader* (Belmont, CA: Wadsworth Publishing Company, 2000), 86.

Ask Appropriate Questions

As you listen for information and attempt to understand how another person is feeling, you may need to ask questions to help clarify your conclusions. Most of your questions will serve one of four purposes: (1) to obtain additional information ("How long have you been living in Buckner?"); (2) to check out how the person feels ("Are you frustrated because you didn't get your project finished?"); (3) to ask for clarification of a word or phrase ("What do you mean when you say you wanted to telecommute?"); and (4) to verify that you have reached an accurate conclusion about your partner's intent or feeling ("So are you saying you'd rather work at home than at the office?").

COMMUNICATION AND TECHNOLOGY

Can Computers Listen Emphathically

Is it possible for a computer to listen and respond sensitively to others? Although there is software that permits you to speak words that your personal computer will then print, computers do not yet have the sophistication to listen and respond with the same sensitivity as people. But computer programmers are working on it. Stanford University professors Clifford Nass and Byron Reeves have been working since 1986 to help PCs interact with people in human ways. They have summarized research regarding how people respond to other people and have been trying to translate these research conclusions into strategies that can be used by a computer to interact with others in real-time dialogues. Professors Nass and Reeves have identified four major personality types—dominant, submissive, friendly, and unfriendly—and have pro-grammed computers to respond to the computer user. The researchers are trying to match more than personality. As Professor Nass explains, "Personality is one aspect. Gender, politeness, cooperation, and even humor are other factors. We decide what the agent [computer user] is going to do, then develop a backstory—each character's likes and life history. This guides the scripting, voice type, animation, and interaction style." The researchers are also working on integrating computer-generated speech into the program. Although computers may not yet listen with the sensitivity and empathy of your best friend, researchers are working on software that can emulate human interaction and responses. So, for now, realize that the opportunity to listen to others is something that can't be delegated to a virtual friend.

Here's another suggestion for sorting out details and trying to get to the emotional heart of a dialogue: Ask questions to help you (and your partner) identify the sequence of events. "What happened first?" and "Then what did he do?" can help both you and your partner clarify a confusing event.

Your ability to ask appropriate questions will demonstrate your supportiveness of your partner, as well as signal that you are interested in what he or she is sharing. Of course, if you are trying to understand another's feelings, you can just ask how he or she is feeling in a straightforward way. Don't ask questions just for the sake of asking questions. Also, monitor the way in which you ask your questions. Your own verbal and nonverbal responses will contribute to the emotional climate of your interaction.

Paraphrase the Content

After you have listened and asked questions, check whether your interpretations are accurate by paraphrasing the content you have heard. Paraphrasing is restating in your own words what you think a person is saying. Paraphrasing is different from repeating something exactly as it was spoken; that would be parroting, not paraphrasing. Your paraphrase can summarize the essential events, uncover a detail that was quickly glossed over, or highlight a key point. Typical lead-ins to a paraphrase include statements such as:

"So here is what seemed to happen. . . ."
"Here's what I understand you to mean. . . ."
"So the point you seem to be making is. . . ."

"You seem to be saying. . . ."

"Are you saying. . . ."

Here's an example of a conversation punctuated by appropriate paraphrases to enhance the accuracy of the message receiver:

Nikki: I'm swamped. My boss asked me to take on two extra projects this week. And I already have the Henrikson merger and Affolter project. I promised I'd arrange to have the lawnmower fixed and pay the bills. I also don't see how I can take the dog to the vet, pick up the kids after school, and get Keshia to the orthodontist at 7 A.M. I'm up to my neck in work. Can you help?

Mark: So you'd like me to take care of the stuff around the house so you can focus on office assignments.

Nikki: Well, some of them, yes. Could you take on a couple of things I said I'd do?

Mark: You'd like me to help around here more?

Nikki: Yes, could you?

Mark: Okay. I'll take care of the kids and run several of the time-consuming errands.

We are not suggesting that you paraphrase when it's not needed or appropriate, only when you need to confirm your understanding of a murky message or to help the speaker sort out a jumbled or confusing situation. When a listener paraphrases the content and feelings of a speaker, the speaker is not only more likely to ensure the message is understood but also will be more likely to trust and value the listener.

Paraphrase Emotions

The bottom line in empathic responding is to make certain that you understand how someone is feeling—not their health, but their emotional state.

"So you feel. . . ."

"So now you feel. . . ."

"Emotionally, you are feeling. . . ."

These are typical lead-in phrases when paraphrasing feelings.

We have discussed empathic responses and the active listening process from a tidy step-by-step typical textbook approach. Realize that in practice, it won't be so neat and tidy. You may have to back up and clarify content, ask more questions, and rethink how you would feel before you summarize how someone feels. Or you may be able to summarize feelings without asking questions or summarizing the content of the message. A sensitive communicator doesn't try to let his or her technique show. Overusing paraphrasing skills can slow down a conversation and make the other person uncomfortable or irritated. But if used with wisdom, paraphrasing can help both you and your partner clarify message accuracy.

Reflecting on the content or feeling through paraphrasing can be especially useful in the following situations:

Before you take an important action

Before you argue or criticize

When your partner has strong feelings

When your partner just wants to talk

When your partner is speaking "in code" or using unclear abbreviations

When your partner wants to understand your feelings and thoughts

When you are talking to yourself (you can question and check your own emotional temperature)

When you encounter new ideas

When you ask questions and paraphrase content and feelings, keep the following additional guidelines in mind:

Use your own words—don't just repeat exactly what the other person says.

Don't add to the information presented when paraphrasing.

Be brief.

Be specific.

Be accurate.

Don't use reflecting skills if you aren't able to be open and accepting; if you are using paraphrasing skills and simply try to color your paraphrased comments to achieve your own agenda, you aren't being ethical.

Don't be discouraged if your initial attempts to use these skills seem awkward and uncomfortable. Any new set of skills takes time to learn and use well. The instructions and samples you have seen here should serve as a guide, rather than as hard-and-fast prescriptions to follow every time.

DEVELOPING YOUR SKILL
PUTTING PRINCIPLES INTO PRACTICE

Listening and Reflecting Content and Emotion

Working in groups of three, ask person A to identify a problem or conflict that he or she is having (or has had) with another person (coworker, supervisor, spouse, or family member) or talk about a goal he or she wants to accomplish. Person B should use questioning, content paraphrasing, and emotion paraphrasing skills to explore the problem. Person C should observe the discussion and evaluate person B's listening and reflecting skills, using the Observer Checklist. Make a check mark next to all of the skills that person B uses effectively.

Observer Checklist

Nonverbal Skills		Verbal Skills	
Direct eye contact	_____	Appropriate questions	_____
Open, relaxed body posture	_____	Accurate paraphrase of content	_____
Uncrossed arms	_____	Accurate paraphrase of emotion	_____
Uncrossed legs	_____	Didn't interrupt the speaker	_____
Appropriate hand gestures	_____		
Reinforcing head nods	_____		
Responsive facial expression	_____		
Appropriate tone of voice	_____		
Appropriate volume	_____		

RECAP

How to Respond with Empathy

Responding with Empathy	Action
Understand Your Partner's Feelings	Ask yourself how you would feel if you had experienced a similar situation or recall how you did feel under similar circumstances. Or recall how your partner felt under similar circumstances.
Ask Questions	Seek additional information to better understand your partner's message.
Reflect Content by Paraphrasing	Summarize the essence of the information as you understand it for your partner.
Reflect Feelings by Paraphrasing	When appropriate, try to summarize what you think your partner may be feeling.

Listen
When I ask you to listen to me and you start giving advice,
you have not done what I asked.
When I ask you to listen to me and you begin to tell me why I shouldn't
feel that way you are trampling on my feelings.
When I ask you to listen to me and you feel you have to do something
to solve my problems, you have failed me, strange as that may seem.
Listen! All I asked, was that you listen. Not talk or do—just hear me.
Advice is cheap: 50 cents will get you both Dear Abby and Billy Graham
in the same newspaper.
And I can do for myself; I'm not helpless. Maybe discouraged and faltering,
but not helpless.
When you do something for me that I can and need to do for myself, you
contribute to my fear and weakness.
But when you accept as a simple fact that I do feel what I feel,
no matter how irrational, then I quit trying to convince you
and can get about the business of understanding what's behind this irra-
tional feeling.
And when that's clear, the answers are obvious and I don't need advice.
Irrational feelings make sense when we understand what's behind them.
Perhaps that's why prayer works, sometimes, for some people because God
is mute, and doesn't give advice or try to fix things,
God just listens and lets you work it out for yourself.
So, please listen and just hear me, and, if you want to talk,
wait a minute for your turn: and I'll listen to you.   —*Anonymous*

SUMMARY

An important principle of communication is to listen and respond thoughtfully to others. Listening is the process of making sense out of what we hear. It includes the processes of selecting, attending, understanding, remembering, and responding to others. We listen for a variety of reasons, including to enjoy, to learn, to evaluate, and to empathize with others.

Most people struggle with the skill of listening. Barriers to effective listening include focusing on our personal agendas, being distracted by emotional noise, criticizing the speaker, daydreaming, and being distracted by information overload and external noise.

To become a better listener, consider three simple processes: Stop, look, and listen. To stop means to be mindful of the message and avoid focusing on your own distracting "talk," which may keep you from focusing on the messages of others. To look is to listen with your ears—to focus on the nonverbal information that provides a wealth of cues about emotional meaning. To listen involves the skill of capturing the details of a message while also connecting those details to a major idea.

The other half of listening is responding to others accurately and appropriately. To respond thoughtfully means to stop and consider the needs of the other person. Check the accuracy of your listening skill by reflecting your understanding of what your partner has said. Responding skills are especially important if the goal is to empathize with and support others. Responding skills include understanding the feelings of others, asking appropriate questions, and paraphrasing the message's content and the speaker's feelings. Responding effectively does not mean being a parrot and repeating a message exactly as it was spoken. Paraphrasing means summarizing the gist of the message. The most effective responses to others are carefully timed, provide usable information, avoid cluttering details, and are descriptive rather than evaluative.

For Review and Discussion

1. What is the difference between listening and hearing?
2. What are some of the key barriers that keep people from listening effectively?
3. Name the four goals of listening.
4. What are similarities and differences between listening for information, to evaluate, to enjoy, and to empathize?
5. List the essential skills to improve your listening, and discuss which strategies will help you improve your listening skills.
6. What are suggestions for improving your ability to empathize with others?
7. What are suggestions for effectively paraphrasing or reflecting messages back to others?
8. How do you appropriately and thoughtfully respond to others?

Activities to Develop Skills and Apply Principles

1. Letting your emotions get the best of you is one of the problems that inhibits effective listening. Make a list of several emotion-arousing words that affect your listening competence. Share your list with other class members. Identify strategies to keep your emotions in check when you hear words or phrases that keep you from listening well.

2. Spend a certain period of time (for example, one hour, one morning) noting those times when you are not listening at your best. Keep a log describing those times when your attention waned. Then note why you think your listening ability was affected. Using the strategies mentioned in this chapter, identify how you can enhance your listening skill.

3. In a group, assign one student to speak very slowly on a difficult or demanding subject (such as a passage from a textbook other than this one). Write down short summaries during pauses in the speech, then compare the summaries with those of others in the group.

4. List the things in your home—TVs, stereos, computers, newspapers, and so on—that might distract from conversation. Bring a radio into class and try conversing with a partner with music and news broadcasts in the background. Then have a conversation without the extra noise. Compare the difference.

5. On pages 184–193 we noted several barriers to listening. Rank order these barriers, with 1 being the most problematic. After you have identi-fied your top three or four barriers, identify at least one specific strategy for overcoming your problematic listening behavior.

6. Charting Your Listening Cycle

Are you a morning person or an evening person? Use the chart in Figure 10.3 to plot your listening energy cycle. Draw a line starting at 6:00 a.m., showing the highs and lows of your potential listening effectiveness. For example, if you are usually still asleep at 6:00 A.M., your line will be at 0 and start upward when you awake. If you are a morning person, your line will peak in the morning. Or perhaps your line will indicate that you listen best in the evening.

After you have charted your typical daily listening cycle, gather in small groups with your classmates to compare listening cycles. Identify listening strategies that can help you capitalize on your listening "up" periods. Also, based upon information you learned from this chapter and your own experiences, identify ways to enhance your listening when you traditionally have low listening energy.

FIGURE 10.3
Your Listening Energy Cycle

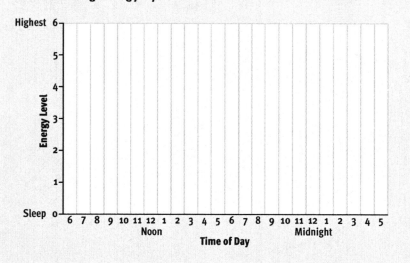

PART THREE

Interviewing

CHAPTER 11

What is Interviewing?

WHAT IS INTERVIEWING?

An **interview** is a form of interpersonal communication in which two people interact, most often face to face, largely through a question-and-answer format to achieve specific goals. While interviews usually involve two people, some involve more. At job fairs, for example, where many people apply for the few available jobs, interviewers may talk with several people at once. Similarly, couple and family counselors frequently interview entire families while counselors in the workplace often interview groups of coworkers or other related individuals.

Although most interviewing is done face to face, much interviewing now takes place via computer—through e-mail and on Internet Relay Chat groups. For example, you can use e-mail or IRC groups to conduct an informative interview with people living in different parts of the world. The Internet allows employers to interview candidates in different parts of the world all for the price of a few local phone calls. And, of course, it allows candidates to explore employment opportunities from their own desks. With advanced hardware and software enabling audio and video exchanges over the Internet, the computer-mediated interview will very closely resemble the traditional face-to-face situation.

The interview is different from other forms of communication because it proceeds through questions and answers. Both parties in the interview can ask and answer questions, but most often the interviewer asks and the interviewee answers. The interview has specific goals that guide and structure its content and format. In an employment interview, for example, the interviewer's goal is to find an applicant who can fulfill the tasks of the position. The interviewee's goal is to get the job, if it seems desirable. These goals guide the behaviors of both parties, are relatively specific, and are usually clear to both parties.

Interviews vary from relatively informal talks that resemble everyday conversations to those with rigidly prescribed questions in a set order. You would select the interview structure that best fits your specific purpose or combine the various types to create a new interview structure tailored to your needs (Hambrick, 1991):

- The *informal interview* resembles conversation; the general theme is chosen in advance, but the specific questions arise from the context. It's useful for obtaining information informally.

- The *guided interview* deals with topics chosen in advance. The specific questions and wordings, however, are guided by the ongoing interaction. It's useful in assuring maximum flexibility and responsiveness to the dynamics of the situation. An example is the interviews on television talk shows.

- The *standard open interview* relies on open-ended questions whose order is selected in advance. It's useful when standardization is needed—for example, when interviewing several candidates for the same job.

- The *quantitative interview* uses questions that guide responses into pre-established categories. For example, questions may contain multiple-choice responses that the interviewee selects from or may ask for a number from 1 to 10 to indicate an interviewee's level of agreement. It's useful when large amounts of information (which can be put into categories) are to be collected and statistically analyzed, as, for example, in a marketing survey of customer satisfaction.

We can also distinguish the different types of interviews by the goals of interviewer and interviewee. Some of the most important types of interviews are persuasion, appraisal, exit, counseling, information, and employment. You'll probably come into contact most often with information and employment interviews, so these are covered in more detail. In the information interview, we concentrate on the role of the interviewer and in the employment interview, on the role of the interviewee, roles you are likely to experience. Of course, the principles for effective information and employment interviews will also prove useful for other interview types.

The Persuasion Interview

In the **persuasion interview,** the goal is to change a person's attitudes, beliefs, or behaviors. One way to accomplish this is for the interviewer to ask questions that will lead to the desired conclusion. So, for example, if you go into a showroom to buy a new car, the salesperson may ask you questions that are obviously and favorably answered by the car he or she wants to sell: "Is safety an important factor?" "Do you want to save a bundle?" Another way is for the salesperson to become the interviewee, explaining the superiority of this car above all others in answer to your questions about mileage, safety features, and finance terms, for example.

All interviews contain elements of both information and persuasion. When, for example, a guest appears on *The Tonight Show* and talks about a new movie, information is communicated. But, there is also persuasion. The performer is trying to persuade the audience to see the movie.

The Counseling Interview

Counseling interviews provide guidance. The goal is to help the person deal more effectively with problems involving work, friends or lovers, or just the hassles of day-to-day living. For the interview to be of any value, the interviewer must learn about the interviewee's habits, problems, self-perceptions, goals, and so on. With this information, the counselor tries to persuade the person to alter certain aspects of his or her thinking or behaving. The counselor may try to persuade you, for example, to listen more attentively to relationship messages or to devote more time to your class work.

▌▚ THE INFORMATION INTERVIEW

In the **information interview,** the interviewer tries to learn something about the interviewee or some information that the interviewee has. You might interview politicians to discover their position on education or scientists to discover recent technological advances. Examples of such interviews often appear in magazines, in newspapers, on the Internet, and on television. The television interviews conducted by Conan O'Brien, Rosie O'Donnell, Larry King, and Diane Sawyer as well as those conducted by a lawyer during a trial are all information interviews.

You might also interview potential baby-sitters before leaving your child in their care, financial consultants before entrusting your savings to them, or health care workers before hiring them to look after an aging parent. In these cases, the information you seek is whether the interviewee is suitable for a particular job.

In all these situations, the interviewer asks the interviewee a series of questions designed to elicit his or her views, beliefs, insights, knowledge, background, perspectives, predictions, life history, and so on. Each interview aims to gather specific information from someone who supposedly knows something others do not.

Information interviews are also commonly used to gather information about a specific career field in order to evaluate employment opportunities. Let's say that you're conducting an interview to get information about the available job opportunities in and the preparation you would need to get into desktop publishing. Here are a few guidelines for conducting such an information interview.

Secure an Appointment

To select a person to interview about desktop publishing, you might, for example, look through your college catalog to see who teaches a desktop publishing course. Or you might call a local publishing company and ask for the person in charge of desktop publishing. Try to learn something about the person before the interview. For example, has the instructor written a book or articles about the field? Look at the book catalog, at indexes to periodicals, at relevant websites.

Call, send a letter to, or e-mail the person you select to request an interview and to identify the purpose of your request. For example, you might say, "I'm considering a career in desktop publishing, and I'd appreciate an interview with you to learn more about the business and your company. The interview should take about 20 to 30 minutes." By stating up front a limited time for the interview, you make the interviewee know that it will not take too long.

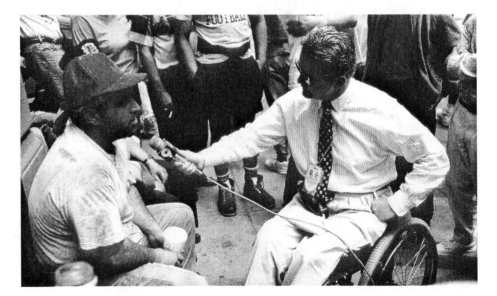

How would you evaluate the effectiveness of one of the popular television interviewers, for example, Rosie O'Donnell, Oprah Winfrey, Jay Leno, Larry King, Charlie Rose, or Geraldo Rivera?

Because you are asking the favor of the interviewee's time, it's best to be available at her or his convenience. So, indicate flexibility on your part: "What time is good for you? I'm available any day next week after noon."

If you find it necessary to conduct the interview by phone, call to set up a time for a future call. For example, you might say, "I'm interested in a career in desktop publishing and I would like to speak to you about job opportunities. If you agree, I can call you back at a time that's convenient for you." In this way, you don't run the risk of interrupting the interviewee's busy day and asking her or him to hold still for an interview.

Prepare Your Questions

Preparing questions in advance will ensure that you use the time available to your best advantage. If appropriate, you might also send these questions in advance to the person you're going to interview to allow him or her time to think about them. Of course, as the interview progresses, you may think of other questions, and you should pursue these as well. But a prepared list of questions (which can, of course, be altered or even eliminated as the interview progresses) will help you obtain the information you need in a reasonable amount of time.

Use open-ended questions that give the interviewee room to discuss the issues you want to raise. Instead of asking a question that requires only a simple yes or no answer—such as "Do you have formal training in desktop publishing?"—ask open-ended questions that allow the person greater freedom to elaborate—such as "Could you tell me about your background in this field?"

Establish Rapport with the Interviewer

Open the interview by thanking the person for making the time available and again stating your interest in the field and in learning more about it. Many people receive numerous requests, and it helps to remind the person of your specific purpose. You might say something like "I really appreciate your making time for this interview. As I mentioned, I'm interested in learning about job opportunities in desktop publishing, and learning about your expertise and experience in this area will help a great deal."

Ask Permission to Tape the Interview

Generally, it is a good idea to tape-record the interview. It will ensure accuracy and allow you to concentrate on the interviewee rather than on note taking. But always ask for permission first. Even if the interview is being conducted by phone, ask permission if you intend to tape the conversation.

Close and Follow Up the Interview

At the end of the interview, thank the person for making the time available and for being informative, cooperative, and helpful. Closing the interview on a positive note makes it easier to secure a second interview should you need it. Within the next two or three days, follow up the interview with a brief note of thanks. You might express your appreciation for the person's time, your enjoyment in speaking with the person, and your accomplishing your goal of getting the information you needed.

TOPIC 2: TAKING STATEMENTS

Questions and Answers

Good Question 1: When should an officer obtain a **statement**?

Answer 1: At a criminal offense and noncriminal incident, an officer should obtain a **statement.**

Good Question 2: From **whom** should statements be taken?

Answer 2: Offenders, witnesses, victims and other officers are individuals from whom statements are obtained.

Good Question 3: What information should be gathered regarding a **suspect's description?**

Answer 3: Race, sex, age, height, weight, scars, disabilities, and clothing should be included in **descriptions of suspects.**

Good Question 4: What information should be gathered regarding a **vehicle's description**?

Answer 4: Make , model, style, color, tag number, and marks should be included in **descriptions of vehicles.**

Good Question 5: What questions should be asked at a criminal offense or a noncriminal incident?

Answer 5: Who, what, when, where, why, and how are questions asked for a **criminal offense** or **noncriminal incident.**

Good Question 6: What type of information should be gathered regarding **property description**?

Answer 6: Type, characteristics, estimated value, inscriptions, and owner's name are information needed in **descriptions** of **properties.**

Good Question 7: What are the **basic procedures** officers should follow when taking statements?

Answer 7: Review notes, evidence, statements, and rights are **basic procedures** to follow when taking statements.

Good Question 8: What are the **methods** used for obtaining statements?

Answer 8: Methods for obtaining statements include tape recordings, videotapes, and dictation as well as written statements by officers or by persons being interviewed.

Good Question 9: Should someone be present when an officer takes a **juvenile's** statement?

Answer 9:	Yes, a parent should be present when an officer takes a statement from a **juvenile.**
Good Question 10:	What information should an officer gather regarding a case involving **injuries**?
Answer 10:	When it comes to injuries, officers should address the nature, extent, cause, and seriousness of the **injury.**

ESSENTIAL INTERVIEWING SKILLS

1. Preparation.

Before you begin an interview, arrange an appropriate setting. Both you and the person you're talking to should be seated comfortably so that you're both at eye level. In an investigation, privacy is essential; so is trust. If you are trying to establish rapport, avoid having physical barriers between you, such as a vase of flowers, briefcase, or desk. Such objects inhibit communication.

Remember that you are being judged. Your actions should demonstrate that you're a trustworthy professional. Experienced officers often begin an interview with courteous, casual conversation about a subject of mutual interest—sports, unusual weather, or family life. In a person's home, you can admire some feature of the architecture, setting, or furnishings. Avoid controversial subjects such as politics, religion, or social problems.

In dealing with a victim, allow some time for feelings to be ventilated. You don't have to offer solutions to the problems at hand. Nod encouragingly, make eye contact, and express your concern. Then, at an appropriate time, say, "I'd like to get the facts about what happened" and begin your interview.

2. Concentration.

If you're not paying attention, you may miss something important—a fact, a feeling, or other vital information. Factual errors caused by inattention can be especially embarrassing in court. Even if you're simply discussing an everyday problem with a citizen, poor listening skills may damage your image.

Most people have never fully developed their listening potential. Fortunately, concentration increases with practice, and opportunities to improve occur constantly. The next time you attend a movie, watch a TV news show, or eavesdrop on a conversation, practice tuning in completely to what is said. Test yourself by trying to repeat what you heard. This simple self-improvement program can (and should) be a lifetime project—one that will reward your efforts again and again.

3. Focusing.

Listening is difficult when someone rambles, overwhelms you with irrelevant information, or talks incoherently. When you interview an anxious citizen at a crime scene, you may have trouble sorting out the jumble of events and facts you are hearing. You can improve your listening comprehension by making your own connections between the citizen's information and your observations at the scene. Appropriate questions (but not too many) can be helpful as well.

You may find it helpful to list five headings, with space after each, on your notepad when you begin your investigation: victims, witnesses, suspects, evidence, and disposition. By entering facts under the appropriate headings, you will experience less confusion when you are recording information.

4. Neutrality.

Don't let preconceptions weaken your listening skills. Train yourself to set aside your opinions when you are listening. This advice is particularly important when the speaker is different from you in some significant way. Don't allow yourself to be influenced by ethnic, economic, religious, sexual, or educational barriers. A person who is mentally ill, unemployed, or disabled may provide valuable information. Biases about a person's age, lifestyle, or previous history can prevent you from learning important facts.

Avoid exposing your own attitude toward what you're hearing. Don't influence a citizen's statement by nodding, asking leading questions, or excitedly taking notes about the details you find important. Don't immediately challenge a statement that seems deceptive. A defensive, argumentative witness is unlikely to help your investigation. When the citizen has completed his or her statement, you can choose an appropriate way to deal with the deception.

5. Accuracy.

Many officers mentally divide interviews into two parts: storytelling and verification. They find it helpful to allow witnesses to tell their stories freely, with a minimum of interruptions for questions and notetaking. In the second phase of the interview, they verify the facts, ask questions about gaps in the story, and record basic information: names, addresses, and so on. Premature or excessive notetaking can be an obstacle to communication. Try to record most of your notes near the end of the interview.

6. Decoding mixed messages.

Sometimes a speaker will communicate one message through words and a contradictory one through body language. For example, a suspect may assure you that she's not angry and has no desire to hurt anyone. But her loud voice, aggressive posture, and clenched fists may convey a different message. Similarly a battered woman may refuse to press charges against her husband, insisting that the dispute was a minor one. But you may perceive fear in her anxious eyes, nervous hands, and quavering voice. When in doubt, trust body language rather than verbal messages.

7. Closing the interview.

Don't be too abrupt. Ask if there's any other information to be shared—you may learn valuable information that way—and thank the person for cooperating. Many officers close an interview on a professional note by offering a business card in case further communication is necessary.

CHAPTER 12

Interviews and Interrogations

INTRODUCTION

Interviews and *interrogations* are unique forms of communication that usually occur only in a law enforcement agency. These information-gathering techniques are critical in apprehending and obtaining criminal convictions. They are distinguished from each other by purpose and the circumstances surrounding the collection of the desired information.

An *interview* is a systematic questioning of an individual to gather information regarding an actual or suspected crime. An *interrogation* is a systematic questioning of an individual *who is in custody or is deprived of freedom in any significant way* for the purpose of gathering information regarding an actual or suspected crime. As the preceding definitions indicate, the difference between the two types of inquiry centers on the fact that during an interrogation the person is not free to leave. The following sections examine, compare, and contrast the interview and the interrogation and analyze special issues that arise concerning a law enforcement officer's communication skills.

MIRANDA AND ITS EFFECT

Before the U.S. Supreme Court decided *Miranda v. Arizona,* confessions and the accompanying interrogations were decided on a case-by-case basis. This approach reviewed the circumstances surrounding the interrogation to determine if the suspect's will was broken by the police. The interrogation was considered improper if it violated the suspect's due process rights.

Pre-Miranda Techniques

In *Brown v. Mississippi,* the defendant was taken to the crime scene, where he was questioned regarding his involvement in a murder. After denying guilt, he was hung by a rope from a tree. He continued to claim innocence and was tied to the tree and whipped. He was released, but was subsequently again seized and whipped until he finally confessed. The court held that the interrogation and confession were products of *coercion* and brutality and violated the defendant's Fourteenth Amendment due process rights.

In *Ashcraft v. Tennessee,* the defendant was taken to the police station and questioned continuously for two days regarding the murder of his wife. The officers questioned Ashcraft in relays because they became exhausted during the interrogation; however, the defendant was denied rest and sleep during the entire time. The court held that the prolonged interrogation of Ashcraft was coercive and, therefore, the confession was *involuntary* and inadmissible.

In *Spano v. New York,* the defendant was suspected of a murder. Spano informed a friend, who was a rookie police officer, that he had in fact killed the victim. Spano was arrested, and the rookie officer was instructed to tell Spano that he was in trouble and might lose his job unless Spano confessed. Spano finally confessed to the killing. The Supreme Court held that the use of deception as a means of psychological pressure to obtain a confession was a violation of the defendant's constitutional rights; therefore, the confession was ruled involuntary and was suppressed.

In *Escobedo v. Illinois,* the defendant was arrested for murder and interrogated for several hours at the police station. During the interrogation, Escobedo repeatedly requested to see his attorney—who was also at the police station, demanding to see his client. The police refused both requests and finally obtained the confession. The court held that Escobedo was denied his right to counsel and, therefore, no statement obtained from him could be used at a criminal trial.

Escobedo was confusing because it was unclear when this right to counsel attached during the interrogation. Trial courts began interpreting the meaning of Escobedo differently. Thus, the stage was set for the U.S. Supreme Court to clear up the confusion that resulted from its previous rulings.

Miranda

In *Miranda v. Arizona,* the U.S. Supreme Court established certain safeguards for individuals who are being interrogated by police. Most people know that the Miranda decision requires police officers to advise defendants of their constitutional rights. In reality, Miranda established a four-prong test that must be satisfied before a suspect's statements can be admitted into evidence. The test requires affirmative answers to all four of the following questions:

1. Was the statement voluntary?
2. Was the Miranda warning given?
3. Was there a waiver by the suspect?
4. Was the waiver intelligent and voluntary?

Unless all these questions are answered in the affirmative, none of the suspect's statements can be admitted into evidence. In Miranda, the defendant was arrested at home in Phoenix, Arizona, in connection with the rape and kidnapping of a female and was taken to a police station for questioning. At the time, he was 23, poor, and basically illiterate. After being questioned for two hours, he confessed to the crime. The Supreme Court issued its now-famous Miranda warning requirement, stating:

> We hold that when an individual is taken into custody or otherwise deprived of his freedom . . . , the privilege against self-incrimination is jeopardized. . . . He must be warned prior to any questioning that he has a right to remain silent, that anything he says can be used against him in a court of law, that he has a right to an attorney, and that if he cannot afford an attorney one will be appointed for him prior to any questioning if he so desires.

The *Miranda* decision drew a bright line for admissibility of confessions and admissions obtained during investigations. It changed the way police interrogate suspects. While the decision was sweeping in its scope, it still left questions unanswered.

In *Berkemer v. McCarty,* the Supreme Court held that the *Miranda* warning must be given during any custodial interrogation. The court held that a person subjected to a custodial interrogation must be given the warning regardless of the severity of the offense, but questioning a motorist at a routine traffic stop does not constitute custodial interrogation.

The *Miranda* decision has generated both support and criticism since its inception. Supporters argue that it protects the rights of those accused of crimes, while detractors claim that it allows the guilty to go free because an officer may not have followed all the rules. In recent years, the courts have begun to allow statements to be admitted into evidence despite the absence of the *Miranda* warning.

The Eroding of *Miranda*

Miranda did not prevent statements obtained in violation of its rules from being used to impeach the credibility of a defendant who takes the witness stand. In *Harris v. New York,* the court held that it was proper to use such statements so long as the jury was instructed that the confession was not to be considered as evidence of guilt, but only to determine if the defendant was telling the truth.

Voluntary statements made by the defendant without having received the *Miranda* warning are admissible, even though the defendant is later advised of his rights and waives those rights. In *Oregon v. Elstad,* the defendant was picked up at his home as a suspect in a burglary and made incriminating statements without receiving his *Miranda* warning. After being advised of his rights, he waived them and signed a confession. The Supreme Court held that the self-incrimination clause of the Fifth Amendment did not require suppression of the written confession because of the earlier unwarned admission.

In *Illinois v. Perkins,* the Supreme Court held that an undercover officer posing as an inmate need not give a jailed defendant the *Miranda* warning before asking questions that produce incriminating statements. The court held that there is no coercive atmosphere present when an incarcerated person speaks freely to someone whom he believes is a fellow inmate. The court added that the *Miranda* warning does not forbid strategic deception by taking advantage of a suspect's misplaced trust.

In *Arizona v. Fulminante,* the U.S. Supreme Court held that the harmless error rule is applicable to cases involving involuntary confessions. The harmless error rule holds that an error made by the trial court in admitting illegally obtained evidence does not require a reversal of the conviction if the error was determined to be harmless. The burden of proving harmless error rests with the prosecution and must be proved beyond a reasonable doubt.

In *Davis v. United States,* the U.S. Supreme Court considered the degree of clarity that is necessary for a suspect to invoke his *Miranda* rights. Agents of Naval Investigative Service were questioning the defendant in connection with the death of a sailor. He initially waived his rights, but approximately 90 minutes later stated, "Maybe I should talk to a lawyer." The agents asked clarifying questions; when the defendant stated that he did not want an attorney, the interrogation resumed, eliciting incriminating statements. The court held that an equivocal request for a lawyer is insufficient to invoke the right to counsel and that there is no need for clarifying questions before proceeding with the interrogation.

After years of allowing suspects to avoid police interrogation by invoking their *Miranda* rights, the Supreme Court is beginning to take a more reasonable and practical approach to this controversial issue. Police officers must carefully tailor their interrogations so that they obtain information while at the same time protecting the suspect's constitutional rights.

INTERVIEWS

Interviews are a key part of any investigation. Various techniques are used during interviews to elicit information from the different types of witnesses. No single method will work for all officers or be effective on all witnesses. While the general rules regarding interviews also apply to crime victims, special consideration must be given to their needs and feelings. A successful interview is composed of tact, sensitivity, and determination.

Interviewing Witnesses

A witness interview does not occur without preparation and hard work on the part of an officer. However, before a witness can be interviewed one must be found.

Identification of Witnesses One of the cardinal rules in law enforcement interviewing is to locate witnesses to a crime as soon as possible. There are several reasons for this principle. First, locating and interviewing witnesses immediately after the commission of the crime allows officers to broadcast the suspect's description to other officers. The greater the lapse of time from the incident to the witness interview, the greater the chance that the witness will not recall all that was observed. Another reason for interviewing witnesses as soon as possible after the crime is to prevent them from comparing stories with other witnesses and changing their accounts of what they saw.

Witnesses may be located in a number of different places; however, the crime scene is the most obvious place to begin. Normally, people who remain at crime scenes are willing to provide information to the police. The officer should approach the most obvious witness first; this will normally be someone who is excited or talkative. Avoid asking, "Did you see what happened?" A more open-ended question will elicit a wider response. A question such as "What happened here?" may lead to other witnesses. The first question may be answered by a simple "No," while the second question may provide other information: "I didn't see who fired the shot, but the janitor saw everything." Thus, the technique of how the initial question is posed may determine the citizen's answer or level of cooperation.

Officers should consider revisiting the crime scene on a daily basis for a week after the crime was committed. If at all possible, this visit should occur at the same time that the crime originally occurred. Pedestrians, school-children, and other people who may have been in the area at the time of the crime should be questioned. The officer should approach these citizens with an understanding attitude and stress the need to cooperate with the police during this period of time.

A third technique in locating witnesses is canvassing the neighborhood. This normally occurs only after a serious crime, such as homicide, has been committed. Since this is a staff-draining exercise, the police administrator will be called on to justify this use of officers. When contacting neighbors, the officer should present identification, explain the reason for the visit, relate the time of the crime, and ask if the witness saw or heard anything unusual. If the answer is in the affirmative, the officer can then proceed to more specific questions regarding the crime.

Finally, the victim or suspect's friends or relatives should be interviewed in an attempt to locate witnesses. The officer should approach these citizens in a professional manner and begin the interview with open-ended, nonspecific questions. If one of these persons has any knowledge about either the victim or the suspect, the officer should then proceed to specific areas of inquiry. This allows the officer to develop a well-rounded picture of either the victim or the suspect. Identifying potential witnesses is the first step in the process of interviewing witnesses.

Interview Preparation The officer cannot always select the interview location. Therefore, the officer must rely on communication skills and control the communication process in order to elicit the needed information. The officer must have as much information as possible prior to conducting any interview. Depending on the situation, the officer may conduct the interview at the scene of the crime, at a witness's home, or at the police department. The officer should control the interview and ensure that critical items of information are obtained. At the same time, the officer must not be so rigid in questioning as to miss a witness's offhanded remark that might lead to information that will assist in the arrest of the suspect.

In situations where there are numerous distractions, the officer should attempt to obtain only the basic facts and should schedule a follow-up interview to gather other information. A basic description of the suspect, what the witness observed, and the witness's name, address, and both work and residence telephone numbers may be all the information the officer is able to obtain in these situations.

The follow-up interview is a vital phase of the interviewing process. The officer should review all available information prior to conducting this interview. The normal procedure for such an interview is to follow a structured or logical sequence of questioning. Random questioning is rarely used because it lacks direction and fails to obtain all pertinent information. Witnesses should be allowed to relay all the information in their possession before the officer begins to ask questions. When interrupted during a statement, a witness may forget a fact or pick up the narrative at a different point.

Preparation is critical to the efficient, productive interview of witnesses. The officer must be prepared for the interview by knowing the facts surrounding the incident. The officer must also know when and where a brief interview is appropriate and when a more thorough interview is necessary.

Conducting the Interview The actual interview should flow very smoothly if the officer has prepared properly. The officer must remember to remain courteous, attentive, and professional. If the witness is uncomfortable relating the facts of the incident, the officer should offer supportive comments. If the witness seems reluctant to talk, the officer can remind the witness of a citizen's obligations. An officer may use many techniques during the interview process but the primary duty is to make sure the lines of communication with the witness remain open.

Evaluating Witnesses One of the tasks of the interviewing officer is to evaluate the credibility of the witness. Credibility can be defined as the believability of the witness. In other words, what are the personal characteristics that render this witness's testimony worthy of belief by an impartial party? These characteristics include truthfulness, opportunity to observe, accuracy in reporting what was observed, and motive for testifying.

Four factors may determine credibility: (1) opportunity, (2) attention, (3) personal knowledge, and (4) physical characteristics. The officer should evaluate each of these factors when judging a witness's credibility.

Opportunity refers to the witness's awareness of his surroundings. Was he in a location that allowed for an unobstructed view of the crime? Did he see only part of the act? Can he contribute facts that, although not specific to the crime, assist the investigators in putting together a complete picture of the incident?

Attention requires that the witness be aware of the incident. What brought the event to the witness's attention? The witness may have paid attention to only part of the incident, and the officer must resist the temptation to put words in the witness's mouth regarding something that the witness did not observe. For example, if a witness states, "The first time I saw him was when he shoved the shotgun in the teller's face," the officer should not attempt to have the witness testify regarding when the suspect entered the bank.

Personal knowledge relates to those facts that the witness observed or experienced. The officer should ensure that the witness actually observed what she states she saw, heard, or felt. To do this, the officer may want to determine where the witness was located in relation to the incident, the location of other persons, and any other facts which may show that the witness was where she states she was and that she had an unobstructed view of the scene of the crime.

Physical characteristics concern the witness's ability to observe and relate what he saw. Does the witness wear glasses, contact lenses, a hearing aid? Is the witness color-blind? If so, is it critical to his testimony?

Once the interviewing is completed, the officer should compare the witnesses' statements against each other to assist in evaluating their credibility.

Successfully interviewing witnesses is more an art form than a science. However, general principles regarding the interview process will assist the officer in communicating with witnesses. Locating witnesses, preparing for the interview, conducting the interview, and evaluating the credibility of witnesses are necessary steps in this process.

Interviewing Victims

Many of the same techniques discussed in the preceding apply when interviewing victims of crimes. Victims are also witnesses to the crime in many situations. However, victims must be treated differently than witnesses for a variety of reasons.

Some victims will experience emotional or mental problems as a result of the crime. Many crime victimization studies have examined the effects of sexual assault on victims, but consensus is being developed among experts that victims of serious nonsexual crimes may also experience demonstrated psychological effects as a result of the offense.

Post-traumatic stress syndrome came into our consciousness as a result of the Vietnam War. Returning veterans reported flashbacks, severe depression, and other symptoms. Post-traumatic stress syndrome is now recognized as a mental disorder. There might be some confusion between the words *syndrome* and *disorder*. *Syndrome* connotes a collection of symptoms, while *disorder* is the clinical diagnostic term. The *Diagnostic Statistical Manual of Mental Disorders–IV* states that the essential feature of post-traumatic stress disorder (PTSD) is the development of characteristic symptoms following a psychologically distressing event that is outside the range of usual human experience. The victim usually experiences intense fear, terror, and helplessness. The characteristic symptoms involve flashbacks in which the patient relives the experience, avoidance of stimuli associated with the event, or numbing of general responsiveness.

Several studies have found that many victims of violent crimes suffer from PTSD. Dean Kilpatrick and his associates found that over 57 percent of all rape victims and 27 percent of nonsexual assault victims suffered from PTSD within one month after the assault. Victims of crimes have reported experiencing anger, fear, anxiety, intrusive imagery and nightmares, sleep disturbance, guilt, and impairment in social functioning following the crime.

It must be stressed that victims suffering from PTSD are not necessarily psychotic or deranged; rather, they are attempting to cope with a highly stressful event or series of events in their lives. An understanding and awareness of a crime's psychological impact will help peace officers obtain information and investigate the case. Investigators should understand that, like other forms of trauma, a victim suffering from PTSD may not exhibit a total disappearance of the symptoms over time; rather, the victim will feel a reduction in their frequency and intensity. As these symptoms lessen, crime victims may be able to resume their places in society but they will often harbor terrifying memories. Law enforcement officers can assist victims in this transition by being sensitive to their needs, concerns, and fears.

INTERROGATIONS

The key to success in interrogating suspects is careful preparation. Just as preparation for interviewing witnesses is necessary, a complete review of all facts is a requirement for an effective interrogation. As with many aspects of police work, interrogation is more of an art than a science; however, certain broad guidelines will assist officers in this area.

Unlike in the movies, successful interrogations do not always end with a confession. Statements given by a suspect may be exculpatory in nature. That is, the suspect may deny any wrongdoing or guilt. The suspect may also admit guilt, but plead justification for those actions. Finally, an interrogation may produce a complete confession. The various degrees of statements that come from an interrogation require investigating officers to effectively utilize their communication skills to the fullest extent possible.

Interrogations should occur in a location that is free from distractions or interruptions. Most modern police departments have rooms that are designated as interview/interrogation rooms. Many are equipped with tape recorders and some have one-way mirrors so superiors or other officers working on the case can view the questioning. These rooms should be sparsely furnished, well-lit, and secure.

Numerous interrogation techniques are available to police officers. Normally, an interrogation is conducted by two officers. One officer is the primary interrogator and the second officer acts as a recorder/witness. Depending on the suspect's reaction, the officers may switch roles during the interrogation. The officers should agree before the interrogation which role each of them will take. Following is a brief summary of some of the more common interrogation techniques.

Factual This is a straightforward approach in which the officer points out all the facts that show the suspect committed the crime. The officer explains the nature of the evidence and how it conclusively proves the suspect committed the act. The officer then explains that the suspect's only alternative is to cooperate with the police and that it is in the suspect's self-interest to do so. The interrogation should be conducted in a businesslike manner, with little or no emotion displayed by the officer. The officer should not make any deals or indicate that the suspect's cooperation will be brought to the attention of the district attorney.

Sympathetic In this technique, the officer acts understanding toward the suspect's position or justification for carrying out the acts. The officer should speak in a mild voice, sit close to the suspect, and may want to occasionally touch the suspect in an understanding way. This approach offers the defendant a friendly face during the interrogation.

Face-Saving or Justification The officer using this approach encourages the suspect to state the reason for committing the act. Again, the officer should never indicate that the defendant will receive a lesser sentence or go free after explaining the reasons for the act. The officer can, however, ask questions in such a manner as to imply that what the suspect did was a natural, everyday occurrence—that anyone facing the same set of facts would do the same thing.

These interrogation techniques are usually not employed in a strict, mechanical method. The officer may have to switch from one approach to another depending on the suspect's reaction or mental state. Veteran police officers understand the need to remain flexible in this critical area of law enforcement investigation and utilize their interpersonal and communication skills to the maximum.

How the suspect's statement is recorded affects the communication process between the officer and the defendant. Several of the more common techniques to record a suspect's statement follow.

Interrogating Officer Records Statement This method requires the interrogating officer to take notes while conducting the interrogation. This can be distracting to both the suspect and the officer. It may interrupt the free flow of the discussion and cause the suspect to become concerned about what the officer is writing down. One advantage to this approach is that the officer is able to testify to personally recording the suspect's statement in his or her own handwriting. However, the disadvantages of this method outweigh that simple fact, and this technique is not used when two officers are available to interrogate the suspect.

Assisting Officer Records Statement This is one of the most common methods used to record the suspect's statement. The officer who is not doing the talking writes down what the defendant says during the interrogation. The problem with this approach is that unless the suspect is ready to give a complete confession, the situation might require both officers to ask questions at different times during the interrogation. An advantage of this technique is that it allows for uninterrupted questioning by one officer while the other takes notes. The questioning officer can concentrate on the suspect and not be diverted by having to write down what is said.

Statement Is Transcribed by Court Reporter This is one of the most accurate ways to record the suspect's statement. However, it is normally used only when the officers feel the suspect is ready to make a confession. Normally, the suspect has to agree to this method. The disadvantage of this approach is that it requires a certified court reporter to take the statement from the suspect. In addition, since the suspect usually has to agree to this procedure, it is not used until a confession has been obtained.

Statement Is Tape Recorded There are two alternatives available to tape recording a suspect's statement. The traditional method uses a common cassette tape recorder. With the advent and increased use of videotape recorders, more and more modern police departments are turning to this approach to record interrogations. This method may be either clandestine or obvious. The clandestine method usually places the video camera behind a one-way mirror. The obvious technique involves obtaining the suspect's permission prior to taping the interview. With either approach, the officer should state the time, date, and location of the recording.

The advantages are obvious: a video is a pictorial record of the suspect's demeanor as well as the statement. Also, videotapes are now used by average citizens, and jurors are more understanding and appreciative of the medium.

Accurately recording the suspect's statement is vital to the successful prosecution of the criminal case. The interrogating officers should ensure that the suspect is treated in a courteous manner and that the suspect's rights are preserved. Interrogating a suspect is one of the most critical stages of any criminal investigation and requires the officer to react in an appropriate manner at all times.

Interrogation skills, like interviewing skills, take time and practice to develop. However, once sharpened, they will serve the officer and the department well.

SUMMARY

Conducting an interview is an essential step in any criminal investigation. This encounter provides law enforcement with vital facts surrounding the commission of a crime. Many times, the interview will take place in an atmosphere charged with emotion. Victims of violent crimes may be under a great deal of stress and law enforcement officers must be sensitive to their plight, yet at the same time must proceed, gathering enough information to go forward with the investigation. This dilemma requires police officers to use all the communication skills they possess to obtain the necessary information.

Interrogating a suspect is more an art than a science. It is true that officers can learn the mechanics of an interrogation; however, knowing when to switch approaches comes only with experience and knowledge. No one technique will work on all suspects. The officer must understand this and pattern the interrogation accordingly. Even when interrogations do not produce confessions, they provide law enforcement with sufficient information to request the filing of charges by the prosecutor's office.

REVIEW QUESTIONS

1. Explain the rationale behind the *Miranda* decision.
2. Do you believe the *Miranda* warning is still a valid concept? Why?
3. What are some of the keys to success in interrogating a suspect?
4. How are interviews and interrogations distinguished from each other?
5. Explain some of the popular techniques used in interviewing potential witnesses.

CHAPTER 13

Legal Issues in Interviewing

The duty of law enforcement is to investigate crime, but investigation has no purpose unless the information obtained can be used to prosecute the criminal. Police departments are organized in quasi-military structures with definite lines of authority. Individual officers generally act on their own without being required to consult with supervisors or legal counsel prior to taking action. Officers commonly focus their energy on collection and preservation of evidence to enhance this criminal prosecution. Unless they have been trained in the aspects of the law regarding the collection and preservation process, serious errors may occur and criminals may go free.

The officers assigned to tasks of interviewing and interrogation must be able to communicate and empathize with both the victim and the family of the offender. The purpose of interviewing is to collect and preserve critical information while the purpose of interrogation is to get a confession. Both techniques require a specialized knowledge and skill of the communication process. Officers must use systematic efforts when identifying, analyzing, measuring and displaying the outcomes of a police-suspect interview. Once this is accomplished, the evidence collected is often reviewed by a prosecutor or agency attorney. The prosecutor or agency attorney frequently assist in drafting documents such as search warrants, preparing witnesses for trial and providing general guidance and direction. Tactics used must be such that the courts will rule the evidence admissible.

With tasks defined, attention is now turned to what evidence must be collected and preserved and how the process is accomplished. Before law enforcement officers can investigate a crime, they must first determine if a crime has been committed, and if so, who is likely to have committed it. To answer these questions, the officer must acquire certain information. That information can include demographics, crime scene evidence, witness statements, and documents. Items collected must be obtained legally so as not to destroy their useful purpose in court. There are different rules for different types of evidence. Three such rules are those dealing with confessions, interviews with children, and search and seizure.

CONFESSIONS

The United States Constitution sets forth many of the "rights" which must be preserved if evidence is to be used against an offender. Perhaps the strongest of these, was the 1966 Supreme Court Ruling known as the *Miranda Rule* which indicated that for confessions to be admissible in court, officers had to follow a certain set of rules which stated that if a suspect was in custody, or deprived of his freedom of action in any way, he must be advised that:

- He has the right to remain silent
- If he gives up his right to remain silent, anything he says can and will be used as evidence against him in court.
- He has the right to consult an attorney and to have the attorney present during any questioning by the police; and
- If he is unable to afford an attorney, he can have one appointed to represent him during the investigation and questioning, free of charge.

However, even prior to the *Miranda Rule,* the Supreme Court, in the 1964 case *Escobedo vs. Illinois* held that a person's right to counsel commences at the moment an "investigation begins to focus on a particular suspect". More specifically, Chief Justice Warren elaborated on these issues by saying:

> "... we deal with the admissibility of statements obtained from an individual who is subject to custodial police interrogation and the necessity for procedures which assure that the individual is accorded his privilege under the Fifth Amendment of the Constitution not to be compelled to incriminate himself."

Chief Justice Warren further goes on to say:

> "... The difficulty in depicting what transpires at in-custody interrogations stems from the fact that in this country, they have largely taken place incommunicado". "... by custodial interrogations, we mean questioning initiated by law enforcement officers after a person has been taken into custody or otherwise deprived of his freedom of action in any significant way."

In conclusion, Chief Justice Warren indicated:

> "... In dealing with statements obtained through interrogation, we do not purport to find all confessions inadmissible. Confessions remain a proper element of law enforcement. Any statement given freely and voluntarily without any compelling influence, is of course, admissible as evidence ... There is no requirement that the police stop a person who enters a police station and states he wishes to confess to a crime, or a person who calls the police to offer a confession or any other statement he desires to make."

Although there is no requirement that someone sign a waiver of these rights, having the suspect sign such a form will prevent him from later denying he was advised of them. Remember, however, that even if a suspect signs a waiver, he still has the right to stop an interrogation at any time. After all these conditions are met, should a suspect confess, be sure to have the confession typed and signed by the suspect.

INTERVIEWS WITH CHILDREN

In most states, the law considers anyone under the age of 18 a child. This means that initial interviews or interrogations with children are delicate situations requiring skill and tack. While some officers may have natural abilities with children, special training is needed to promote understanding of the situation. Many state laws dictate that children cannot be questioned with a parent being present. Law enforcement officers need to follow specific guidelines during the process of interviewing or interrogating a child. Officers should:

- Be sure that the setting for the interview is chosen as carefully as possible.
- Be sure that, if the child is a younger child, the interview setting should be a neutral setting where the child fees comfortable and safe. The

interview should be set around the younger child's schedule as much as possible.

- Ensure that as few people as possible should be present during the interview.
- Guarantee that interviews or interrogations do not take place until a parent or legal guardian is present.
- Be sure that if the child or the child's parent/legal guardian requests an attorney, the interview or interrogation must stop.
- Conduct the interview or interrogation in a quiet setting where minimal disruptions may occur.
- Keep in mind that children rarely feel free to disclose information when a parent is present
- Minimize the number of interviews or interrogations and remember that child become tired more easily than adults.
- Be extremely careful in how they react to the child's statement. Children are very perceptive and "pick up" on even the most subtle reactions. Children may use this reaction as a reason to stop talking about the very issues that necessitated the interview or, on the other hand, may use the reaction to their own benefit.
- Realize that body language and facial responses must be carefully controlled by the interviewer.
- Conduct the interview in the child's language.
- Remove all weapons prior to the interview or interrogation.
- Documented fully by the interviewer. All notes taken should be as exact as possible using the specific words of the child rather than an interpretation.
- Not stand above the child unless he/she wants to exert authority,
- Established rapport on whatever level is appropriate. The level of rapport will differ from small children to teenagers.
- Ascertain the development level of the child. Children do not mature at the same rate and an understanding of level of the particular child is important and can dictate how the rest of the interview or interrogation should proceed.
- Not initiate physical contact with any child during questioning.
- Encourage clarification. Children will often make vague references to the incident they have witnessed or participated in.
- Not use bribes or enticements, this will jeopardize the case in court.
- Ask specific questions which have been previously tailored to the situation.
- Encourage the child to use pictures to tell what happened if the child is very young
- Not ask leading questions—use open-ended questions.
- Remember that often times the child fears for their safety.
- Consider how any when the child is disciplined by parents or legal guardians.

- Proceed with caution if the child a run-away or a child-of-the-street?
- Use his/her words and demeanor to encourage, not discourage, open communication

In addition to the above guidelines, officers must take into consideration a child's "beliefs". These beliefs may greatly hinder an investigation. Officers should be sensitive to:

- the child's beliefs as to what will happen if they disclose information. Many child may have been threatened,
- the child's past experiences with police,
- the fact that a child may believe the police represent authority. This can produce a positive or a negative reaction.
- the child may view the police as a symbol of protection.

In the final analysis, the skill and tact required by law enforcement officers dealing with children are significantly different than those expected of officers in the investigation adult criminal activity.

SEARCH AND SEIZURE

The Fourth Amendment to the United Stated Constitution states:

The right of the people to be secure in their persons, houses, papers, and effects, against unreasonable searches and seizures, shall not be violated, and no Warrants shall issue, but upon probable cause, supported by Oath or affirmation, and particularly describing the place to be searched, and the persons or things to be seized.

But what is "probable cause." Neither the Constitution for the federal statutory provisions define it. The meaning simply comes down to judicial creation. If an officer believes that the law is being violated on the premises to be searched; and if the facts are set out in an affidavit as factual and practical considerations that any reasonable and prudent person would understand, then a search warrant may be issued. Evidence obtained without a proper search may be ruled inadmissible in court. But what is a search warrant and when they are necessary and when are they not necessary.

SEARCH WARRANTS

A search warrant is simply an order signed by a judge authorizing police officers to search for specific objects or materials at a definite location at a specified time. Police officers obtain warrants by providing a judge with a sworn statement called an Affidavit. The affidavit provides either the officer's own observations, reports from or police information from undercover informants. The information set forth in the affidavit should demonstrate the reliability of the information. (*Illinois v. Gates,* U.S. Sup. Ct. 1983.) If the judge believes that an affidavit establishes "probable cause" to conduct a search, the warrant will be issued. Only then will the information and/or items obtained be admissible in court.

Even though the Fourth Amendment to the U.S. Constitution placed limits on the power of the police to make arrests; search people and their property; and seize objects, documents and contraband , the terrorists attacks on 9-11-2001 changed things.

EFFECT OF THE PATRIOT ACT

On October 26, 2001, President George Bush signed the USA Patriot Act (USAPA) into law. This law gave sweeping new powers, particularly in the areas of online communications and activities, to both domestic law enforcement and international intelligence agencies and have basically eliminated the checks and balances that previously gave courts the opportunity to ensure that these powers were not abused.

While some of the changes will expire on December 31, 2005 unless renewed by Congress, many will not. At the writing of this Chapter, many Civil Rights organizations are challenging the validity of new powers.

PART FOUR

Negotiation

CHAPTER 14

Hostage Negotiations

Unfortunately, greed, misplaced ideals, or simple incompetency can lead to situations where a criminal is placed in the position of taking an innocent party hostage. Negotiation with individuals or groups holding citizens as hostages requires special communication skills. These skills are discussed in this chapter.

INTRODUCTION

Hostage negotiation is one of the most publicized actions of law enforcement agencies, not only in the United States, but throughout the world. It is also one of the most misunderstood actions that peace officers undertake. Hostage negotiation is truly a test of the communication skills of a law enforcement officer.

On February 28, 1993, in Waco, Texas, agents of the Bureau of Alcohol, Tobacco, and Firearms (ATF) attempted to serve a search warrant on David Koresh, leader of the Branch Davidian group, at the group's compound. The raid on the compound involved more than 100 federal agents and was deemed a failure by some: four ATF agents and six Davidians died. For the next 50 days, federal agents attempted to negotiate with Koresh for his surrender. Finally, on April 19, 1993, agents fired tear gas into the compound. Within moments, the building was in flames and more than 70 sect members died inside.

The FBI was involved in a standoff at Ruby Ridge, Idaho, with Randy Weaver, an alleged white separatist. In August 1992, marshals went to Weaver's cabin to arrest him for failing to appear on a gun charge. A gunfight broke out, and Weaver's son and a federal deputy marshal were killed. The next day, Weaver's wife was accidentally shot by a federal agent as she stood unarmed in the cabin's doorway. Weaver subsequently surrendered after an 11-day standoff.

While the Davidian incident and Weaver situation may not have involved hostages in the traditional sense, both of these situations highlight the importance of communication skills during critical incidents. The Good Guys in Sacramento, the *Achille Lauro* hijacking, the bombing of TWA Flight 840, the Rome and Vienna airport attacks, and the Atlanta and Georgia prison sieges by Cuban inmates are examples of well-known hostage situations. Just listing some hostage situations brings memories of terror, death, and, in some situations, failure to save the hostages.

COMMUNICATION IN HOSTAGE SITUATIONS

The FBI classifies hostage situations in four broad categories: (1) the terrorist, (2) the prison situation, (3) the criminal, and (4) the mentally disturbed. However, the techniques utilized in each incident are the same. All officers should have a fundamental understanding of hostage negotiations, since they may find themselves involved sometime in their career and because hostage negotiations are a specialized form of communication. Police administrators must also understand these principles in order to effectively supervise their departments.

Police officers are trained to take charge and control the situation. They are taught that their lives and the lives of others may depend on their ability to manage any situation. However, when those same officers are involved in a hostage negotiation situation, they must understand that their ability to completely control the events in question may be limited. The officer on the scene must attempt to contain the situation until trained negotiators arrive.

An officer's communication skills play a critical part in hostage negotiations. The officer must attempt to get the suspect to talk. The ability to communicate with the suspect is an absolute requirement in a hostage situation.

If hostage negotiators are part of a team, they should train together as often as possible. This allows trust and effectiveness to build within the hostage negotiation team. All training should be evaluated and constant efforts made to improve the performance of each team member.

Training for hostage negotiators should be wide ranging, including briefings from the local telephone company on new designs and features of any communications system, and insights into personality disorders and techniques for communicating with distraught individuals from mental health professionals and members of the clergy. The department's legal advisor or the county prosecutor should discuss the legal aspects of hostage negotiations and update the members on any changes in the law. Hostage negotiators should also train by attending critiques of actual incidents.

Goals in Hostage Situations

The officer must strive for three primary informational goals in setting the stage for a successful negotiation. First, the officer must attempt to obtain specific information about the incident so the department can negotiate with the suspect on a realistic basis. The officer should attempt to determine the motivation and intent of the hostage taker through discussions with the suspect. Is the hostage taker mentally ill and suffering from delusions? Is he wanted by the police and attempting to use the hostages as leverage? Was he caught in the act of committing a crime and holding the hostages as a reaction to the situation? The answer to why the suspect is holding the hostages allows the officer to react according to the suspect's demands. The negotiator should also obtain as much information as possible about the suspect from outside sources. All of this information helps the officer find triggers to the suspect's personality and understand what personal tack to take.

Second, and similar to the first goal, the officer must attempt to gain as much information as possible from the suspect during the negotiations. The officer should not ask closed-ended questions that the hostage taker can answer with a simple yes or no. A question such as "We can't get you a million dollars, will you accept five hundred thousand?" can be answered quickly and in the positive or negative by the suspect. However, a question like "We will try to get the million, but if we can't get all of it, what else do you want?" requires explanation and engages the suspect in a discussion with the officer. In addition, this adds to the suspect's belief of being in control of the situation and able to dictate the terms of the negotiations.

The final goal of any communication effort is for the officer to express interest in what the suspect is saying. While police officers should avoid face-to-face negotiations whenever possible, the situation might arise where the officer is in close contact with the suspect. The officer will want to obtain as much information as possible about the situation if there is a chance to meet with the suspect. However, the officer must also remain attentive. Verbal and nonverbal skills come into play in this situation. By maintaining eye contact with the hostage taker instead of looking around and casing the location, the officer will give the impression of being sincerely interested in what the suspect is saying. By appearing to be interested in the suspect, the officer takes the first step toward establishing a relationship with the defendant.

The relationship between the suspect and the officer who negotiates for the release of the hostages is a delicate one. The officer must appear to be professional and neutral. The suspect will realize that a hostage taker's goals and those of the officer are distinctly different, but may begin to believe that the officer can be trusted if the officer appears willing to enter into a neutral relationship for the purpose of gaining the release of the hostages. The hostage taker understands the objectives of the officer and the mission of the police, and will therefore constantly evaluate the officer's statements and actions during the negotiations. The suspect will not readily believe the officer, but will hesitantly accept the officer's role, because the suspect needs the officer in order to accomplish any goals of this action and reach an acceptable settlement.

A suspect who believes the officer is lying will not proceed with negotiations. The officer should attempt to maintain credibility by agreeing to only those demands that the suspect could reasonably be expected to accept. For example, the officer should not agree to give the suspect the Hope diamond. However, the officer might be able to convince the suspect that several one-carat diamonds could be obtained. Open and credible communication between the officer and the suspect leads to the beginning of a relationship. The officer has taken the first step toward establishing that relationship when he and the suspect can rationally discuss alternatives.

Time is not of the essence in hostage negotiations. Just the reverse—the officer should do everything possible to consume time. From a tactical perspective, the longer the negotiations take, the more likely the suspect is to make an error that will lead to apprehension.

The lapse of time allows the officer to establish a relationship with the hostage taker. One technique is to explain to the suspect that all requests must be cleared by headquarters. This allows for a delay between receiving a request and having to act on it.

Delaying the negotiation will wear down the suspect. The passage of time requires the suspect to continue to watch the hostages, anticipate police responses to demands, and worry about the consequences of these actions. This stress on the hostage taker may allow the officer to negotiate a deal. It should be obvious, however, that this can be a two-edged sword, in that stress may also cause the suspect to act irrationally and harm one of the hostages. The officer must be able to anticipate the suspect's moods and intentions and react accordingly.

In the best of all possible worlds the officer should be able to offer the suspect a deal in which it appears to the hostage taker that both parties win. A win–win solution is very hard to achieve. Hostage negotiation is simply a bargaining process in which each side has a bottom line. Most negotiations center on moving from stated unrealistic demands to finding appropriate points of agreement. The negotiator must attempt to steer the suspect's demands away from absolutes to acceptance of certain realistic demands in exchange for other alternatives. For example, in a situation where a hostage needs medical attention, the negotiator may obtain the release of that hostage in return for a minor concession in another area, such as giving the suspect special food. This bargaining process is part of establishing a relationship between the suspect and the officer.

Many negotiators do not believe offering the suspect access to a radio or television is a wise tactical decision. They like to cut suspects off from the outside world and therefore make them more dependent on the negotiator. Additionally, news media coverage of the situation might impair negotiations.

Normally, the officer is replaced by trained negotiators during the incident. However, the officer must be prepared to carry out all the negotiations if no other trained personnel are available and must be ready to accept the suspect's surrender at any time. If the suspect indicates a desire to surrender, the officer must communicate the procedure in a clear, professional manner that is reassuring to the suspect. If, as part of the surrender, certain concessions or agreements with the suspect were made, the officer should endeavor to abide by them whenever practical. For example, if the officer agreed to allow the suspect to meet with a representative of the media, that agreement should, if possible, be honored. The purpose of honoring such agreements is simple—other potential hostage takers will understand that the police keep their promises in such situations.

Guidelines for Negotiation

- Stablilize and contain the situation.
- Select the right time to make contact.
- Take your time when negotiating.
- Allow the subject to speak; it is more important to be a good listener than a good talker.
- Don't offer the subject anything.
- Be as honest as possible; avoid tricks.
- Never dismiss any request as trivial.
- Never say "no."
- Soften the demands.
- Never set a deadline; try not to accept a deadline. If a deadline is set, let it pass without comment if possible.
- Do not make alternative suggestions.
- Do not introduce outsiders (non–law enforcement) into the negotiation process.
- Do not allow any exchange of hostages; especially do not exchange a negotiator for a hostage.
- Avoid negotiating face to face.

Profile of Hostage Negotiation Teams

In February 1992, hostage negotiators and members of special operations teams gathered to exchange information and experiences. There is little comprehensive data regarding hostage negotiation activities in the United States. Therefore, members attending the February conference agreed to complete a survey to learn more about the needs of hostage negotiation teams.

The survey was a 44-page questionnaire asking specific questions regarding issues that affect negotiation teams. The survey was based on input from FBI hostage negotiators. The survey was reviewed by those negotiators, as well as other experts, to ensure its accuracy.

The survey revealed that very few females served on hostage negotiation teams. The ethnic composition of the teams was primarily white. Most team members were assigned to investigation or patrol, with some in administration. Only 41 percent of those surveyed stated that their department had any written negotiator selection policy. Once selected to serve on a hostage negotiation team, very few of the members received more than 10 days of training. Once a team member, the amount of training did not improve. The majority of team members received less than 5 days of inservice training each year.

This survey points out the importance of effective communication in hostage situations. Many hostage negotiation teams may have very little training in crisis management; therefore, the ability to communicate with the perpetrator becomes critical. Failure to communicate effectively may have deadly results.

The Critical Incident Negotiation Team

In 1985, the Crisis Management Unit at the FBI Academy established the Critical Incident Negotiation Team (CINT). This team is a small, highly trained, and mobile group of experienced FBI negotiators. The FBI negotiates approximately 45 bank robbery and hijacking hostage incidents each year. The original CINT members were selected from more than 350 FBI agents nationwide on the basis of law enforcement background, personal interviews, psychological testing, and negotiation experience. Twenty-five negotiators were selected. The Crisis Management Unit arranged and coordinated semiannual training seminars for team members.

The FBI deploys CINT negotiators both within and outside the boundaries of the United States. Negotiators have been used at Ruby Ridge, Idaho; Waco, Texas; and in other high-profile, emotionally charged situations. Additionally, negotiators have assisted in the release of American hostages held in Ecuador, Chile, El Salvador, and other countries.

CINT negotiators are also engaged in training international police forces. They have met with police forces around the world to provide training in crisis management as it pertains to kidnapping and hostage incidents.

Protracted hostage situations require special skill and training. The FBI Critical Incident Negotiation Team is one federal agency's response to this demand. Training and consultation may prevent the loss of innocent lives in such a situation.

▊ SUMMARY

Hostage negotiation is one of the most difficult situations any officer will have to face. It involves tact, understanding, and patience. More important, it requires all of the officer's communication skills. All police officers should be familiar with the communication skills involved in hostage negotiations. The officer on patrol may have to begin and carry out such negotiations while waiting for specially trained negotiators to arrive at the scene.

▊ REVIEW QUESTIONS

1. What are the personal characteristics of a good negotiator?

2. At what point in a hostage situation should the negotiator call for armed intervention instead of negotiations?

3. How much training should hostage negotiation teams receive?

PART FIVE

Written Communication and
Report Writing

CHAPTER 15

Effective Report Writing

THE PROBLEM AND THE SOLUTION

Many law enforcement professionals regard writing as a necessary evil. It's the "dreaded paperwork" that's best done quickly and gotten over with. As people of action, police don't relish the quiet, slow work that good writing demands. Moreover, written reports, if not precisely done, can jump up and bite their writers when these reports are used by clever attorneys to undermine a painstaking investigation. No wonder that many police officers wish that they could avoid writing altogether.

Yet good writing is in key ways the backbone of law enforcement. Without good reports, there is no case. Without full and accurate records, there is no history, no precedent. Without clear, careful memos, there is no communication within the organization; efficiency erodes and morale crumbles.

Writing, like all other main elements of police work, demands care, precision, and smart work habits. We intend this brief guide to help all law enforcement professionals build writing as a skill that they can use with confidence and no waste of time or effort.

TOP ELEVEN REASONS WHY YOU SHOULD WRITE WELL

1. You are a professional.
2. Professionals are expected to write well.
3. You represent a prominent department.
4. Well-written reports lead to solid convictions of defendants.
5. Well-written reports are used for promotional consideration.
6. Well-written reports help investigations.
7. Well-written reports reflect efficiency and knowledge.
8. You will most likely write each day during your career.
9. Reports are public record.
10. You will gain respect from supervisors, colleagues, and citizens.
11. You owe it to yourself to write well!

RULES OF SPELLING

Since there are many exceptions in English spelling, no one set of spelling rules will cover all cases. When you are in doubt, use a dictionary. However, the following rules will help you in many situations.

ie or *ei*

When the sound is long *ee*, use *i* before *e*, except after *c*. Remember the old folk rhyme that says:

Use *i* before *e*	(e.g., believe, field, piece)
Except after *c*	(e.g., receive, ceiling, deceive)
Or when sounded like *a*	
As in *neighbor* and *weigh*.	(e.g., freight, reign)

LEARNING TIP

There are 10 exceptions to the above rule. It would be helpful for you to memorize them.

Exceptions: either, neither, leisure, seize, weird, foreign, height, counterfeit, forfeit, science

---

Prefixes

A prefix consists of one or more letters added before the root word to make a new word. You do not have to worry about single or double letters; simply write the prefix and add the root word as it is normally spelled.

EXAMPLES:

PREFIX	ROOT WORD	NEW WORD
un	known	unknown
un	necessary	unnecessary
mis	spelled	misspelled

Suffixes

Suffixes are one or more syllables added after the root word. Unfortunately, adding a suffix is not as simple as adding a prefix.

Final Silent *e:* When adding a suffix to the word, you drop the final silent *e* if the suffix begins with a vowel (*a, e, i, o, u*).

EXAMPLES:

ROOT WORD	SUFFIX	NEW WORD
come	ing	coming
imagine	ary	imaginary
berate	ed	berated

When adding a suffix to a word, keep the silent *e* if the suffix begins with a consonant.

EXAMPLES:

ROOT WORD	SUFFIX	NEW WORD
hope	ful	hopeful
late	ly	lately
shame	less	shameless
close	ness	closeness

y to *i*

You change the *y* to *i* when you add a suffix preceded by a consonant. The exceptions are adding *-ing* or *-ist*.

EXAMPLES:

ROOT WORD	SUFFIX	NEW WORD
happy	ness	happiness
party	es	parties
try	ed	tried
study	ing	studying
copy	ist	copyist

When adding a suffix to a word that ends in *y*, keep the *y* if the letter before the *y* is a vowel.

ROOT WORD	SUFFIX	NEW WORD
valley	s	valleys
attorney	s	attorneys
deploy	ed	deployed

Exceptions: Some words ending in *-ay* are exceptions. There isn't any rule to identify them. When in doubt, you should check the dictionary.

EXAMPLES:

lay/laid, pay/paid, say/said, day/daily

Most verbs ending in *-ie* are exceptions to the change *-y* to *-i* rule. In verbs such as lie and die, you change the *-ie* to *-y* before adding *-ing*.

EXAMPLES:

lie/lying, die/dying

Final Consonants: When a word ends in a consonant, sometimes the consonant is doubled and sometimes it is not when you add a suffix.

Double Consonants: When the following conditions are present, you double the final consonant:

You are adding a suffix that begins with a vowel.

EXAMPLES:

-ing, -ed, -er, -est, -ist, -able
run*ning*, skip*ped*

The word to which you are adding the suffix is only one syllable or if it has more than one syllable, the accent is on the final syllable.

EXAMPLES:

be*gin*, oc*cur*, com*pel*
begin*ning*, occur*ring*, compel*ling*

The word's last two letters must be one vowel and one consonant.

EXAMPLES:

commit + ed = committed, stop + ing = stopping

When adding -*ly* to a word ending in -*l,* keep the final -*l.*

EXAMPLES:

careful + ly = carefully, brutal + ly = brutally

When adding -*ness* to a root word ending in -*n,* keep the final -*n.*

EXAMPLES:

open + ness = openness, green + ness = greenness

Not Double Consonants: When the following conditions are present, you do not double the final consonant:

When the word ends in two or more consonants.

EXAMPLES:

jump + ed = jumped, find + ing = finding

When two or more vowels precede the final consonant.

EXAMPLES:

contain + ing = containing, appear + ed = appeared

When the word ends in a single accented vowel and a consonant and the suffix begins with a consonant.

EXAMPLES:

regret + ful = regretful, equip + ment = equipment

If the accent is not on the last syllable of the root word.

EXAMPLES:

quarrel + ing = quarreling, bigot + ed = bigoted

Plurals

You make singular nouns plural using several different spelling guidelines.

Adding -s: You add -*s* to make most nouns plural.

EXAMPLES:

books, automobiles, guns, suspects

Adding -es: You add -*es* to nouns ending in *s, ch, sh, x,* or *z.*

Joneses, boxes, flashes, churches, inches, buzzes

Words ending in o: When words end in the letter *o,* use *-s* if a vowel comes before the final *-o.* If a consonant comes before the final *o,* use *-es.*

EXAMPLES:

radios, scenarios, studios
heroes, potatoes, vetoes

LEARNING TIP

There are four exceptions: memos, pros, pianos, solos.

Words Ending in f or fe: For some words ending in *f* or *fe,* you change the *f* to *v* and add *-s* or *-es.* Some words don't change the *f* to *v;* just add *-s.*

EXAMPLES:

knife/knives, wife/wives, chief/chiefs, staff/staffs

Irregular Plurals: Some nouns have irregular plurals.

EXAMPLES:

foot/feet, child/children, man/men, woman/women

Unchanged Nouns: Some nouns do not change when you form the plural.

EXAMPLES:

sheep, moose, series, species

Compound Words: You make the last part of the compound word plural when the word is not hyphenated or written as two separate words. When they are written as two separate words or hyphenated, you make the most important part of the word plural.

EXAMPLES:

briefcases, mailboxes, brothers-in-law, bus stops

LEARNING TIP

Simple plural forms *never* have an apostrophe (') before the *-s* ending.

Examples:

Two boys left.   (correct)
Two boy's left.   (incorrect)

Seed Words

Words ending with the *seed* sound are usually spelled *-cede*.

EXAMPLES:

concede, intercede, precede, accede

There are only four exceptions: supersede, exceed, proceed, and succeed.

Words Commonly Misspelled in Police Reports

abduction
accelerated
accessories
accident
accommodate
achievement
acquire
acquitted
affidavit
altercation
among
apparatus
apparent
arguing
argument
arson
assault
belief
believe
beneficial
benefitted
bureau
burglary
category
coercion
coming
commission
comparative
complainant
conscious
conspiracy
controversial
controversy
conviction
corpse
counterfeit
criminal
defendant
define

definitely
definition
describe
description
disastrous
dispatched
disposition
drunkenness
effect
embarrass
embezzlement
emergency
environment
exaggerate
existence
existent
experience
explanation
evidence
extortion
fascinate
forcible
fraudulent
height
homicide
indict
interest
interrogate
intimidation
intoxication
investigation
its (it's)
juvenile
larceny
led
legal
lieutenant
lose
losing

marriage
marshal
mere
necessary
occasion
occurred
occurrence
occurring
offense
official
opinion
opportunity
paid
particular
patrolling
pedestrian
penalize
performance
personal
personnel
possession
possible
practical
precede
precinct
prejudice
premises
prepare
prevalent
principal
principle
privilege
probably
procedure
proceed
profession
professor
prominent
prosecute
prostitution
pursue
pursuit
quiet
receive
receiving
recommend
referring
repetition
resistance
rhythm

robbery
sabotage
scene
seize
sense
sentence
separate
separation
sergeant
serious
sheriff
shining
similar
statute
strangulation
studying
subpoena
succeed
succession
suicide
summons
surprise
surrender
surveillance
suspect
suspicion
techniques
testimony
than
their
then
there
they're
thieves
thorough
to/too/two
traffic
transferred
trespassing
truancy
unnecessary
vagrancy
victim
villain
warrant
woman
write
writing
written

Homonyms

Homonyms are words that sound alike, but have different meanings and are spelled differently. You should learn the difference and use the correctly spelled word.

beat/beet
boar/bore
board/bored
bread/bred
break/brake
bridal/bridle
buy/by/bye
capital/capitol
ceiling/sealing
cent/sent/scent
cereal/serial
cite/sight/site
chord/cord
corps/corpse
council/counsel/consul
current/currant
dear/deer
hole/whole
idle/idol
its/it's
knew/new
knot/not
know/no
lain/lane
lessen/lesson
liable/libel
lie/lye
loan/lone
made/maid
maybe/may be
meat/meet
medal/meddle
muscle/mussel
naval/navel
oar/or/ore
ordinance/ordnance
pail/pale
pain/pane
pair/pare/pear
pause/paws
peace/piece
peal/peel
pedal/peddle
peer/pier
plain/plane

pray/prey
presence/presents
pride/pried
principal/principle
rain/reign/rein
raise/rays/raze
rap/wrap
real/reel
right/rite/write
road/rode/rowed
role/roll
sail/sale
scene/seen
seam/seem
sense/cents
serf/surf
shear/sheer
shone/shown
soar/sore
sole/soul
stairs/stares
stake/steak
stationary/stationery
steal/steel
straight/strait
tail/tale
taught/taut
team/teem
tear/tier
their/there/they're
throne/thrown
through/threw
tied/tide
to/too/two
toe/tow
vain/vane/vein
vale/veil
vial/vile
wail/whale
waist/waste
wait/weight
waived/waved
way/weigh
weak/week
wear/where

Abbreviations

Three Rules for Abbreviations

1. Spell out all titles except Mr., Mrs., Mmes., Dr., and St. (saint, not street).
2. Spell out street, Road, Park, Company, and similar words used as part of a proper name or title.
3. Spell out Christian names (William, not Wm.).

Standard Abbreviations   You should exercise caution when using abbreviations. While they may shorten reports, using incorrect or unfamiliar abbreviations can lead to misunderstandings. When in doubt, spell it out.

Dates, Time, and Measurement

Jan.	Apr.	Jly.	Oct.
Feb.	May	Aug.	Nov.
March	June	Sept.	Dec.

Mon.	Thurs.	Sun.
Tues.	Fri.	
Wed.	Sat.	

1st	6th
2nd	7th
3rd	8th
4th	9th
5th	10th

yr.	year	wk.	week
yrs.	years	wks.	weeks
mo.	month	hr.	hour
mos.	months	hrs.	hours

min.	minute	in.	inch
mins.	minutes	ft.	feet/foot
sec.	second	yd.	yard
secs.	seconds	mi.	mile
		g.	gram
		kg.	kilogram
		km.	kilometer
		lb.	pound
		lbs.	pounds
		oz.	ounce
		meas.	measurement
		doz.	dozen
		l.	length
		wt.	weight
		hgt.	height
		w.	width

Common Abbreviations

administration	admin.
all points bulletin	APB
also known as	AKA
amount	amt.
approximate	approx.
assistant	asst.
assist outside agency	AOA
attempt	att.
Attempt to locate	ATL
attorney	atty.
be on the lookout	BOLO
birthplace	BPL
building	bldg.
burglary	burg.
captain	capt.
caucasian	cauc.
central	cen.
chief of police	COP.
Colonel	Col.
Company	Co.
convertible	cvt.
court	ct.
date of birth	DOB
dcad on arrival	DOA
defendant	def.
degree	deg.
department	dept.
Department of Motor Vehicles	DMV
detective	det.
description	descp.
director	dir.
district	dist.
division	div.

driver's license	DL
Doctor	Dr.
doing business as	DBA
driving under the influence	DUI
driving while intoxicated	DWI
eastbound	E/B
enclosure	encl.
example	ex.
executive	exec.
federal	fed.
general broadcast	GB
government	govt.
headquarters	hdq.
highway	hwy.
hospital	hosp.
identification	ID
informant	inf.
inspector	insp.
junction	junc.
junior	jr.
juvenile	juv.
last known address	LKA
left	L
left front	LF
left hand	LH
left rear	LR
license	lic.
Lieutenant	Lt.
Lieutenant Colonel	Lt. Col.
location of birth	LOB
Major	Maj.
manager	mgr.
maximum	max.
medium	med.
memorandum	memo
middle initial	MI
misdemeanor	misd.
modus operandi	MO
National Auto Theft Bureau	NATB
National Crime Information Center	NCIC
no further description	NFD
no middle name	NMN
northbound	N/B
not applicable	NA
number	no.
numbers	nos.
officer/official	ofc.
Ohio driver's license (NMDL, FDL, etc.)	ODL
opposite	opp.
organization	org.
package	pkg.

page	p.
pages	pp.
passenger	pass.
permanent/personal identification number	PIN
pieces	pcs.
pint	pt.
place	Pl.
place/point of entry	POE
point of impact	POI
police officer/probation officer	PO
quantity	qty.
quart	qt.
received	recd.
required/requisition	req.
right	R
right front	RF
right rear/rural route/railroad	RR
road	Rd.
school	sch.
section	sect.
Sergeant	Sgt.
serial	ser.
southbound	S/B
subject	subj.
Superintendent	Supt.
surface	sur.
symbol	sym.
tablespoon	tbsp.
technical	tech.
teletype	TT
transportation	tran.
treasurer	Treas.
University	Univ.
unknown	unk.
vehicle identification number	VIN
veterinarian/veteran	vet.
village	vil.
volume	vol.
weapon	wpn.
wholesale	whsle.

TIPS

The following seven tips should help you improve your spelling.

Speller's Journal: When you get a report back with misspelled words, write those words (correctly spelled) in the back of your notebook. We use the same words over and over, and soon you will correctly spell those words.

Dictionary: When in doubt, always use a dictionary to verify spelling and meaning.

Speller/Divider: Speller/dividers are pocket-sized books that list the words correctly spelled. They don't have any definitions. Most officers know what a word means, but may not know how to spell it.

Thesaurus: A thesaurus is a book of synonyms, words with similar meanings. Use by police officers improves spelling and makes reports more interesting. It also helps you find a word with the exact meaning you need.

Misspeller's Dictionary: If you have trouble finding correctly spelled words in a dictionary, try a *Misspeller's Dictionary.* The words are listed incorrectly spelled, followed by the correct spelling, for example, *newmonia/ pneumonia.*

Electronic Spellers: Hand-held, battery-powered electronic spellers are available. The more sophisticated models include a dictionary and thesaurus. They will correctly spell a word, but may not differentiate between homonyms.

Proofreading: Proofread your own work or have someone read it for you. Proofreading will greatly reduce spelling errors.

TEN EASY WAYS TO IMPROVE YOUR SPELLING

Good Point 1.   Refer to the list of commonly misspelled words in the workbook.

Good Point 2.   Refer to a dictionary.

Good Point 3.   Use an electric spelling device.

Good Point 4.   Learn one new spelling rule each week.

Good Point 5.   Practice spelling words commonly used in the profession.

Good Point 6.   Substitute an easy word for a difficult word.
(I spell concurrence: A-G-R-E-E)

Good Point 7.   Look for hints in the word.
(The word *tomorrow* is the spelling of three words: tom/or/row.)

Good Point 8.   Help your colleagues improve their spelling by posting a weekly list of misspelled words that appeared on reports or memos. (That will get their attention!)

Good Point 9.   Spell words that are giving you difficulty into a tape recorder. Each evening, listen actively to the tape.

Good Point 10.   Maintain a positive attitude and practice, practice, practice!

▌ CHAPTER REVIEW

You have learned that accurate spelling is essential in police report writing. You learned some of the rules of spelling to help you correctly spell common words that may cause you trouble. You also learned the importance of correctly using homonyms and abbreviations.

▌ DISCUSSION QUESTIONS

1. What is a homonym?
2. How can homonyms cause trouble in your reports?
3. What are some of the resources you can use to check your spelling?

▌ EXERCISES

Add the suffixes -*ed* and -*ing* to the following words:

raid _____
prevent _____
describe _____
rob _____
try _____
identify _____
study _____
die _____
allege _____
hope _____

Add -*able* to the following words:

rely _____
note _____
remark _____
work _____
excite _____

Write the plural form of the following:

officer _____
witness _____
child _____
man _____
attorney _____
knife _____
party _____

box   _____

radio   _____

shelf   _____

Circle the correctly spelled words from the choices you are given:

accellerated	excelerated	accelerated
all right	allright	alright
burglary	burglery	berglary
dialated	dilated	diliated
homocide	homicide	homacide
lisence	license	licence
preceeded	preceded	precceeded
sargent	sergent	sergeant
secratery	secretary	secretery
warrent	warrant	warent

Circle the correct homonym.

1. If the suspect walks down that (aisle, isle, I'll), I'll meet her at the front of the theater.

2. Reporters should not be (allowed, aloud) to leak information before a trial.

3. Smith refused to pay the (fair, fare) because she said the amount wasn't (fair, fare).

4. Officers found the jewel-encrusted (idle, idol) in the suspect's closet.

5. The (knew, new) recruit said he (knew, new) some of the local ordinances.

6. The witness was very (pail, pale).

7. He (passed, past, pasted) the detour because he drove right (passed, past, pasted) it.

8. This time, the detective obtained the (right, writ, write) (right, writ, write) so the judge didn't have to (right, writ, write) another.

9. The defense attorneys were unable to save (their, there, they're) client because (their, there, they're) wasn't evidence to refute the charges.

10. She said the (vial, vile) man had thrown the (vial, vile) of acid at her.

CHAPTER 16

Police Reports

USES AND PURPOSES OF REPORTS

Police reports are written at the scene of many events and, as a result, are used for a wide variety of reasons. You should remember that every report you write might be the one that "goes around the world" and is read by everyone.

Criminal Investigations

When you write a report documenting a criminal act, that report becomes the basis for coordination of the complete investigation and prosecution of the crime. It is also used to gain information for statistical reporting and crime analysis. Whether the investigation is conducted by patrol officers, general investigators, or a specialty unit of investigators, the original crime report is the source document. Initial crime reports are also used to compare past and current crimes to determine *modus operandi* and identify suspects.

Newspapers and the Media

Crime reports, and in some cases all reports, are available to the press and media. In most states, some parts of the crime reports may be deleted, for example, names of juvenile suspects and victims and the victims of certain crimes. However, in general, the press has the right of access to reports. The result is they read exactly what you have written, including misspellings and grammatical errors.

Reference Material

Because reports are permanent documents, they provide an excellent source of historical information. They may be used to document the agency's actions, refresh your memory, or determine liability.

Statistical Data for Crime Analysis

The rapid development of computer technology, including expert systems and automated pin maps, has resulted in improved crime analysis. The source document for that information remains the crime report you write in the field. Your reports are used to identify trends, locations, and methods of operations. The result of that analysis may be directed patrol.

Documentation

Reports are used to document the action of the department and its officers. Because police departments are typically reactive, reports document what actions were taken to stop the criminal activity or arrest the suspect. They provide evidence of the department's responsiveness to the community and its needs.

Officer Evaluation

It is common for supervisors to use reports to evaluate an officer's performance. An experienced supervisor can determine your ability to organize information, level of education, technical knowledge, intelligence, and pride in the job. A report discloses an officer's weaknesses, weaknesses the officer may not even realize he or she has.

Statistical Reporting

Crime reports are the source document for the collection of statistical data. Agencies report crime statistics to various state and federal agencies. Statistical reports may also be generated for budget purposes, city council briefings, and other special-interest groups.

Report Writing Audience

Your reports must be self-explanatory because numerous people make decisions based on the information in your reports. Depending on the nature of the event, any or all of the following may read your report:

Police departments: Supervisors and administrators of both your department and those cooperating in investigations

Attorneys: Prosecution, defense, civil, and judges—all attorneys who may read your reports

Jurors: In both criminal and civil trials

Administrators: From your department and jurisdiction, as well as from city, county, and state jurisdictions

Medical professionals: Doctors, psychiatrists, and psychologists

Corrections: County jail and state and federal prison staff, including probation officers and parole agents

Insurance companies: The parties involved in claims

Media: Newspapers, radio, and television

Regulatory agencies: Motor vehicle departments, insurance commissioners, alcohol beverage control, consumer affairs

If any part of your report requires further explanation, you have failed to accomplish your objectives. When you have to write a supplemental report to explain your original report, you create an air of skepticism. Your credibility may become questionable in the eyes of the court. You must not evade the necessity of well-written reports. It is important that you understand the merits of effective report writing and recognize the significance of reports in the total criminal justice system.

CHAPTER 17

Basic Reports

As indicated in other chapters, administrators utilize law enforcement reports when making decisions regarding departmental policies and missions. Individual police reports form the basis for decisions by policy makers. At the other end of the spectrum is the use of reports by officers when testifying in court. However, while court testimony is critical in convicting the offender, it is only one aspect of report writing. Law enforcement reports are used by individual officers in a number of ways: they are the principal source of information in conducting investigations, they provide the basis for transferring cases from one officer to another without loss of valuable information, and they are an accurate reflection of the individual officer's training, skill, and capabilities.

Reports are important at all levels in law enforcement. There are many different types of reports. Each has a designated purpose. These various reports mandate different responses and efforts by the police officer who is writing them. In addition, each law enforcement agency has its own particular rules and regulations regarding the writing of reports. This profusion of different rules, jurisdictions, and reports makes it difficult to set forth requirements that apply to each and every department and report. However, certain basic principles do apply to all law enforcement reports. In police report writing, there are two important types of reports. The next section discusses these two classifications of police records.

Common Errors in Report Writing

Listed below are the most common errors in report writing. Note that most of them are the result of oversights caused by simple carelessness.

1. Failure to provide sources of information.
2. Failure to report significant details.
3. Failure to write neatly and clearly.
4. The use of poor English.
5. Failure to maintain objectivity.

TYPES OF REPORTS

There are as many methods of classifying police records as there are law enforcement agencies. This is because there is no one single rigid system of reports that will work for every police department. However, general guidelines exist that can assist a police supervisor who is assigned the responsibility of administrating or establishing a records division.

While all police records are aimed at accomplishing the department's mission of protecting the public and preserving the peace, some records fall into the realm of general support: those records that assist in the administration of the department. Other records are operational—that is, they are directly connected to the apprehension and conviction of persons who commit crimes. This is therefore a commonsense and logical separation to make when examining police records.

Initial Police Reports

Often law enforcement agencies will require the use of special forms for initial police reports. While the reports vary among agencies, there are common practices to note. Normally, when the police receive a call for assistance or discover a crime, they are aware of the general nature of the misconduct. Accordingly, depending on the nature of the incident or crime, one of the following standard forms is used in reporting the incident:

- Case report
- Traffic citation
- Animal control violation
- Stolen vehicle report
- Arrest report
- Juvenile arrest report
- Stolen bicycle report
- Hit-and-run report
- Vehicle accident report
- Minor property damage accident report
- Petition for emergency commitment

The *case report,* or *crime report,* is used to provide a written record of crimes reported to the police, including details of the crime and the police action. The case report is generally used unless one of the previously listed special reports can be used. In some cases, both a case report and a special report are required.

In completing the case report, the preliminary investigator must determine if an offense has actually been committed by determining and documenting the elements of a crime. Often, reference to particular criminal codes is used to accurately describe the offense committed.

Case reports are generally coded in a manner that will alert the supervisor who reviews the reports as to the seriousness of the case.

Since the investigator on the scene generally has no information regarding the background of the suspects, standard case reports have a section to be completed by the department's records section after a records check has been made.

Operational Reports

Operational reports are directly connected with the apprehension and conviction of persons who commit crimes. The term *conviction* is included since part of the criminal justice system involves the officer testifying in court before a judge or jury. In almost all instances, the officer will rely on the written report prepared at the time of the incident. The officer may not have had anything to do with the arrest of the defendant, but testimony concerning the scene of the crime as recorded in the officer's report may be an essential part of the prosecutor's case and a necessary ingredient in the conviction of the defendant.

There are two distinct types of operational reports: the offense report and the follow-up or supplemental report. The *offense report* is the original record detailing facts surrounding the commission of a crime. The *follow-up* or *supplemental report* sets forth information concerning any subsequent investigation and the results of that investigation.

The preceding section briefly introduced the two primary types of operational reports utilized by a majority of law enforcement agencies. In addition, there are specialized operational reports that do not fit within this classification but should be considered as follow-up or supplementary reports. These reports concern the recording of such criminal activities as narcotics, intelligence, and, in some instances, sex cases. For the most part, offense reports do not initiate the investigation in these cases. Many of these types of crimes are handled by trained specialists who are involved in the case from the beginning to the trial of the offender.

Most of this text focuses on the operational aspects of policing and report writing. However, the cop on the street is unable to operate absent a formalized organizational structure. This structure, the police department, utilizes administrative reports to function.

Administrative Reports

Administrative reports are just as important as operational reports. Without administrative reports the department would grind to a halt and no law enforcement activities could be carried out.

Administrative reports can be subdivided into two areas: those that provide information concerning the agency's mission of protecting the public and those that set forth internal rules for the operation of the agency. The former documents are usually reports to top-level management; the latter documents involve procedures, orders, memorandums, or manuals that set forth departmental policy.

Following is a brief examination of administrative reports that establish internal rules within a department:

Standard Operating Procedures (SOPs) These administrative records are directives that establish a uniform procedure for the operation of the department in a certain area or situation. They are normally established for an indefinite period of time and may be revised or updated depending on changed circumstances. Some departments have no SOPs, while others may have 100 or more. For example, the Los Angeles Police Department has over 100 SOPs. Standard operating procedures concern such operational matters as use of force, when an officer is authorized to go to Code 3 response (lights and siren), and other similar issues.

Temporary Operating Procedures (TOPs) These administrative records set forth short-term directives for the operation of the department. They differ from SOPs in that they have a specific starting and ending date. TOPs might be used to instruct departmental personnel on how to respond to an unusual event, such as the visit of an international dignitary or the arrival in the department's jurisdiction of a large outlaw motorcycle club. Unlike SOPs, temporary operating procedures have a definite termination date.

General Orders (GOs)   These administrative records are utilized to pass information to lower level personnel within the department, rather than to set forth operational instructions. Additionally, general orders have traditionally been utilized to define or redefine the duties and responsibilities of officers. For instance, a GO might be issued that revises existing departmental policy and requires patrol officers to conduct a limited amount of the initial investigation of a crime before the case is referred to detectives. The basic distinction between GOs and SOPs is that SOPs are concerned with specific operational situations; GOs may affect the operations of a department, but they do so in an indirect manner. General orders may be utilized to pass information regarding court legal rulings or information received from another agency which requires coordination between that entity and the police department. This information then causes the officers to react differently in the field.

Special Orders (SOs)   These orders are specific and temporary in nature. SOs are similar to general orders in that they are used to pass information rather than to dictate direct operational policy. They might be used to inform all personnel of transfers, promotions, or upcoming promotion examination dates.

Memos (memorandums)   Memos are utilized to pass instructions or information from one party in the department to another. They may be of limited duration and are routinely utilized as a method of ensuring that all personnel understand the item being discussed. They are more effective than oral communications, especially when there are multiple districts and overlapping shifts. If the memo becomes a procedure it should be reformatted into a SOP or GO, depending on its content.

Duty Manual   This administrative record is known by many names: procedures manual, department rules manual, operations manual, and so forth. This document has been defined as follows:

   Duty manual: Describes procedures and defines the duties of officers assigned to specific posts or positions. . . . Duty manuals and changes in them should be made effective by general order; the changes should be incorporated into the first revision of the duty manual.

   All standard operating procedures and general orders should be included in the duty manual. In addition to containing a table of organization, duty manuals normally contain a job description for each departmental position. This establishes the duties and responsibilities of all members of the department. For example, the duty manual lists the responsibilities of a lieutenant assigned to patrol. The manual also lists the responsibilities of a lieutenant assigned to narcotics. As one can well imagine, the duties of these two lieutenants are substantially different.

   The other form of administrative report provides information to high-level management regarding the operation of the department. The following three reports fall within this classification: (1) daily reports, (2) monthly reports, and (3) annual reports.

Daily Report   This administrative record is utilized to present an up-to-date report of the major crimes reported in the last 24 hours. This report usually includes statistics showing the number of major crimes committed during the month to date, the number of major crimes committed during the year to date, and the number of major crimes committed in the last year up to the date of the report.

Daily reports also include information regarding the number of arrests for the same time periods. This report is an extremely effective tool for informing the chief of police and the department's upper management of the extent of criminal activity within their jurisdictions. The daily report serves as the basis for compiling the monthly and annual reports.

Monthly Report   This report is a key management tool. While the daily report serves to keep the police administrator informed of the extent of criminal activity, the monthly report allows administrators to determine trends in both departmental functions and criminal behavior. For example, the monthly report may indicate a sudden rise in burglaries. This could alert the department to the need to adjust patrol boundaries within a district or might cause the burglary division to start inquiries on the street as to whether a new gang is operating in the area. The information contained in the monthly report forms the basis for the annual report.

Annual Report   This report presents information concerning the operation of the department for the preceding year. It is considered an indispensable management tool in the profession.

The preceding section described various types of police records which are found in most law enforcement agencies. The following sections examine the types of information that may be contained in these reports.

REQUIRED INFORMATION

As indicated previously, different reports are utilized for different purposes. However, all initial reports should contain certain building blocks of information. This information forms the basis for any arrest, follow-up investigation, and presentation of the case to the district attorney. This information can be classified under six separate headings: (1) *who*, (2) *what*, (3) *when*, (4) *where*, (5) *how*, and (6) *why*.

Who

Who is much broader than *who committed the crime*. This is an all-inclusive category that requires special attention by the responding officer. The question *who* is not answered by simply listing the name of the person suspected of committing the crime.

Who requires the officer to identify certain persons involved in the offense. *Who is the victim?* Many times, officers respond to a call and talk to a witness to a potential crime, but discover that finding the victim may be time consuming and, in some situations, futile.

Who is the offender? Is the person known to the victim, witness, or other persons? Can the officer obtain a name, description, or other information that may identify the offender?

Who are potential witnesses? Will they volunteer information, or are they afraid of retaliation by the offender? They should be identified by name, address, employment, and other information that will assist other officers if a follow-up or a second interview of the witnesses is required.

The officer must also ensure that law enforcement personnel who responded to the scene of the crime are identified. *Who was the first officer on the scene? Who conducted the investigation? Was any evidence collected and who was it turned over to?* All officers involved in the investigation must be identified and their roles explained.

Answering the question of *who* involves identifying the complaining party, victim, suspect, witnesses, and any involved law enforcement personnel. This identification should include residence and home addresses, telephone numbers, physical descriptions, and occupations where appropriate.

What

What is a broad question that covers a number of areas. The officer must ensure that all of these aspects are answered in any report. Many times citizens will call and report what they believe to be a certain type of crime. For example, a citizen may call and report being robbed. The officer who responds and interviews the victim may discover that the citizen has been the victim of a burglary instead of a robbery. Therefore, the type of offense reported and the offense actually committed may be different. Injuries, damage, or other physical aspects of the crime or the crime scene observed by the officer must be included in any report.

The officer must determine what evidence is available and what evidence was not obtained. The evidence may be oral, visual, or physical in nature. *What was done with any evidence?* Is there a chain of custody? Has it been properly marked, tagged, stored, and disposed of according to departmental policy and regulations?

The officer must also review what, if any, further police actions are required. *What agencies responded to the call? What agency assumed jurisdiction for the crime? What section or officers will conduct any necessary follow-up investigation?*

What type of offense was committed? Was it a crime against a person or property? An accident, natural disaster, or intentional act?

When

The question of *when* is more than the date, day, and time of the offense. The officer must examine this question from the perspectives of the offense, the citizens involved in the offense, and the law enforcement agency responding to the call for assistance. Each of these areas should be reviewed and basic information documented regarding when they became involved.

When was the offense committed or discovered? When was it reported? Was there a significant delay between discovery and reporting? If so, the officer needs to inquire into the reasons for this delay.

What persons were observed at the scene of the crime is a critical piece of information. What time did they arrive, how long did they stay, and when did they leave are questions and answers that should be sought by the officer. Was the victim at the scene or did he arrive at that location at a certain time? Did any witnesses have an opportunity to view the scene of the crime before the officers arrived? If so, what was the time and how long did they view the scene? Did they observe the incident? If so, for how long and from what location?

When did law enforcement officers arrive at the scene of the crime? How much time had passed since the commission of the crime, the report of the crime, and the arrival of the police? *When did the officer contact the victim, witnesses, or other parties and take their statements?* Recording this information may be critical if the victim or witness later changes the story. The fact that the officer obtained a statement within minutes, hours, or days immediately after the incident when the crime was fresh in their minds may become important in court if the witness or victim testifies differently during trial.

Where

This area of inquiry must cover the offense, persons involved in the incident, and police agencies. The officer must answer questions regarding the location of all these variables in the police report.

The most obvious question to be asked is *where was the offense committed?* The officer should not automatically assume that the location of the property or body is where the offense occurred. Where the offense was discovered may be different from where it took place. Where any crime occurred, was discovered, and where it was reported may be three distinct locations. The officer should ensure that any report clearly indicates the location and type of activity involved: *where the crime occurred, where it was discovered,* and *where it was reported.*

The location should be described by street address, intersection, or exact location in any building. What is the difference between a living room and a family room? The officer should ensure that the location is clear and understandable by any person who reads the report.

The officer should ensure that all available information is obtained regarding persons involved in the incident. The locations of the victim, witnesses, and suspect are critical to any investigation. Where they reside, their work addresses, all phone numbers, and other information necessary to contact them should be gathered and recorded by the officer. In addition, the location of all the parties at the time of the crime is important. Exactly where they were located may have a significant impact on their testimony. For example, a witness who was located across the street may not have been able to observe the color of the suspect's eyes.

The locations and activities of the police should be carefully recorded. Where they interviewed victims, witnesses, and suspects is important. Where they arrested the suspect may become critical. If it was inside a residence, did they have a warrant? Where evidence was observed, marked, and stored is important to follow-up investigators. Simply listing where the crime occurred is only the beginning of answering this query.

How

How the offense was committed is important for modus operandi files. What tools were used and how they were used are often critical pieces of evidence that may tie the offense into other similar crimes. *How was the offense discovered? How was it reported?*

How various persons were involved in the crime is often overlooked by inexperienced officers. *How was the victim transported to the hospital? How did the suspect arrive and depart the scene of the crime? How did witnesses happen to be at the location of incident?*

How police agencies responded at the scene of the crime is also important. *How did the officer identify the victim, suspect, and witnesses? How did they locate these individuals?*

Why

Motive, or *why a person commits a crime,* is not traditionally one of the elements of any offense. However, prosecutors and jurors want to know why the crime was committed; therefore, officers should attempt to answer this question if possible. *Why was the offense reported?* Was it for insurance purposes, to seek revenge, or other reasons? *Why did the suspect commit the crime in that manner?* Was there an easier method to accomplish the crime, and why didn't the suspect use it? *Why did witnesses come forward?* Is there any bias, prejudice, or motive to their cooperation?

As the preceding discussion indicates, there are several different ways of asking the same question. If the officer approaches report writing in this method, it will ensure that there is no gap or missing piece of information in the report. Simply put, gathering information is only the first step in writing a complete report. Once the information is obtained, the officer must organize it. The organization and structure of police reports is the subject of the next section.

ORGANIZATION OF REPORTS

All departments or agencies have standard forms that assist the officer in organizing and writing reports. Many of these reports have boxes or spaces for specific information regarding the crime and further information gathered by the officer. This format is to ensure consistency and completeness in law enforcement reports. However, after the first page of these reports is filled in, the officer is expected to write a summary or detailed account of the crime. This requires that the answers gathered during the initial investigation be organized and set forth in a clear and readable fashion.

Drafting the Report

The officer must learn to quickly and accurately place the information obtained at the crime scene into a readable document. This report should flow logically and be a complete record of the officer's involvement. To accomplish this the officer should utilize four principles in drafting any report: (1) start at the beginning, (2) write in chronological order, (3) place details in supplemental reports, and (4) write in the past tense. By using these principles, the officer will avoid leaving out valuable information and ensure that any person reading the report will understand what occurred.

The officer should begin any summary or narrative with his or her initial involvement: "Responded to a call for assistance," and so forth. This sets the stage for the reader to follow the officer's actions from the beginning to the end of the report. It also establishes when the officer became involved in the incident.

The officer should then proceed to write the report in chronological order. Starting at the beginning, the officer can proceed to the present time or the end of the report. This principle gives an easy order to the material and also ensures that the officer does not forget some item of information that might be left out if the report jumped from the beginning to the end and back to the middle of the officer's involvement.

General Rules on Report Writing

1. Law enforcement reports are generally written about past events. Accordingly, under most circumstances they should be written in the past tense. Rather than write that the car is black, state that the car was black. (It may have been repainted since that time.)

2. Be specific in quantifying an individual's behavior in your reports. While the subject may be "aggressive" or "combative," those words have different meanings to different people. For example, reporting that the subject "took a boxer's stance, tightened his lips across his teeth, was breathing rapidly, and brought up clenched fists" is a better description of the subject's conduct than the comment that the subject was "combative."

3. The officer writing the report should write in the first person. Report writing should be similar to speaking. When speaking to a colleague, you would not say "this officer." The third-person "fly on the wall" report is more cumbersome to write and not as easy to grasp for officers being trained in how to write reports.

4. When you are writing reports that contain statements of others (witnesses, suspects, or other officers) use the third person to refer to the others. "Officer Smith stated that the weapon belonged to him."

5. Use complete sentences in your report. All sentences should have subjects and verbs and convey complete thoughts. Do not write in sentence fragments. Sentence fragments are groups of words that begin with capital letters and end with periods but are not complete sentences.

6. If the subject is singular, the verb in that sentence should also be singular. If the subject is plural, the verb must also be pural.

7. Collective nouns are always singular, therefore their verbs should also be singular.

8. Indefinite pronouns are always singular

9. Use adjectives to alter, give additional meaning to, or modify nouns and pronouns. Use adverbs to alter, give additional meaning to, or modify verbs, adjectives, and other adverbs.

10. Most words ending in -ly are adverbs. Not, never, and very are adverbs.

11. When deciding whether to use an adjective or an adverb, find the word being modified. If the word is a noun or pronoun, use an adjective. If the word is an adjective or adverb, use an adverb.

12. Do not use run-on sentences. Run-on sentences are sentences that contain two or more sentences in one long sentence.

13. Eliminate comma splices. Comma splices occur when two complete sentences are joined with commas without connecting words such as *and* or *but*.

14. Use correct punctuation in your reports. Poorly punctuated reports can be confusing and misleading.

15. Use apostrophes to show possession. Possessive pronouns (e.g., *his, hers, ours, yours, theirs,* and *its*) do not need apostrophes.

16. Many people do not understand the rules for using brackets. Accordingly, as a general rule do not use them in law enforcement reports.

17. Use quotation marks in reports only to enclose exactly what a person said.

18. Do not use abbreviations in reports that can be confusing to people who are unfamiliar with the subject matter. When in doubt, spell it out.

19. Poor spelling creates doubt about the report. One method of eliminating misspelling is through your choice of words.

20. If any force is used, the report should contain all the specifics of how and why the officer used force.

21. If handcuffs are used, the officer should report that fact. For example, one career law enforcement officer recommends the use of language similar to the following:

> Mr. Jones submitted to my handcuffing him. He was handcuffed with his hands behind his back with his palms facing outward. I then checked the handcuffs to see that the handcuffs were on properly and double-locked the handcuffs and checked that they were double-locked. I asked Mr. Jones how the handcuffs felt and he did not reply to my question. I placed the tip of my right little finger between each of Mr. Jones's wrists and the handcuffs were on properly (Edward Nowicki, "Report Writing: Keep Excessive Force Litigation at Bay," *Police* (Nov., 1999): 48).

The officer should cover only the main points in the initial report. Other details should be placed in supplemental or follow-up reports. This allows the reader to gain a quick understanding of the incident without getting bogged down in details. In addition, the officer is able to concentrate on explaining exactly what happened without weaving numerous details into the report. Details are important and may be critical in solving the case or convicting the offender. However, they belong in supplemental reports rather than the initial crime report.

The officer should write the report in the past tense since it has already occurred. This also assists the officer in maintaining the chronological order of events.

Format

As indicated previously, most law enforcement agencies have standard forms that the officer will use in drafting reports. Filling in these forms is relatively simple. Unfortunately, there is not an accepted form for all reports in the United States. However, the different forms used by various agencies normally include the following sections.

Front Sheet   This is a preprinted form with short empty spaces, boxes that are checked, and space for short names, addresses, and other information. This portion of the report is relatively easy to fill out, since it requires the officer to fill in the blanks and limits the choice to a few common selections.

The front sheet is used by the records section to maintain statistical information about the type and number of crimes within the jurisdiction. It also provides any reader with a quick summary of the parties, the nature of the crime, and other pertinent information.

Narrative Section   This is a blank portion of the report that is used by the officer to flesh out the front sheet information. It provides a chronological history of the officer's involvement.

The officer should follow the principles set forth previously in drafting the report in this section. It must be clear, concise, and understandable. This section does not include every conceivable detail about the crime. Within the narrative section, the officer will refer to other portions of the report or separate supplemental reports for more detail or information.

Conclusions and Recommendations   This is the section that allows the officer to express opinions and/or recommend a course of action. At this point the officer may state, "Recommend case be referred to the D.A. for filing of P.C. 459 [burglary]." This is the officer's opinion or conclusion that a crime has been committed and that further action is necessary.

In addition to the three basic portions of any police report, there are three other sections that many departments include in initial reports. These are separate sections that detail witnesses' statements, property involved, and evidence collected by the officer or other officers.

Witness Statements   This section sets forth any witness statements. Whenever possible, the officer should use direct quotes and not substitute words for those of the witness. The officer must ensure that facts are separated from opinions in this section. The witness may state, "I heard two loud sounds." The officer should record that statement and not substitute "I heard two gunshots." If the witness states, "I heard two shots," the officer should follow up with questions as to why the witness knew or recognized the sounds as gunfire. This adds to the witness's creditability and saves everyone embarrassment later.

Property   This supplement is used to describe any property that was stolen or damaged. The property should be listed separately and described in detail. For example, if the property stolen was a man's watch, *one man's watch* does not fully identify the property. A more complete description would be: *One man's yellow gold watch, Balwin, Model No. 334, Serial No. 55555.*

The nature and extent of any injury to the property should be explained in detail. If photographs were taken, refer to them and where they are located; for example, *photographs attached* or *photographs taken and maintained by crime lab personnel, contact Technician Smith.*

Evidence   This section refers to any evidence obtained during the investigation. It should be itemized, identified, and its locations listed. If possible,

INITIAL CRIME REPORT

HARRISBURG POLICE BUREAU

☐ CRIMES AGAINST PERSONS   ☐ CRIMES AGAINST PROPERTY

1. UCR NO.	2. SECTION NO.	3. NAME OF CRIME	4. DATE OF INCIDENT	5. TIME INCIDENT OCC.	6. INCIDENT NO.
			MO. DATE YEAR DAY		

7. REPORT GRID	8. WEATHER	9. STATUS	10. EXACT LOCATION	11. DATE OF REPORT	12. TIME OF REPORT	13. DA NO.
	☐ RAIN ☐ SNOW ☐ CLEAR ☐ CLOUDY ☐ OTHER TEMP_____	☐ EXCEPTIONAL CLEARANCE ☐ CLEARED ☐ OPEN UNFOUNDED MO. DATE YEAR	☐ INSIDE ☐ OUTSIDE			Badge No.

14. REPORTED BY

15. NAME	16. RESIDENCE ADDRESS	17. CITY	18. STATE
☐ MR. ☐ MRS. ☐ MISS.	19. TELEPHONE	20. R/S/A	21. DATE/TIME DISCOVERED	22. CODE
23. BUSINESS ADDRESS	24. CITY	25. STATE	26. TELEPHONE	27. OCCUPATION

28. COMPLAINT

29. NAME	30. RESIDENCE ADDRESS	31. CITY	32. STATE
☐ MR. ☐ MRS. ☐ MISS.	33. TELEPHONE	34. R/S/A	35. CODE	35A. WORK HOURS
36. BUSINESS ADDRESS	37. CITY	38. STATE	39. TELEPHONE	40. OCCUPATION

41. COMPLAINT

42. NAME	43. RESIDENCE ADDRESS	44. CITY	45. STATE
☐ MR. ☐ MRS. ☐ MISS.	46. TELEPHONE	47. R/S/A	48. CODE	48A. WORK HOURS
49. BUSINESS ADDRESS	50. CITY	51. STATE	52. TELEPHONE	53. OCCUPATION

54. VICTIM NO. I

55. NAME	56. RESIDENCE ADDRESS	57. CITY	58. STATE
☐ MR. ☐ MRS. ☐ MISS.	59. TELEPHONE	60. R/S/A	61. CODE	62. WORK HOURS
63. BUSINESS ADDRESS	64. CITY	65. STATE	66. TELEPHONE	67. OCCUPATION

68. NO. OF OFFENDERS COMPLETE SUSPECTS PORTION	69. HOW & WHERE ENTERED	70. HOW AND WHERE EXIT MADE	71. FORCE USED	72. TYPE OF WEAPON/FORCE	73. CRIME SCENE SEARCHED
			☐ YES ☐ NO		☐ YES ☐ NO

74. PRINTS TAKEN	75. PHOTOGRAPHS TAKEN	76. TYPE OF PREMISES	77. PREMISES PROTECTED BY ALARM
☐ YES ☐ NO BY:	☐ YES ☐ NO BY:	☐ HOME ☐ OFFICE ☐ APT. ☐ OTHER	☐ YES ☐ NO

78. TYPE OF INJURY (DESCRIBE IN NARRATIVE)	79. CONDITION OF VICTIM	80. NEXT OF KIN NOTIFIED	81. CORONER NOTIFIED	82. DA. NOTIFIED	83. HOSPITAL AND/OR DOCTOR TAKEN TO
	☐ GOOD ☐ FAIR ☐ POOR ☐ DECEASED	☐ YES ☐ NO	☐ YES ☐ NO	☐ YES ☐ NO	

WAS THERE A WITNESS TO CRIME? [ ]

84. WITNESS

86. NAME	87. RESIDENCE ADDRESS	88. CITY	89. STATE
☐ MR. ☐ MRS. ☐ MISS.	90. TELEPHONE	91. R/S/A	92. CODE	
93. BUSINESS ADDRESS	94. CITY	95. STATE	96. TELEPHONE	97. OCCUPATION

98. WITNESS

99. NAME	100. RESIDENCE ADDRESS	101. CITY	102. STATE
☐ MR. ☐ MRS. ☐ MISS.	103. TELEPHONE	104. R/S/A	105. CODE	
106. BUSINESS ADDRESS	107. CITY	108. STATE	109. TELEPHONE	110. OCCUPATION

CODES:
1. ARRESTED
2. INCARCERATED
3. OUT ON BAIL
4. INTERVIEWED
5. NOT AVAILABLE FOR INTERVIEW

6. DOES NOT WISH TO BE INTERVIEWED OR INVOLVED
7. WILLING TO PROSECUTE
8. NOT WILLING TO PROSECUTE
9. RECOMMENDED TO BE SUPONEAD FOR COURT
10. SOBER (5)

11. HAD BEEN DRINKING (HBD)
12. INTOXICATED (I)
13. ON CONTROLLED SUBSTANCE (OCS)
14. ACCUSED BEING SOUGHT
15. CAN MAKE POSITIVE IDENTIFICATION OF ACCUSED OR SUSPECT
16. MENTALLY DISTURBED

POLICE 22/FORM1

---

photographs or photocopies of any physical evidence should be attached to the report.

All of this information is critical, to allow other officers to continue any follow-up investigation. It provides a standard format and flow of information that is easy to understand and ensures that vital information is not omitted. The next section examines the content of any law enforcement report.

INCIDENT NO.		EXISTENCE OF A SIGNIFICANT MO IDENTIFICATION OF SUSPECT				
☐ SUSPECT ☐ ACCUSED						

110. NAME ☐ MR. ☐ MRS. ☐ MISS	111. ADDRESS	112. R/S/A	113. HT.	114. WT.	115. CODE
116. OTHER CHARACTERISTICS					

A. SUSPECT NAME OR GOOD DESCRIPTION   B. KNOWLEDGE OF SUSPECT LOCATION   A. ☐   B. ☐

☐ SUSPECT   ☐ ACCUSED

118. NAME ☐ ☐ ☐	119. ADDRESS	120. R/S/A	121. HT.	122. WT.	123. CODE
124. OTHER CHARACTERISTICS					

PRESENCE OF A DESCRIPTION WHICH IDENTIFIES THE VEHICLE USED BY THE SUSPECT

125. VEHICLE	126. NAME	127. TYPE	128. COLOR	129. YEAR OF VEHICLE	130. REGISTRATION NO. & STATE
	131. OTHER CHARACTERISTICS		132. OWNER		
133. OWNER ADDRESS			134. TOWED TO		
135. TOWED BY			136. VEHICLE INVENTORIED ☐ YES ☐ NO	136A PROPERTY RECORD SHEET COMPLETED ☐ YES ☐ NO	137. DATE

A LIMITED OPPORTUNITY TO COMMIT THE CRIME
A LIMITED NUMBER OF PERSONS AS POSSIBLE SUSPECTS
BELIEF THAT A CRIME CAN BE SOLVED WITH REASONABLE INVESTIGATIVE EFFORT
BELIEF THAT A CRIME CAN BE SOLVED WITH PUBLICITY
PRESENCE OF SIGNIFICANT PHYSICAL EVIDENCE
PROPERTY WITH IDENTIFIABLE CHARACTERISTICS, MARKS OR NUMBERS WHICH CAN BE TRACED
POSITIVE RESULTS FROM A CRIME SCENE EVIDENCE SEARCH

NARRATIVE: DESCRIBE IN FURTHER DETAIL ANY CONTENTS PLACED IN BLOCKS, SUCH AS WEAPONS USED, HOW THEY WERE USED, ETC. DESCRIBE MEANS OF ATTACK, DIRECTION IN WHICH SUSPECT(S) FLED, FURTHER TRADEMARKS OF OTHER DISTINGUISHING POINTS OF SUSPECT. GIVE STATEMENTS OF VICTIMS, WITNESSES, SUSPECTS, AND THEIR LOCATION AT THE TIME OF THE CRIME. EXPLAIN FACTS OF ARREST--SUMMARIZE CHRONOLOGICAL DETAILS OF OFFENSE, OBSERVATIONS MADE AT THE SCENE, ETC. GIVE ITEMS RECOVERED IN GENERAL TERMS AND PLACED ON PROPERTY RECORD. (USE ADDITIONAL SHEETS OF 8 1/2 X 11 PAPER IF NECESSARY).

138. CASE CLOSED ☐ YES ☐ NO	139. ARREST(S) MADE ☐ YES ☐ NO	139A. WITNESS SHEET ATTACHED ☐ YES ☐ NO	139B. PROBABLE CAUSE AFFIDAVIT ATTACHED ☐ YES ☐ NO	140. FURTHER ARREST(S) TO BE MADE ☐ YES ☐ NO	141. CONTINUATION REPORT ATTACHED ☐ YES ☐ NO	142. RECOMMEND DET ASSIGN ☐ YES ☐ NO
143. RECOMMEND YOUTH AID ASSIGN ☐ YES ☐ NO	144. RECOMMEND COM. RELA. ASSIGN ☐ YES ☐ NO	145. RECOMMEND SERVICES DIVISION ASIGN ☐ YES ☐ NO	146. RECOMMEND PAT ASSIGN ☐ YES ☐ NO	147. FOLLOW UP NECCESSARY ☐ YES ☐ NO	148. SERVICE BY SUMMONS REQUIRED ☐ YES ☐ NO	149. COMPLAINT (TYPING NEEDED) ☐ YES ☐ NO
150. TYPING BY COMPLETED ☐ YES ☐ NO	151. STATEMENT. CONFESSION ATTACH ☐ YES ☐ NO	152 CRIME PREVENTION INFO REQUESTED ☐ YES ☐ NO	152A VICTIMS/WITNESS HANDBOOK DISTRIBUTED ☐ YES ☐ NO	153 SECURITY SURVEY REQUESTED ☐ YES ☐ NO	OFFICER'S FULL NAME	BADGE NO.
SUPERVISOR'S FULL NAME			BADGE NO.	DATE		

☐ I FULLY AGREE WITH THE CONTENTS OF THIS REPORT
☐ I DO NOT AGREE WITH THE CONTENTS OF THIS REPORT

POLICE22/FORM

ENTERED BY

![] **CONTENT**

This section does not discuss how to write the numerous reports required of law enforcement officers; rather, it explains how that information should be set forth. As indicated in previous chapters, police reports serve a variety of purposes. To meet these various objectives, they are read, reviewed, and acted on by different individuals and agencies. It is therefore necessary that any police report contain all the necessary information. Police reports must be *accurate, complete,* and *fair.* The following sections will discuss each of these concepts.

Accuracy

Accuracy in a police report requires that it be written in an objective manner. The officer must verify information contained in the report. An item as simple as the date versus the day can be critical in a police report.

Accurate reports must be clear and understandable. Spelling, grammar, and sentence structure add to the accuracy of any report. Use of correct grammar ensures that the reader understands what the officer is attempting to communicate. The difference between *there* and *their* may not seem like a major mistake to a civilian, but it can make a difference in a police report.

Accuracy also implies that the report is turned in to the department in a timely manner. Adding information to the initial report after it has been filed is unacceptable. If additional information is discovered after the initial report has been completed, the officer should submit a supplemental report and explain why the information was not included in the initial report.

Completeness

All police reports should be complete. The reader should be able to pick up any initial report and answer all the questions listed previously. While the report must be complete, the officer must not be so detail oriented as to confuse the reader. Therefore, completeness includes the principle of *conciseness.*

The officer must learn when to leave information in the main body of the report and when to place it in a supplemental report. The report cannot be so brief and full of references that the reader must constantly flip back and forth between different attachments. Additionally, the report should not be so lengthy and full of details that the reader must wade through the unimportant to find the useful information.

Fairness

It is difficult, but the officer must constantly keep in mind the obligations to be fair to everyone involved in the criminal justice system. This includes the suspect. The officer is not an advocate for one side or another. As Joe Friday of *Dragnet* fame used to say, "Just the facts" really applies to report writing.

Fairness in a police report requires combining accuracy and completeness to ensure that all relevant information is reported. The officer's credibility and reputation will outlive any single report; therefore, their integrity should never be compromised on any case.

The report should clearly distinguish between facts, inferences, opinions, and judgments. *Facts* are those items that can be independently verified. Facts are information the officer has obtained or observed. *Inferences* are suppositions of what "probably" occurred. These are statements the officer makes which are drawn from facts. Personal *opinions* of the officer are personal beliefs and should never be placed in a report. However, the officer may place the personal opinions of witnesses or victims in the report so long as they are clearly indicated to be opinions and not facts. The officer's personal approval or disapproval of certain acts are considered *judgments* and do not belong in police reports.

SUMMARY

Every agency has its own special rules for writing reports. However, many agencies incorporate certain basic principles or require the same or similar information in their reports. Every law enforcement officer must understand how to approach the report-writing task. Like many other personal skills, effective report writing is achieved only with practice and a conscious effort to improve.

All reports should contain the basic information necessary for supervisors to make informed decisions. This information includes *who, what, when, where, how,* and *why.* This information is necessary for a variety of reasons, including modus operandi, follow-up investigation, and departmental use.

Officers must ensure that all reports are *accurate, complete,* and *fair.* As will be discussed in other chapters, the credibility of the officer may depend on his or her ability to write an intelligent report. Report writing is probably one of the least favorite and most avoided activities in a police agency. However, the benefit of a well-written police report may be the conviction of a violent criminal.

REVIEW QUESTIONS

1. What is the most important fact in any report—*who, what, when, where, how,* or *why?* Justify your answer.
2. If why a person commits a crime is not part of the elements of the crime, why should police officers be required to spend their time attempting to answer this question?
3. Which of the four principles of drafting is the most important? Why? If you had to eliminate one of these principles, which one would you choose? Why?
4. Explain why departments have separate reports for different aspects of a crime, such as a separate sheet for witness statements.
5. The section dealing with content lists three basic areas that all police report writers should ensure are present—*accuracy, completeness,* and *fairness.* Which is the most important and why?

Law Enforcement Records

Any decision made in a law enforcement agency is, or should be, based on the evaluation of all available information. Information or data is located in several places: an individual's memory, written works, or electronic storage. The law enforcement agency's records division is the primary location for all related information on which police officers base their operational and administrative decisions. All authorities in the field of police report writing agree that an efficient and effective records section is an essential part of the planning and execution of operations.

Law enforcement records systems vary from city to city and serve different purposes depending on the level or responsibility of the agency. Records for a local police department will be different from those maintained by a federal agency. However, certain basic principles should remain the same no matter where the agency is located or at what level it operates.

CRIMINAL JUSTICE RECORDS SYSTEMS

Any records system should incorporate certain standard criteria into its operation. Scholars and authorities in the field recommend the following two standards as a minimum:

1. Consolidation of all records into one division. This allows for centralization of authority and responsibility within the department. One administrator should be responsible for this division.
2. Standardization of all records and reporting systems within an agency. This provides for ease of administration and ensures the proper reporting of all necessary information.

Adoption of these standards will ensure that a records system is operational. Additionally, any valid police records system should allow the police administrator to carry out certain tasks. The following 14 functions are critical objectives of any records system:

1. Ascertain the nature and extent of crime within the jurisdiction of the agency.
2. Update the staffing level of the department.
3. Provide a means to control the reporting and investigation of crimes.
4. Arrest offenders by analysis of their modus operandi.
5. Report and analyze traffic accidents with the objective of working with other city departments to correct dangerous intersections or roads.
6. Follow up on arrests and the disposition of cases.
7. Predict trends in crime to maximize the use of law enforcement personnel by properly deploying them to the areas of greatest need.
8. Detect unusual trends within the department and the community.
9. Assist in the assignment and promotion of personnel.
10. Provide information for use in criminal investigations.
11. Ascertain the level and maintenance of police equipment.
12. Predict future trends in criminal activity.

13. Prepare the department's annual budget.
14. Provide information to citizens and elected officials regarding matters of concern.

Police records systems must ensure that any communication is clearly understandable. Most operational and administrative communication takes the final form of written documents. Written documents are preferable to oral statements because there is less chance for misunderstanding in a properly drafted document. Additionally, written reports, orders, or policies allow members of the police force to refer to the document if there is any question concerning its application, effect, or content. Written documents may take many forms.

Some law enforcement agencies combine oral statements with written reports. Patrol officers in the St. Louis County Police Department telephone headquarters and orally report to a trained specialist. The information is entered on a preformatted computer system that electronically processes the report.

However, the mere collection of data or information without subsequent action does not assist a department in carrying out its mission. The following section examines how certain types of police records are processed.

PROCESSING OF REPORTS

Processing police reports in a timely and accurate manner is one of the most important functions of the records division. This section gives a brief overview of using computers to process certain types of reports.

A police department, by its very nature, generates a large number of reports. These reports are normally stored in the records division. Without an efficient system of storage, retrieval, and analysis, any law enforcement agency can be overwhelmed by a sea of paper.

Computers and Arrest Records

If paperwork can be seen as the mother's milk of bureaucracies, the Garden City, New York, Police Department is in the process of weaning itself, using a computer software program to reduce the time and tedium involved in arrest-related paperwork.

The JetForm software used by the department to process arrest paperwork is one of the agency's latest applications of computer technology, reports the April edition of *PC Publishing* magazine, and has cut from 4 hours to 40 minutes the time spent processing the myriad of forms that arrests generate.

Officer Al Perez, who has been in charge of the department's computerization effort since 1987, pointed out that JetForm can be used for a variety of tasks, including designing new forms when needed.

"We are doing most of our arrest forms, pedigree information sheets, vehicle accident reports, court information manuscripts, and the like in the program," said Perez. The JetForm program is compatible with the agency's PC-clone microcomputers, as well as the on-line printers in use by the agency, added Perez.

HARRISBURG POLICE BUREAU
FIELD TRAINING AND EVALUATION PROGRAM

DAILY OBSERVATION REPORT

Recruits Last Name, First Initial	Badge No.	F.T.O. Last Name, First Initial	Badge No.	Date MM/DD/YY

Assignment or Reason for no Evaluation:_____

RATING INSTRUCTIONS: Use below scale to rate trainee. Comment on any category you wish. However, **SPECIFIC** comments **MUST** be made on the reverse side if a rating of 1,2,6, or 7 is indicated **OR** if "Failure to respond to training" is indicated. During Phase IV comments **MUST** be made on all ratings except a 4.

Rating Scale-------------Not Acceptable   Acceptable   Exceptional
(circle most appropriate)   1 2 3   4   5 6 7

	Rating	None Observed	Remedial Training (Time)	Responding To Training
APPEARANCE				
1. General Appearance	1 2 3 4 5 6 7	☐		YES☐ NO☐
ATTITUDE				
2. Toward Police Work and Criticism	1 2 3 4 5 6 7	☐		YES☐ NO☐
KNOWLEDGE				
3. Knowledge of Bureau Policies and Procedures	1 2 3 4 5 6 7	☐		YES☐ NO☐
4. Knowledge of Rules of Criminal Procedure	1 2 3 4 5 6 7	☐		YES☐ NO☐
5. Knowledge of Crimes Code (Title 18)	1 2 3 4 5 6 7	☐		YES☐ NO☐
6. Knowledge of Vehicle Code (Title 75)	1 2 3 4 5 6 7	☐		YES☐ NO☐
7. Knowledge of City Ordinances	1 2 3 4 5 6 7	☐		YES☐ NO☐
PERFORMANCE				
8. Driving Skill: Normal, Moderate, High Stress Conditions	1 2 3 4 5 6 7	☐		YES☐ NO☐
9. Knowledge of City Geography / Response Time to Calls	1 2 3 4 5 6 7	☐		YES☐ NO☐
10. Report Writing: Accuracy, Timeliness, Grammar, Spelling, etc.	1 2 3 4 5 6 7	☐		YES☐ NO☐
11. Field Performance: Stress / Non-Stress Situations	1 2 3 4 5 6 7	☐		YES☐ NO☐
12. Investigative Skills: Interview and Interrogation	1 2 3 4 5 6 7	☐		YES☐ NO☐
13. Self Initiated Field Activity	1 2 3 4 5 6 7	☐		YES☐ NO☐
14 Officer Safety: General, Susp. Person, Voice and Physical Skills	1 2 3 4 5 6 7	☐		YES☐ NO☐
15. Problem Solving and Decision Making	1 2 3 4 5 6 7	☐		YES☐ NO☐
16. Radio: Listens-Comprehends and Articulates Transmissions	1 2 3 4 5 6 7	☐		YES☐ NO☐
RELATIONSHIPS				
17. With Citizens in General and other Ethnic Groups	1 2 3 4 5 6 7	☐		YES☐ NO☐

TRAINEE'S NAME (PRINT)	Badge No.		Date MM/DD/YY

Acknowledgement of review of this evaluation report

Harrisburg Police Bureau Daily Observation Report. An example of a small agency's reporting form. *(Courtesy of Chief Richard Shaffer, Harrisburg, Pennsylvania Bureau of Police.)*

VANCOUVER POLICE DEPARTMENT
INVESTIGATION REPORT

BULLETIN   CRIME INFO [ ]   FILE [ ]

FILE NO. [ ]
INCIDENT NO. [ ]

PAGE _____ OF _____

SECTION 1 — OCCURRENCE INFORMATION

1. LOCATION		TEAM AREA	2. DATE OF OCCURRENCE	TIME
			FROM:	
3. OFFENCE / OCCURRENCE		VPD CODE	TO	
		UCR CODE	4. DATE INVESTIGATED	

PERSONS CODE   V - VICTIM   R - REPORTEE   P - PARENT / GUARDIAN   W - WITNESS   CIRCLE APPLICABLE CODE

#1

5. NAME (SNME, G1, G2 OR BUSINESS NAME)				LANGUAGE ASSISTANCE	STATEMENT YES ☐ NO ☐	VWSU CARD

	RACE	SEX	D.O.B.	AGE	HEIGHT	WEIGHT	HAIR	EYE	UTI. ALCH. ☐ DRUG ☐	TOURIST
V										
R	RES. ADDRESS (NO. DIR. NAME, TYPE, APT/STE, CITY)				POSTAL CODE	RES. PHONE		I.D. TYPE-NUMBER		
P										
W	BUS. ADDRESS					BUS. PHONE		OCCUPATION		WORK HOURS

#2

6. NAME (SNME, G1, G2 OR BUSINESS NAME)				LANGUAGE ASSISTANCE	STATEMENT YES ☐ NO ☐	VWSU CARD

	RACE	SEX	D.O.B.	AGE	HEIGHT	WEIGHT	HAIR	EYE	UTI. ALCH. ☐ DRUG ☐	TOURIST
V										
R	RES. ADDRESS (NO. DIR. NAME, TYPE, APT/STE, CITY)				POSTAL CODE	RES. PHONE		I.D. TYPE-NUMBER		
P										
W	BUS. ADDRESS					BUS. PHONE		OCCUPATION		WORK HOURS

#3

7. NAME (SNME, G1, G2 OR BUSINESS NAME)				LANGUAGE ASSISTANCE	STATEMENT YES ☐ NO ☐	VWSU CARD

	RACE	SEX	D.O.B.	AGE	HEIGHT	WEIGHT	HAIR	EYE	UTI. ALCH. ☐ DRUG ☐	TOURIST
V										
R	RES. ADDRESS (NO. DIR. NAME, TYPE, APT/STE, CITY)				POSTAL CODE	RES. PHONE		I.D. TYPE-NUMBER		
P										
W	BUS. ADDRESS					BUS. PHONE		OCCUPATION		WORK HOURS

#4

8. NAME (SNME, G1, G2 OR BUSINESS NAME)				LANGUAGE ASSISTANCE	STATEMENT YES ☐ NO ☐	VWSU CARD

	RACE	SEX	D.O.B.	AGE	HEIGHT	WEIGHT	HAIR	EYE	UTI. ALCH. ☐ DRUG ☐	TOURIST
V										
R	RES. ADDRESS (NO. DIR. NAME, TYPE, APT/STE, CITY)				POSTAL CODE	RES. PHONE		I.D. TYPE-NUMBER		
P										
W	BUS. ADDRESS					BUS. PHONE		OCCUPATION		WORK HOURS

INJURED PERSON   ENTER APPLICABLE PERSONS CODE AND NUMBER

CODE	9. TAKEN TO	10. TRANSPORTED BY	11. DESCRIBE INJURIES	12. REFUSED TREATMENT YES ☐ NO ☐
#	13. TIME OF DEATH	14. PRONOUNCED BY	15. IDENTIFIED BY	
16. NEXT OF KIN		17. ADDRESS	18. RELATION	19. PHONE	20. NOTIFIED YES ☐ NO ☐

NOTE: FOR ADDITIONAL PERSONS USE ADDITIONAL PERSONS PAGE

SECTION 2 — SOLVABILITY FACTORS   PLACE (X) IF ANSWER IS YES

1. ( ) WAS A SUSPECT(S) ARRESTED?
   IF '1' IS YES AND NO OTHER SUSPECT(S) GO TO '6'
2. ( ) IS THERE A POSSIBLE SUSPECT(S)?
3. ( ) CAN A SUSPECT(S) BE NAMED?
4. ( ) CAN A SUSPECT(S) BE LOCATED?
5. ( ) CAN A SUSPECT(S) BE DESCRIBED?
6. ( ) IS THERE A WITNESS TO THE CRIME?
7. ( ) CAN THE SUSPECT(S) BE IDENTIFIED?
8. ( ) IS THERE A SUSPECT VEHICLE LICENSE NO?

9. ( ) IS THERE A SUSPECT VEHICLE DESCRIPTION?
10. ( ) IS THE STOLEN PROPERTY IDENTIFIABLE?
11. ( ) IS THERE A SIGNIFICANT M.O.?
12. ( ) IS THERE SIGNIFICANT PHYSICAL EVIDENCE?
13. ( ) HAS EVIDENCE BEEN SENT TO / OBTAINED BY IDENT?
14. ( ) HAS EVIDENCE BEEN SENT TO / OBTAINED BY CRIME LAB?
15. ( ) ARE THERE OTHER FACTORS THAT NECESSITATE A FOLLOW-UP INVESTIGATION?
16. ( ) IS THERE A SIGNIFICANT REASON TO BELIEVE THAT THE CRIME WILL BE SOLVED?

SECTION 3 — REPORTING OFFICER

1. NAME	2. RANK PIN	TEAM/SQ	3. ACCOMPANIED BY	4. RANK PIN
				DATE

SECTION 4 — FOLLOW UP INVESTIGATION

1. CASE ASSIGNED TO	2. CASE ASSIGNED BY	3. DATE ASSIGNED	4. B.F. DATE

COPIES TO	2	3	4	5	6	7	8	9

QUALITY CONTROL   DATA ENTRY   CASE REPORTS   RECORDS

Vancouver Police Department Investigation Report. An example of a Canadian reporting form. *(Courtesy of Chief Constable W. T. Marshall.)*

ARIZONA DEPARTMENT OF PUBLIC SAFETY
CRIMINAL SUPPLEMENT TO TRAFFIC
ACCIDENT INVESTIGATION

1. DR. NO.

2. DATE & TIME OCCURRED	3. LOCATION OF OCCURRENCE	4. TYPE OF OFFENSE/INCIDENT	5. COUNTY

6. DUI ☐   HIT & RUN ☐   AGGRAVATED ASSAULT ☐   ENDANGERMENT ☐   HOMICIDE ☐   **7. B A**

SUSPECT

8. NAME		9. ADDRESS						
10. BUSINESS ADDRESS		11. OCCUPATION	12. SEX	13. RACE	14. WGT.	15. HGT.	16. EYES	17. HAIR
18. SOCIAL SECURITY NUMBER	19. DRIVERS LICENSE NUMBER	20. PLACE OF BIRTH				21. DATE OF BIRTH		
22. HOME PHONE	23. BUSINESS PHONE	24. ALIAS, MARKS SCARS, TATOOS, ETC.						
25. LOCATION OF ARREST		26. DATE AND TIME OF ARREST		27. LOC. BOOKED OR REF.		28. CITATION NO.(S)		

VEHICLE

29. SUSPECT	30. COLOR	31. YEAR	32. MAKE	33. BODY STY.	34. LIC. NO.	35. STATE	36. OTHER ID.	37. VEHICLE DISPOSITION
38. VICTIM	39. COLOR	40. YEAR	41. MAKE	42. BODY STY.	43. LIC. NO.	44. STATE	45. OTHER DI.	46. VEHICLE DISPOSITION

VICTIM

47. NAME		48. ADDRESS						
49. BUSINESS ADDRESS		50. OCCUPATION	51. SEX	52. RACE	53. WGT.	54. HGT.	55. EYES	56. HAIR
57. SOCIAL SECURITY NUMBER	58. DRIVERS LICENSE NUMBER	59. PLACE OF BIRTH				60. DATE OF BIRTH		
61. OTHER				62. HOME PHONE		63. BUSINESS PHONE		

64. LIST ALL OTHER SUSPECTS/WITNESSES/INVESTIGATIVE LEADS/EVIDENCE

65.	66. OFFICER(S)		I.D.	DISTRICT	67. REVIEWED BY:
☐ PENDING					
☐ CLOSED BY ARREST					68. DATE & TIME TYPED
☐ CLOSED, OTHER					69. CLERK NO.

DISTRIBUTION: WHITE: DEPT. RECORDS;   YELLOW: PROSECUTOR;   PINK: WORK COPY   802-04059 10/91

Arizona Department of Public Safety Traffic Accident Report. An example of a large agency's reporting form. *(Courtesy of Director F. J. "Rick" Ayars and Officer F. A. Stewart.)*

But the JetForm program is used most to process arrests, which require filling out local, state, and federal forms with pertinent data. Much of the data is redundant, but JetForm saves time by inserting repetitious items in the appropriate spaces of all of the various forms.

"Using the program greatly reduced the amount of time required to process an arrest. That's a welcome benefit," Perez said, noting that it saves overtime costs and hastens the return of the officers to patrol duties.

JetForm has features that allow the transfer and capture of information from one field to another—a capability that Perez said is "very handy."

"Scanning a form, tracing it out and using it as a template has worked out well, too," he added.

Perez said the 44-officer department will soon have its computer capabilities linked into a local-area network, and there are plans to acquire mobile data terminals, or laptops, for police cruisers. The terminals will be connected to a radio frequency and the local-area network at headquarters.

"Officers in the vehicles will be able to transmit information back to the department instantly, and that should boost the speed at which forms are processed," Perez explained.

The department's computerization program has streamlined the way paperwork is processed, Perez noted. "We produce anywhere from 6 to 100 forms daily. I could not imagine going back and doing things the old way."

The preceding article indicates how computerization of certain records can save the department an immense amount of time.

Some departments began to utilize computers in certain sections of their records divisions in the early 1970s. Even if those areas were modernized within the last 10 years, their status should be reviewed with technical experts to ensure that recent advances have not made them obsolete.

There are several areas of internal administration within a police department that can be computer enhanced with very little effort or expense.

Training Records   Individual officer training records are maintained by the department. These records may be entered into a computer and updated with very little effort. Many states require periodic training for all officers or advanced training for officers when a certain number of years has elapsed after their initial training. Computerized training records offer the department the ability to track the level and amount of training administered to each officer.

Personnel   Personnel records, like training records, require a large amount of time to maintain and update. By placing these records in a computer, the department can quickly update and cross-reference them to other files, such as training records.

Scheduling of Personnel   This used to be a cumbersome task that had to be redone every time a change was made. Computers allow a department to insert personnel changes and modify scheduled hours with a minimum of effort. Numerous factors that go into scheduling a 24-hour-a-day patrol can be entered into a computer to assist in determining the schedule.

Community Relations This area is gaining more importance in police work. A computer may assist the department by updating speaking schedules and maintaining lists of community associations and citizens who work with the department in solving community issues.

Vehicle Maintenance The ability to track maintenance schedules and repair costs is becoming more and more important in this era of tightening municipal and federal budgets. Tracking routine vehicle maintenance schedules and identifying the cost of upkeep is simplified with readily available software. Computerized systems allow immediate costing out of vehicle maintenance.

Purchasing The ability to keep track of items purchased by the department is closely related to the next area—budgeting. Purchasing and inventory control of such items as agency-supplied uniforms, paper, pencils, and so forth is a task requiring attention to detail and subject to multiple mistakes in accounting. Computers provide a method to update constantly changing inventories and cross-check figures.

Budgeting This is becoming a most critical area for every law enforcement agency. The need to project expenses (and in some cases revenues) accurately is an ideal requirement for software spreadsheet programs. Even if the department relies on the city finance or treasury department for final figures, many administrators feel the need to have their own in-house method. A typical spreadsheet program will cost $100 to $500 and is well worth the investment.

Payroll Closely related to budgeting is preparation of the departmental payroll. In many departments, this service is carried out by a centralized office outside the agency. Typically, the finance or treasury department will prepare payrolls. Similar to the use and preparation of budgets, some departments may desire to track payroll records to include sick time used, vacation taken, and other information that typically appears only on paystubs but which may be of interest to administrators.

A computerized records system standing by itself does not automatically ensure a more efficient records division. Computers will not think for humans. They process information that has been placed in the software program. Therefore, it is absolutely necessary that an effective records processing system be utilized in addition to putting information into computers. There are many variations concerning records processing within a police department. No matter what form or name they take, these records processing systems should include the ability to cross-reference all criminal activities. Cross-referencing or indexing criminal records requires that certain key information be indexed with other information so that anyone searching the database will be supplied with all other pertinent facts.

All crime indexing should include the following information:

1. The full name of the victim or complaining party.
2. The full name of the person arrested or suspected of committing the offense.
3. The name of the officer who took the offense report.

4. The name of the investigating officer.

5. The full names of all witnesses.

6. The classification of the crime.

Cross-indexing of crimes is critical to properly utilizing the *modus operandi concept*. Briefly stated, modus operandi is the method of operation. Certain people commit similar crimes using the same method each time. This leaves a "fingerprint" which assists the department in determining how many crimes have been committed by the same person, and in some instances may lead to the capture of the criminal. For example, a pattern or method of operation may be established showing that a rapist attacks young women and wears a stocking mask during the assault. Additionally, he may utter the same words to each victim at the same time during the rape. This becomes his MO. Even though some of the victims cannot identify his face, this MO may be sufficient for arrest and conviction of all the rapes he committed using that method.

Whenever the department cross-indexes crimes according to modus operandi, the method of operation should be further divided into the following areas:

1. Location—where the crime was committed.

2. Person or property attacked.

3. Time of the attack.

4. How the attack was carried out.

5. Method of attack.

6. Object of the attack.

7. Any special characteristics.

Every crime should be indexed. Once the information is input, the computer can analyze the data and produce variations that may assist in the capture of the offender.

Report processing is more than simply filling out forms in the correct manner. It involves indexing the information and utilizing computers to assist in the detection of criminal activity.

CONFIDENTIALITY OF RECORDS

The final aspect of law enforcement records that should be examined is the issue of confidentiality of police records. Many states have freedom-of-information laws that require all public records to be open for inspection by members of the public. Most of these statutes, however, set forth certain exceptions. Police records have traditionally been exempt from disclosure. The reasons for this exemption are obvious. If anyone could view investigative files, ongoing criminal investigations might be compromised.

Another area that causes friction between law enforcement officers and the media concerns the confidentiality of information regarding juveniles accused of committing crimes. Juvenile proceedings, as well as all the facts surrounding the case, are confidential. This protection is established by various state statutes. The rationale behind keeping juveniles' names and criminal acts confidential is that publicizing these incidents could stigmatize the juveniles and possibly prevent rehabilitation. This area continues to be debated and will undoubtedly continue to generate high public emotion.

The confidentiality of records is an area of high emotion when the department deals with members of the media. The media will argue that the public has a right to know, and that the police department does not have the right to refuse to release information, especially if the case has been referred to the district attorney for the filing of criminal charges.

Confidentiality and Police Informants

Informants expose crimes that otherwise may go undetected. When properly used and controlled, they provide information that improves police efficiency, assists in the apprehension and prosecution of criminals, and sometimes even prevents crimes from taking place.

However, to use informants effectively, agencies must establish and maintain strict, written departmental policies on handling informants. Even when operating under tight controls, informants can quickly go bad or become unreliable. When they do, they create significant legal and public relations problems.

Only those with a need to know should be advised of an informant's identity. In practical terms, this means investigators and their alternates who work closely with the source. The squad supervisor or first-line manager should be encouraged to meet the informant, so that the source knows there are people in authority who support the program, and so that the manager has a general "feel" for the informant. The person who controls the informant file room must also know an informant's identity in order to handle the filing and other paperwork. These employees should be the only people who routinely handle informant information and who need to know the informant's identity.

To ensure secrecy, informants should be assigned code numbers and code names. These take the place of the source's real name on all documents and reports, and also in personal conversations. Any information provided by the source must be documented and recorded using code numbers and code names.

The files created must be maintained in secure rooms and access to them must be strictly controlled by an employee specifically assigned to control access. Only the informant's handler or alternate handler and the immediate supervisor should be allowed to examine those files routinely. A daily record that lists everyone who enters the secure room should also be maintained. This control is not implemented to create a bureaucratic roadblock, but to protect sources by limiting the number of people who know their identities. Institutionally, it also reinforces the importance of protecting informants' identities.

Source: Adapted from Harry A. Mount, Jr., "Criminal Informants, An Administrator's Dream or Nightmare," *FBI Law Enforcement Bulletin* (Dec. 1990): 12.

The department may be concerned that releasing the results of an investigation prior to a conviction may influence members of the public and impact the prosecutor's ability to find an impartial jury. For the most part, this area of the law is controlled by statutes that govern the withholding of information and set forth specific guidelines for the release of police department files.

SUMMARY

Basic law enforcement records may vary from jurisdiction to jurisdiction, but the principles behind their utilization will remain the same. There are two basic types of reports—operational and administrative. Each serves a vital purpose, and to neglect one in favor of the other is to destroy the effectiveness of any records division—and ultimately the operational capability of the agency.

Law enforcement, by its very nature, involves access to or use of confidential information. Many times this information is recorded in reports. This may cause a conflict with members of the media who would like access to those records. However, criminal justice professionals must keep those records confidential if they are to retain their credibility.

REVIEW QUESTIONS

1. What is the most important aspect of a police records system?

2. Should law enforcement agencies use computers and not maintain any paper records? Why? Why not? Read the chapter dealing with management information systems and determine if that changes your mind.

3. This chapter contains examples of reports from a small, a large, and an international law enforcement agency. What are the differences in the forms? What are the similarities?

4. List some reasons why police records should remain confidential even after the case has been sent to the prosecuting attorney.

Report Writing Techniques

INTRODUCTION

The previous chapters provided you with English composition skills and general knowledge about the types of police reports. In this chapter you will learn to apply your skills and knowledge to write police reports. Police report writing is considered technical writing, and as such you will need to develop special skills and techniques. Police report writing is the backbone of criminal investigations and prosecutions.

Objectives

At the end of this chapter, you will be able to do the following:

1. Define and explain interpersonal communications.
2. Identify the five parts of the report writing process.
3. Define chronological order.
4. Identify and write active-voice sentences.
5. Identify appropriate word usage for police reports.
6. Identify the advantages of first versus third person.
7. Properly use a tape recorder for note taking and report dictation.

INTERPERSONAL COMMUNICATIONS

You must understand the interpersonal communication process before you learn to conduct interviews and interrogations. One of your most valuable tools as a police officer is your interpersonal communication skill.

Definition of Communications

Generally, communication is defined as the use of language, spoken or written, to exchange ideas or transfer information. The transfer of information or ideas from one person to another includes the transmission and receipt of a message to effect some type of action or change.

Reasons for Communication

There are four reasons you communicate with other people.

1. *To provide adequate information for group living:* Police services are delivered to multicultural communities that include a growing elderly population. Your role as a police officer is rapidly changing from the traditional enforcer of laws to that of a service provider.

2. *To clarify perceptions and expectations:* The exchange of ideas and information is essential to clarify your perceptions and expectations and those of the community you serve.

3. *To stimulate creative thinking through feedback:* The human mind requires stimulation. You receive that stimulation from the feedback you receive during the communication process.

4. *To maintain your balance in the world:* During the communication process, you receive reinforcement or reassurance that you are okay.

Communication Process

The communication process contains a *sender, receiver,* and the *feedback loop.* There is a continuous line of communication between the *sender* and *receiver.* They are linked together by the *feedback loop.* When you begin an interview, you are the *sender* because you ask questions. The person you are interviewing is the *receiver.* Both of you listen to and watch each other, which provides you *feedback.* When the person you're interviewing answers, your roles in the communication process change. Feedback includes the answers to questions, gestures, and expressions.

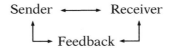

Types of Communication

You use verbal and nonverbal communication when dealing with people. Remember that you not only give off communication clues, but you should also practice reading the clues others give you.

Nonverbal Communication: You use three types of nonverbal communication: gestures, facial expressions, and body language.

Your gestures should be nonthreatening, using an open hand, for example. Facial expressions reveal your true feelings, so master appropriate expressions for every situation. Body language is easily read by others and conveys both your feelings and meanings. Positive use of body language will encourage people to talk and improve your ability to gather information.

Verbal Communication: You may not realize it, but there are many different types of verbal communication. It is important for you to recognize and understand each type.

One-way communication is lecture or direction. It is effective in limited situations, especially where compliance without feedback is necessary. An example would be felony or high-risk car stops.

Two-way communication includes speaking and listening. You typically exchange information or ideas in two-way communication.

Oral-in-person communication means you can see and hear the other person you are speaking to. You have the opportunity to use both verbal and nonverbal communication skills.

Oral-Telephone communication is just what it sounds like, talking on the phone. The disadvantage is nonverbal communication is eliminated.

Written communication is the most difficult to master. You always disclose something about yourself in your writing. Typically, you disclose your ability to organize information, your educational level, and your technical expertise.

Practice

Team up with another student in the class and alternate between each other, doing the following:

Look at your partner and use your eyes and facial expressions to convey warmth and caring.

Look at your partner and use gestures to convey that "you mean business."

Look at your partner, smile, and say, "I'm going to fire you."

Look at your partner, smile, and say, "I'm always here to help you."

REPORT WRITING PROCESS

Police report writing is a five-step process. They are (1) interviewing, (2) note taking, (3) organizing and planning, (4) writing the narrative, and (5) proofreading. Your preliminary investigation includes report writing. During the investigation you must complete each of the steps, or your final report will not be acceptable.

Interviewing

Interviewing is the first step in the process. Your interviews of victims, witnesses, and suspects are the backbone of your preliminary investigation. Frequently, the first officer at the scene of a crime has the best opportunity to solve the crime by conducting a thorough preliminary investigation. If you do not conduct successful interviews, your preliminary investigation and police report will not be acceptable.

Three-step Interview Method: The three-step interview method is an easy way for you to conduct interviews. It is structured to allow your informant to speak at ease while you have control over the interview. While you are learning, practice on simple interview situations. After you feel comfortable, you will be able to use the three-step method for interviews and interrogations.

1. *Subject tells the story:* You listen, keeping the subject on track, and giving verbal and nonverbal clues to keep the story flowing. You don't attempt to take notes during this first step. During this step, you accomplish the following:

   Establish rapport with the subject.
   Determine what crime, if any, occurred.
   Determine what agency has jurisdiction.
   Detect signs of untruthfulness or discrepancies.
   Determine what action you should take.

2. *Subject retells the story and you take notes:* You gather identifying information about the subject and ask questions about the incident as you guide the subject through the story a second time. During this step, you accomplish the following:

   Determine the chronological order of the event.
   Establish the *corpus delicti* of the crime.
   Ask questions in the order you want to write the report (thereby organizing your report as you take notes).

3. *You read your notes to the subject:* When you do this, you are actually writing your report for the first time. What you are reading is going to be what you write in your report. During this step, the subject can correct errors or remember additional information, and you can correct errors or ask additional questions.

LEARNING TIP

Use of the three-step interview method adds credibility to your courtroom testimony. You can testify that you always use the same method, following the same three steps, in all the interviews you conduct. If there is a discrepancy in the informant's courtroom testimony and what you've written in your report, your use of the three-step method documents your actions.

Interrogation: In general, there is one difference between an interview of a subject and the interrogation of a suspect: *focus.* An interrogation is a planned interview with the primary focus being to obtain a confession or eliminate the person as a suspect. A secondary focus may be to find incriminating evidence. Generally, when you interview a victim or witness, you are not sure what he or she is going to tell you. When you interrogate a suspect, you have probably already collected substantial information about the incident and have a pretty good idea what the suspect is going to say. During most interrogations, police officers don't ask questions they don't know the answers to. That doesn't mean you will get the answer you anticipated.

You use the same interpersonal communication skills in both situations. That's why it is important for you to develop the ability to use both your verbal and nonverbal skills. In some cases you may have several questions written down to ask a suspect during the interrogation. There is nothing in an interrogation to justify coercion, excessive force, or violation of a suspect's constitutional rights. Because case law changes rapidly and may vary from state to state, you should review legal updates and department training bulletins regularly.

Note Taking

Notes are defined as brief notations concerning specific events that are recorded while fresh in your mind and used to prepare a report.

Types of Notes: There are two types of notes: *permanent* and *temporary*. If you use permanent notes, you must keep those notes in a safe storage place. If you elect to use temporary notes, you must discard your notes after completing your report. Whichever type of notes you elect to use, you must not change back and forth based on the type of report. If you do change the type of notes you take from call to call, defense attorneys may attack your credibility by asking why you keep some notes and discard others.

It is recommended you use permanent notes. Recording your notes in a note pad or steno pad provides you with a reference and resource book. You will always have access to your original source of information.

Purposes of Notes: Notes are the basis for your report. You take notes to assist your memory with specific details, such as names, dates of birth, serial numbers, addresses, and phone numbers. If you take neat and accurate notes, and they are subpoenaed into court, they add to your credibility and demonstrate your high level of proficiency and professionalism. A good defense attorney may attempt to develop impeachable inconsistencies between your notes and your report.

Scratch Outlinings: You should use a *scratch* or informal outline for taking notes. Scratch outlines provide a simple, structured, easy way to organize the information on your note pad during step 2 of the three-step interview method.

A scratch outline has a key sentence followed by supporting points. The supporting points are written under the key sentence and indented from the left margin. Neither the key sentence nor supporting points are numbered or lettered.

EXAMPLE:

Key sentence	Ofc. Cleveland arrested Rusty Hodges for burglary
Supporting points	victim saw Hodges
	Hodges ran from Ofc. Cleveland
	Cleveland caught Hodges
	Hodges had the victim's license

Scratch outlines don't have a set format. Use your own style and develop something useful for you.

The questions you ask in step 2 of the interview are generally your key sentences. The informant's responses are your supporting points. Don't try to write down everything the subject tells you, unless you're going to quote him. Remember, notes are *brief notations,* just enough to remind you at a later time when you are writing your report.

Scratch outlining may sound familiar to you. Teachers use a similar method to teach writing and paragraphing. A key sentence is the same as a topic sentence. The difference between police report writing and English compositions is the source of information and the method used to collect it. Most of the information in a police report comes from interviews you conduct.

When you are taking notes, remember to leave spaces between the lines and don't try to use every inch of the page. You may need to add additional information or correct something you have already written down. You will also need space when you begin to organize your report.

Organizing and Planning

The organizing and planning of your report are the third step. If your report is properly organized and planned, it will be clear, easy to read, understandable, and concise. The small amount of time you spend on organizing and planning greatly reduces the time you spend rewriting reports.

Organizing and planning your report begins during the three-step interview method. During step 2, ask questions in the order you want to include the information in your narrative. Organizing and planning your narrative are closely related to chronological order, which is discussed later in this chapter. Ask questions in the order the event took place, which is the chronological order of the event, and it will make writing your narrative much easier.

Once the informant has told you his or her story during step 1 of the three-step interview, you can begin organizing and planning your report. You will know the chronological order of the event, so ask questions in that order during step 2 of the interview.

Review your scratch outline and verify the information you will need to include in the narrative. You may want to underline, number, or otherwise mark important points in your notes. In some cases you may even draw arrows to remind you where to include information in the narrative. You should also consider the information you want to omit from the narrative.

Writing the Narrative

You may not believe it, but writing the narrative should be the easiest part of report writing. If you have carefully followed the three-step interview method (properly taken notes), and spent a few minutes organizing and planning, writing the narrative is almost anticlimatic. If you use the methods described above, you will be prepared to write reports using the one write system, dictation, or a lap-top computer.

Just before you begin to write the narrative, stop and think about what you have done and what you have left to do. You have collected all the appropriate information, determined your actions, taken notes, and actually recited the report out loud during step 3 of the interview. Your notes, in scratch outline format, are the road map for writing the narrative. The key sentences generally remind you to start a new paragraph, and the supporting points are used to write the sentences. If you practice following these steps, you will find writing the narrative really is the easiest part.

Proofreading

You may think writing the narrative is the final step, but it's not. When you have finished writing the narrative, proofread it. Most officers are just thankful to have finished the report and don't take the additional moment or two to review their work. Think about who else is going to read the report. Depending on the type of report and whether or not you've arrested a suspect, your report will be read by sergeants, investigators, prosecutors, defense attorneys, and judges. If you have made an arrest, the defense attorney's best chance to defend his or her client comes from your report.

Check for the following when you proofread:

Correct report form(s) and format

Probable cause to stop, detain, arrest, search, and seize

Corpus delicti, the elements of the offense

Correct spelling

Active-voice sentence structure

Proper punctuation

The last things to ask yourself when proofreading are as follows: Is this report the best I can do? Would I want to read it to the chief of police or to a jury? Is there anything else I can do to make it better?

Practice

Team up with another student in the class and use one of the following questions to interview each other. Use the three-step interview method and scratch outlining for note taking.

Tell me everything you've done today, from the time you woke up.

Tell me about your last job.

CHRONOLOGICAL ORDER

You must understand chronological order to write coherent and accurate police reports. Your reports should not skip around or jump from topic to topic. Frequently, officers' reports will jump from interview to interview, which makes the report confusing and difficult to follow. If you use the three-step interview method and scratch outlining, you shouldn't have any trouble with chronological order.

Definition

For the purposes of police report writing, chronological order is defined as the arrangement of events and/or actions in order by the time of their occurrence. Simply stated: in order, what happened and when.

There are usually two chronological orders to an event: the order of the officer's activities and the order of the event. The exception is when you

initiate the activity, for example, an observation arrest, and you become a participant in the event.

Officer's Order of Activity

The order of your activities should be the easiest for you to follow. You will not only have your memory, but also your notes. It is recommended that you write your reports in the order of your activity. This style is frequently called narrative style report writing. (Category style is discussed later in this chapter.)

Think of a residential burglary where the victim calls the police and wants to make a report. What do you do after you receive the radio call?

Interview the victim.

Search for and interview any witnesses.

Search for and possibly arrest the suspect.

Account for your activities.

You would write the narrative in the above example in that same order. First, write about the victim interview, then your search for witnesses, their interview(s), your search for the suspect(s), and so on.

Order of the Event

The order of the event is the arrangement of occurrences and/or actions as they occurred during the crime. When did the suspect enter the house, what did he take, when did he leave, what was he driving, and what was his direction of travel? Every witness may have a different version of the chronological order of the event because they may not have seen the same things.

Using the above example, the following scratch outline demonstrates the chronological order of an event as you might write in your notes.

EXAMPLE:

Victim:	left at 7 P.M. to go to the movies
	returned at 10:30 P.M.
	front door was open
	VCR and camcorder were missing from family room
	called police
Witness:	lives next door at 9380
	8:00 P.M. saw suspect walk across victim's yard
	carried camcorder to car
	white Chevrolet, license ABC 123
You:	11:00 P.M. saw suspect car on Main St.
	verified license number
	stopped and arrested suspect
	saw VCR and camcorder on seat
	Mirandized suspect and interviewed
Suspect:	went to house at 8:00 P.M.
	no one answered door bell
	twisted knob with vise grips
	took VCR and camcorder
You:	booked suspect at county jail
	returned property to victim

Officer-initiated Activity (Observation)

When you make an observation arrest or see an event take place, you become an active participant and there is only one chronological order. A good example would be if you saw someone smoking marijuana. Your observations and actions are part of the report. You document your actions and those of someone else.

EXAMPLE:

You:	see suspect sitting on a park bench
	smoking a marijuana cigarette
	confiscate the dope
	interview the suspect
Suspect:	admits it is his dope
You:	arrest suspect
	book the evidence

Spatial Order

Spatial order defines the position of objects within a given environment. At a crime scene, it means the location of all physical evidence and objects. The spatial order you should be aware of is the location of items of evidence in relationship to each other. When you describe the crime scene, you would move logically from left to right, top to bottom, and so forth. You always want to describe what you see in a logical order, not jump from one object or location to another, so the reader has a clear picture of the crime scene.

I approached the open bedroom door, looked inside, and saw the following: The light switch was on the left wall, and the switch was on. To the left of the light switch, I saw a hole in the wall. I saw a sofa along the same wall under the hole. There wasn't anything else in the room. The light on the ceiling was broken. I saw a blood-stained area on the carpet beneath the ceiling light.

Category Style

You may work for an agency that prefers officers write in category style. Category style requires you to use specific subheadings in the specific order dictated by your department's report writing manual.

EXAMPLE:

Source: I received a radio call about a subject in the park smoking marijuana.
Officer's observations: I arrived at 1345 hours and saw Jones sitting on a park bench. He was smoking what appeared to be a marijuana cigarette.
Suspect statements: Jones said it was his marijuana.

While category style can be cumbersome and inconvenient, it does provide a guide or checklist for you to follow.

Practice

The following facts are pertinent to a theft report. Read each statement and decide the correct chronological order for your report. Place 1 by the first fact, 2 by the second, and so on, until all statements have been put in order.

_____ The red & white bicycle was worth $100.00.

_____ The movie was over about 2:15 and she rode straight home.

_____ She came out of the house about 30 minutes later.

_____ No one had permission to take the bicycle.

_____ She left it parked on the front porch.

_____ The bicycle was gone.

ACTIVE VOICE WRITING STYLE

Police reports should be clear and concise. Clear means plain or evident to the mind of the reader. Concise means your report says as much as possible, in as few words as possible. The best way to accomplish both of these qualities in your reports is to write in active voice. If you use active voice, your reports will be easier to read.

The alternative to active voice is passive voice. Passive voice sentences are weak and confusing and may not identify the doer of the action.

Active voice writing style allows you to:

Reduce sentence length by 20 percent.

Directly answer the question, Who did the action?

Eliminate punctuation errors.

Avoid weak and awkward sentences.

EXAMPLE:

I wrote the citation. (active voice)

The citation was written by me. (passive voice)

THREE STEPS TO DETERMINE ACTIVE VOICE

Use the following three steps to write in the active voice.

1. Locate the *action* (verb) of the sentence.
2. Locate who or what is doing the action. This is the *doer* (subject) of the sentence. If the *doer* is implied and not written in, or it is being acted on by the *action,* the sentence is weak or passive. If the *doer* is written but not located just in front of the action, the sentence is *weak.*
3. Put the *doer* immediately in front of the *action.*

EXAMPLES:

The officer wrote the citation. (active voice)
The dispatcher repeated the address. (active voice)
A suspect was arrested. (passive voice)

Using the above steps, correct the last statement:

1. What is the *action* of the sentence? *was arrested*
2. Who or what is the *doer* of the action? The sentence doesn't have a *doer,* so who made the arrest? *I*
3. Put the *doer* immediately in front of the *action:* I arrested the suspect.

Practice

Determine if these sentences are active or passive voice. Use an A for active and P or passive.

_____ The sergeant read the crime warning.

_____ The suspect didn't resist arrest.

_____ The meeting was called by the chief.

_____ It was determined by the victim what was missing.

_____ Several citations were written by the motor officer.

While you may write only factual statements in your reports, it is possible they are not objective. In your police reports, objective means you weren't influenced by emotion or prejudice. Your writings are fair, impartial, and not opinionated.

Your reports can lose objectivity because of poor word usage, omission of facts, and uncontrolled personal feelings. You maintain your objectivity by using nonemotional words, including both sides of every story, and remaining a professional during all investigations.

Nonemotional Words

You should use *denotative* words, words that are explicit and nonemotional. Emotional words are called *connotative* because they suggest or imply something beyond the explicit or literal meaning of the word.

EXAMPLES:

bureaucrat, blubbered, scream, wail (connotative)

public employee, civil servant, cried, wept, yell (denotative)

Slanting

You slant your report when you fail to include both sides of the event. You must include statements from all the witnesses, victims, suspects, or participants. When you omit all or part of someone's statement, no matter how unusual, you have slanted your report and lost objectivity.

Practice

Circle the denotative word in each example.

woman/broad, officer/cop, confused/crazy, uncooperative/hostile, argue/verbal confrontation

WORD USAGE

Police officers from all regions of the country tend to use similar words and phrases. Unfortunately, these words and phrases are not necessarily the best choices for clarity, objectivity, and conciseness. In most cases, officers don't use them in everyday conversation. While you shouldn't write the way you talk, you should try to use everyday words that everyone will understand.

Deadwood Words

These words and phrases are fancy, formal, or grand expressions that usually serve no purpose. You should use common, everyday words that are understood by everyone, especially judges and jurors.

Instead of:	*Try:*
abeyance	delayed or held up
accomplish, execute, perform	do
accordingly	therefore, so, that is why
accumulate	gather
acquaint	tell
acquire, secure	get
additional	added
ad infinitum	endlessly
adverse	poor, bad
advise	write, inform, tell
afford an opportunity	allow, permit, let
aforementioned, aforesaid	these
aggregate	total
a good deal	much
a great deal of the time	often
a limited quantity of	few
all of	all
along the lines	like, the same way
alteration, revision	change
altercation	fight
ameliorate	improve
analization	analysis
answer in the affirmative	say yes
anticipate	foresee
apparent	clear
appears that	clear
appended	added
applicable	apply to
are desirous of	want
are in receipt of	have received
as a matter of fact	in fact
ascertain	discover, find out
as per	according to
assistance	aid, help

Instead of:	*Try:*
assuming that	if
at a later date	later
at an early date	soon
at such time	when
at the present time	now
attached you will find	attached is
attribute	due
balance of	remainder, rest
basis, based on, on the basis of	on, by, after, for, because
be in position to	can
beneficial aspects of	benefits
broken down into	divided into
bulk of	most
by means of	by, with
check into	check
classifications	classes
close proximity	near, or just "close"
cognizance	knowledge
cognizant of	know
commence	start
commitment	promise
compensate, compensation	pay
concur	agree
consensus of opinion	consensus
consequently	so
consider favorably	approved
considerable	much, serious, grave
construct	build
contacted	spoke to, visited
contingent upon receipt of	when we receive
continuous basis	continually
contribute	give
deleterious, detrimental	harmful
demonstrate	show
despite the fact that	although
direct effort toward	try
due in large measure to	due largely
due to the fact that	because
during the course of	during
during the time that	while
effect a reduction of	reduce
employ	use
encounter	meet
endeavor	try
equivalent	equal
excessive amount	too much
exit	leave
expedite	hasten, hurry, speed

Instead of:	*Try:*
expense	cost
explicit	plain
facilitate	make easy, simplify
feasible	possible
feels	believes, thinks
finalize	finish, end
following	after
forthcoming	coming
for the purpose of	for, to
for the reason that	because, since
found to be	are
forward, furnish, transmit	send
frequently	often
furthermore	also, in addition
gainfully employed	working, employed
give consideration to	consider
give instruction to	instruct
have a need for	need
henceforth, hereafter	from now on, in the future
herein	here
hereinafter	after this
hereinbefore	until now
heretofore	up to now, until now
herewith	with this, now
imminent	near (in time)
implement, implementation	carry out, set up, enforce
in advance of, prior to	before
in accordance with	with, by, as, under
in a most careful manner	carefully
in a number of cases	some, many
in a timely manner	promptly
in connection with	with
in the amount of	for
inasmuch as	because
indebtedness	debt
indicate, state	show, tell, said, noted
initial	first
initiate	begin, start
in large measure	largely
in lieu of	instead of
in many cases	many
in order that	so
in order to	to
in regard to	concerning
in relation to	about
in spite of the fact that	although
institute	start, begin
in the affirmative	yes, agreed
in the course/case of	in, at, or, during, while

Instead of:	*Try:*
in the event of/that	if
in the magnitude of	about
in the majority of cases	usually
in the matter of	in, about
in the time of	during
in the very near future	soon
in the vicinity of	near
in this day and age	today
in view of the fact	since, because
is as follows	follows
it is my understanding that	I understand
it is our opinion	we feel, believe
it should be noted that	furthermore
justification for	reason for
kindly arrange to send	please send
locality	place
locate	find, put
likewise	and also
maintenance	upkeep
make a decision	decide
make a determination	determine
make application for	apply
make inquiry regarding	ask
modification	change
negative results	found nothing
nevertheless	but, however
nonavailability of	unavailable
notwithstanding	despite, in spite of
numerous	many
objective	aim
obligate	bind
obligation	debt
observed	saw
obtain	get
occasion	cause
on a few occasions	occasionally
on behalf of	for
on the basis of	by, from, because
on the grounds that	because
on the occasion of	when
on the part of	for, among
on the subject of	about
optimum	the most for the least
orientated	oriented
outside of	outside
owing to the fact that	because
participate	take part
per diem, per annum	per day, a year

Instead of:	*Try:*
pertain	about, on
peruse	read
place emphasis on	emphasize
possess	have
preventative	preventive
prior to	before
proceed	go
procure	get
provided, providing	if
regarding	about
realize a savings of	save
reimburse	pay
related with, relates to, relating to, relative to	on, about
render aid or assistance	help
reported	said, told
resided	lived
residence	house, apartment
responded	answered, said
sibling	brother, sister
subject matter	subject, topic
submit	send, give
subsequently, subsequent to	later, afterward, then, next
sufficient	enough
summarization	summary
sustained	received
take action	act
terminate, terminated	end, ended, stopped, ending
the question as to whether	whether
the reason is due to	because
thereafter	after that, then
therein	there, in it
thereof	of it
thereupon	then
this is a subject that	this subject
transmit	send
transported	took, drove
under date of	on
under the circumstances	because
until such time as	until
utilization, utilize	use
vehicle	car, truck
visualize	see, think of, imagine
whereby	by which, so that
wherein	in which, where, when
whether or not	whether
wish to advise, wish to state	(avoid, do not use)

Instead of:	*Try:*

with regard to,
    with reference to,
    with respect to
	about, regarding, concerning

with the result that	so that
without further delay	immediately, soon, quickly
would seem, would appear	seem/appear (try to avoid these)

Slang

Slang is usually a coinage or nonstandard vocabulary developed by a group of people. You may be familiar with street slang, drug slang, and police slang. It is inappropriate to use slang in your report, unless you are quoting someone.

EXAMPLES:

ran/split, arrested/busted, in possession/holding, under the influence/down

Jargon

Jargon is usually the specialized language of a profession. Criminal justice professionals, just like other professionals, use a great deal of jargon. You should not use jargon in your reports.

EXAMPLES:

undefined penal codes; 187 PC

radio codes; 503, 1199

drunk driver; deuce

Word Meanings

You should always make sure you know the correct definition and spelling of the words you use in your reports. The following words are frequently misused because of a lack of understanding of correct meaning, definition, or usage.

Already: By this or a specified time
All ready: All things are ready

Among: three or more in a group
Between: in a position between two or an interval separating

Appear to: to come into view, become visible
Seems to: to give the impression of being

As: to the same extent or degree, equally
When: at what time

Canvas: a heavy, coarse fabric
Canvass: to examine thoroughly or to solicit

Counsel: consultation or a lawyer
Council: a body of people elected by voters

Effect (noun): result, the way something acts on an object
Affect (verb): to have an influence on, impress

Elude: to evade or escape
Allude: to make an indirect reference to

Past: no longer current
Passed: to move on ahead, proceed

Principle: a basic truth, a law
Principal: foremost in rank or worth, a person

Stationary: not moving, not capable of being moved
Stationery: writing paper

Trustee: a person or agent in a position of trust
Trusty: an inmate worker in prison or jail

Upon: on, to put on top of
When: at what time

Euphemisms

A euphemism is a polite or diplomatic way to say something that might otherwise be taken as an insult or uncomplimentary remark. You should be specific and professional in your reports and avoid using euphemisms. Euphemisms can mislead the reader.

Officers frequently are embarrassed or self-conscious when investigating sex crimes or child-abuse cases, and they will use euphemisms for anatomical parts of the body. You should use the correct terms.

EXAMPLE:

penis/private parts, bra and panties/unmentionables,

used/previously owned car, obese/weight problem,

argue/verbal confrontation, refused to answer/uncooperative

FIRST PERSON AND THIRD PERSON

You may write your reports in either the first- or third-person style. Both are acceptable; however, first-person style is preferred and the most widely used. You should refer to yourself as an active participant. Third-person writing style for police reports is archaic and outdated. "I" isn't poison.

The alternative to first person is third person. You refer to yourself as assigned officer, reporting officer, or this officer.

Usually, department policy specifies which style you use. If given the choice, use first person. Police reports should be written in an easily understandable style. When we interview a victim, witness, or suspect, we are actively involved.

EXAMPLES:

I talked to Mrs. Smith.   (first person)
Officer Jones and I searched the building.   (first person)
This officer talked to Mrs. Smith.   (third person)
Assigned officer and his partner searched the building.   (third person)

PARAGRAPHING

You may want to review the section on note taking and the use of the scratch outline. Scratch outlines have key sentences, and those key sentences are generally topic sentences in paragraphing. If you take good notes during the interview process, you should have no trouble understanding paragraphing.

A paragraph is a group of sentences that tells about one topic. The topic sentence tells what the sentences in the paragraph are about. Usually, it is the first sentence in the paragraph. Paragraphing is a method of alerting the reader to a shift in focus in the report.

Steps in Writing a Paragraph

First, your notes provide the key or topic sentence and the outline for the paragraphs. Check for completeness and rearrange sentences if necessary.

Second, write the paragraph in active-voice style, using 12- to 15-word sentences. Paragraphs in police reports generally have five to seven sentences or approximately 100 words. However, it is acceptable in police reports to write one- or two-sentence paragraphs. One- or two-sentence paragraphs are used to mark a transition in reports, from one topic or section to another: typically, going from the interview of the victim to the interview of a witness.

Indent the beginning of each paragraph or skip one or two lines between paragraphs.

Unity: Preserve the unity of the paragraph. A paragraph should develop a single topic, the key sentence. Every sentence in the paragraph should contribute to the development of that single idea.

Coherence: Compose the paragraph so it reads coherently. Coherence makes it easy for the reader to follow the facts and events. It reflects clear thinking by the report writer. A clearly stated chronological order of events makes the paragraph, and therefore the report, coherent.

Development: Paragraphs should be adequately developed. The first step is to consider the central idea. Present examples or specific quotes. Include relevant facts, details, or evidence. Explore and explain the causes of an event or the motives of the suspect. The result may be an explanation of how the event occurred. Finally, describe the scene, injuries, or other pertinent information.

Consider the following suggestions:

Repeat key sentences from paragraph to paragraph.

Use pronouns in place of key nouns.

Use "pointing words," for example, *this, that, these,* and *those.*

Use "thought-connecting words," such as *however, moreover, also, nevertheless, therefore, thus, subsequently, indeed, then,* and *accordingly.*

Arrange sentences in chronological order.

Third, proofread your work. If necessary, correct mistakes and rewrite the paragraph or report.

USE OF TAPE RECORDERS

You may consider using a tape recorder for both note taking and report dictation.

Note Taking

The use of a tape recorder for field note taking is generally discouraged. The biggest problem with tape recording field notes is that you capture too much unnecessary information. You may elect to use a tape recorder for note taking if you are interviewing a suspect in an involved or serious crime.

If you use a tape recorder for interviews, at the beginning of the interview always include the following:

Your name

Rank

Department

Date and time

Case number and type of case

Tape recorders may play an important role in obtaining unsolicited suspect statements where there is no violation of their constitutional rights. Under current case law, a suspect has no reasonable expectation to privacy in a police car. Therefore, officers may place a tape recorder in a patrol car and record suspect conversations.

Remember, there is no substitute for good note taking.

Report Dictation

You will find that dictating reports is much easier if you follow the three-step interview and scratch outline note-taking methods. The combination of these two methods is called a *dictation tree.* Some agencies now use dictation systems that have limited word-processing capabilities.

Eleven Dictation Tips

1. Organize your thoughts by reviewing your notes.
2. Relax for a few minutes after reviewing your notes.
3. When you first begin to dictate, state the type of report (what form to use) and your name and badge number.
4. Follow the order of the blocks on the form.
5. Slow your speech slightly.
6. Speak clearly; spell out names and words that are not easily understood.
7. Do not lose concentration: Don't try to listen for radio calls and the like.

8. Do not smoke, drink, chew gum, or eat during dictation.
9. If you make a mistake, pause; then tell the operator that you need to make a correction.
10. When finished, restate your name and badge number.
11. Use simple courtesy, "Thank you, operator."

CHAPTER REVIEW

In this chapter you learned to apply your skills and knowledge to write police reports. You can define and explain interpersonal communications, identify the five parts of the report-writing process, define chronological order, identify and write active voice sentences, identify appropriate word usage for police reports, identify the advantages of first versus third person, and properly use a tape recorder for note taking and report dictation.

DISCUSSION QUESTIONS

1. Explain why interpersonal communication skills are important to police officers.
2. Identify two of the four reasons we communicate, and discuss their importance and meaning.
3. Define and explain nonverbal communication.
4. What are the three steps in the three-step interview method and what does each accomplish?
5. Explain the value of three-step interviewing and scratch outlining when writing paragraphs.

EXERCISES

Revise the following sentences so they are clear, concise, and jargon and slang free.

1. The subject exited the stolen vehicle post hastily.

_____

2. A theft in amount of $34.83 was reported.

_____

3. The officer detected the odor of burning marijuana.

_____

4. Officers contacted Lewis at his home.

_____

5. The detective named Robinson as their primary suspect on account of the fact that his fingerprints matched those detectives found at the crime scene.

_____

_____

Replace each of the following words or phrases with a simple word or phrase:

Adjacent to _____

Altercation _____

Transported _____

Observed _____

Ascertain _____

Choose the correct word in each of the following sentences:

1. The (affect/effect) of the medication began to (affect/effect) his judgment.
2. The burglar parked the car in the (alley/ally).
3. The driver said he could not (brake/break) in time to avoid the accident.
4. As the mortally wounded victim was (dying/dyeing), he named his assailant.
5. The building was a strange (local/locale) for the gathering.
6. Always use a (stationary/stationery) object when you need a point of reference.
7. The investigators made a (through/thorough/through) investigation.
8. Officers will (advice/advise) the suspects of their rights.
9. The forgery suspect tried to (altar/alter) his appearance.
10. The whole neighborhood could (breath/breathe) easier once the police caught the escaped murderer.

Determine if these sentences are active or passive voice. If they are passive, rewrite them in active voice.

1. All the money was given to the suspect by the teller.

   _____

2. The suspect took the money and ran out the door.

   _____

3. A radio broadcast of the suspect's description was put out by me.

   _____

4. Two blocks away the suspect was stopped by Officer Wright.

   _____

5. The suspect was identified by the witness.

   _____

CHAPTER 20

Writing Investigative Reports

Prologue: The Need for a New Perception

Paperwork! Merely hearing the term causes many a brave police officer to shudder, seemingly with good cause. Horror stories of cases lost and careers ruined because of poor writing permeate the profession. Local, state, and federal agencies all share this attitude; neither an organization's size nor its affiliation seems to matter.

For many investigators, report writing epitomizes this problem, and no wonder. The sheer size of many reports would overwhelm anybody. Just the thought of reading them, much less writing them, boggles the mind. Combined with the knowledge that even minor errors can destroy an entire case, it becomes easy to understand the nearly universal dislike of report writing. Law enforcement must solve this problem if it is going to improve its effectiveness.

The solution must begin with a change in perception. Officers cannot look at the investigative report as a single entity. Instead, they must view it as a compilation of many pieces derived from individual investigative actions such as surveillances, searches, and especially interviews. This viewpoint makes the term *report writing* a misnomer. Officers do not write reports; they assemble them, and that is a far less daunting chore. Once you realize this, it will allow you to concentrate on gathering the facts and recording them during each step of the investigation. The following material is meant to help you do this.

Writing: Real Police Work

The keen competition for jobs in law enforcement has allowed police departments to test and eliminate candidates who cannot convey their thoughts in writing. Despite this screening, the lament, "Cops can't write," continues to be heard throughout many departments both large and small. At least in some cases, events confirm this opinion. Incidents, some comic and some tragic, seemingly caused by inept writing by police officers, appear in the news all too frequently.

These criticisms can and have affected subsequent investigations, sometimes causing officers to tailor their findings to facilitate their writing. A story from the 1920s illustrates this: While walking his beat in New Orleans, a police officer discovered a dead horse on Tchoupitoulas (that's pronounced chop-o-TOOL-is) Street. He immediately found some wharf workers and had them help him drag the horse to Julia Street. A fellow officer saw this operation and asked him why he had done it. The man replied, "I knew I would have to write a report about the dead horse and I had no idea how to spell Tchoupitoulas."

The low opinion of officers' writing, whether justified or not, has prompted agencies to look for ways to simplify it, often by trying to reduce all writing to a few fill-in-the-blanks forms. When this strategy fails, departments find themselves creating more and more forms.

One federal agency developed more than two thousand forms for reporting information, each designed to make life easier for its agents. Needless to say, this plan did nothing to increase the effectiveness of that organization, nor did it make life easier for its investigators. The diversity and complexity of investigations preclude any such simplistic and universal solution.

In addition to disliking writing because of its consequences, many officers view writing as a hindrance to "real police work." They fail to see or refuse to accept that without proper documentation, most investigations have little value. By examining various aspects of law enforcement writing in a systematic way and by presenting writing as an integral part of the investigative process, we hope to remove some of the mystery and diminish the disdain for it. Only with understanding can a change in attitude occur, and attitude is the real problem in police writing.

Purpose and Style in Investigative Reporting

Using only words, novelists might convey feelings and events with such skill that they earn the highest literary honor in the world, the Nobel Prize for Literature. Scientists, on the other hand, although they too must provide written accounts of their findings, receive awards not for their writing but for the work it describes. By contrasting the two disciplines, we may gain some insight into problems and solutions regarding paperwork for law enforcement.

Examining works of fiction will provide little information for law enforcement to use when developing a model for writing. Creativity and the ability to tell a story in a convincing fashion play little part in effective police writing. In fact, using these talents can lead to disaster.

A scientist's situation, however, offers an excellent example for illustrating an investigator's position. Even though scientists' plaudits result from their discoveries rather than from their reports, unless they articulate those findings to the satisfaction of those who would act upon them, their work will go unrecognized. This coincides with the burden facing today's police officer, who must "discover" the facts and then record them for use by others.

No aspect of police writing creates as much impact as the investigative report, either in terms of publicity or, more importantly, in terms of outcome. Verdicts of guilt or innocence often depend as much on how investigators document their findings as they do on the quality and quantity of evidence obtained. Unfortunately, even in this specialized arena, officers find few rules for recording the results of their investigations that apply to all situations. Therefore, we will examine some of these diverse investigative activities and then suggest some standards or guidelines for documenting them.

The Interview

Throughout history, police have tried to gather the facts needed to solve crimes. Just as other researchers would do, they methodically searched for clues and methodically recorded the results. Although made more effective by improved techniques and equipment, today's investigators do many of the same things in much the same way.

Despite the years of practice at gathering physical evidence and the recent advances in forensic science, today as in the past *the interview solves more crimes than all other techniques combined.* People provide the solutions to crimes; they tell investigators "who done it." This very nonmethodical technique remains the primary research tool of most successful investigators.

Almost every investigative agency has at least a few members whose fellow officers describe them as "really good on the street but not worth a damn on paper." These people seem to have the ability to talk with anyone, but their writing, if it exists at all, has little value. Many of these officers spend their entire careers being touted for their expertise while contributing little to the mission of their organizations. An examination of this all-too-common phenomenon may provide some insight for avoiding the stigma of not being "good on paper."

How do these types manage to exist in an environment that relies to such a large extent on paperwork? Often they do so by limiting their efforts to superficial encounters and then moving on, leaving the gathering of details and their subsequent documentation to others. They justify this behavior by defining their mission as one of "greasing the skids." This evasive ploy enables them to survive and in some cases even to flourish. Departments can be well served by using these officers in positions where their ice-breaking skills are paramount. Some of these types make excellent informant developers or liaison officers.

Some investigators really do lack the basic skills and knowledge needed for writing, thus justifying their efforts to avoid any situation in which they must write. However, for most the inability to write has little to do with ineptness. Instead, they fail because they have nothing worth writing despite their willingness to talk with anybody they meet.

Fundamentals of Interviewing   To understand why these bright, likable, enthusiastic people fail so miserably requires us to examine the fundamentals of interviewing; often it is here that their difficulties with writing begin. Their encounters with people ignore the second part of the widely accepted definition of an interview, a conversation with a purpose. They concentrate so much on the conversation that they fail to guide it to the relevant topics, let alone pursue them in depth. Instead they "chat" (some have other, less flattering terms for what they do) extensively about any number of things, declare the interview completed, and depart.

If such officers were to produce a written document based on their efforts, it would leave most readers bewildered. Recognizing this fact, they usually try to avoid writing anything by characterizing the results of their efforts as inconsequential. If this fails, they write either an exceedingly brief account or one that rambles on interminably. The absence of relevant information is the commonality of either effort.

Preparation for the Interview   It is difficult to imagine scientists beginning work on a project without first defining what they hope to achieve and reviewing the work of those who preceded them. So, too, must interviewers consider their purpose for interviewing a person and review all relevant information, such as the facts of the case and the background of the subject to be interviewed prior to beginning that interview. Unlike a scientist, who can usually pause to review previous data, once an investigator has begun the interview, the time for preparation has passed.

Careful planning not only provides interviewers with a clear understanding of their purpose for conducting an interview, but it also helps them to decide *how*, *when*, and *where* to conduct it, all variables that can contribute to the success or failure of an interview. Unfortunately, investigators who fail to realize this fact, usually those for whom meeting people comes easily, often spend their careers "winging it" and thus rarely obtain the needed information; no amount of writing skill can rectify this. *Failure to obtain the needed information probably accounts for more inadequate reports than all writing inadequacies combined.*

The antithesis of those who "have never met a stranger" are those who fail to grasp the other prong of the interview definition, that *an interview is a conversation.* Their interviews consist of nothing but questions, and they justify this technique on its presumed efficiency. However, treating people as if they are some sort of data bank that will spew forth information on demand rarely succeeds. It did not work when Jack Webb as Sergeant Friday of *Dragnet* popularized it some forty years ago, and it does not work today. Furthermore, a quest for "just the facts" has the added detriment of alienating nearly everyone subjected to it.

An encounter with a representative of the law, no matter how routine it may seem to the officer, is far from routine in the minds of most people, whether they are suspects, victims, or witnesses. This encounter, often the result of some traumatic event, serves to heighten already existing feelings such as fear, guilt, and embarrassment. These as well as many other emotions inhibit a person's ability to provide information. Many investigators choose to ignore these feelings and stick to "just the facts" because it is easier. However, *unless interviewers deal with their subjects' feelings, they will never learn the facts.*

The Dangers of Preprinted Forms   The ultimate technique for avoiding personal involvement during an interview is the use of the preprinted fill-in-the-blanks form. It contains spaces for everything, usually beginning with the person's name and date of birth and proceeding through every conceivable bit of background information about that person. Each blank is usually numbered and the investigator must dutifully start with number 1 and work through the list. If the form is designed for a victim or witness, it will then often move to a series of blanks designed to enable the investigator to obtain a complete description of the culprit or culprits. To make this process logical and systematic, these forms usually start at the top, asking for the suspect's hair color and style and then work their way down the body to the feet. Unfortunately, few people have thought patterns that conform to the order of the preprinted form. By trying to force recall in this manner, the investigator will stymie the witness's memory and thus fail to get the needed information.

At the end of the fill-in-the-blanks section, these forms usually have a space for the investigator to record the witness's narrative account. By the time the investigator gets to this point, the questionnaire has often conditioned the witness to talk in sound bites. Brevity becomes the standard, and cooperative witnesses comply by severely editing and condensing their information. The investigator will record it, move onto the next interview, and at the end of the day proudly announce the completion of a significant number of interviews.

Despite deadlines and other factors that lend a sense of urgency to a case, *the completeness, accuracy, and clarity of the subsequent report usually determine the outcome of the case.* Failure to obtain the information precludes the possibility of meeting these standards and reinforces the criticism that officers cannot write—they cannot write what they do not know.

Preparing Questions in Advance   Some investigators, aware that no preprinted form can suffice for conducting an effective interview, prepare a list of questions in advance. Although the absence of any visible list of questions can sometimes lend an air of spontaneity to the interview, staunchly adhering to the list often becomes as inhibiting as the preprinted form. Interviewers who compose questions in advance and equate this to preparation miss the point. Dianne Sawyer, noted journalist and television commentator, suggested that interviewers are truly prepared only when they feel free to throw away that preparation. They must be so comfortable with the person and the situation that they have no reservations about where the conversation may take them. Only then can they get the facts they seek.

If preparing a list of questions helps you prepare for the interview, write the list. Indeed, doing so can help you tailor the interview to the person with whom you'll converse and help you make decisions about the how, when, and where of the interview. But be sure not to use the list as a crutch during the interview itself.

Listening   Some years ago, a newly commissioned federal investigator, a former local deputy from the Northeast, received her assignment to an office in the South. Unfortunately, she did not meet the local preconceived notion of a federal agent at that time. She was petite, the "wrong" gender, and had a "strange" accent. As a result, through no fault of her own, few people took her seriously despite her training and experience. Remarks such as, "Hey sweetie, why didn't they send a real agent?" frustrated her on a regular basis. However, at last she located a potential witness who did not question her credibility, a tenant farmer who answered her questions without hesitation. In fact, while standing in a field beside his tractor, he spewed forth such a torrent of information that she had difficulty grasping all of it. As a result, while trying to record this valuable data, she ignored the unintelligible phrase "washemans" that he periodically interjected into his monologue. The farmer seemed to use this phrase, accompanied by a slight nod of the head, in lieu of punctuation. Both the phrase and the gesture were lost on the agent.

To her chagrin, the credibility that she so desperately sought and for once had achieved disappeared when the fire ants began gnawing at her ankles. In his understated way, the farmer had been trying to warn her that she was standing beside an anthill; "watch them ants" was what he had been saying. According to the agent, dignity played no part in dealing with that situation; fire ant bites hurt. She resolved never again to ignore any part of what a person says during an interview. She had learned in one incident what many investigators never grasp—that a successful interview and the resulting written account depend on effective listening. It makes no difference what is asked or how it is answered; only what is heard and understood matters.

Failure to listen effectively during an interview may not always have the immediate reaction that the fire ants triggered, but it can often have even more painful results. Cases can and do go unsolved and criminals go unpunished, not because the needed information was not available, but because the investigator failed to "discover" it, often despite its being provided during an interview.

Investigators must concentrate on the witness's words and actions, rather than on formulating the next question, allowing their minds to wander, taking detailed notes, or assuming they know what the witness will say. Nothing that goes unheard during an interview will appear in any subsequent writing. Although this is certainly not the result of poor writing skills, it often gets categorized as such; after all, the writing is flawed.

Note Taking during Interviews   Note taking interferes with interviewing. A scientist's laboratory specimens may not object, but taking notes tends to inhibit people while they are being interviewed. It also interferes with the flow of a conversation and prevents effective listening by the interviewer. *However, if investigators hear relevant information that they did not already know and will not otherwise be able to remember, they must record it.* If they do not, it will not appear in any subsequent report.

This apparent conflict may not be nearly the dilemma it seems.

Absent some complicated topic involving numerous facts and figures that require contemporaneous recording, effective interviewers usually *limit* or *completely avoid* note taking during the conversation. After they have thoroughly discussed the topic with the person being interviewed, they move to another necessary phase of the interview, the *verification*. During this phase, while they confirm that they heard and understood what the interviewee said, *they record only the items they will need as prompts for writing the subsequent account.* To record more is counterproductive, and trying to produce a verbatim transcript will completely frustrate the interview process.

However, the second stage of note taking, that of *summarizing* one's notes—in this case, summarizing the interview soon after it has occurred—can be invaluable toward remembering what occurred.

Having discussed the primary technique for obtaining information here, we will deal with some areas that writers should consider before committing their findings to paper.

PREDRAFTING CONSIDERATIONS

The Importance of Written Reports

When scientists know for certain that their work has succeeded, they must experience feelings of satisfaction. They must want to shout to the world, "We did it!" However, their work is far from finished. Their methods as well as their results must be reviewed, tested, and scrutinized by many experts before their findings will be accepted. Much of this scrutiny centers on the written account of their research and its results. Knowing this, it is hard to imagine that they would assemble it in a haphazard fashion. With their having devoted so much time and effort to a project, we can presume that their findings will be presented in a meticulous, well-organized fashion designed to make understanding as easy as possible for scientific reviewers.

Police officers, too, must submit a report of their findings, and these findings can be the culmination of many investigative steps. A report may contain written accounts of

- numerous interviews
- surveillances
- searches
- arrests

done by many people; nevertheless, it is ultimately one person, often called the *case officer* or *lead investigator,* who has responsibility for it. Although scientists may have skeptics and critics, the latter might seem supportive compared to some who read police reports. Defense attorneys, for example, hope to discover any errors either in the methodology or the results and to use these flaws to attack the credibility of the investigators. Because of the adversarial nature of this process, officers need to devote the same energy to their writing that they do to solving their cases.

Predrafting/Preparation

Just as with interviewing, effective investigative writing depends to a large extent on preparation. An absence of planning becomes obvious to readers, who are often left wondering just what the writing was about. Bewilderment should rarely be the effect a writer seeks. Reports that have this effect lack value; they become reports for their own sake, a far too common situation. To avoid this outcome, writers should consider several items before they begin writing.

Readers and Their Roles   Interviewers cannot afford to concentrate on facts to the exclusion of the human element, and neither can writers. Writers must determine who will read their material and tailor it accordingly. Will an investigator read the material looking for leads to further develop the case? Will supervisors use it to make decisions about devoting additional resources to a case? Will a prosecutor use it to decide if and how to present some evidence in court? Will defense attorneys and their clients have access to the information and try to extract items to impeach the investigatoror witness?

Unlike many other situations in life, answers to these questions come easily. However, the answers come only if the writers ask the questions. The solution lies in the asking, and writers who do so and then maintain an awareness of the answers will write more effectively. They will be better able to focus their efforts on a specific purpose and eliminate meaningless and therefore confusing material.

Content: What to Leave In and What to Take Out   Scientists' reports surely omit much of what they did during their research; after all, they may have worked on the project for many years and explored many avenues that lead nowhere. Including all of these elements would overwhelm many readers by sheer volume. Confusion and boredom would beset the rest.

Investigators, too, must decide what to include and what to omit. They might reduce a three-hour interview to a single paragraph; they should if that is all that pertained to the case. While preparing documents, writers should ask and answer the question, "Does this matter?" They should then exclude anything that does not. *This principle does not give writers a license to exclude facts just because the facts do not support their agendas.* Investigators must strive to discover and then record the complete truth regarding an issue. However, much of the information gathered during interviews and other investigative procedures has no relevance to the case and should be omitted.

Getting Started

A blank sheet of paper is an intimidating thing. Clichés about a journey of 1000 miles that begins with a first step and the first sentence of a novel as the hardest to write apply equally to investigative writing. When it comes to writing, many people, including competent investigators who have gathered the relevant facts, have difficulty getting started.

Much of the difficulty of starting comes from the fear of failure, a fear often learned in elementary school. Many adults remember the feeling of terror they experienced as students when they struggled with a writing assignment while their teachers roamed the classroom. These teachers would detect the slightest flaws and correct them, often in a voice that oozed contempt and with sufficient volume for all to hear.

The teachers did not limit their criticisms to content; in fact, they often concentrated on grammar, spelling, and even penmanship. Most people find it difficult to think about facts and ideas and commit them to paper while having to worry about the mechanics of writing at the same time. This preoccupation can produce enough stress that the thought process falters, causing a lack of ideas and the resulting blank page.

Many students ultimately realized that the blank page often prompted less criticism than one that bore any imperfect prose. As a result, as time passed, they became more and more reluctant to begin writing; it was safer not to. Although the teachers have long since gone, the effects of their criticisms remain; the intimidation of the blank page endures.

Outlining and Other Ways to Defeat Writer's Block Investigators must develop some strategy for overcoming the inhibitions of the blank page. Exercises and the regular practice a writing log affords toward working through this difficulty. Another strategy—preparing an outline—also works for many report writers, particularly in instances where a large amount of information contributes to the sense of being overwhelmed that many investigators encounter. It has the appeal of being logical and systematic, a characteristic many law enforcement officers share. Outlining can be especially valuable in dealing with incoherent and seemingly irrelevant information, as often results from interviews. For example, the debriefing of a long-time hoodlum who has reached out to the police because he has fallen from grace with his organization and suspects he has become a target for "retirement" might fit this category. In a case like this, the hoodlum, because of his fears and his efforts to demonstrate his value, may provide a torrent of information, much of which may be only vaguely familiar to the investigator whom he has chosen as his confessor. Likewise, he will probably spew forth his information in a haphazard way, moving from topic to topic and back again with no hint of logic or organization.

Although the initial conversation is hopefully only the first of many debriefings in such a situation, the investigator must document any information initially provided. After all, the guy may be right about his life expectancy; there may be no second chance. This leaves the investigator with the challenge of reducing myriad facts from cryptic notes taken in the same disjointed fashion that the hoodlum provided them. The sheer quantity of the information as well as its lack of organization add to the stigma of the blank page. Where to begin becomes a major concern.

Outlining may solve this problem. By breaking the information into logical categories of manageable size, the chore becomes less daunting. For instance, the investigator might begin by giving the outline an overall title such as "The First Debriefing of Mr. X." Just doing this removes the blank page syndrome. The investigator can then consider the general topics the hoodlum discussed. Perhaps the general topic would be "Criminal activities and the people involved." The writer now has two major subheadings. By looking at them separately, the writer may begin to see some logical way to proceed—such as listing the criminal activities (loan sharking, gambling, and prostitution) and then subdividing these. Under the subhead "Gambling," the investigator might list the various gambling activities to include casinos, sports betting, horse racing; then continue subdividing each until the information has been exhausted. Here is what a portion of the outline might look like:

First Debriefing of Mr. X

    People involved
    Criminal activities
        Loan sharking
        Gambling
            Casinos
            Sports betting
                basketball
                football
                    line information
                    book makers
                        identities
                        locations

By repeating this process for each topic and always leaving space for additional entries, you can ultimately develop a skeleton of the entire session. You can then flesh out the skeleton by converting the words into sentences and the sentences into paragraphs. This systematic approach eliminates the feeling of being overwhelmed and adds some order to what had been chaos.

Freewriting   Some investigative actions, particularly interviews, pose a writing problem not because of the magnitude and complexity of the material but rather because of a lack of such substance. Often an extended interview may consist mostly of rambling conversation interspersed with a few relevant facts. Furnishing the facts in a succinct fashion and still enabling readers to understand what transpired poses problems for many writers.

In such cases, the outline does not offer a solution: the writer does not have enough details to make one. This situation conjures up the same hesitancy as that caused by the elementary school teacher who assigned an essay but refused to provide a topic. This indecision combined with the need to create an error-free document stifles both young students and experienced officers.

Freewriting, a technique that encourages the writer to adopt the attitude that mistakes do not matter, may offer the best solution to this dilemma. Many achieve this attitude by assuring themselves that nobody else will ever see their document, that they are writing it only for their own eyes. Therefore, they need not pay any attention to grammar, spelling, punctuation, or penmanship. The freedom to ignore these long-time inhibitors makes starting much easier.

Others pretend that they are *writing a letter* about the incident to a trusted friend. Trusted friends do not critique letters; they appreciate them. This technique might work well for the First Debriefing of Mr. X, where only vague and sparse information was obtained. People in those circumstances may be so anxious and tense that although they talk incessantly, they provide few substantive facts. Freewriting rather than outlining offers a more effective technique for getting started in such a situation. The result of such an approach might resemble the following:

> Just talked with Mr. X who is scared to death that he might get killed—he wants help and is willing to provide info in return. Will name names—rambled about why they are out to get him. Mentioned various activities including gambling—Mr. X was a successful bookie and went into great detail about the art of bookmaking—insists that being a gentleman of honor is the key—went into detail about his break with the mob—they think he is a snitch. . . .

The investigator could continue on in this manner until memory is exhausted and notes provide no further information. Continuing to write without pausing to evaluate provides the key to successful free writing. Writers must force themselves to ignore the hated but engrained concerns about recording anything in less than flawless fashion.

When they are finished freewriting, writers can review their narrative and highlight those points worth documenting. Then they can extract these items and place them in some logical sequence, perhaps by using the previously discussed outlining process. They can then convert the outline to sentences and paragraphs. For most investigators, this kind of conversion presents little difficulty once the facts are on paper. These ploys and any others that help the writer to begin are acceptable, such as the *dummy drafting.*

After overcoming the difficulties of getting started, the writer must now produce the document. The actual preparation of an investigative report, including the recording of individual investigative steps and the assembling of these into a finished product.

Selecting From the Case File

Nearly every law enforcement agency maintains a separate file for each case under investigation. This case file serves as a repository for all information that pertains to that case. It will not only have the results of both productive and unproductive investigative actions such as interviews and surveillances, but it will also often include administrative material. The file could contain such diverse items as notes taken during an interview, photographs of the crime scene, newspaper clippings about the case, laboratory reports, and a letter from the prosecutor requesting a briefing about the case's progress. Regardless of the complexity, diversity, or magnitude of the file's contents, the case officer bears the responsibility for maintaining and understanding it.

At some point during an investigation, other people such as supervisors or prosecutors may need to know the details of the case. Rarely can the case officer merely hand the file over to the interested party. For some, the irrelevant material would be indistinguishable from the pertinent, and for others, the file might contain material that they have no authority to see. For example, the file might contain information that could reveal the identity of a confidential informant, information that must be limited to those who have a "need to know." The case officer has the responsibility to select the appropriate material from the case file and to disseminate it in report form to the appropriate people.

Arranging the Documents

Regardless of the complexity of a case, an investigative report should consist of the file's pertinent documents arranged in a logical order. Report recipients should not have to read irrelevant material, flip-flop back and forth among the pages, nor refer to other documents. *Thus in most cases, the document that initiates the case serves as the first page of the report.* This document, usually prepared by the person who received the information, may have resulted from such diverse sources as a 911 call to a dispatcher, an observation by an officer on patrol, or a discovery by a detective while conducting a search. After selecting this document, the case officer merely adds each relevant document in the logical order, usually *chronological.* However, some cases are so diverse and complex that the case officer must arrange the report in some other way, such as by *types of crimes, locations,* or *suspects.*

Cover Memo and Table of Contents To complete the report, about the only writing the case officer needs to do is to prepare some type of cover sheet. It may identify the case officer, the suspect(s), the victim(s), and the dates covered by the investigation. Inclusive dates are particularly helpful if subsequent reports become necessary because they enable the reader to place the reports in chronological order. Sometimes cover sheets also contain a one-paragraph summary of the case.

Here is a sample cover sheet for a burglary report:

XYX Police Department

Case Number	Burglary—1234–97
Case Officer	Detective John Smith
Inclusive Dates of the Report	xx/xx/98–xx/xx/99
Primary Suspects	William James Joseph Johnson
Victim	Neighborhood Computers, Inc. 555 Maple Street (Merriwether Plaza)

Summary: On xx/xx/98, the above store was burglarized sometime during the early morning hours. Numerous printers, computers, and other hardware valued at over $30,000 were taken. Suspects apprehended three months later while trying to sell some of the proceeds to an undercover officer in a sting operation. Both suspects have been charged with grand larceny and are in custody awaiting trial. Others are suspected of being involved, and investigation is continuing.

Distribution:
1—Burglary Squad Supervisor
1—District Attorney
1—Case File

Whether or not the investigative report includes other items depends on the magnitude of the case. A report may contain dozens of interviews, numerous surveillances, and other investigative accounts as well as lab reports. In such instances, a *table of contents* may be appropriate.

Witnesses Section   Some cases may have so many potential witnesses that a separate section that *lists* witnesses, their addresses, and phone numbers and provides a *brief synopsis* of the nature of their testimony would prove invaluable to a prosecutor when preparing for trial.

Other Tips for Writing Component Parts of Reports

As previously indicated, report writing is a misnomer. Instead of writing a report, the case officer selects the appropriate material and assembles it. Therefore, compiling good reports results from good judgment, not from good writing. The actual writing was done by the participants in the case as they documented their actions and discoveries.

Investigators may not write full reports, but they still must write the individual pages that make up those reports. The critics of inept report writing are actually criticizing these individual accounts. However, merely knowing that the critics have used incorrect terminology does little to remove the anxiety many officers feel. Fortunately, recognizing this error in terminology offers the key to the solution. By viewing writing as a series of manageable steps instead of one overwhelming project, officers can identify and overcome their shortcomings. The following sections identify some of the areas of concern for many police writers and offer some suggestions for dealing with these problems.

Using First Person   Before considering the various techniques involved in documenting the results of an investigation, perhaps we should consider the issue raised most often by police officers in a recent survey conducted by one of us among participants in an e-mail list server discussion group. Asked about writing difficulties in their profession, they universally agreed on a need for clarity, but they could reach no accord as to what that means. Much of the dispute hinged on the question of whether police reports should be written in first or third person. Although the comments implied that many respondents had varying interpretations of those terms, most wondered whether report writers should refer to themselves by name, by title, or by the pronoun *I*. The responses revealed no clear consensus on this issue. Some stressed that using first person contributed to a report's clarity, while others argued in favor of the supposed objectivity afforded by the use of third person. The next section offers an acceptable solution regardless of style preference.

Using Preambles   Some writers manage to satisfy the desire to personalize their writing and still present an aura of detached objectivity by using an introductory paragraph to achieve the former and subsequently employing a journalistic approach to convey the latter. Their introductory paragraph or *preamble* gives the investigators a nearly automatic beginning for recording the results of any investigative action and further reduces the barrier of the blank page. They need only adapt the wording of the preamble to fit the specific type of investigation. Preambles for the investigative activities that make up a finished report can take various forms.

Interview Preamble   A preamble for an interview might read as follows:

> John Doe, of 100 Elm St., Smallville, Michigan, was contacted at his home by Smallville officers William Jones and Mary Smith on month/day/year. After introducing themselves and telling Mr. Doe they were interested in what he had seen at the convenience store the previous morning, Mr. Doe furnished the following information:

This format, or some variation of it, serves many useful functions, and it can be used for almost any interview.

This preamble allows the reader to avoid scanning extensive text to learn the identity of the interviewee; the name appears at the beginning.

In a report that contains dozens or even hundreds of interviews, such a tactic can save a great deal of time for the reader who is looking for a specific interview. It also sets forth where, when, and why the person was interviewed, questions that many readers wish to have answered early on.

The preamble also resolves the issue about using first person or third person by rendering it irrelevant. The wording of the preamble identifies the interviewer(s) by name and position, and thus achieves the clarity and personalization desired by some officers. Furthermore, it eliminates any need to make reference to them again. The writer need not say either "Doe told Officers Smith and Jones" or "Doe told us." The reader already knows that, and thus the writers can now merely relate what they learned, much as a newspaper account would do. This strategy lends an air of objectivity to the writing that some officers prefer.

Lastly, the preamble makes it clear that the person interviewed provided all the information that follows it. This makes any further reference to the source of the information unnecessary. The preamble eliminates the need for the writer to use phrases such as "he said" or "he advised," phrases that typically occur throughout many reports and often distract the reader. This format makes them not only unnecessary but also redundant. For instance, at the end of the preamble, the wording "furnished the following information" allows the writer to say, "Doe arrived at the store" not, "Doe said he arrived at the store." The preamble already attributes the information to Mr Doe.

Search Preamble   Obviously a preamble intended for an interview cannot be copied verbatim for the text of some other investigative activity. However, the same principles do apply. An account of a search might begin:

> Based on a warrant issued on month/day/year by Judge John Brown of the municipal court of Smallville, Michigan, a search was conducted at 100 Elm Street by Officers Mary Smith and John Jones from 2 p.m. to 4 p.m. on month/day/year. As indicated below, the following items were found and retained.

This introductory paragraph sets forth the authority for the search, identifies the searchers, and furnishes the specifics of the search regarding date, time, and location. Like the interview preamble, it allows readers to easily decide whether this document will contain the information they are seeking.

Subsequent paragraphs could then set forth the results of the search using the same criteria as in reporting an interview.

Listing Items Found in a Search.   Qualities such as relevance, objectivity, and clarity apply to all investigative writing, and writers must decide the style and format that best achieves these goals in each instance. For example, an investigator might report the items seized during a search of a gambler's office as a simple list of items found. However, the investigator might record the search of the home of a suspected serial killer in a completely different manner. The potential relevance of the specific location of various items and their proximity to each other might mandate an extensive, step-by-step narrative account of the search and a detailed description of each item seized. Case circumstances would determine the most appropriate format.

Arrest Preamble

On month/day/year, John Doe was arrested without incident at his residence, 100 Elm Street, by Officers John Jones and Mary Smith of the Smallville police department. The arrest was based on a warrant issued on month/day/year by Judge William Brown of the municipal court of Smallville, Michigan. After the arrest, Mr. Doe was immediately taken to the Smallville jail where he was fingerprinted, photographed, and detained pending a bail hearing.

As in the examples of other activities, this introductory paragraph regarding an arrest covers most issues. It not only answers the who, what, where, when, and why questions, it also tells how. It does this with the simple phrase "without incident." These two words enable the writer to omit any details of the tactics used. Giving details about tactics such as locating, handcuffing, and searching a suspect needlessly provides the defense with material to use during cross-examinations.

On the other hand, if the arrest did not occur "without incident," if resistance was encountered, the writer could modify the preamble to immediately alert the reader of this fact. The preamble might read: "After initially struggling with the officers, John Doe was subdued and . . ." Later, the writer could provide the details in the appropriate section of the text. By mentioning the resistance in the preamble, however, the writer ensures that the reader will not overlook it.

Interrogation Preamble
Technically, interrogations are a type of interview. However, their adversarial nature raises some unique issues and mandates some specific requirements. Writers must consider these requirements, such as issuing a Miranda warning, when composing a preamble for an interrogation.

Policies regarding advising people of their rights against self-incrimination vary from one department to another, and many go far beyond what the court mandated. However, all must adhere to the court requirement that people in custody be told of these rights and waive these rights prior to any questioning that could lead to admissions against themselves. By documenting that they did this, officers will not eliminate allegations of misconduct, but they can reduce the number and credibility of such allegations.

John Doe was contacted at the Smallville jail by Officer Mary Smith on month/day/year. Officer Smith identified herself to Mr. Doe and informed him of the reason for her visit. She then gave Mr. Doe a copy of a form entitled "Waiver of Rights," which he read, stated he understood, and then signed. Mr. Doe then furnished the following information.

Had Mr. Doe refused to sign the form or if Officer Smith had spent time explaining it or even reading it to him, the preamble should also indicate this. The writer should try as succinctly as possible to give the reader a clear understanding of what happened at the outset of the interrogation.

Three Issues: Relevance, Order, Lists

While using preambles can solve some formatting issues in reports, this section notes three other common concerns and offers suggestions for dealing with them.

Relevance   After setting the stage with an introductory paragraph, writers must now present whatever information they possess that relates to the case. They should include little if anything else. As they review their notes, outlines, or freewritten drafts, they should continually ask themselves if a point matters to the reader. Doing so will help them avoid cluttering their writing with extraneous information and will enhance its clarity.

Order of Information   Writers must also decide the proper order in which to present their material. Investigative activities have a beginning, middle, and an end; so does the information they produce. As a result, a *chronological* accounting of an event usually works best. This ordering rarely presents a problem in recording the results of interviews, inasmuch as witnesses and victims usually provide accounts of events as they occurred. However, sometimes they do not. For instance, a cooperative suspect may begin his story by discussing his recent arrest. He may then talk about his associates and move from there to how he initially got involved. Even so, if interviewers take the time to verify and understand what they heard, they can usually rearrange these bits of information into some orderly fashion, chronological or otherwise. The previously discussed *outlining* technique can often facilitate this organization process. *Investigators should feel no obligation to report items as they received them. Instead, they should always strive for clarity for the reader, and presenting items in a logical order can help achieve this goal.*

Handling Lists of Information   Many writing manuals stress the importance of using clear, concise, grammatically correct sentences. The preamble and body of an account of an investigative effort should usually meet this criterion. Because of the need for clarity, however, not all documentation of investigations lends itself to sentences and paragraphs. For instance, if Mr. Doe had given a detailed description of an associate during his interview, putting that data in paragraph form would look something like this:

> His associate is a white male, about forty years old, nearly six feet two inches tall who weighs approximately 230 pounds. He has dark-brown hair that is short on top and long on the sides. He has brown eyes, a fair complexion, a heavy mustache, a one-inch circular scar just below his right eye and a tattoo of an eagle on his right shoulder.

This description requires more than a cursory glance by readers to know what the person looked like; they would probably have to read it several times. Contrast this description with the following:

Race	White
Sex	Male
Age	40 (approximately)
Height	6'2"
Weight	230 lbs.
Hair	Dark brown (short on top, long on sides)
Eyes	Brown
Complexion	Fair
Scars	One-inch, circular below left eye
Tattoos	Eagle on right shoulder
Other	Heavy moustache

By putting the description in column format, the writer makes it much easier for the reader to envision the man. The more detailed the description and the greater the number of such items, the more important this clarity becomes. Imagine reading a paragraph that gives the results of a spot check of a parking lot, one that contained dozens of cars. Looking at that many cars of various makes, models, years, colors, and license plates in paragraph form would overwhelm most readers. More important, imagine the difficulty this kind of description would cause for someone charged with entering the data into a computer.

Although setting out descriptive data in columns aids readability, inserting these columns within the body of the narrative detracts from the overall appearance of a document. Writers can avoid this problem by putting all such descriptions at the end of the document. This method requires only a brief explanation such as:

Descriptions obtained during the interview, including that of Mr. Doe, are set forth below.

Obtaining Feedback on Drafts

When police officers tell "war stories," particularly traumatic ones, about their work, their partners almost always play a significant role. Officers develop extremely close relationships with their partners, often closer in many ways than with their own families. They have few if any secrets from each other. Yet few officers ever ask their partners to review their writing even if it recounts an event in which they worked together.

After having gone through the process of preparing a document, few people, including investigators, want somebody else to read it, much less change it. After all, they are the ones who did the investigation, and it should be reported in their style. Besides, they have read it several times and have even run it through spell-check; that should suffice.

Unfortunately, the adage about attorneys who defend themselves having fools for clients also applies to writers who edit their own work. Writers tend to read what they meant, rather than what they wrote. Writers need somebody else to find their mistakes, but ego or a reluctance to impose often prevents them from asking for help. Given the opportunity, defense attorneys will gleefully fill this role, but few officers relish this kind of "help." Defense attorneys will use the writers' mistakes to attack their credibility, offering the errors as evidence of incompetence and dishonesty.

To avoid this outcome, officers need to take advantage of the relationships they have developed with their partners—to trust others with your life but not trust them to critique your writing seems absurd. Besides, having one's mistakes corrected by a trusted friend in no way approaches the discomfort experienced when being cross-examined on the witness stand. Furthermore, by offering to reciprocate, officers can remove the stigma of imposition. They can also make the review process easier *by asking their reviewer specific questions* about the document and by noting any areas of concern. This technique not only helps reviewers focus their attention, it encourages them to provide concrete suggestions rather than generalized observations. Typical questions could include:

1. Which parts did you have to read more than once?
2. Where are there gaps in the information or any conflicting statements?
3. What in the report might a defense attorney readily misinterpret?
4. Would you be comfortable testifying based on this document, or would you change it?

Even when they are carefully written and logically assembled, reports can still contain stumbling blocks that detract from their effectiveness.

College Greek societies subject their prospective members to initiations and secret rites that foster both loyalty and a sense of uniqueness. Often the worse the ordeal, the stronger the allegiance. Law enforcement personnel also belong to a tightly knit community, one that occasionally subjects them to life-threatening ordeals. Members of this society often acquire their own vocabulary, codes of conduct, and prejudices. Sometimes these unique characteristics find their way into writing intended for readers outside the group. Officers need to be alert to this tendency and guard against several manifestations that would reflect poorly on the writers or their departments.

PITFALLS

Policespeak

"The alleged male perpetrator proceeded to exit said vehicle." The e-mail survey of law enforcement officers from around the world suggested that many people view a sentence like this as the epitome of what is wrong with much of the writing done by police officers. Although most officers know that a better version would be, "The man got out of the car," they disregard this knowledge as soon as their writing becomes official business. Much police writing continues to resemble an oldtime movie script written for Leo Gorcey, the leader of the Bowery Boys. His use of such phrases as "aforementioned prestidigitations" baffled everybody and enlightened no one. The scriptwriters did this to amuse the audience—police reports have no such purpose.

The tendency to write in *policespeak* occurs throughout law enforcement. Neither size or type of department nor officers' experience level seems to inhibit it. Many officers attribute this convoluted writing style to the nature of their opposition—defense attorneys. In an effort to "outlawyer the lawyers" by sounding sophisticated and judicial, officers sacrifice clarity and conciseness. Defense attorneys take advantage of this flaw and use it to attack the officers' credibility, the very attribute they were trying to emphasize.

Regardless of the cause of the poor prose, officers must overcome this misguided inclination for creating confusion, not an easy task. Having a partner review the draft rarely works; after all, the partner belongs to the same society. Even the department's clerical staff become conditioned to this style of writing and will thus fail to correct it. One technique that often helps depends on the writers' willingness to look at each sentence and ask themselves if there is a simpler and clearer way to write it. Some successful writers view each sentence as if it were intended for their twelve-year-old son or daughter. Just asking this question provides the answer: "Would I ask my daughter to *secure the rear exit to our residence* or would I would I ask her to *lock the back door?*" The key to success is in the asking.

Tactical Talk

Another problem comes from officers' desire to sound official in their writing. When involved in "operational situations" (i.e., real police work), officers value efficiency in both words and actions. Prompt, decisive actions provide a margin of safety, and succinct radio messages help make them possible. Officers do not want to hear long rambling radio transmissions when a few words would do.

Those who try to duplicate this operational style when writing can produce documents that read like the dialogue from a grade-B cave-dweller movie: "Saw suspect in house, arrested him." Eliminating subjects, verbs, adjectives, and adverbs from a written narrative of an event does not convey a professional image. Instead, it gives the impression that the writer thinks that a capital letter followed by a period equals a sentence.

In some instances, the desire for brevity stems from defensiveness. Investigators, particularly those who have been brutally cross-examined, often adopt the philosophy that the fewer words they write, the less they will have to defend. Unfortunately, good defense attorneys can also detect omissions and may use them to attack the writer's integrity by implying some type of coverup. Regardless of investigators' intentions, an overzealous effort to minimize their writing can result in the omission of facts as well as words, facts needed by the prosecutor or other readers for whom the account was written.

Wordiness

Just as some officers attempt to convey professionalism by being too brief, others take the opposite approach. They assume, as do members of many other professions, that a document's importance depends on its volume and the size of its words; in each case, the bigger the better. Writers who use this philosophy produce vague, convoluted documents that defy understanding. Bewildering a reader rarely enhances a writer's stature.

Investigators can reduce this bewilderment by viewing their documents as crime scenes that the reader must examine for evidence. Just as irrelevant items clutter a crime scene, vague or excessive words clutter a document. In either case, the more clutter, the more difficulty. Before Lincoln gave his Gettysburg address, he was preceded by a famous orator who spoke for two hours. How many people now know who that person was or what he said? Good writers, like good speakers, use only the words needed to convey their ideas.

Jargon

Any outsider who has ever listened to a technocrat can understand why research companies hire writers to describe their products. Without these writers, the company's products would go unsold because many of the researchers lack the ability to articulate their work in lay terms. Police officers also face this problem. Much of their language, particularly acronyms and abbreviations that they take for granted, has little meaning to outsiders. "The decision was made at SOG, rather than by the SAC": The writer of this sentence intended to tell the reader that responsibility for the decision lay with headquarters (seat of government, or SOG) rather than a field office (special agent in charge, or SAC). Even though the writer understood this, few people outside the organization would have.

Even worse, much police terminology has multiple meanings, thus forcing readers to puzzle out an interpretation. "The unit remained operational" could refer to a tactical team's readiness, or it might mean that the officer's car was still drivable. "We secured the area" could mean they established a perimeter, or it might mean that they departed the scene. The reader must put these sentences into context to determine their meaning. Use of such language increases the chance of misunderstanding.

Prejudices

The process of dealing with criminals on a daily basis makes cynics of most officers. Sooner or later they come to regard everyone as a criminal—all are guilty until proven innocent, and even then they are probably guilty of something. This attitude hinders investigators by destroying their objectivity in dealing with people and in evaluating the information they collect. Then they reveal this cynicism in their writing, and it hurts their credibility.

If most of their work involves specific ethnic, racial, or other cultural groups, this cynicism can also lead to the acceptance of stereotypes. Indicators, some subtle and some blatant, of these prejudices can creep into investigators' writings, and defense attorneys will use them to divert the court's attention from the issue of guilt or innocence. Instead, the officer's character and suitability become the issue. Defense attorneys have gotten more than one acquittal using this ploy.

Police cynicism does not stop with the general public. They often perceive that judges, politicians, and their own bosses place unreasonable restrictions on them while demanding ever-expanding services. These perceptions, justified or not, affect the actions of some officers. They sometimes respond with acts of malicious obedience that can cause problems for them. A police officer who drags a traffic violator from his car and forces him to a spreadeagle position, a procedure clearly intended for dangerous criminals, will get no more support than a coach who demands that girls on an adolescent sports team obey the rule requiring players to wear jock straps.

The same principle holds true for police writing. Not just blatant terminology but any language designed to ridicule a portion of society has no place in a police report. No matter how harmless or amusing it may seem to some, its presence hurts the image of the writers and their profession. For example, officers who refer to manhole covers as personhole covers leave no doubt about their attitudes on a mandate to avoid sexist language.

Although most officers do not deliberately try to offend others with their writing, they sometimes do so inadvertently. They can be oblivious to the offensive nature of words and phrases. On other occasions, writers offend through a misguided attempt at political correctness. Although use of the term policewoman lacks the sarcastic intent of *personhole cover*, it still distinguishes an officer by gender. Failing a valid reason for making such distinctions, writers should try to avoid them, and they usually can. In this instance the term *police officer* works quite well.

Unfortunately, writers have difficulty detecting these kinds of problems even when they look for them. Because *they* do not feel offended, they fail to understand or even notice that their words might insult others. To overcome this discrepancy, they must adopt the attitude of the public speaker, who, faced with the question of whether or not to use some material, should already know the answer: if you need to question material, do not use it. Not only will this tactic eliminate offensive words, it will help writers to select more precise terms and thus enhance the quality of their writing.

Assumptions

Officers often make assumptions during their investigations. If they see *A* and *C*, they correctly assume that *B* must also have occurred. However, during a fast-moving, tension-filled situation, the difference between an observation and an assumption can become blurred. This failure to distinguish between the two can cause problems.

During a surveillance, an agent watched two people, one of whom was carrying an envelope, enter a restaurant. When the couple left the restaurant, the agent saw the other person carrying the envelope. The agent's account indicated that one individual had given the envelope to the other. However, under cross-examination the agent admitted that he had not seen the envelope change hands. Following this admission, the defense forced him to acknowledge that he had recorded an assumption as a fact. The defense then asked, "What other facts in this report are really assumptions?" followed by, "Is there anything in this report that is not an assumption? Can we believe any of it?" Nobody who has experienced this type of treatment ever wants to endure it again.

To solve cases, investigators must combine their observations and experiences to reach conclusions and make decisions. However, in reporting their results they must take care to avoid confusing facts with suppositions. "Do I know this happened or do I think it happened?" is the question writers must continually ask themselves. Maintaining an awareness of the tendency to commit such mistakes is often sufficient to prevent them from occurring, or at least it helps one detect and correct them.

Judgments

Readers make judgments based on the facts provided by the investigators. Investigators must not provide the conclusions. Officers who have worked road patrol know this fact well. Regardless of how drunk a driver might appear, they refrain from classifying the driver as drunk. Instead, they describe the symptoms that led them to that conclusion. Their writing will show that the driver had slurred speech, emitted a strong odor of alcohol, and could not walk a straight line. The readers will conclude that the driver was drunk.

One situation in which officers have difficulty omitting their opinions occurs when they conclude that a person has lied to them. The feel compelled to tell their readers, particularly other officers, of their opinion because they know that merely relating what they heard will be misleading. Rather than inadvertently reporting an assumption as a fact, they deliberately include an opinion despite awareness of the possible - consequences.

They could avoid this dilemma by rejecting the fallacy that interviews consist solely of words. The nervous mannerisms, a lack of eye contact, and whatever else they saw all contributed to the interviewer's knowledge; they are part of the interview process. Had they reported these observations, the reader could have reached the same conclusion they did—the person lied.

Misuse of Quotes

Using the exact words of a recognized figure in giving a speech or writing an essay can add impact and credibility. In an investigative report, a criminal's exact words may occasionally reveal a uniqueness that could prove valuable later on. Lacking this type of situation, writers should use quotes sparingly, if at all, and they should never use them to disguise investigative shortcomings.

To Conceal Vagueness If interviewers hear ambiguous words or phrases during an interview, they must clarify them. Failure to do so will present problems when they try to reduce the interview to writing. A bank teller may say that she "buzzed out" during a robbery. Quoting this phrase will not help the reader to understand it. Did the teller faint, make a phone call, or escape using an exit that had a hidden electronic lock? The reader cannot determine the distinction, but the interviewer could have. Quotation marks will not salvage poor verification during an interview.

To Justify Obscenities Even though criminals often direct obscene language at their victims, investigators rarely need to repeat these obscenities in their written documents. Some investigators justify doing so on the basis that it helps to convey the callousness of the criminals and their deeds. Others include them for their shock value. The loss of professionalism and respect caused by the presence of obscenities in the investigative report more than offsets any value they provide. Putting the obscenities in quotes does not negate this negative effect.

An investigative report consists of a compilation of written accounts of the various activities performed by those involved in the case. If the investigators effectively gathered the information and properly recorded it, assembling the report poses few problems. Assembly rarely involves more than arranging the separate accounts in a logical order and preparing a cover page. This principle holds true regardless of the complexity of the case. However, if the investigators performed poorly either in the collection of the data or in recording it, no amount of shuffling of the pages will remedy these flaws.

CHAPTER 21

Writing Memos

THE NEED FOR STRONG INTERNAL COMMUNICATION

"I know you need more help; you and everybody else on this squad. Put your request on paper and I'll consider it along with all the others." Law enforcement paperwork goes far beyond recording investigations. Officers must document actions, provide explanations, and make requests of many kinds. The old adage "If it's not on paper, it doesn't count" still holds true. Even in the age of the computer, which proponents said would reduce reliance on paper, the number and size of documents—paper as well as electronic—have dramatically increased. Stated goals notwithstanding, the greater the ease of communication, the more documents organizations tend to produce—especially internal documents.

Even the effort to reduce an organization's reliance on memos and reports can lead to more paperwork. Consider the following anecdote: At an all-department meeting, executives of a large investigative agency stressed the need to reduce that agency's paperwork. They suggested that eliminating needless duplication of documentation would make a significant contribution to this goal. As an example, they said that if they recorded information furnished to them by an employee, the employee should not document the same information. They also recommended that employees reduce the size of documents by restricting them to the issue at hand rather than providing a lot of needless information; if they asked what time it was, they said, they did not want to know how to build a watch.

Then the executives solicited ideas about addressing these problems. Somebody suggested that the training department teach all new employees how to write concisely, a skill few had. A training department representative disputed this contention. He pointed out that although he did not know the exact numbers, he was certain that he could get the data showing that his division had tested many trainees and that few had significant writing deficiencies. The executive asked the trainer to get the test results to him as soon as possible.

The following day the trainer phoned the executive and said that the training department had tested 1,112 trainees and that only six had shown serious writing deficiencies. The executive replied, "Can you put that on paper and send it to me?" The trainer prepared a memo setting forth the results of the testing and forwarded it to his boss for approval. The boss returned it with the notation, "Beef this up a bit before we send it to headquarters. Tell them about some of the great stuff we are doing here with our trainees."

As Pogo said, "We have met the enemy, and they are us."

MEMO FORMAT

Predrafting, outlining, drafting, and revising can often improve writing regardless of the document or the profession. Clarity, conciseness, and grammatical accuracy also contribute to the quality of any document.

Formats for internal documents vary greatly from one agency to another; nevertheless, many have common features that merit consideration here.

Headings

Horror stories abound about documents gone unread until too late, either because they were misdirected or because they were in an inbox where they gradually sank to the bottom. Although nothing can guarantee this fate will not happen to any given memo, the writer can reduce the chance of either of these outcomes by *making the recipient and topic noticeable* at a glance in the *heading*.

Unless the agency uses a preprinted form or, more likely, a template on a computer, the writer should

1. *Date* the memo.
2. Using official names and titles, list the recipient at the top, followed by the *sender* and the *topic*.

Writers have little if any leeway regarding the first two categories, but how they word the topic or title may determine the attention the memo will get. Consider the following memo titles: "Need for Vigilance" versus "Enemy Attack Expected." Although the contents might be the same, the latter title will probably get a quicker response. Headings should never merely announce a general topic; they should *alert the reader to the type of action needed.*

References

Writers often produce memos whose effectiveness depends on information contained in other documents, which sometimes require furnishing copies of those documents or restating their information. If writers know that their recipients have access to the other information, however, they can merely *call attention* to it. Most readers would prefer reading one line on a memo— "Reference my report of October 18"—to receiving an attached report of sixty pages, a report they already had received.

Getting to the Point

Despite administrators' constant demand for full documentation, few want to spend much of their time reading the material they insisted the officers produce. As prime minister of Great Britain during World War II, Winston Churchill reputedly insisted that his advisors limit their memos to one page. Although writers deal with many topics they cannot cover adequately in one page, they should strive for brevity whenever possible.

Many administrators regard themselves as action-oriented people who want to get to the bottom line; they often say they "skimmed the material." Few have taken speedreading courses, so what they really mean is that they read the first few sentences and then skipped to the bottom of the page. Writers must take advantage of this practice by *immediately stating their main point or premise* and following this statement with supporting data. If they have a specific *request* based on the data, they should put it either at the beginning—if the request is the main point of the memo—or at the end, the other likely place that a busy reader will look. *Never bury the request in the middle of a page or document.*

Such careful placement improves the chances of the request's being granted or at least considered, simply because it is more apt to be read.

Copies

If writers send copies of a memo to several recipients, they should note this fact on the memo. Sometimes just knowing that somebody else—especially someone whose good will your recipient wants to keep—has received a copy can prompt action that might otherwise not happen. *Caution:* While sending a copy of your memo to your recipient's boss may prompt your recipient's action, judge carefully the risk of needlessly antagonizing your recipient before sending copies up the office hierarchy.

Moreover, writers should *always make a second copy* for themselves. In the age of computers, this copying can take the form of an electronic copy instead of a printed page. However, most computer experts recommend that the copy be stored on a separate disk rather than, or as well as, on the computer itself. One failed hard drive can obliterate years of records.

Sample Memo

Although many formats can fulfill a memo's requirements, a generic memo based on the points we have discussed might resemble the following:

Date: xx/xx/xx

TO: Sgt. Marie Jones, Fraud Squad II
FROM: Det. William Smith
TOPIC: Overtime for surveillance team
REF: Position Paper of Chief Jakob dated xx/xx/xx

BODY: The surveillance team became entitled to overtime pay as of two weeks ago. As mandated in the referenced paper, each member of the team has worked the required number of hours for each of the last four pay periods. These hours were devoted exclusively to surveillances requested by Fraud Squad II. It is requested that you execute the necessary forms for overtime to be paid to the surveillance squad.

COPIES: 1—Chief Jakob, 1—Detective Smith, 6—Surveillance Squad

---

PURPOSES/TYPES OF MEMOS

Writers must consider the purpose of their memos and tailor the contents accordingly.

Depending on their purposes, memos dealing with the same topic can vary substantially. The following section deals with three typical types of memos that correspond to differing purposes. We include a short sample of each type.

Memos to Document

Officers prepare some memos with the absolute certainty that nobody will ever read them. *Memos to document* are often regarded in this manner, because they merely provide supporting data or evidence of action taken rather than initiating new action or making a request. For example, such a memo may result from a requirement that officers notify their organization that they attended some mandatory training program. Officers know that a clerk will glance at the title, check an appropriate block on some form, and file the memo where nobody will ever see it again. As a result, they pay almost no attention to the contents when they write it.

Sooner or later, disaster results. Three years after the writing of the innocuous training memo, a lawsuit makes it a big issue. Dates of the course and topics covered, along with numerous other things that the officer could have documented in a few sentences, become critical. Unfortunately the memo does not contain that information, and its writer learns the hard way that "if it ain't on paper, it didn't happen."

Sample Memo   A chief asks the head of the burglary squad to give him an account of the current situation. The memo text might run as follows:

Sample Memo to Document

TO: Chief McMillan
FROM: Lieutenant Suarez, Burglary Squad
TOPIC: Current Situation
DATE: xx/xx/xx

The burglary situation in this precinct is not encouraging. The number of burglaries reported during the past two years has nearly doubled from the previous two-year period, but the number of solutions has remained constant. Of the 315 reported burglaries, over 200 were of residences, 75 were of businesses, and the rest were distributed among schools, churches, and automobiles.

Copies: 1—Lieutenant Suarez

Despite the brevity of this text, it achieves the intended purpose: providing the reader with an understanding of the nature and scope of the problem. A one-sentence memo, "Things are bad and getting worse," although accurate, would not. On the other hand, the writer avoids cluttering the document with irrelevant data. The memo contains no details regarding specific cases, investigative incentives, or other information the chief had not requested.

Memos to Explain

Because everybody makes mistakes, sooner or later all officers find themselves in the uncomfortable position of having to explain some transgression. Many such incidents have no real consequences and require *memos of explanation* only because they happen to be a pet peeve of the boss. Much of what many in law enforcement hate about paperwork falls into this or some similar category: what they call "paper for its own sake." Officers must beware of treating these memos of explanation in too cavalier a manner or, worse, using them as a means of ridiculing authority. For instance, a chief may regard the department's weight standards as critical, and when officers weigh in over the limit they must write memos of explanation on what they are doing to correct the problem. One officer might respond that because the weight limit is based on a height-to-weight ratio, he is not trying to lose weight but is instead doing everything in his power to grow taller. What could have been a three-sentence explanation becomes an ongoing battle with the boss. No good ever comes of such contests.

Because of the perceived triviality of many required memos, some officers tend to regard all of them, particularly those requiring explanations, with contempt. This contempt leads them to write superficially to meet the requirement for submission while providing little real information. Years later, when the incident results in an administrative or legal action, writers have none of the details they need to defend their actions. Now they must write memos to explain the lack of earlier explanation, but these belated efforts lack credibility.

Sample Memo   A memo in response to a chief's question, "What are we doing about the burglary situation?" would differ from the previous request for a status report. Again, although a one-line response such as "We are devoting considerable resources to the problem" might be accurate, it would not likely satisfy the chief. A better option might read:

Sample Memo to Explain

TO: Chief McMillan
FROM: Lieutenant Suarez, Burglary Squad
TOPIC: Actions to Respond to Increase in Burglaries
DATE: xx/xx/xx

As a result of the increase in burglaries, we have doubled the number of officers assigned to work these cases. Because the largest increase is in house burglaries, patrols have been instructed to devote a greater percentage of their time to residential areas. In addition, detectives have been told to increase their efforts to develop informants in these areas. We have also been in touch with several insurance companies who have agreed to provide significant cash rewards to anyone who assists in recovering stolen goods.

COPIES: 1—Lieutenant Suarez

Memos to Request or Propose

As indicated earlier, organizations function because of paper, much of it internal. Not just administrators but also street-level officers, if they are to be successful, must write effective *memos to request;* that is, proposals. Whether or not they get the needed assistance in a complex case, obtain permission to change shifts, or receive authorization to attend an in-service training program may depend on how well they write their requests. Using some of the techniques described in the following paragraphs may increase a writer's approval rate.

Memos to Persuade

Some law enforcement personnel consistently get suspects to admit willingly to otherwise unprovable crimes. Officers who are able to do this understand the art of persuasion. Yet many of these same officers, when confronted with the need to write a memo designed to convince others to do their bidding or honor their requests, fail miserably. They provide suspects with good reasons to confess but do not give administrators good reasons to approve their proposals. They abandon the very skills that make them good interrogators.

Successful *memos to persuade* often result from the same persuasive techniques interrogators use, and examining some of these tactics can help enhance persuasive writing. The intent of this section is not so much to teach new skills as to make you aware that the skills you already use in one arena can apply to others. Officers who can sell suspects on the idea of going to jail should certainly be able to sell an administrator on the approval of any reasonable request.

Interrogators do not get confessions by asking, "Did you rob the store?" Instead, they try to offer the suspect logical or emotional reasons to confess. One such ploy, *creating a sense of urgency,* can sometimes prompt an admission. In the case of the robbery, they might suggest a need to react quickly: "You were not alone in this, and we got two of your partners. The first one who talks might get a break; after that, cooperation will mean nothing. Who's going to get some consideration, you or one of those other guys?"

This same sense of urgency can often be applied in a memo. For instance, in requesting resources for a sting operation, the writer might suggest, "Experience shows that the peak season for burglaries is in the next three months. If we are to take advantage of this fact, we need to begin our operation at once, something we cannot do until the resources have been allocated. The results we can get with the same efforts three months from now will pale in comparison to what we could achieve right now."

Interrogators sometimes succeed because they manage to create the impression that they are entitled to a confession, that *the suspect owes it to them* in return for something they have done for them. "I believe you when you tell me you did not get any money from the robbery. You know why? Because this wasn't your idea—you just went along for the ride, and I am going to make sure the prosecutor knows that; I am not going to let him blame you for planning this thing. You were just along for the ride, weren't you?" By accepting the suspect's version of the crime and offering to defend it to others, the officer has put the suspect in his debt.

By the same token, the memo writer might note, "During the past six months our squad has conducted more investigations and cleared more cases than at any time in the past. This performance earned plaudits from the front office for the entire squad. However, the squad now needs some relief, or the quality of their work will begin to suffer." Supervisors who read such comments may well recognize that their success has resulted from the efforts of others and feel indebted to them.

Good interrogators *use the suspect's own words* to compel a confession. "You just told me you were at the scene. Now I am telling you we can show that there was only one person at the scene, the one who did it. You also told me you were a man who accepts responsibility for his actions. Based on what you said, that you were there and that you are a responsible man, then you must admit that you did it."

Similarly, the memo to the supervisor might say, "As you indicated in your all-personnel directive of six months ago, 'Anyone who can get the cases will get the resources needed to work them.' Since then, my partner and I have opened far more cases than needed to meet your directive. Based on your statement, we are requesting the assistance needed to work them." This approach has a much better chance of success than a memo whose wording amounts to, "Give us the help you promised."

ADOPTING A POINT OF VIEW

Interrogators, sales representatives, and writers of memos have one thing in common: they lack the authority to demand compliance. Absent this power, they are left with only the opportunity to persuade; successful ones do it effectively. They achieve this effectiveness not just by using various persuasive techniques but also by tailoring their presentations to the individual who can grant their requests.

Unlike investigative report writers, who must write in an objective manner devoid of opinion, memo writers often have no such restriction. They strive to convey their opinions, to convince others of the correctness of their views, and to influence the behavior of their readers. *Memo writers have a perspective* and often have no reason to convey opposing views with the same zeal that they do their own.

Although writers of both investigative results and memos must consider their audiences, the former have to deal with a variety of readers with different backgrounds and agendas, while the latter usually have a more select readership, often only one person. This narrow focus offers memo writers an opportunity to tailor their writing to that person's style and taste. Just as investigators should learn as much about their subjects as they can before interviewing them, memo writers should invest the time needed to understand the recipients of their efforts.

Readers and Personality Type

Although we must avoid the temptation to stereotype any profession or role, realizing that people tend to gravitate to careers that suit their personalities can sometimes help in dealing with them. The following section compares just one aspect of two different personality types and their tendency to assume different roles within law enforcement. Perhaps this example will illustrate how a writer's awareness of the reader's perspective, value system, and style can contribute to successful memo writing.

Understanding Your Own Personality

Writers need first to recognize their own perspectives and values before trying to understand those of other people. Although every person is unique, a variety of instruments designed to quantify various aspects of personality reveals an amazing number of similarities among most law enforcement personnel. One such instrument, designed by David Keirsey and Marilyn Bates, classifies people into four categories or temperaments, which they label "guardians," "idealists," "rationals," and "artisans."* When the Kiersey-Bates survey was administered to over 1,000 law enforcement personnel, the results placed well over 90 percent of them into one group, the "guardians," a category that makes up only 38 percent of the general population.

Guardians display a mix of characteristics that distinguishes them from the other temperaments. Other temperaments lack some of these traits or possess them to a lesser degree. These characteristics include:

1. A reliance on senses rather than on intuition
2. A respect for traditions
3. A desire for clearly defined parameters of behavior
4. A philosophy expressed by the motto "If it ain't broke, don't fix it"

However, the dominant characteristic of the guardians is their *sense of duty,* their need to serve. Knowing that something needs to be done provides them with sufficient motivation to act. The degree to which they feel this obligation to contribute sets them apart from all others.

Successful investigators, most of whom belong to the guardian type, realize that these values have little impact on criminals. Respect for rules and duty has little appeal for most confirmed lawbreakers. Although criminals may give these values lip service when it benefits them to do so, the values of the personality group Kiersey and Bates label "artisans," such as excitement, adventure, and a freedom from restrictions, have more appeal for lawbreakers. Ineffective investigators ignore this difference and instead often berate criminals with the refrain, "It's the right thing to do." This tactic rarely works regardless of how often or how loudly investigators say it. Instead, the statement "Although it might be a bit dangerous, there is good money involved, and it could provide a real rush" offers a better chance of success. Whether developing an informant or seeking a confession, good investigators appeal to the criminals' values rather than their own.

The Personalities of Proposal Readers

Unfortunately, many effective investigators who know that their values hold little appeal to criminals fail to realize that their value systems may not always appeal to their fellow officers, either. Members of the law enforcement community represent various personality profiles, including a category Kiersey and Bates refer to as "rationals." Unlike the guardians, rationals rely on intuition rather than on their senses, and they are more motivated by a desire for improvement than by a need to serve. Although they make up about 12 percent of the general population, experience shows that the number of rationals in law enforcement is far fewer.

Though few in number, the rationals should not be ignored by the rest of law enforcement: the rationals' desire for improvement combined with the intuitive thinking that enables them to envision their organization's futures makes them prime candidates for promotion; rationals tend to achieve leadership roles. An informal survey of the membership of a state police agency showed that although the department had only a few rationals, they headed thirteen of the department's sixteen divisions. Thus, the memos written by guardians are often destined to be read by rationals.

Although rationals may appreciate the concepts of duty and a need to serve that the guardians value so highly, they are far less motivated by these ideals. Instead, rationals tend to look for the big picture and the bottom line. "What will be the total impact of my approval or rejection of this request?" may well be the question that the administrator asks before making a decision. Writers who have addressed this question have a better chance of gaining approval.

Although a reader's perspective may be a minor concern when writing memos to document or explain, it becomes paramount in writing proposals or requests. Consider the following versions of a memo designed to obtain additional resources:

Version 1

The number of burglaries in this precinct has increased dramatically in the past two years. Citizens are afraid to leave their homes for fear that nothing they own will be there when they return. As the burglaries have increased, so have the insurance rates, and most people can no longer afford adequate coverage. Our citizens have a right to expect to feel free to come and go as they wish, and it is our duty to ensure that they can. By setting up a storefront to serve as a fence for stolen goods, we could identify most of the major players and get them off the street. The resources needed to meet this responsibility are . . .

Version 2

During the past two years, despite doubling the number of officers on patrol, house burglaries have tripled while cases cleared have remained stagnate. Meanwhile, many higher-profile cases that may determine how headquarters will allocate support remain inactive. Establishing a storefront operation would enable us in three months to make more arrests and recover more merchandise than our precinct has done in the past two years. This improvement would reduce the burglary problem to a level that would enable us to reassign officers to the priority programs. The resources needed to solve this problem are . . .

Depending on the reader's perspective, either the first memo, which stresses obligation, or the second, which emphasizes outcome, has a better chance of approval. The advantage does not depend on the quality of the request but on the reader's outlook. Administrators must carefully choose how to allocate their limited resources, and they tend to approve requests that are in harmony with their own perspectives.

Based on the Kiersey-Bates analysis of temperaments, the odds would favor the second memo (directed to a rational type), but writers need not play the odds. If, instead, they make the effort to ascertain their readers' perspectives and write accordingly, they will consistently get their requests approved.

*David Kiersey and Marilyn Bates, *Please Understand Me* (Del Mar, CA: Prometheus Nemesis, 1984).

PART SIX

Testimony

CHAPTER 22

Testimony Defined

TESTIMONY

The opinions or conclusions of witnesses or recognized authorities is referred to as **testimony.** Speakers use testimony to support or reinforce points they want their audiences to accept. The value of the testimony is related both to the listeners' opinion of its acceptability and to the speaker who presents it. Consider this opening of a student's speech:

> You try to stop yourself, but for some reason you can't! The child keeps on screaming, "Mommy, Mommy, please don't hit me anymore!" You've lost control and until your rage subsides, you can't stop, even though you know you should. Not until you are caught or you do something severely harmful is anything done about it. When it's all over, you have inflicted the worst kind of human atrocity on your own child. How do I know this? Because I used to beat my own child until I got help.

The young woman who gave this speech had her audience's attention not only because of the story she was recounting but also because she had the courage to relate what she had done and how she had overcome it. Her abuse of her own child did not enhance her believability and create acceptance for what she was saying, but her willingness to admit that she was personally involved in her topic did.

The use of testimony usually adds trustworthiness to what a speaker says—a necessity for all speakers who are not yet established as experts on their chosen speech topic. The speaker's own experience can be an excellent form of testimony as in the previous example. When the speaker's reputation and experience are insufficient, the use of a recognized and trusted authority can be invaluable in gaining listeners' acceptance.

Testimony can either support or clarify material or both. Here is an example of testimony that does both:

> The following statement by the American Automobile Association sums up experiments too numerous to mention and represents the best current professional opinion on automotive safety: "We know that seat belts, if used properly and at all times, can save hundreds of lives each year. By 'used properly' we mean that both the shoulder and seat belts must be fastened."

Here the speaker adds support by citing the American Automobile Association as a source of information, and clarifies what seat belts can do, and explains the meaning of the phrase "used properly."

Testimony can be either quoted directly or paraphrased. Paraphrasing is an effective method of condensing a long text or clarifying a passage that is too technical for audience members to understand. Sometimes audience members tune out speakers who use long and complex quotations. Restating long quotations in your own words helps make the source's words fit the tone of your speech. If you paraphrase, be sure not to violate the meaning of the original statement.

Certain statements are so well phrased that they cannot be stated any better. An example is the forceful and unforgettable statement made by John F. Kennedy in his 1961 presidential inaugural address: "Ask not what your country can do for you; ask what you can do for your country." Always quote such statements word for word. Misquoting someone can be embarrassing, but even worse, it can destroy your believability. Double-check every quotation for accuracy and source, and never use a quotation out of context.

Testimony should meet two essential tests: The person whose words are cited must be qualified by virtue of skills, training, expertise, recognition, and reputation; and the expert's opinion must be acceptable and believable to your listeners.

The person you quote should be a qualified authority on the subject. For example, an athlete's endorsement of tennis shoes and a movie star's endorsement of cosmetics are fairly believable because they use such products in their work. But when celebrities advertise products completely unrelated to their area of expertise, their opinions becomes less believable. Avoid using celebrities' names solely because they are well known. The best testimony comes from a person whose knowledge and experience are related to the topic and who is recognized by your listeners.

For maximum believability, testimony should also come from objective sources. The objectivity and neutrality of authorities is particularly important when your subject is controversial. For example, in trying to persuade an audience that today's automobiles are safer than those of a decade ago, it is more convincing to quote the American Automobile Association or the National Safety Council than the president of an automotive company. Listeners tend to be suspicious of opinions from a biased or self-interested source.

COURT TESTIMONY

Now that general testimony has been briefly explained, what is Court testimony and how does it differ from general testimony. Remember that general testimony is the opinion or conclusions of person as witnesses or individuals recognized as experts. Presentation of this testimony in a court setting or during a deposition requires skill, preparation, and persuasion and delivery techniques.

Deposition Testimony

Each side of a lawsuit has the right to ask questions to the opposing parties, prior to and during trial, regarding the facts, issues and circumstances involved in a case.

A deposition is a legal proceeding very similar to giving testimony on the stand in court. All information is recorded by a Court Reporter and can later be used in court for testimony or impeachment purposes. Before any questions are asked or answered, the Court Reporter will administer an oath to tell the truth. Not telling the truth after the oath is administered has penalties of perjury. This is the same oath that will be administered during court testimony. Opposing parties request depositions to find out what facts are know by other parties. Court testimony is actually giving testimony on the stand during trial. The Judge or the Judge's clerk will administer the oath in this setting.

In preparation for giving testimony, whether it is in deposition or in court, there are a number of "dos" and "don'ts" which need to be explained to the person giving testimony.

DO's

1. Keep it simple. Never attempt to explain or justify an answer.
2. Take your time in responding to any question. Think about your answer before you give it.
3. Wait a few minutes (2 or 3 minutes) prior to responding to a question. This gives your attorney time to object to any question. If your attorney objects to a question, do not answer the question until instructed to do so by your attorney.
4. If you do not know the answer to a question, or have doubts about your answer, simply say "I don't know". Saying "I don't know" is perfectly acceptable.
5. Stop speaking whenever your attorney starts to speak.
6. ALWAYS tell the truth.
7. Listen carefully to the question before answering.
8. Be polite.
9. Dress conservatively and appropriately.
10. If you need a break, ask for it.
11. Correct an answer if you have misstated it.
12. Speak slowly and clearly.
13. Discuss the deposition or trial procedure with your attorney prior to testimony
14. Discuss the nature of the case with the attorney
15. Review important items of chronology.
16. Discuss key points with the attorney.
17. Discuss any prior depositions taken in the case.
18. Discuss favorable point in the case you need to remember.
19. Be aware of what is happening.

DON'Ts

1. Do not refer to any notes or bring any documents with you unless your attorney has asked you to do so.
2. Do not give an opinion or guess an answer to any question
3. Never state something as a fact unless you are certain that it is a fact.
4. Do not let the other side make you feel angry or excited.
5. Never joke in deposition or on the stand. Opposing counsel may try to get to you joke. This is a ploy to get you to talk more—don't do it.
6. Do not volunteer information, simply answer the question with a "yes" or "no".
7. Do not guess as to time, speed, distance, place, etc.

8. Do not talk with opposing counsel or parties before, during or after your testimony.

9. Don't answer any question you don't understand.

10. Do not argue with opposing counsel or parties.

11. Do not chew gum.

12. Do not exaggerate.

13. Never say "never".

Remember, even though the experience of testifying in deposition or court may be new, it is helpful to be relaxed and honest.

23

Using Reports
in Court

Numerous television shows attempt to portray what it is like in courtrooms. Police officers are sometimes shown as cool professionals who do not recant their positions under fierce cross-examination. Unfortunately, real life bears little resemblance to television. Many times, officers do become frustrated and flustered on the witness stand, especially if they have not properly prepared for the hearing. In court, officers have identified the wrong person as the perpetrator, forgotten to mention important details, and made other embarrassing and avoidable mistakes. Many of the mistakes made during court hearings are the direct result of an officer either failing to prepare for court or failing to discuss the case with the prosecutor before taking the stand.

The following dialogue is an example of what can happen in court if several key words are incorrectly spelled in the police report:

"Now officer, will you explain to the court why you attacked the victim after she had already been injured?"

"I did not attack the victim."

"But isn't this your signature on the report as the reporting officer?"

"Yes."

"Now, officer, your report reads 'I raped her in a blanket and called for an ambulance.' "

"But sir, I meant *wrapped*."

"Then your report is in error?"

"Yes sir."

"How many other errors are in your report?"

INTRODUCTION

The criminal legal process begins with the apprehension of the suspect. Once an arrest is made, the officer must fill out a report, have it approved by the sergeant, and file it with the records division. The report and any follow-up will then be forwarded to the city attorney or district attorney's office for review, to determine if a criminal case should be filed.

The prosecuting attorney may reject the case for a violation of some technical rule or simply for insufficient evidence. The case may be returned to the arresting officer or to the detectives assigned to the case for additional follow-up prior to filing. Finally, the prosecutor may file the case.

Once the case is filed, there will be a series of hearings regarding the defendant's plea, bail, and willingness to settle the case. During this process, the arresting officer and assigned detectives continue to work on other cases or assignments. The legal system is notorious for moving slowly. Days, weeks, and months may pass before the officer is called to appear in court. For a police officer, the court appearance is the final step in the criminal justice process. It will tax the officer's communication skills to the limit.

Police officers—good police officers—do not simply arrive in court the day of the trial, do battle with the defense attorney, and convince the jury they are telling the truth and the defendant is lying. They prepare for court. During their careers officers can expect to testify in court about everything from simple traffic tickets to homicides. While the magnitude of the cases may be different, the principles regarding trial preparation are the same.

Preparing for Court

Prior to going to court, the officer should review, in detail, the report. The officer cannot expect to sit in front of a judge in a court trial, or a jury in a jury trial, and read the report. Citizens do not understand that the officer may have made numerous other arrests since this one. After all, the defendant's liberty is at stake and the defendant will testify to remembering the incident clearly; therefore, the reasoning goes, so should the officer. Depending on the seriousness of the case and how well the officer remembers the scene, it may be prudent to drive by it prior to coming to court. The officer should be able to pronounce the defendant's name and be familiar with any other unique pronunciations of words in the case. As will be seen, this adds to the officer's credibility.

Dress regulations vary, depending on the jurisdiction. Some departments require the officer to appear in court in uniform. Others give this discretion to the officer. Prosecutors have their own personal beliefs about how an officer should dress for court. Some prosecutors believe that the police uniform adds an aura of credibility; others believe it makes the officer look like the gestapo. If the officer is to appear in uniform, it should be clean and pressed. When wearing civilian attire, the officer should strive for a professional, conservative look. Remember, the jurors should pay attention to the testimony and not what the officer is wearing. Flashy clothes, rings, gold chains, or other out-of-the-ordinary dress may cause a juror to concentrate on the officer's clothing at a critical part of the testimony instead of listening. The officer does not have to wear a three-piece suit with white shirt, but should dress in a manner acceptable for court. Cowboy boots, jeans, or a leather miniskirt are definitely out—unless the officer was working undercover and the prosecutor believes the jury needs to see how the officer was dressed when the arrest was made.

Coordinating with the Prosecuting Attorney

The officer should attempt to contact the prosecutor on receiving the summons to appear in court. In most large cities and counties, prosecutors—like the police—are overworked and understaffed and may not return any phone calls before meeting the officer in the court hallway. The officer should not depend on the prosecutor to make the job of testifying easy. The prosecutor may not have examined the file prior to appearing in court and may be depending on the officer to carry the day. If there is a critical aspect of the case that is not evident from reading the report, the officer should ensure that the prosecutor is informed of it *prior* to the start of the trial—

not just before the officer takes the stand. The reason for this is obvious: the prosecutor may be engaged in last minute plea-bargaining or may make an opening statement to the judge or jury that will later turn out to be false if not made aware of all the important facts surrounding the case.

Depending on the jurisdiction, the officer may have the opportunity to sit next to the prosecutor during the trial and act as an *investigating officer* or *trial assistant.* Instead of thinking of this experience as wasted time away from normal assignments, the officer should rejoice! This is an opportunity to observe the entire trial from start to finish. The experience gained from acting as an investigating officer on a case will improve the officer's courtroom demeanor immeasurably.

After discussing the case with the prosecutor, the officer will await his or her turn to testify. Depending on the nature of the case, and the prosecutor's preference, the officer may testify first or last. If at the counsel table as the investigating officer, the officer should remain attentive and assist the prosecutor whenever possible. If in the seats reserved for the general public, the officer should also remain attentive and professional. While jurors are not supposed to consider anything that is not admitted into evidence, they will sometimes form unofficial opinions of persons based on their observations of them. If required to remain outside the courtroom, the officer should also remain attentive and professional. In addition, the officer should avoid joking with other officers—and especially avoid laughing with the defense attorney. Jurors who observe these antics may believe that the officer is not serious about what is occurring in the courtroom and therefore may discount the officer's testimony.

Having reviewed the report, refreshed the memory, and talked with the prosecutor, the officer is ready to take the stand and testify.

TESTIFYING IN COURT

Some of us are uncomfortable standing or sitting in front of a group and talking. That is exactly what every police officer must master. There may be occasions when the officer testifies in a deserted courtroom with only the court personnel present. This might happen in a closed hearing where the officer is testifying regarding a confidential informant. However, the great majority of the officer's testimony will occur in public. Moreover, the officer will be subjected to cross-examination by the defense attorney, who will attempt to destroy the officer's credibility.

Even if we did not belong to the debating team in high school or college, with proper training all of us can learn to communicate in a professional manner while testifying. This oral skill can be mastered with practice, if the officer is familiar with the purposes of both direct examination and cross-examination. The following sections briefly discuss this aspect of the criminal justice process.

Direct Examination

To testify in court effectively, all officers should understand the aims or goals of direct examination. There are two generally accepted objectives that most prosecutors attempt to satisfy during all direct examinations:

1. Present all legally sufficient evidence to support the charges filed against the defendant.
2. Convince the factfinder of the integrity of the evidence and, ultimately, the truth of the charge.

Direct examination is the prosecutor's opportunity to present favorable evidence to the jury. The officer is responsible for telling the truth and leaving the jury with a good impression of professionalism and honesty. Many prosecutors hand lists to lay witnesses outlining what is expected of them during direct and cross-examination. Unfortunately, prosecutors assume that since police officers have been through academy or other formal training they understand what occurs in a courtroom. This is not necessarily the case. Following is a list of what have been called the "Ten Commandments" for witnesses:

1. *Tell the Truth* In a trial, as in all other matters, honesty comes first.
2. *Don't Guess* If you don't know, say so.
3. *Be Sure You Understand the Question* You cannot possibly give a truthful and accurate answer unless you understand the question.
4. *Take Your Time and Answer the Question Asked* Give the question such thought as is required to understand it, formulate your answer, and then give the answer.
5. *Give a Loud, Audible Answer* Everything you say is being recorded. Don't nod your head yes or no.
6. *Don't Look for Assistance When You Are on the Stand* If you think you need help, request it from the judge.
7. *Beware of Questions Involving Distance and Time* If you make an estimate, make sure everyone understands that you are making an estimate.
8. *Be Courteous* Answer *Yes* or *No*, and address the judge as *Your Honor*.
9. *If Asked If You Have Talked to the Prosecutor, Admit It Freely If You Have Done So.*
10. *Avoid Joking and Wisecracks* A lawsuit is a serious matter.

These commandments are as valid for a seasoned police officer as they are for a rookie. Each rule is based on both common sense and years of court experience by prosecutors.

The first and most basic rule of testimony requires that the officer tell the truth. While it appears obvious that peace officers should always tell the truth, reality and emotions can sometimes cause officers to slant their testimony in order to assist the prosecutor or to ensure that the defendant is portrayed in a bad light. Failure to testify truthfully has several consequences. The most obvious issue is that the officer is sworn to tell the truth. Violation of this oath can lead to criminal charges or the destruction of the officer's reputation. Additionally, the officer's credibility may be destroyed in front of the court or jury, with the result that they disbelieve all of the officer's testimony and acquit the defendant. This is the exact opposite of what the officer intended when slanting or stretching the truth to help out the prosecutor or place the defendant in an unfavorable light. Who can forget the problems caused in the O. J. Simpson case when it was learned that Detective Furman of the LAPD had "forgotten" using racial slurs in the past.

Very close to the first rule is the second, which requires that the officer not try to help the case by guessing. If the officer is unsure, a simple statement to that effect is sufficient. Additionally, this type of statement shows the jury that the officer is human and may not have all the answers to every single question.

The third rule simply requires that the officer understand the exact question that is asked. This appears simple at first glance; however, many times attorneys will ask several questions in one sentence. If the officer is unsure of the exact question, a request should be made to repeat or clarify the question.

The fourth rule requires the officer to think through both the question and answer before blurting out a response. There is nothing wrong with taking a few seconds to form your answer in your mind before responding to the question.

The fifth requirement mandates that the officer answer in a loud and clear voice. Remember, appellate courts have only the written transcript of what occurred when they review a case on appeal. The court reporter will not transcribe a nod of the head or estimate the distance between the officer's hands when demonstrating a gesture or action of either the officer or the defendant. If the officer is going to use motions during the testimony, they should be accompanied by an accurate verbal description.

The sixth commandment may seem harsh, but it is there for the officer's benefit. The officer must understand that no one but the judge can intervene during direct- or cross-examination. The attorneys may raise objections, but the court must decide if they are valid or not.

The seventh rule is one that every rookie will violate at least once. Typically, the officer may state a distance during direct examination. For example, in response to a question by the prosecutor regarding the distance between the officer and the defendant, the officer may state, "The defendant was twenty feet from me when I observed the weapon." On cross-examination, the defense attorney may ask the officer to point out an object in court that is 20 feet from the witness stand. If the officer is mistaken about that distance, the defense attorney will go to great pains to point it out and will end up asking how the officer could be certain about the distance between the officer and the defendant on the night in question when he or she cannot even make an accurate estimate in the calm and secure setting of a courtroom.

The eighth commandment is basically common sense, but can also build an officer's credibility. The officer should be seen as a professional and not someone who does not respect authority.

The ninth rule ties in with the first rule in that it requires the officer to answer every question truthfully. There is absolutely nothing improper in discussing the case with the prosecutor before testifying.

The last commandment goes to the officer's credibility. The defendant's liberty is at stake during the trial. The officer should be professional and calm in answering every question.

Once called to testify, the officer should approach the witness chair or, as it is sometimes called, witness box, and turn to the clerk or judge to be sworn in. The officer will be asked to swear or affirm to tell the truth, the whole truth, and nothing but the truth. Once sworn in, the prosecutor, clerk, or judge will tell the officer to be seated. The officer should wait for this invitation, as it shows respect for the court and allows the prosecutor to appear to be in control of the courtroom.

Once the officer is seated, the prosecutor will ask a series of questions regarding the officer's knowledge of the crime or the defendant. This is known as *direct examination.* Following is a series of preliminary questions most prosecutors will use to start the questioning:

- Would you state your full name for the record?
- What is your occupation?
- How long have you been employed by the X police department?
- On the (date and time in question) what was your assignment?
- On that date and time did you observe anything unusual?
- At what location did you observe this occurrence?
- Is that location in the (city, county, state) of X?

The purpose of these questions is to allow the officer to become comfortable on the stand and give the jury some background information regarding the officer. It also sets the stage for the more critical testimony regarding the officer's observations and reactions. In some jurisdictions these questions are known as *foundational questions,* in that they establish the officer's jurisdiction and authority to act.

When a party—in this instance, the people of the state through the prosecutor—calls a witness, they are allowed to ask only direct questions (with some minor exceptions that are not relevant to this text). This is accomplished through direct examination. A direct question is open ended and does not suggest the answer to the person being questioned. Once the prosecutor has finished with direct examination, the defense attorney has a right to cross-examine. Cross-examination allows asking either direct or leading questions. A *leading question* is phrased in such a way as to suggest an answer to the person being questioned.

After establishing the jurisdiction for the officer to act, the prosecutor will question the witness about his or her knowledge of the crime. The officer should listen to each question and ensure that he or she understands what is being asked. If it is not clear what the question is, the officer should state that and ask the prosecutor to restate the question. "I'm not certain I understand your question; would you please restate it?" is one way to ask for clarification. A review of the previous chapters will indicate that such a question is a form of feedback.

If the question is understood, the officer should pause for a second and then answer. This pause should follow every question; as will be discussed, it becomes very important during cross-examination.

In answering the question, the officer should only answer exactly what was asked. Following is an example of an officer answering more than was asked:

Did you observe anyone at that location?
Yes, as I pulled up to the service station, he saw me and fled from the scene. I then lost sight of him for several minutes, but observed him one block from the scene of the crime.

Not only is the officer's response defective on several grounds, it creates more questions than it answers. Furthermore, without clarifying some of the issues in the officer's answer, the prosecutor may have opened the door for the defense attorney to question whether the defendant was really the same person who fled from the service station. Following is a specific series of questions dealing with the issues the officer raised:

Did you observe anyone at that location?
Yes, I did.

Who did you observe?
I saw the defendant.

Would you point to that person if he is in court and, for the record, describe what he is wearing?
Yes, it is the person sitting next to the defense attorney, wearing a blue suit.

How far away were you when you saw the defendant?
I was about fifteen feet from him.

What was he doing when you first saw him?
He was backing out of the service station office.

What, if anything, did he do next?
He looked towards my marked patrol vehicle and fled.

Where did he go?
He ran south on Broadway Street.

What did you do at that time?
I entered the service station to check on the welfare of the people inside and was informed by Mr. Smith that the defendant had just robbed them at gunpoint.

Once you heard this, what did you do?
I called for backup on my police radio.

Is that the only thing you did—call for backup?
No, I broadcast a description of the defendant, including his height, weight, color, and clothing.

Where did you receive that information?
I observed the defendant when I drove into the location, and broadcast that information.

What did you do next?
I proceeded south on Broadway and observed the defendant standing behind some boxes in the alley.

After you saw him, what did you do?
I pulled my service weapon and ordered him to put his hands in the air and turn around.

The difference between the two sets of questions is apparent. The second set provides the jury with more complete facts surrounding the incident and establishes why the officer could recognize the defendant even though she lost sight of him for several minutes.

Cross-Examination

Once the officer has finished answering the questions posed by the prosecutor, the defense attorney has the right to ask questions on cross-examination. Unlike trials in the movies, cross-examination very seldom breaks down witnesses and gets them to recant their previous testimony. Rather, it is a series of questions designed to attack the credibility of witnesses by showing weaknesses in their original testimony or by establishing a motive or bias on their part.

There are several purposes to cross-examination. All officers should be aware of these objectives, to better understand the questions being asked them by defense attorneys. Depending on the jurisdiction, some questions or issues may not be raised on cross-examination. However, the general objectives of cross-examination include, but are not limited to, the following points:

1. To develop favorable matters that were left unsaid on direct examination.
2. To introduce all of a conversation or document, if the witness has testified to only a part of the content.
3. To demonstrate that the witness is lying.
4. To establish that the witness could not have seen or heard what he or she has claimed.
5. To test the witness's ability to hear, see, remember, and relate facts with accuracy.
6. To establish the witness's bias or prejudice.
7. To establish any interest the witness may have in the outcome of the case.
8. To impair the credibility of the witness.
9. To impeach the witness by any means permitted by law.

Just as with direct examination, the officer should pause before answering any question. This pause is critical, in that it allows the prosecutor to object to the question and prevent its answer from coming before the jury. There are numerous tactics or techniques that defense attorneys can and will use to discredit the officer's testimony. However, this is not a chapter on courtroom survival. Rather, it concerns communication; therefore, only general principles will be discussed in this area.

The officer should know the facts surrounding the case. It is not professional and it is embarrassing for the officer to say, "I don't recall, but I put it in my report." Rest assured, the defense attorney will know the facts—and will have the opportunity to read the report again while the officer is testifying. In addition, the defense attorney has the defendant's version to draw on. While defendants do not always tell their attorneys the complete truth, the defense attorney is provided with another perspective on the facts which can be used to attack the officer.

Always maintain a professional, courteous attitude. Some attorneys will argue with witnesses, others will be condescending, and some may even sneer. No matter what tactic is utilized, the officer should never, ever lose his or her temper. The officer must be prepared for these types of defense ploys and respond in a positive manner. This reinforces in the jury's mind that the officer is a professional simply doing a job.

If the officer makes a mistake during testimony and is caught by the defense attorney, the officer should readily admit to the mistake. There is nothing that damages credibility more than letting a defense attorney lead an officer down a path of rationalizations in an attempt to justify an obvious mistake.

The officer's voice and body language should convey the attitude of a calm professional. The voice should be loud enough for all the jurors to hear, but not so loud as to distract from what is being said. The officer should avoid squirming on the witness stand. If the testimony has proceeded for over two hours and the officer has to use the rest room, the officer should politely ask for a brief recess.

The officer should not despair if it appears that the defense attorney is "winning." After cross-examination, the prosecutor is allowed to conduct *redirect*. This is the prosecutor's opportunity to clarify any issues that may have been raised on cross-examination.

Preparing for and testifying in court are everyday experiences for some officers. Even when it becomes a common occurrence, the officer must understand that unless the information can be conveyed to the jury in the proper manner, all the work done during the arrest, questioning, and charging of the defendant may be wasted. This experience can be one of the most challenging and exciting aspects of police work.

SUMMARY

The law enforcement officer's testimony in court is the final step in the criminal justice procedure. The officer should carefully prepare for this event and always remember to present a professional image to the court and jury. The officer's professional reputation—and the department's—goes on the line every time the officer testifies.

Preparing to testify is as important as the actual testimony. The officer must never assume the case will be easy or that the defendant's attorney will not attack the officer's credibility. Whenever possible, the officer should discuss the case with the prosecuting attorney before entering the courtroom.

Direct examination and cross-examination have distinct purposes. The officer should be prepared for both types of questioning and follow the "Ten Commandments" as closely as possible. There are various techniques that all officers should remember when testifying. These will become second nature to most officers after they have testified in court several times.

REVIEW QUESTIONS

1. What is the most appropriate attire for an officer testifying in court? Why?
2. Which of the "Ten Commandments" is the most important? Why?
3. If you had to delete one of the "Ten Commandments," which one would you delete? Why?
4. Which is more important—direct examination or cross-examination? Why?
5. What effect can a simple reporting error have on an officer's testimony?